LYRIC IN ITS TIMES

Also published by Bloomsbury

The Late Cantos of Ezra Pound, Michael Kindellan
Literature as Cultural Ecology, Hubert Zapf
On Modern Poetry, Robert Rowland Smith

LYRIC IN ITS TIMES

Temporalities in Verse, Breath and Stone

John Wilkinson

BLOOMSBURY ACADEMIC
LONDON • NEW YORK • OXFORD • NEW DELHI • SYDNEY

BLOOMSBURY ACADEMIC
Bloomsbury Publishing Plc
50 Bedford Square, London, WC1B 3DP, UK
1385 Broadway, New York, NY 10018, USA

BLOOMSBURY, BLOOMSBURY ACADEMIC and the Diana logo
are trademarks of Bloomsbury Publishing Plc

First published in Great Britain 2019
Paperback edition published 2021

Copyright © John Wilkinson, 2019

John Wilkinson has asserted his right under the Copyright,
Designs and Patents Act, 1988, to be identified as Author of this work.

For legal purposes the Acknowledgements on p. ix constitute
an extension of this copyright page.

Cover design: Eleanor Rose
Cover image: Lanyon Quoit, an ancient burial chamber near
Penzance in Cornwall, UK © Getty Images

All rights reserved. No part of this publication may be reproduced or
transmitted in any form or by any means, electronic or mechanical,
including photocopying, recording, or any information storage or retrieval
system, without prior permission in writing from the publishers.

Bloomsbury Publishing Plc does not have any control over, or responsibility for,
any third-party websites referred to or in this book. All internet addresses given
in this book were correct at the time of going to press. The author and publisher
regret any inconvenience caused if addresses have changed or sites have
ceased to exist, but can accept no responsibility for any such changes.

A catalogue record for this book is available from the British Library.

A catalog record for this book is available from the Library of Congress.

ISBN: HB: 978-1-3500-9391-1
PB: 978-1-3502-1155-1
ePDF: 978-1-3500-9392-8
eBook: 978-1-3500-9393-5

Typeset by Integra Software Services Pvt. Ltd.

To find out more about our authors and books visit
www.bloomsbury.com and sign up for our newsletters.

In Affectionate Remembrance of Neil Reeve

CONTENTS

List of Figures	viii
Acknowledgements	ix
Chapter 1	
BREATHTAKING POETRY	1
Chapter 2	
PETRIFACTION AND WAVE POWER	15
Chapter 3	
ANTI-MEMORIAL ELEGY	33
Chapter 4	
LAPIDARY	61
Chapter 5	
ON A RAISED BEACH	93
Chapter 6	
STONE THRESHOLDS	117
Chapter 7	
DILAPIDATION AND SINGING STONES	141
Chapter 8	
A SHOWER OF NEEDLES	179
Chapter 9	
ON THE TIP OF THE TONGUE	201
Chapter 10	
TRYING TIMES	225
Notes	236
Bibliography	255
Index	266

LIST OF FIGURES

1	Ian Hamilton Finlay, 'The Present Order'	30
2	Ian Hamilton Finlay, 'Marble the Revolution'	32
3	Aaron Siskind, 'New York, West Street 14'	101
4	Aaron Siskind, 'Martha's Vineyard 1954'	104
5	Aaron Siskind, 'Martha's Vineyard 4'	107
6	Paulo Veronese, *Hermes, Herse and Aglauros*	118
7	Paulo Veronese, *Mars and Venus United by Love*	122
8	Peter Lanyon, *St Just*	225

ACKNOWLEDGEMENTS

Although the seeds of this book lie in my earlier collection of essays *The Lyric Touch*, it was at the National Humanities Center in 2007–08 that its ideas emerged in the process of writing about the poetry of George Oppen, developing subsequently through a series of essays whose shared thinking was not always apparent to me, several of them responding to invitations to contribute to edited collections. The book as a whole came together and much additional material was written when I returned as an Associate to the National Humanities Center in 2017–18. My debt to the National Humanities Centre is therefore great, and to the friendships I was fortunate to make among its fellows, especially Judith Farquahar and Elizabeth Helsinger during my first visit, and Anne Reynolds and Harleen Singh during my second. Maud Ellmann has been beside me throughout the decade of this book's gestation, encouraging me to believe in the worth of my critical writing as well as providing a model of lucid and witty prose I cannot hope to emulate.

The changing membership of the Poetry and Poetics graduate seminar at the University of Chicago and the lecture series inaugurated by Richard Strier titled 'History and Forms of the Lyric' have been vital resources. The University of Chicago's community of poet-scholars, Srikanth 'Chicu' Reddy, Jennifer Scappettone, Edgar Garcia, Rachel Galvin, Rosanna Warren, Peter O'Leary, Nathan Hoks and Lynn Xu, along with my colleagues in Creative Writing, Vu Tran, Rachel DeWoskin, Rachel Cohen, Dan Raeburn, Augustus Rose, Ling Ma and Will Boast, comprise the most congenial intellectual and creative environment I can imagine; and I am immensely grateful to the administrative staff of Creative Writing, Annie Janusch, Jessi Haley and Starsha Gill for always having my back. I have been fortunate to have acute and sympathetic critical readers in Matt ffytche and, until the last revision of this book's manuscript, the late Neil Reeve, and I am especially grateful for the generous responsiveness of my colleague Edgar Garcia.

Footnotes have been reduced here to a minimum, removing evidence of quarrels with authorities likely to interest only scholars, but also erasing acknowledgement of many debts to previous writers and to my students. These may be consulted in the original papers incorporated into this book and listed below. To previous acknowledgements I need to add that the discussion of Aaron Siskind originated in a paper for a panel convened by Sam Ladkin at the Modernist Studies Association in Amsterdam, 11 August 2017. My thanks to Sam Ladkin and to my fellow panellist James Boaden for their helpful comments. Chapter 8 benefited from comments by Drew Milne, Matt ffytche and Edgar Garcia, Chapter 9 from comments by Richard Strier, and an early draft of the first chapter from an acute reading by Anne Janowitz. I am grateful to my student Nathaniel Schmidt for so willingly taking on proofreading chores, and to Bill Hutchison for producing an authoritative bibliography from my sketchy endnotes.

For previous publication of some of this material, I wish to thank the editors of *Cambridge Literary Review, Chicago Review, Critical Inquiry, Critical Quarterly, Textual Practice* and *Thinking Verse*; and Edward Allen, the editor of the collection where my paper on Dylan Thomas appeared. These original publications have in several cases been abbreviated and revised.

Finally, I am grateful to the anonymous reviewers of the first draft of this book. Their contradictory advice has forced me to make fundamental decisions that have altered the book substantially, including the writing of a new final chapter. Yet again I have been brought to realize the greater value of pointed criticism than of kind approval.

Some parts of this book were first published in earlier versions as follows:

'Faults and Somersaults', *Cambridge Literary Review*, Vol. III, No. 6 (Easter 2012), pp. 125–134.

'The Glass Enclosure: Transparency and Glitter in the Poetry of George Oppen', *Critical Inquiry*, Vol. 36, No. 2 (Winter 2010), pp. 218–238.

'Glossing Gloss and Its Undertow', *Textual Practice*, Vol. 24, No. 4 (2010), pp. 749–764.

'Lost and Found in *The Türler Losses*', *Chicago Review*, Vol. 53 & 54, Nos. 1/2 (Summer 2008), pp. 98–106.

'Repeatable Evanescence', *Thinking Verse*, Vol. IV, No. i (2014), pp. 23–49.

'Stone Thresholds', *Textual Practice*, Vol. 31, No. 4 (2017), pp. 631–658.

'Wave Power: The Effacement of the Caesura in Dylan Thomas's Poetry', in *Reading Dylan Thomas*, ed. Edward Allen. Edinburgh: Edinburgh University Press 2018, pp. 15–34.

…

Works by Ian Hamilton Finlay are reproduced by courtesy of the Ian Hamilton Finlay Estate. 'Marble the Revolution' is in the collections of Glasgow Museums.

Works by Aaron Siskind are reproduced by permission of the Aaron Siskind Foundation.

Paolo Veronese, *Hermes, Herse and Aglauros*, after 1576. Oil on canvas. © The Fitzwilliam Museum, Cambridge. Paolo Veronese, *Mars and Venus United by Love*, 1570s. Oil on canvas. The Metropolitan Museum of Art, John Stewart Kennedy Fund, 1910. www.metmuseum.org.

St Just by Peter Lanyon © Sheila Lanyon. All Rights Reserved, DACS, London/Artists Rights Society (ARS), New York. Photograph © Tate, London 2018.

Cody-Rose Clevidence, 'from "By Gaze"', © Cody-Rose Clevidence 2017. Reproduced by courtesy of the author. Andrew Crozier, 'Blank Misgivings', with kind permission of the Estate of Andrew Crozier. W. S. Graham, 'Dear Bryan Wynter' from *New Collected Poems* © 2004 The Estate of W. S. Graham. By courtesy of Rosalind Mudaliar. Barbara Guest, 'A Noise of Return' from *The Collected Poems of Barbara Guest* © 2008 by Barbara Guest. Reprinted with permission of Wesleyan University Press. Mark Hyatt, 'Puberty of Puck', copyright Estate of Mark Hyatt, used by permission. Excerpt from 'Buried at Springs' from COLLECTED POEMS by James Schuyler. Copyright © 1993 by the Estate of James Schuyler. Reprinted by permission of Farrar, Straus and Giroux. 'Poem in October' by Dylan Thomas, from THE POEMS OF DYLAN THOMAS, copyright © 1945 by The Trustees for the Copyrights of Dylan Thomas, first published in POETRY. Reprinted by permission of New Directions Publishing Corp. John Wieners, 'Trimeters', by courtesy of Raymond Foye for the Estate of John Wieners.

Chapter 1

BREATHTAKING POETRY

This first chapter introduces *Lyric in Its Times* thematically, archivally and methodologically. Thematically it focuses on time and rhythm, contending that life in lyric poetry depends on the co-existence of multiple temporalities. Archivally it identifies the book's central poets and artists as working in New York and St Ives in the mid-twentieth century, although the book ranges widely in American, British and other European poetry and visual art since the Renaissance. Methodologically the chapter argues for an ahistorical approach starting with aesthetic response, although historical, political and biographical contexts support and explicate such readings. Poems by Frank O'Hara and Barbara Guest allow a demonstration of my procedure.

*

This book began in a group of essays and a seminar series about lyric poems as objects and events, extending occasionally to visual art while pursuing their thinking through metaphors associated with rock, stone and glass. Originally, this train of thought was motivated by attachment to a processual poetics opposed to Objectivism in poetic practice and to Historicism in theory, participating in a return to aesthetics associated with philosophers and literary critics influenced by (among others) Alfred North Whitehead, Gilles Deleuze and Bruno Latour. Subsequently, I have come to think of poems as object events, where 'object' is informed variously by the extended meanings accorded by Object Orientated Ontology, Bruno Latour's Actor Network Theory and the object relations psychoanalysis of W. R. Bion; in short, the status of poems as things or events can be regarded as mutative according to angle of view. Even so, it is the promise of an aesthetic event that has ever compelled me to read poems, and it is the experience of such an event which I wish to communicate at a time critical discourse appears often to produce (unintentionally or with the best of intentions) ways of protecting readers from aesthetic experience. This observation is made not to disparage historicist readings or to protect art from challenge by political critique, but to assert this book's primary engagement with what I experience only in the workings of art.

What follows is therefore ahistorical according to present disciplinary understandings of 'history' in literary studies, although critical writing openly avowing its time's preoccupations surely is thereby historical. Tone matters, and the contingency of wider cultural and political forces as well as the polemical field of poetics to which this writing responds, shapes its occasional vehemence even as I recognize that laying down the law on something as shifty as a poem is likely to be a mistake. 'Historicist' poetics has rightly pushed back against the tone of *ex cathedra* interpretative authority, but its tendency to treat history as a succession of temporal configurations, situating poems according to the material context of their early publication and the genre assumptions of their first readers, can in turn become over-authoritative. Some historicist critics hold that present-day readers fall into error owing to anachronistic genre assumptions; lyric, according to such accounts, is conceived not on the page of a modern edition but in the distorted eye of a beholder primed to see verse in a particular way – whether this causes her to recoil or to seek identity with a poem's 'voice'. If the work of poetics should properly be to approach poems as linguistic cryptograms figured out for evidence of the ideological assumptions saturating them at birth, readings that fail to acknowledge their own contrary and distorting desires indeed are to be deplored. But this book does not aim to use poems to such evidentiary ends. Poems written centuries ago are here read as emerging into contemporaneity, resonating with our times, because they are hybrid and recurrent object-events. 'History continually arrives as differently as our most recent minute on earth' as W. S. Graham, a poet central to this book, declared.[1]

History and aesthetics stand in a false antithesis. A prime interest in aesthetic effect does not require artworks to be considered eternal; many poems that resonate most powerfully with me and with other present-day readers have previously been derogated as incoherent, superficial, undisciplined or incomprehensible. Oddly, this is true of the majority of poets whose work these pages discuss. My enthusiasm as a schoolboy for Shelley was ridiculed by my teachers, Shelley being the very type, in their eyes, of the irresponsible, politically posturing and rhetorically confused poet. Frank O'Hara's poetry was admired in a small circle but dismissed as lightweight outside it; both Dylan Thomas and W. S. Graham suffered occlusion as, in the one case a mere media sensation and in the other, a marginal hangover from the 1940s. The resonance of these once-disparaged poets is clearly evident as I write, with O'Hara and Graham disturbing the once-settled ascendancy of Robert Lowell and Philip Larkin – not deleting them from the historical record but surpassing them in their poems' effect on present-day readers. Emily Dickinson is our closer contemporary than Lowell, I dare say. 'Relevance' is not the issue here, although I have not been shy, for example, of reading Graham from the present pitch of ecological crisis. My reading of Graham accords with what J. Hillis Miller calls 'anachronistic reading', adding the eloquent gloss that

> such future chiming is also […] a sign to sign relation, an anticipatory allegory or prophecy, or, perhaps, a miniature apocalypse in the etymological sense of an enigmatic unveiling of what has not yet happened.[2]

Relevance then may be revelatory, and serve the point of this book, which is the strange feeling that poems live – they are entities sponsoring life in their readers, emotional, cognitive and creative, or even a 'miniature apocalypse', and this disruptive power is more salient than their conditioning by circumstances of their writing and first reception. Disruptive means 'bursting asunder' and aesthetic experience is disruptive of both poem and reader, creating a new, if fleeting, amalgam changing each element through a sundering of their boundaries; I distinguish in this book between the preservative stance of contemplation or appreciation, and aesthetic experience in its disruptiveness.

While by no means a work of psychoanalytical theory, this book refers frequently to the writing of psychoanalysts interested in aesthetics and in thought-processes, notably D. W. Winnicott and W. R. Bion, and to an art critic steeped in Kleinian psychoanalysis and obsessed by stone, Adrian Stokes. Stone is crucial to this book for several reasons. Proverbially stone and rock epitomize obdurate objecthood, but erosion makes even such kickable objects exemplary of slow events. Headstones commemorate the dead in several religious traditions, and by extension, marble and alabaster have deathly associations while also connoting living fame, especially in Renaissance poetry. Stone is a material for art making in statuary, but is linked by Stokes with natural process, 'the sculpting effects of water upon limestone', and with the externalization of emotion in classical art.[3] Stokes's work becomes prominent towards the end of this book, shadowed as it is by our contemporary apprehension of running out of time. Writing on 'The Future and Art' just before his death in 1972, in a paper to which I shall return, Stokes remains deeply anxious about the threat of nuclear Armageddon felt so strongly in the 1950s and '60s. Moreover, he addresses the incipient perils of what has come to be called the Anthropocene, situating the start of a slow catastrophe in the Industrial Revolution – pollution, overpopulation and 'the threat of the imminent depleting of the earth's riches' while 'surrounded by human triumph, in means of communication, in possibilities of health and comfort'. With remarkable prescience Stokes conceives that 'since a varied connectiveness involves doubts rather than assurance, many of us long to be enveloped, even brow-beaten, carried away'.[4]

Art works done in the New York and St Ives of the late 1950s and early 1960s form the generative core of this book, and Adrian Stokes had an important role in the history of St Ives art, having brought Ben Nicholson, Barbara Hepworth and Naum Gabo in 1939 to stay at his home near this remote fishing town. In the subsequent generation of painters associated with St Ives, personal links developed with New York Abstract Expressionists; the Cornish painter Peter Lanyon was given a party in his honour by Robert Motherwell on a visit to New York in 1959, major artists such as Mark Rothko, Philip Guston, Adolph Gottlieb and David Smith attending, and the Rothko family stayed at Lanyon's home on a visit to Cornwall later that year. Patrick Heron first encountered the dogmatic American art critic Clement Greenberg in London in 1954, entering into a sometimes testy correspondence; in 1959, Greenberg visited Heron in Cornwall and met other St Ives painters. As an artistic colony, the origins of St Ives' mid-century flourishing therefore involved both Stokes and Naum Gabo, a Russian Jew escaping Nazism in Germany. Gabo's constructivist aesthetic is visible in Hepworth's piercing-open of stone and, as my last chapter shows, less obviously in the painting of Bryan Wynter and Peter Lanyon.

When St Ives artists discovered their edgy common cause with Abstract Expressionism, it was the time of Cold War and nuclear terror. Adrian Stokes' essay 'The Future and Art' points to analogies with present times; the prospect of annihilation in a spectacular excess of energy is overshadowed in the present by the prospect and discernible reality of annihilation as entropic and as self-inflicted through exploitative excess. As reflected in Chapter 8, it is a strange feature of the present that the risk of nuclear annihilation is greater by orders of magnitude than during the period of greatest nuclear anxiety, not only in the size of arsenals and the destructive power of individual missiles, but also in the risk of the acquisition of nuclear weapons by non-state actors impelled by apocalyptic religious beliefs. Even so, it is feedback from human activity in weather systems and from the relentless exploitation of 'soil the cumulative evidence of life processes, a recursive matrix & husky skin of utility stretched over the original rock' that haunts consciousness and presses on the skin in privileged enclaves throughout the world, while in less protected zones destroying livelihoods and lives by drought and flood.[5] These twinned temporalities of instantaneity and 'the original rock' meet also in Chapter 5's discussion of documentary and photography in the work of Muriel Rukeyser and Aaron Siskind. Associated with Abstract Expressionism, whose critical advocates exalted the value of event and action above the making of objects, and working in a medium that snaps and catches the ephemeral, Aaron Siskind dwells on rock and walls in his photographs, often using serial composition to complicate the relationship between rock's obduracy and the medium's instantaneity. Rock changes every time you look at it, even commemorative rock, as evidenced in James Schuyler's elegy 'Buried at Springs' discussed in Chapters 3 and 5, and that's so of poems too in their 'repeatable evanescence'—a key term for this book, presented to me during my reading of Barbara Guest.

Poems like tardigrades can rest long dormant before reviving. I have on my desk a just-published pamphlet, where Shelley's 'The Mask of Anarchy' sponsors a blistering and prosodically relentless arraignment of Western military, economic and political depredation, a poem from which the following lines are extracted:

> In our stanzas and our days
> What would Shelley find to say
> Of murder met with on his way?
>   Beyond the Privy Council hall
> And its barred and bolted door
> There sits a weaver in the darkness
> Far from tenterground and market
> Who must sigh in sadness till
> Rivers dry and cease to run
> And all the rocks melt in the sun

So do not harien her and hector
The watches of the night to fill
She weaves a rug for Manchester
For the riots of Bengal
For Kazakh, Kyrgyz and Uzbeck
Or Afghan, where the Helmand shines
And high above its silver line
Glittering and serpentine
Above the *juis* and *karez*
Chinook, Lynx, Apache turn
Their fearsome blades against the sun[6]

To not fade away, a poem must maintain at least a recognizable blur of object-integrity; for sure, there are different editions, errors of transmission, failures of memory and various media contexts, but the life of 'The Mask of Anarchy' inheres in its lasting potential for return. The present light passing over it releases an energy never exhausted but variously expressed as it meets different readers in their times – and the new inclusion of 'The Mask of Anarchy' in the 2018 edition of *The Norton Anthology of Poetry* responds to this poem's suddenly and disruptively audible return to life. To pass over and bring into the light art works consigned to oblivion by the sex or racial designation of their writers is one of a critic's most valuable tasks, and it is any reader's privilege and pleasure to illuminate the long-occluded as well as to restore life to what might have frozen into a cultural fetish. But with 'The Mask of Anarchy', we have a different case, of a poem notably vulnerable to relegation into an archive of responses to the occasion of the Peterloo Massacre – along with newspaper reports, memoirs, letters, etc.; Shelley positively invites such contextualizing by establishing at the start his geographical distance from the event that urges his enraged writing ('As I lay asleep in Italy | There came a voice from over the Sea'). His adoption of (or adoption by) a popular form in ballad also invites generic relegation to an example of the period's political balladry. Such taxonomy may be meat and drink to the literary historian, but does not concern us here: What motivates Martin Thom's verse is the singularity of 'The Mask of Anarchy'. Only the singular can deliver the charge of disruption. For readers who experience its energy an event occurs where Shelley's singular poem and the reading self together constitute a temporary amalgam which may or may not have a longer-lasting effect on self or poem or both – and may or may not become a matter of record. But even if the formation is evanescent, the poem can induce an aesthetic effect (not the *same* effect because the reader will not be same) again and again. In Jonathan Culler's words, 'The singularity of the work is what enables it to be repeated over and over in events that are never exactly the same', eventuating in relation to the like singularity of the reader.[7] Evidently Martin Thom, author of the lines above, was changed by 'The Mask of Anarchy' and 'The Mask of Anarchy' is changed by encounter with Martin Thom. Thom does not merely 'appropriate' Shelley on account of perceiving a likeness between Eldon, Sidmouth and Castlereagh, and the Iraq War-era British politicians Blair, Straw and Hain; his feeling and thinking have been re-configured by Shelley's poem into this amalgam. How can this be? What makes this amalgam distinctly a poem's work rather than the work of, say, a powerful article in *New Left Review*?

That is a question agitating this book from start to finish. But why should anyone care? A first response is unashamedly individual: experience of being reconfigured in reading a poem or seeing a picture goes beyond attachment and beyond connectedness, reaching a state where subject and object become indistinguishable, where object and event become a wave, a flux, where the composed present departs from time so that death and absolute love are identical in their transient implicature. Such an experience in encounter with art is rare and unpredictable, and it is a besetting problem of writing about 'poetry' that the word can be taken to apply either to all the mass of utterances and writings that anyone tags with the category or to an archive defined by certain testable characteristics (academically, but also in the eyes of people offended by a lack of rhyme for instance), or to a very small group of poems described as having had a transformative effect on a particular writer. This ambiguous designation explains why it is possible to be sick of 'poetry' and at the same time, for particular poems to have changed one's life and maybe to do so again. And it suggests why it is a paradoxical undertaking to argue for a poem's value by showing how its components work; accountancy can never recreate nor make a proxy for fascination, although it might explain the principles and technology behind a run-of-the-mill poem. Derek Attridge observes that the singular work of art 'comes across as different from any other work we know, even though its materials – the various components of the techne that the artist deployed in creating it – may be familiar'.[8] And therein lies a problem for the critic seeking to describe how singularity arises from familiar components. To convey how particular poems that do poetic work surpassingly do so (rather than extrapolate what they might be deemed to say) requires metaphor, and sometimes, extravagant rhetoric of a kind literary criticism has found embarrassing since it aspired to science with I. A. Richards or to ideological critique in recent decades, and which Creative Writing finds embarrassing in teaching poetry as a craft skill. Not only is this book ahistorical, but also is often over-the-top. Some detailed arguments for its claims must and will be entered, however, since belles-lettrist effusions have a blanketing quality liable to reduce every transcendent experience to the One. If aesthetic force brings about an amalgam between a particular work and an individual or, more questionably, a collective (aspired to by 'The Mask of Anarchy' and some poems discussed towards the end of this book), each such amalgam must be singular – and singular every time it recurs, if it does, between that artistic work and that individual or roused collective. The challenge therefore is to use over-the-top rhetoric and metaphor in ways specific to each poem discussed – the experience cannot be reproduced but can perhaps be conjured at an angle. I cannot hope though to have achieved a singularity of discursive address, in part because the poems that sponsor my aesthetic experiences must surely answer the needs in me, largely unconscious, that are invariant and insatiable.

A focus on aesthetic experience does not deny a social value for art – as distinct from insisting art must assert its utility. In a moving essay in the *New York Times*, the novelist and Iraq veteran Kevin Powers wrote of art as a tether, which drew him back from a living death in post-combat isolation: 'I have sometimes heard art described as anything created without discernible utility, but my experience tells me otherwise. I have found books to be profoundly and incomparably useful in my life, for they helped me hold on to it.'[9] In this regard, art belongs with sex, religion and political solidarity, and my experience chimes with Powers's in denying another truism that artworks are distinct (*must* be regarded so) from their creator. In large measure, their creator is created anew through her artworks in their reception, but it would be absurdly stiff-necked to deny loving a writer. I love Frank O'Hara, as I know him through his poems and also in memoirs. Aesthetic experience can devolve perilously towards disembodied abstraction or drown in unreticulated oceanic feeling. Such oblivion would negate the aesthetic, rendering unable to touch another or respond to others' responses, unable to touch land, 'losing it' as in sex, religion and political solidarity when disruptive force is forestalled by deathly submission and fails to meet the force-field of another person, thing or event. What distinguishes the particularity of an amalgam from the oblivion that could overwhelm it?

An idea about coextensive and mutually influencing and interfering rhythms and temporalities recurs in this book; the 'wave power' of at least two rhythms in their relations is held to enliven or incarnate a poem's obdurate or mediating materials and so counter any drift towards narcosis or unmooring into abstraction. The story of Western poets' meditation on time from Petrarch through Shakespeare to recent poets and artists as different as Muriel Rukeyser and Ian Hamilton Finlay and the metaphors they have deployed repeatedly of stone, flesh and breath have threaded my thinking through the shocks and contradictions of aesthetic experience. Among poets the book weaves from Blake to Baudelaire and from Dylan Thomas to Cody-Rose Clevidence, and among visual artists from Veronese to Aaron Siskind. Touchstones and lightning flashes denoting the life of lyric are found repeatedly among poems by Percy Bysshe Shelley, Frank O'Hara, Barbara Guest (the contemporaneity of whose poetry has yet to become widely appreciated) and W. S. Graham; their poems return in different contexts. The book's chapters rely on reading and looking closely, and since they present a practice in poetics rather than in theory – a distinction which may be too categorical but will serve – the chapters stand as much in apposition as consecutively, linked by the return of a few exemplary poems as well as by threads of argument.

This book's procedure may be illustrated by thinking through a very well-known poem by Frank O'Hara, which will recur in these pages, 'The Day Lady Died'.[10] What is so compelling about this poem to so many readers? What makes an elegy (which generically is what 'The Day Lady Died' is) live so fully now, although encapsulated as an often-reproduced textual object and seemingly as frozen in its moment as a snapshot? No denying one advantage it possesses, shared with other poems by O'Hara and his distinguished contemporaries: there is a glamour in the New York City of the 1950s and in Frank O'Hara as the cynosure of its extraordinary artistic flowering: Frank O'Hara, John Ashbery, LeRoi Jones, Willem de Kooning, Jackson Pollock, Joan Mitchell, Miles Davis,

Thelonious Monk, John Cage, Merce Cunningham. Not only such names conjure up a milieu, which will always feel more alive artistically than whatever time I or any future reader might inhabit, but also this was the hippest and coolest of times in the hippest and coolest of cities. Post-war New York had transformed into a world city while embodying a peculiarly American economic swagger; and internationalism coupled with rapacious appetite for the world's goods formed the immediate cultural matrix embedding O'Hara's poetry. At the same time, New York was a village where artists, poets and musicians knew or at least would be likely to encounter each other, although 'The Day Lady Died' has something to say about differences within that milieu. Tensions between the international and parochial and especially between black and white contribute to the poem's tight tissue of contradictions; my reading however will focus attention on temporal and prosodic cross-rhythms and how their mutual interruptions allow the poem to be simultaneously admirable and visceral, intelligently alert while nearly overcome emotionally.

The first line of the poem, 'It is 12:20 in New York a Friday' has been much imitated and to various effect. The best-known American imitation or adaptation echoes throughout Ted Berrigan's *The Sonnets* (1964) where time-stamps such as 'It is 5:15 a.m.' repeat and may designate the actual moment of writing as a discipline undertaken at 5.15am (morning after morning) or refer to a particular moment of writing after which the time-stamp becomes conventional and used more to suspend than to mark time.[11] Either possibility or both is plausible, given Berrigan's amphetamine use and sleeplessness. At first sight, use of a time-stamp in sonnets, however irregular their form, may seem disrespectful to the sonnet tradition, but 'our dates are brief' as Shakespeare's Sonnet 123 has it, and Shakespeare's sonnets in their argument between the fleeting and the enduring, in their phrases absorbed into a shared linguistic loam as well as their movement's press against bounds, inevitably shape reading of 'The Day Lady Died' – which at twenty-eight lines suggests a double sonnet in appearance. This poem of busy temporal punctuation and of death and memorialization, of the tension between the desire to continue and the always-destined, almost-seductive halt is therefore already deeply familiar on first reading. 'Lady Day', Billie Holiday, was so named by the saxophone player Lester Young, an inveterate word-player (did he perhaps tease her with being a little la-di-da?), and Lady Day is indeed a Holy Day (Holiday) in the Christian calendar. O'Hara's title flags a temporal disruption in its reversal of Lady Day's name, and expires on a long dying vowel at the end of a short scat sequence – day-dy-die. The title sounds both like a jazz improvisation and devastatingly final. In being retrospective, it casts the opening of the poem into the historical present; 'It is 12:20 in New York a Friday' is not a time-stamp like Berrigan's 'it is 5:15 a.m.' but rather a flashback or a reconstruction. The next line, 'three days after Bastille Day', inaugurates a thread of French cultural references – the French national holiday falls on 14 July and Billie Holiday died on 17 July 1959 – and also rhymes with Friday; Bastille Day recurs annually, commemorating an historical event central to French nationhood, while Friday's recurrence is as arbitrary and predictable as the next line's jingle 'it is 1959 and I go get a shoeshine' where no connection is tenable between date and event. But the very thought of Bastille Day must be hurried past, back to 'yes, | it is 1959' because 'day' is not be dwelt upon or things threaten to come to a breathless halt. Has something worth commemorating occurred on this Friday? Yes, it *will have been* 'The Day Lady Died'. In its last three chapters, this book will return to the future perfect, realized in the aesthetic experience of life *as it would be if it had had existence*; and it is a miracle of this poem and others by O'Hara that a reader can be disrupted into the life she would have had then and there, and that this can feel like life fully realized here and now. At the end of the stanza, rhyme dissolves and the loose four-beat rhythm fades away into a three-beat rhythmic ellipsis after the clock precision of train timetable particulars. Both the train with its passenger and the single-sentence stanza will enter a zone of uncertainty, but this has already happened. The events have occurred already but uncertainty persists through the formal and syntactical break.

The poem resumes with its second stanza retreating from the historical future of 'who will feed me' to the historical present; but what has already been set up is the interplay of two rhythms, a rhythm of conscious, busy and somewhat distracted activity in lines jostling with detail and stuffed with syllables in gaps between beats, and a distinct resisted rhythm, which is as physical and primal as heartbeat and breath. Why resist what composes the poem, the breath that has to be taken anew in order to get moving again, 'I walk up the muggy street beginning to sun'? Resistance can be felt throughout the remaining lines of 'The Day Lady Died' on both the semantic and rhythmic levels. Semantically, what is resisted is a black cultural undertow, from 'the poets | in Ghana' to '*Les Nègres*' and finally 'a NEW YORK POST with her face on it' – a blackness resisted so as to forfend the thought of Billie Holiday's death. The French thread continuing through Verlaine to Gauloises and Picayunes is associated, as Frenchness would have been for a New York sophisticate, with life's pleasures and their persistence, whereas blackness summons both a more intense experience of art than a fretful choice between elegant things and specifically here the end of art (and life) in a death – Billie Holliday's. While Holliday's conscious artistry is displaced into pleasurable things, her intensity is tamped down. Pausing early after the phrase 'these days', again meeting the choke-point of 'day', the stanza then resumes its round – 'I go on to the bank' – ravelling through minor events and consumer quandaries, stepping past the possible obstacle of 'Miss Stillwagon' (an apt name) who waves her customer through his transaction, until his distracting busyness threatens to overwhelm his capacity to manage the day and 'I stick with Verlaine | after practically going to sleep with quandariness'. Sticking anywhere though, re-opens the space or void marked by Billie Holiday in life and death. O'Hara's pedestrian round must pick up again, shopping for liquor and cigarettes until the finally unavoidable 'her face on it' and a pause now invaded by anxiety and distress.

So the historical present confronting news of Billie Holiday's death faces the day, but at once turns to the past. 'I am sweating a lot by now' might reasonably be a result of all the frenetic activity preceding the phrase, but no: here it is the revenge of the body and its deeper rhythms against the rhythms of wilfully distracted thought and physical scurrying. But heart's and breath's rhythms funnel at once into the experience of Billie Holiday singing at the '5 SPOT' in the past (and the club name sounds like a space/time marker), while tenses collapse into a lyric present of sweating and remembering and becoming once again present as Billie Holiday becomes present and simultaneously dies as does the poet in the future and the poem now. The final perfect phrase 'everyone and I stopped breathing' cedes the poem's breathing to a moment of breathtaking. We will all stop breathing, but in the present which the poem can restore, Billie Holiday continues to be breathtaking.

Poised between onrushing and haltingness, sharing the evanescence of aesthetic experience with Billie Holiday's performance here gives pause as if her song had gone unrecorded and this poem were spoken at a particular time and place; rendered nonetheless into this transmissible text, a text that is at once recollection, presence, 1950s New York, the long history of English language lyric resounding with Shakespeare's sonnets. Poised between cultural connoisseurship and a powerfully emotional response to art and loss, 'The Day Lady Died' enfolds a rhythmic confluence that not only determines Billy Holiday will never die, despite the poem's title, but also ensures that like a Shakespeare sonnet 'So long as men can breathe or eyes can see | So long lives this, and this gives life to thee' (Sonnet 18). But Frank O'Hara does not establish a monument; his poem eventuates in what my second chapter terms a 'repeatable evanescence'. Its embeddedness in the Petrarchan and Shakespearian sonnet tradition makes the poem's movement a counter-force to both the ephemera of time-stamps and shopping and the looming of death; it moves across generations. It is important that Billie Holiday was a black female singer and not a white male general or statesman, ensuring that a Renaissance elegiac tenor signifying a lover not a public figure becomes audible even if below conscious identification; and at the same time it is important that Holiday should not be caricatured as a 'troubled entertainer' but hailed as a great artist, for only such great art can take the breath away in life so intense that it challenges death. The poem becomes not a monument inscribed with the name of Billie Holliday, marking one more place where she is interred, but joins with her in a continuing pulse of life that surges up against its own textual ending. As Chapter 3 will show, such a resurgent embodiment is characteristic of O'Hara's elegiac mode.

'Everyone and I' is a striking formulation for lyric, distinct from the canonical 'you-and-I and the other reading this poem', and such capaciousness is consistent with and may derive from O'Hara's social being amid what some call a coterie, a term whose inherent exclusivity is breached in O'Hara's verse through the reader's feeling that she can belong to the 'everyone' and the 'I' all at once. This connects the New York poet with the capaciousness of Whitman, but O'Hara is more radical in his seeming confidence that I, the reader, am another acquaintance of all the people he mentions in passing. His poems' references have become more legible over the years to outsiders, as some of these people have become famous in their own right and as O'Hara's coterie has featured in period memoirs – so for instance I know who Patsy (Southgate) and Mike (Goldberg) are and half-imagine I might bump into them in New York. Even more radical is the effect that I feel I know Frank O'Hara so well that I can be overcome with grief when I recollect he is no longer alive (and the cruel absurdity of his killing by a beach buggy). Shakespeare's sonnets live, but we know nothing of Shakespeare and notoriously his lovers are unidentified; not only do (some of) O'Hara's poems live but they also afford entrance to a living milieu that suggests what a full life might be, impossibly. 'The Day Lady Died' is a concentrated expression of such life, a gay man of Irish American extraction figuring the highest art in a black woman (not to derogate his beloved Rachmaninov) – as elsewhere he does in the female painter Joan Mitchell, the Russian poet Mayakovsky or turning to the Caribbean in his great 'Ode to the French Negro Poets'. This was when the Cold War stoked Russophobia, when glorification of heroic male artistic struggle was at its height, and when, as O'Hara's 'Personal Poem' reminds us, 'Miles Davis was clubbed 12 times last night outside BIRDLAND by a cop'. Urban life in O'Hara's poems stimulates an inexhaustible appetite for encounter that simply obliterates the fear of encounter, fear of the stranger and celebrates living 'as variously as possible' in the face of both internal and external pressures to conform to type.

How does the complex rhythmic temporality of 'The Day Lady Died' connect to stone, a metaphor central to this book? Although an elegy, O'Hara's poem is anything but a memorial slab of verse. Stone and marble are materials long utilized to bespeak the deathless and immemorial in Western art; lyric poetry often is explicit in its ambition to defeat the ravages of time. But once objectification into the beautiful and admirable is achieved, the same medium transforms the deathless and immemorial into the deathly, and into a memorial that cannot fail to advertise common finality. The question then: How to make the rock live, how achieve a 'repeatable evanescence', an experience of life, of beauty time and again, not to be exhausted by one reading of an unambiguous inscription? What is the power 'which turned the rock into a standing water, the flint into a fountain of waters' (Psalm 114 [King James])? Again this book propounds an answer in rhythmic confluence. Water springs from rock in Muriel Rukeyser's *The Book of the Dead*, and in an art which shoots its instant dead-on and transfixes it; Aaron Siskind's photographs of rocks and stones are seen to animate, even to summon to corporeal presence, their obdurate subjects. Barbara Guest is accorded the most extended treatment of a single poet in this book, showing how she can make the rubble of destroyed art and dwellings sing, offering art's dilapidated towers to the reader as *Rocks on a Platter*. By way of further illustration, here is a late, short, and stony poem by Barbara Guest with a brief commentary:

A Noise of Return

We have seen the bowl toppled by morning crickets,
or imagined so, on our imaginary route,
it leads through the mountain.
We are walking on a shadowy line gentle in its way.

Imagination has removed the harshness.
This is a filibuster of routes,

> concealed is the icy stone you tripped on.
> It turns rocks into stone and promises
> to listen to the morning tympanum.
> felicitudes!
> creating another tympanum.[12]

Guest's enigmatic poem celebrates and creates resistance while appearing to move unobstructed along a gentle way mapped out by the iambic pentameter it hovers about rhythmically. Perhaps, the poem was seeded by the celebrated opening lines of Edward Fitzgerald's translation of *Rubáiyát of Omar Khayyám*: 'Awake! For Morning in the Bowl of Night | Has flung the stone that puts the stars to Flight.' If so here is an imaginary landscape where the sound of crickets, produced through friction of their wings, heralds the morning that topples the bowl of night. Fitzgerald's line refers to the flinging of a stone in a cup as the signal in desert life to mount up and ride into the day, even if here the imagined route leads through 'the mountain' (in the singular) and 'into stone'. Before we arrive, we might pause and consider whether, gentle as we are, we get in the way of the 'shadowy line', whether we walk on a line 'gentle in its way', so suggesting it may not be so gentle by other lights, or whether we have become gentle in the way the shadowy line is gentle. In any case, it seems imagination forms 'a shadowy line', which had been harsh and now is made gentle – it is shared, it authorizes the first person plural. A 'filibuster' is a contradictory word, which either makes imagination a 'freebooter' choosing whatever routes appeal, or refers forward to the next line's 'icy stone' as an obstruction, its commonest American usage being an obstructive manoeuvre in Senate. 'It turns rocks into stone' is a puzzling statement since the stone in the preceding line is even more particular than 'rocks', but can possibly be glossed by reference to parts of the ear along with 'tympanum', 'rocks' referring to the crystals of calcium carbonate in the inner ear called otoconia whose displacement results in the vertigo which may indeed follow tripping on an icy stone and getting up again. Turning rocks into stone is what a quarryman does in order to prepare blocks for sculpture; in this way 'our imaginary route' leads through a mountain. While the work is sculpted in stone, it is also shaped from sound, and the 'noise of return' of the poem's title brings into play both the eardrum and the sounds it receives, chiefly 'morning crickets'. Such shaping is shown vividly in the unusual (but first recorded in Middle English) word 'felicitudes!', so this word is a sonic contraction, carved out of the phrase 'filibuster of routes'. Now we arrive at 'creating another tympanum' because as well as an eardrum and insect noise (crickets have tympani on each front leg, just below the knee, to catch sound) a tympanum is a recessed space in a stone pediment or a carving (or textual inscription) in that space. This little lyric therefore at once turns to stone as it reaches the page, and repeats and alters on the breath and in repeated reading. Such a relationship between stone and sound, text and breath will be explored throughout this book. One example in Chapter 7 follows the play around a stone 'pediment and 'gibber' in J. H. Prynne's *Triodes*, where a pediment's dilapidation falls out in 'gibber' which not only refers to loose, nervous talk, but also in Australian English to boulders and loose stone. 'Stone' can be an abstract noun, abstracted from the earth or shaped into an 'abstract' form; Prynne's pediment may collapse into gibber and present impediments, and the stoniness of Guest's 'A Noise of Return' is not so much polished as sharp-edged. This book refuses to abstract stone; it commemorates two mining disasters, the Hawks Nest Tunnel disaster at Gauley Bridge, West Virginia, killing up to a thousand men with silicosis in the late 1920s, and ends with the Levant Mine disaster in Cornwall in 1919 when the 'man-engine' bearing miners to and from the workface collapsed with great loss of life.

Barbara Guest's lyric, like many modern lyrics, obtrudes its resistance to draw attention to its materials, textual and sonic. 'Concealed is the icy stone you tripped on' contrives that we readers end up down in stony gibber while also tripping along on the pavement of the poem's benign, gentle rhythm. 'A Noise of Return' bears traces of Guest's lifetime of thinking about poetry and art, and shows how even the two-finger exercises of such a composer contribute to 'creating another tympanum'. When titling this book *Lyric in Its Times*, what Guest achieves here is what I had in mind: that a lyric poem can transmit sounding, thinking and feeling, and at the same time, shape the tympanum, the mind and body that receive it. And the stone that obstructs our path or that we trip over, halting us in our walking so that we pay attention to 'the morning tympanum' and feel our felicitude, may animate deeply buried meanings emerging from a language's long history, a different rhythm that disrupts a bustling walk through New York, a stroll through the Carrara, its mountains quarried for stone and strewn with gibbers, or a walk down a dark track from a pub in Cornwall. Cross-rhythm causes a catch in reading a poem, where a reader takes up or catches his part in time.

Barbara Guest's stoniness is strongly at odds with Adrian Stokes's love of stone, which belonged to an aesthetics of reparation this book will come to challenge and then to a limited degree re-admit. The granite bedrock and cliffs of the Penwith peninsula of Cornwall, where St Ives is located, is aggressive to farmers, seafarers and miners. Furthermore, granite is radioactive, its radioactive elements decaying into radon gas in a slow, insidious event of what the poet Drew Milne terms 'nuclear implicature'. The book's final chapter finds its themes recapitulated in Peter Lanyon's painting *St Just*: the poetic towers of Chapter 7 are inverted, plunging into destroyed flesh: the tower becomes the Levant mine shaft, while also a birth canal, a windpipe and the vertical plank of a crucifixion. This combination of the visceral and formal is meant to resonate with the extended reading of Dylan Thomas in Chapter 3, for *Lyric in Its Times* consists of folds and pleats. I discover such pleats, such small revelations, in even the most fleeting reference.

Hillis Miller's 'Anachronistic Reading' centres on an ecological reading of Wallace Stevens's 'The Man on the Dump', in particular the final stanza, concluding:

Is it to hear the blatter of grackles and say
Invisible priest; is it to eject, to pull
The day to pieces and cry *stanza my stone*?
Where was it one first heard of the truth? The the.[13]

Guilty of what Veronica Forrest-Thomson describes as 'bad naturalisation' – the itch to secure poems to external referents – Miller asserts that 'the puzzling phrase *"stanza my stone"'* points categorically to the philosopher's stone.[14] As I insist to the contrary in Chapter 9, in a poem an object is always a function. I think Stevens's 'puzzling phrase' works to claim that this stanza, this poem, has made from the dump's incoherent rubbish and from the reasoned-out, piecemeal day, this block, this form; and that '*stanza my stone*' is 'the truth', 'the the', emerging almost miraculously from the now-useless useful junk of which it's made (including old newspapers and forgotten poems). Miller does get there in the end: 'Poetry is the philosopher's stone. We need no other.' The living will be memorialized in stone, but stone returns to life in the work of art – which transcending 'the the' in its facticity conjoins with the reader or listener or looker in a transient amalgam, an event. Such alchemical gold will be recognized in this book as life *as it would be if it had had existence*. Re-reading *Lyric in Its Times* I acknowledge that I have been impatient with Objectivism, understood as trained on enhancing the object-status of a poem, and more generous with kinds of linguistic biomorphism exceeding the bounds of metaphor. But then, there is nothing dispassionate about this way of reading poems. I recognize too that in some way I am seeking to pleat my own life. My life began in the early fifties in Cornwall and took me to New York half-way through my life in the most consequential year of my adulthood. Looking and listening for resonance, I discover it time and again.

Chapter 2

PETRIFACTION AND WAVE POWER

This chapter outlines a post-Renaissance history of lyric poetry's tension between an ambition for formal completion resulting in textual objectification and a contrary desire for utterance to persist in speech or song. Such tension has been often figured in poems through memorializing in stone, a paradoxical practice of enlisting death in the interest of keeping alive and tending to reproduce the human form as statuary, in opposition to the commingled breath of the living lover and poet – and eventually of the reader. The chapter introduces the idea of 'repeatable evanescence' as characterizing aesthetic experience; poets discussed include Shakespeare, Herrick, Baudelaire, John Berryman, Frank O'Hara and Ian Hamilton Finlay.

*

So I was trudging on the elliptical trainer at my gym, listening to a mix-tape of New Orleans classics, when out of Labelle's 'Lady Marmalade' a line estranged itself, whirled out and struck my ear as a line of lyric poetry, unmistakably so if a little too mellifluous: 'May the saddest beast inside roar into the crowd.' As I suspected, this was a case of so-called mondegreen, of creative mishearing, since the line in the song's published lyric is 'Made the savage beast inside roar until it cried.'[1] The misheard line is where this chapter starts, before touching on pieces of poetry setting their course through time and stone, lyric experience and objectification: a song by Robert Herrick, a sonnet by Shakespeare, a stanza of poetry by John Berryman, poems by Baudelaire and Frank O'Hara, and a carved stone text designed and sited by Ian Hamilton Finlay. This discussion comprises the chapter's first section. A second section dwells on the threshold between flesh and stone, marking the moment of transformation either into flesh or stone, through an interpretation of Paulo Veronese's *Hermes, Herse and Aglauros* and that painting's source in Ovid, and through discussion of poems by Georg Trakl and William Blake. The choice of a painting and of Blake's epic verse might suggest an expansion of the terms of argument here from lyric into the fuller category of the poetic.

What is the nature of the line, 'May the saddest beast inside roar into the crowd', a line that was not sung but was misheard in a popular song? Evidently it is not a piece of text, or not until I transcribed my mishearing. At the moment of its adventitious production an event was recognized, an event long-prepared. For this hearer it was prepared as long ago as an adolescent reading of Rilke translations. The force of its iambics and its strong caesura had gathered through the extended history of English poetry. And immediately, the intensity of Patti Labelle's vocal performance intersecting with my body's rhythmic trudging launched this event. A poem is being written, as Eve Sedgwick put it, so after the event this line could make me ask, where am I?[2] Am I with the saddest beast or with the crowd? Surely with neither and both; I am composed somewhere in the exchange and as soon dissolved. This line of a possible poem leans forward into life – it anticipates a fulfilment (or its negative) through its subjunctive form. Its promise does not need to be fulfilled, the saddest lion may stay mangy and torpid; for unacknowledged legislation of the poetic kind works through rhythm's bounds colliding and stirring eddies in time. Rhythm must both bind and unbind, since binding rhythm withdraws into its object and cannot influence futurity. If a poem started with the misheard line, developed a narrative of the crowd withering in the blast of the poet's arraignment, then concluded that the crowd had indeed been troubled, we would face a fixation complete in three ways: first by referring to evidence outside the poem, second by its rhetoric tying together, and third through the reader's regard for a finished poem – an object of admiration.

What is wrong with admiration? Admiring an object may evoke the mental–corporeal, organic–inorganic and subject–object divisions held to characterize Cartesian and modern scientific thinking, but it was Petrarch who wrote the book for admiring poets. The problem, deeply felt by Petrarch, lies in the risk of petrifaction. To admire a poem as an object reduces its potential energy, situating the reader and poem in a space already symbolic, rather than engaging them in creating meaning. Lyric poetry performs a binding and unbinding; the poem and its reader are involved in the event as comprising, however briefly, however tentatively, both a unifying and a freeing. Such an account depends on Freud but is ambivalent about his two terms: '[We] have decided to assume the existence of only two basic instincts, *Eros* and *the destructive instinct* …. The aim of the first of these basic instincts is to establish ever greater unities and to preserve them thus, in short, to bind together; the aim of the second is, on the contrary, to undo connections and so to destroy things.'[3] Should binding be perceived as excessive, in what might be called a fixation, no event can unfold – there is no subsequent position available from which an event can be perceived. If, on the contrary, the unbound character of the poem is such that hope is lost of any binding, however deferred, nothing eventuates. Lyric fails if incoherent, but fails also if bound into object inertia.

The Labelle mishearing was a lyric catch. You cannot step twice into the same river, nor can a river receive the same you twice, but the conditions for this event were so adventitious that the song could never again produce a similar effect. What a lyric poet seeks to contrive is repeatable evanescence, exemplified in the elegy and anti-elegy which is Frank O'Hara's 'The Day Lady Died' – a restorative performing of song and life as evanescent, a repeatable lyric event supervenient on a printed poem. This lyric event entails the binding of particulars into the course of self, for O'Hara makes himself up in the course of the poem and the poem makes the reader up too, and the poem and the disrupted reader make up a strange amalgam: so configured by what it loves the made-up self of O'Hara suffers an almost imperceptible dissolve into a work of art and death, Billie Holliday's, Frank O'Hara's, mine and yours. O'Hara's poem has the paradoxical effect of reconciling a reader to contingency, to the evanescent, *time and again*. To make an event recur, not as a memorial of a moment past, a song dying, a day fading, a lover gone, but to recur in its particularity so a reader's subjectivity can be endued with quotidian details of 1950s Manhattan – this is a lyric achievement. The technical panoply of rhythm, rhyme, assonance, consonance, and so forth generates reliably the kind of experience that engrossed me in the gym; and yet prediction dissolves in the poem's re-reading, time and again.

Through a slight lyric, death can become optional. Here is Robert Herrick's 'To Daisies, Not to Shut So Soone':

> Shut not so soon; the dull-ey'd night
> >   Ha's not as yet begunne
> To make a seisure on the light,
> >   Or to seale up the Sun.
>
> No Marigolds yet closed are;
> >   No shadowes great appeare;
> Nor doth the early Shepheards Starre
> >   Shine like a spangle here.
>
> Stay but till my Julia close
> >   Her life-begetting eye;
> And let the whole world then dispose
> >   It selfe to live or dye.[4]

Night figures as a bailiff approaching the house of light in this beautiful nocturne. Resistance to the watchman or bailiff, a contemporary and evidently a close relative of Descartes, involves resistance to the division between sentient and non-sentient beings, so imbuing flowers, stars and shadows with a restorative animation. The poem resists the categorical line between night and day, death and life. Such a delicate detail as the stress on 'up' in the fourth line anticipates the sun's re-arising. From the titular daisies to *Julia* to *I* to the whole world *It selfe*, all things live or die as they dispose themselves. Of course the diurnal petal closure of daisies and marigolds is hardly a matter of choice any more than human sleep or death's last curfew; flowers and humans share this character, but as flowers fold and Julia falls asleep, shadows and stars appear, to the bailiff's confounding. Julia's eye may be life-begetting like the sun, but when Julia's eyes seal up the Shepherd's Star shines, shedding a lesser light admittedly, like the poet's eye as he watches his Julia. It would be more than two hundred years after Herrick's death that the Shepherd's

Star, Capella, was discovered to be a dyad, and later still before its companion star was descried. This further enriches the lyric event supervening on this poem's text as I now read it, spiralling between night and light, eye and die. Finally the rhyme between 'Life-begetting eye' and 'dye' offers a promise of sexual contentment.

But a poem, as it contrives to make a complex event repeatable, may succumb to seizure and turn into a memorial slab. Poets struggle against this tendency of the material as they work to capture what capture will destroy. Shakespeare's Sonnet 17 embodies this fate of a poem to petrify its contents and itself petrify in a reader's eyes – also in its author's eyes in being written. Reading this poem as for the first time caused me to feel a collapse in its final couplet even as that anticipated flourish wrapped it up. What might condition such an event, emerging in my encounter rather than any subsequent teasing out? Did I respond automatically to the poem's demeanour, its rhythmic temporality, falling into step then stumbling? Demeanour can be treacherous, compromising experience by obtruding a swiftly apprehended, mesmerizing unity. This peril is addressed by Sonnet 17 directly: the sonnet may objectify as a casket, the end-point of human rhythm. Here is a profound tension between a Petrarchan love of the beautiful object, fearing both the object's petrifaction and its Medusa stare, and love of a living creature.

The philosopher Isabelle Stengers writes: 'At every step artists know they are exposed to the risk of betrayal, particularly when, through laziness, ease, impatience, or fear, they believe they can decide on the path, instead of capturing, step by step, the question posed to them at that step.'[5] Surely she demands here a private experience, approaching art as a spiritual exercise. When talking of lyric it seems inadequate to reduce the genre to a drama of the self exposed to the risk of self-betrayal. Lyric poetry then becomes a dance of the split self about its caesura. That's one reason to begin with Shakespeare and a conventional, a social poetic practice. For it is not only yourself who can be betrayed in a work of art. Stengers's persuasive discourse disregards the sociality of lyric performance: far from facing questions, listeners may be caught up in a collective affirmation through rhythm, whether or not in others' company – in 'A Defence of Poetry' Shelley identifies the origins of poetic experience in 'social sympathies'. Even recital can become a temporal site whose structure is linked, step-by-step, to an audience, and through rhythm to wider social sympathies, past and future. Listening to a Chinese student reading Shelley's 'Ode to a Skylark', my heart was in my mouth through a procedure exactly of 'capturing, step by step, the question posed [...] at that step'. A poem calling restlessly to its own dissolution becomes an anthology piece, and then is unsettled again in the particular time and place of its performance. Shelley's rhythmic sociality has been linked to such individual performance by Henri Meschonnic, restating in his different terms the binding–unbinding structure of an event:

> For rhythm is a subject-form(er). The subject-form(er). That it renews the meaning of things, that it is through rhythm that we reach the sense that we have of our being undone [défaire], that everything around us happens as it

undoes itself [défaire], and that, approaching this sensation of the movement of everything, we ourselves are part of this movement.[6]

Rhythm is indeed 'a subject-form(er)' since as Mutlu Konuk Blasing notes in introducing a detailed summary of recent work on rhythm and language acquisition, 'learning language depends on a rhythmic training that precedes and enables meaningful speech. The stage of babbling, where the infant can produce the phonemes of all possible languages, entails recognizing aural sensations and reproducing them orally'.[7] For Meschonnic as for Blasing rhythm subtends linguistic embodiment; but more radically he attributes to rhythm a quickening and thickening of the real, such that subjectivity starts to pulse within all that is concrescent and prepares for the event of its emergence. Rhythm gives birth to new forms out of people conjoined with it historically and also people disposed to respond to it in the future – to child in this way is to believe that a poem will have been read by those longing for its rhythm.

So even where lyric art foregrounds individual risk, any step-by-step movement catching the reader in its concatenation must have been prepared for, although unrecognized until a beat later, *in* the event, or through longer retrospection. Here 'step-by-step' evokes the turnings of poetic line. In present-day prosodic theory, recognizing the work lyric does means attending to line-breaks as though searching for handholds in a rock-face. Such searching counts among the phenomenal data brought into relation when reading a short lyric poem. Formal unity can be held in abeyance during an encounter which joins a poem's demeanour, keeping edges in view, step-by-step. Through demeanour the object of attachment moves with you. Sonnet 17 lends itself to such rhyming, rupture and resumption, and rhythm, since the binding and unbinding I remarked in the misheard line from 'Lady Marmalade' are here situated prominently in line ending and not-ending. When reading step-by-step, Shakespeare's rhyming 'time' and 'rhyme' in his final couplet illustrates the contradictory workings of prosody, this rhyme of rhymes binding and unbinding in one gesture.

17

Who will believe my verse in time to come,
If it were filled with your most high deserts?
Though yet, heaven knows, it is but as a tomb,
Which hides your life, and shows not half your parts:
If I could write the beauty of your eyes,
And in fresh numbers number all your graces,
The age to come would say, 'This poet lies;
Such heavenly touches ne'er touched earthly faces'.
So should my papers (yellowed with their age)
Be scorned, like old men of less truth than tongue,
And your true rights be termed a poet's rage,
And stretched metre of an antique song;

> But were some child of yours alive that time,
> you should live twice: in it, and in my rhyme.[8]

'Who will believe my verse in time to come', opens a temporal horizon beyond the time of reading while putting in doubt the event that opens such a horizon. We might believe this verse in our present, but a gap opens between present and future readings. In time the poem may become discredited. Contrariwise, the poem might discredit the future – and as it emerges in the poem, the future may lack the conditions needed to make the poem credible. The performative drama of this poem brings temporalities into alignment – the poem's enduring, its subject's present being, its subject's perpetuation, the moment of a reader's recognizing a sonnet and knowing its sonic shape, the sonnet read as contemporaneous with its writing, the sonnet read in a conditional future which is ours in 'time to come'. The poet knows that readers know that belief in this poem is not contingent on testing its truth-claims against a pattern in the admired lover; its temporalities can be brought into alignment, bound together through poetic devices calling attention to their own performance. But if felt as contrived, this may too far strain belief.

At the end of the sonnet 'time' and 'rhyme' rhyme in what might seem a fixational clincher. While 'my verse in time to come'. threatened to entomb, 'tomb' is not a resolving rhyme for 'time to come'. The sonnet is Shakespeare's child ('it') and also *your* child (the lover's), the lover is its true begetter, and the sonnet as a whole must rhyme with the lover's visible pattern of beauty (outside the poem in the present and reproduced in time to come). But the lover remains elusive since to rhyme 'rhyme' with 'time' is tautological. Here you are, lover, in time to come, back where you started in a not very tomb-like tomb – indeed at the end you *live* 'in my rhyme', breathing even when immured. But you can never live in my verse because the condition for that is your living outside it, in a child reproducing your pattern. The time to come, 'that time', is the horizon this sonnet promises to extend, while snapping back into alignment.

Formally a Shakespearian sonnet would seem desirous of fixation: 'it is but as a tomb', this poem, if 'filled with your most high deserts', and its prescribed form always risks sepulture.[9] Your parts, or some of them, might make this tomb ornate, but its outline will be made all too secure. A reading may work between step-by-step line-endings and formal unity, but line-endings are not enough; there must be more to life than enjambment. And as we know, whether in the shower or concert hall, there is more to song than the shape of song. An analytical language fixated on edges and the contradiction mobilized by enjambment can lead to a feeling of always crashing in the same car. Reading a lyric poem must stay open to its eventuation, a rhythmic coming together that includes the reader's contingent subjectivity. Sonnet 17 can be a fascinating thing freezing its reader in admiration; or the text for an experience of repeated capture and loss; or an event felt as social, supervening on a lyric poem liable to objectify despite the weak rhyme of 'time to come' and 'tomb'. Thus all of these at once.

A stronger reading of the relationship between casket and death, and lyric and life, may emerge if the dissonant rhyme of 'tomb' and 'rhyme' is heard semantically.

Rhyme then becomes a temporal edge, an aspect of the body's demeanour as it moves forward in time; and rhyme's doubling becomes the sonnet's triumph – it does not merely represent but it childs, a childing which will reveal the pattern of its parenthood. Rhyme accomplishes the state of what will have been. 'If I could write' anticipates 'your true rights' which will have re-written the incredible number of your graces, and will have unbound a binding which threatens to petrify the heart of the poem – 'in fresh numbers number' and 'touches ne'er touched'. Such creeping petrification is not unusual in the sonnets; for instance, Sonnet 43 has 'whose shadow shadows' (l.5) and 'shadow's form form happy show' (l.6), and offers another kind of release in its final line, into the mobility of a dream visitation. More optimistically Sonnet 17 anticipates it will have childed its reader, through its rhythmic call conceiving an embodiment, an embodied chorus which neither dissolves like a mishearing, nor petrifies into a tomb. That is, the last couplet accepts and celebrates the condition of this sonnet extending the 'stretched metre of an antique song'. 'No subject can easily be conceived as extinguished', writes Denise Riley. 'Language doesn't want to allow that thought; its trajectory is always to lean forward into life, to push it along, to propel the dead onward among the living.'[10]

What then of my first sense of everything falling apart? Perhaps this corresponds with Giorgio Agamben's view that a poem's final line inevitably abandons the step-by-step, turning away from the question posed by a line-ending. But this seems too generic an explanation for a sinking feeling which undermines its proleptically hopeful assertion. No, there is a failure here, felt in the phrase 'in it'. Where you place the stress between these two insignificant words scarcely makes a difference, although a stress on 'it' may be marginally worse; but the indifference of the phrase infects 'my rhyme' whose potential dies in so-whatishness. The unbinding is too passive, libidinal energy flags, and no resonance oscillates between ending and not-ending.

Petrifaction stills time and makes a poem a material entity rather than a temporal performance. The contents of a casket may however be heard out through the joint attention of a future readership and speakership; in this prospect the immured being never dies. Shakespeare brings forward an assertive corollary to Sonnet 17 in Sonnet 81:

> Your monument shall be my gentle verse,
> Which eyes not yet created shall o'er-read,
> And tongues to be your being shall rehearse,
> When all the breathers of this world are dead.

'And tongues to be your being shall rehearse' asserts the supervening of performance over a monument thereby made 'gentle', living because lines of verse rehearse (a verb which derives from harrowing, lineating the earth before seeding). An iconoclastic alternative would demand a monument's destruction. The power exercised by P.B. Shelley's sonnet 'Ozymandias' stems from the interplay between object, eternity and the poem's opening to spatial rhythm. 'Round the decay | Of that colossal wreck, boundless and bare, | The lone and level sands stretch far away.' The represented and petrified has been subjected to dismemberment, whose energy invests an undifferentiated eternity, 'lone and level', with a regular rhythmic pulse. The rhyming of 'away' with 'decay' adjusts 'away' to a musical decay, that is a resonant fade-out signifying an event that never ceases. So 'the lone and level sands stretch far away' produces an affirmative pulse by contrast with a decay which here is categorically inorganic. The poet's spatial and temporal distance from the decayed monument is no bar to its continuing half-life.

Verse itself feeds on decay, wriggling through calcified memories and the emotions turning to bric-a-brac. In Baudelaire's 'Spleen II' 'vers' denotes at once poetic verse and earthworms, alike feeding in the charnel house of the poet's brain. But in the second part of 'Spleen II' even the energy of decay wanes, with emptiness and anomie taking on the proportions of immortality. Amid such tedium there remains nothing on which to feed; living matter becomes entirely obdurate, a block of granite. This block however is open to imaginative shaping, surrounded as it is by an overwhelming wave and seen indistinctly through fog in its desert place. The poem performs two parallel sequences of transfiguration, with emotions objectifying into a lumber room of useless memories in the first part, then entering a productive decay as a charnel house where verse can feed; while in the second part emptiness becomes boredom prefiguring the stupidity of immortality, striving for the absolute which converts living matter into a granite block rather than a miscellany of objectified emotions. Hereafter the obelisk, despite its installation in the Sahara, can also become a medium for representation, a work of art which sings even if remote and inaccessible.

Spleen II (Les Fleurs du Mal LXXVI)

J'ai plus de souvenirs que si j'avais mille ans.
Un gros meuble à tiroirs encombré de bilans,
De vers, de billets doux, de procès, de romances,
Avec de lourds cheveux roulés dans des quittances,
Cache moins de secrets que mon triste cerveau.
C'est une pyramide, un immense caveau,
Qui contient plus de morts que la fosse commune.
—Je suis un cimetière abhorré de la lune,
Où comme des remords se traînent de longs vers
Qui s'acharnent toujours sur mes morts les plus chers.
Je suis un vieux boudoir plein de roses fanées,
Où gît tout un fouillis de modes surannées,
Où les pastels plaintifs et les pâles Boucher,
Seuls, respirent l'odeur d'un flacon débouché.

Rien n'égale en longueur les boiteuses journées,
Quand sous les lourds flocons des neigeuses années
L'ennui, fruit de la morne incuriosité,

Prend les proportions de l'immortalité.
—Désormais tu n'es plus, ô matière vivante!
Qu'un granit entouré d'une vague épouvante,
Assoupi dans le fond d'un Saharah brumeux;
Un vieux sphinx ignoré du monde insoucieux,
Oublié sur la carte, et dont l'humeur farouche
Ne chante qu'aux rayons du soleil qui se couche.[11]

Edna St Vincent Millay's brilliant translation of this poem coaxes forward its relationship with 'Ozymandias' in what is effectively an intertext – an intertext which in one direction visits on Baudelaire's sphinx a 'rude and sullen frown' more Shelleyan than Baudelairian, but in the other resonates with alexandrines ('Assumes the shape and size of immortality'). Millay is more expansive than Baudelaire, but her expansions are illuminating; 'fruit de la morne incuriosité' becomes 'fruit of the mind's inert, incurious tree' playing not only with an echo of *Paradise Lost*, but also lodging the mind imagistically in the bracteate, physical brain. Her intermediary text, a distinguished poem in its own right, makes the echo of 'Ozymandias' in the final couplet's sonic decay unmistakable, while also linking Baudelaire to Shelley as poets of energetic decay:

The Sphinx

I swear to you that if I lived a thousand years
I could not be more crammed with dubious souvenirs.
There's no old chest of drawers bulging with deeds and bills,
Love-letters, locks of hair, novels, bad verses, wills,
That hides so many secrets as my wretched head;—
It's like a mausoleum, like a pyramid,
Holding more heaped unpleasant bones than Potter's Field;
I am a graveyard hated by the moon; revealed
Never by her blue light are those long worms that force
Into my dearest dead their blunt snouts of remorse.
—am an old boudoir, where roses dried and brown
Have given their dusty odor to the faded gown,
To the ridiculous hat, doubtless in other days
So fine, among the wan pastels and pale Bouchers.

Time has gone lame, and limps; and under a thick pall
Of snow the endless years efface and muffle all;
Till boredom, fruit of the mind's inert, incurious tree,
Assumes the shape and size of immortality.

Henceforth, O living matter, you are nothing more
Than the fixed heart of chaos, soft horror's granite core,
Than a forgotten Sphinx that in some desert stands,

> Drowsing beneath the heat, half-hidden by the sands,
> Unmarked on any map,—whose rude and sullen frown
> Lights up a moment only when the sun goes down.[12]

In Swinburne's characterization, this verse (whether the original or Millay's translation) 'has the languid, lurid beauty of close and threatening weather – a heavy heated temperature, with dangerous hothouse scents in it; thick shadow of cloud about it, and fire of molten light. It is quite clear of all whining and windy lamentation; there is nothing of the blubbering and shrieking style long since exploded'.[13] Rather, entanglement in this poem endangers its reader: Does she also light up 'a moment only when the sun goes down', when the poem closes? Not so, for this forgotten Sphinx is lit up time and again by a reader's attentions and by its release from her attentions – neglected, forgotten, mere words awaiting revival, a block of text whose lineaments await discernment. Millay's translation tends to obscure the relationship in Baudelaire's verses between the abstraction of a granite block, the dead form of the necessary shape of a universal, and its counterpart in the bric-a-brac of dead particulars. Through casting their attentive light, the moon and the sun become parallel counterparts, reviving the Hegelian Dialectic of the Object between universal and particular and generating both the long worms of verse amid memory's stuff and the manifestation of a Sphinx out of the mists surrounding the obelisk. This revival occurs in the event of the poem as the reader too disperses into the text and pulls back in order to survey it; as the reader is absorbed into its particularities and contemplates simultaneously its intrication with the greater unity and disparity of *Les Fleurs du Mal*.

'There is no subject prior to or outside the expression', as Brian Massumi puts it; while at the same time, according to Alain Badiou, 'the poem presents itself as a thing of language, encountered – each and every time – as an event'.[14] But if the world unifies as an event about a subjectivity itself realized through this particular shaping by time-space, what I have yet to do here is register the effect of these encounters on my subjectivity. The bathos I felt at the end of Sonnet 17 collapsed me into an appraising position, whereas Shelley's sonnet produced an expansiveness which did for a moment feel as though it dissolved subject–object positions and furthermore, divisions between subjectivities in a conjoining and potentially collective rhythm. This distinction begins to challenge the categorical nature of subjectivity: different construals of subjectivity have to be specified, rather than just pressing against the subject–object division. To contemplate a poem does not necessarily serve accountancy; metrical and etymological analysis can connect a poem to a cultural and affective history which enriches its embodiment and its continuing eventuation, unfolding through Allen Grossman's questions: 'What does the poem intend to follow after – what can be thought that could not be thought by the reader before the poem was known to the reader?'[15] How though is it possible here to distinguish the poem from its interpretation, to resist binding the poem to its interpretation, especially that of a reader such as Grossman? Here Grossman seems to imagine the poem not so much as an object but as a transitional object which might at last be abandoned, however reluctantly.

For the poem to still accompany a reader and not be used up, it may need to remain to a degree unassimilable, unmistakably alien to the reader's creativity. How can the poem survive its interpretation without being assimilated? Can the Owl of Minerva forget its perch?

'Knowing' in Grossman's question begs subsequent questions: What does it mean to know a poem by heart? How does the object of poetic artifice differ from the loved and internalized object? Poems solicit remembrance, but should perhaps be forgotten. Writing a commentary on his own psychoanalytical papers, W. R. Bion suggests 'that the papers should be read in the same conditions in which a psycho-analysis should be conducted—without memory or desire. And then forgotten. They can be re-read; but *not* remembered'.[16] If lyric is an art of remembrance, perhaps it is an art of necessarily unconscious remembrance, of the return so well imagined by Mutlu Konuk Blasing, to a place before the sundering experience of linguistic representation, the place where the always-restored good object fills the mouth as wanted.[17] Only the art of forgetting can restore between breaths the poem known by heart, o'er-reading the poem which recital might regurgitate as a hard-edged and uncommunicative object. The poem 'lights up a moment only when the sun goes down', as Millay's translation has it. Cultivated forgetfulness might however herald the death of hermeneutics, advocating worship of the inexpressible and what lies beyond grasping, or else the scholastic typologies of formalist poetics.

Romantic aesthetics are obsessed with dynamism and swear off Eucharistic and grammatical tables alike; they prefer dissolution as experienced through time to either transcendence or petrifaction. Horror of the dead object haunts post-romantic prosody. All eventuates under the sign of contingency and as fast unbinds. That is to distinguish Romantic poetics from a modern but anti-Modernist tendency where fleetingness leads to capture, the snapshot that makes an object of the moment; and which leads towards the insistence on language's materiality in an Objectivist lineage. With Language poetry this will be complicated by linguistic constructivism, but the descent is clear enough – from the Cartesian Modern to New Criticism to a structuralist critic like Veronica Forrest-Thomson, and on to Language and conceptualist poetry. One strange and estranged feature of its vaunted materialism is a cancellation of the material world, a material world occasioning disgust at its failure to be concrete and hard-edged enough.

Appalled by temporality, Objectivist poetics associates the passage of time with death and decay but also with viscera, maternity and the female, whereas Romantic poetics associates objectification with the corpse. Shelley's post-Lucretian organicist philosophy conceives decay as creative, releasing energy – the collapse of despotisms energizes a frozen, adamantine world, burning and rotting are preconditions for growth. The affirmative pulse of 'the lone and level sands' is challenged by desert aridity; the despotism of Ozymandias has been so absolute that the power of decay dissipates across an infertile emptiness, its potential felt rather than realized.

By contrast, nowhere is disgust at decay and fear of the failure of petrifaction more vividly performed than in a poem which like Sonnet 17 rhymes 'time' with 'rhyme', John Berryman's 'Homage to Mistress Bradstreet'.[18] Where this rhyme occurs in stanza 55, an undead organicism infects objects with a radioactive half-life, a continuous particulate dissolution. Attempts to memorialize are confounded by time's depredations. Most frighteningly the categorical division between organic and inorganic is confounded. This stanza may start on a *grand guignol* note but it gathers great force; and after fifty-four stanzas of a seventeenth-century idiom consistent with the teleporting of the poet to a Puritan New England, linguistic anachronism delivers a jarring shock:

> Headstones stagger under great draughts of time
> after heads pass out, and their world must reel
> speechless, blind in the end
> about its chilling star: thrift tuft,
> whin cushion—nothing. Already with the wounded flying
> dark air fills, I am a closet of secrets dying,
> races murder, foxholes hold men,
> reactor piles wage slow upon the wet brain rime.

The world reels and becomes real again in its historical distance, but 'distance' should be in the plural since the poem oscillates between contemporary and early America. 'Headstones stagger' announces a grotesque resurrection that animates commemorative stones, their names and texts passed off for bodies. 'After heads pass out' makes of time a kind of birth canal and the identity of headstones and heads is strongly asserted.

The reduction of grave-mounds to 'thrift tuft, | whin cushion' is followed by a specifically anti-Wordsworthian reduction to 'nothing' – that is, *not* 'Rolled round in earth's diurnal course, | With rocks, and stones, and trees'. But then thrift and whin make living pillows of grave-mounds. The human and the animal collapse too, for 'foxholes hold men'. This phrase is anachronistic for early America; it calls back to 'wounded flying' which begins to sound like body-parts filling the air after a shelling. The 'wounded flying' may also pertain to aerial battles. 'I am a closet of secrets dying' collapses subjectivity and the external world; these secrets seem to be ugly flat truths about recent American history: 'races murder, foxholes hold men'. 'Homage to Mistress Bradstreet' was written at the end of the Korean War where the experience of American troops in foxholes in bitter cold had been horribly traumatic, and at the start of the civil rights movement. 'Great draughts of time' then are staggering the headstones of generations of Americans. The enclosure of 'a closet of secrets dying' becomes hard to distinguish from 'dark air fills'. A histrionic dismissal of the early Americans back into a speechless world, an inrush of contemporary horror and barbarism, may seem to divide the stanza at the caesura of 'nothing', but 'time' and 'rime' bind the temporal confusion together.

The final line moves like sludge. How is this impassable line to be parsed? 'Rime' may have hoarfrost for a primary dictionary meaning, but not primary here. The flaunting of 'rime' in the position of the most insistent rhymes of this poem, as the last word of the stanza, strikes the ear as scornful, disgusted with the demands of poetic form in conditions where 'reactor piles wage slow upon the wet brain'. 'Rime' by this token gestures impatiently towards the formal closing/closeting of the stanza in its rhyme with 'time', comparable to 'reactor piles wage slow upon the wet brain *full stop*'. The line could suggest these very verses 'wage rime' upon the wet brain, that is, immobilize the brain so it swells, sealing it with its pressure of secrets.[19] But the word 'piles' although belonging chiefly to the noun phrase 'reactor piles' could also be read as a verb, rime piled upon the wet brain in waging war against it. This attack on rhyme vandalizes the stanza in both its interior and formal circumference.

On first reading my shock came from the phrase 'reactor piles', so extreme, so unprepared-for, that it felt like a breach not only in the poem's temporal organization, but also in the contract between poet and reader – a contract based on the poem's object status. Hitherto the poem as object had kept its temporal domains and formal procedures clearly demarcated, through a repeated enjambment of Puritan America with the temporality of the poem's composition, an unsituated present. Now the brutality of this stanza's first and last lines performs a headlock; these lines resemble linguistic slabs, unmarked by commas and unmitigated by caesuras. Collapsed headstones become radioactive as 'reactor piles', the ledgers of the dead dealing death down to the present, insidious and 'slow', releasing negative energy into the swelling brain through a kind of shale impaction of syntax.

'Reactor piles wage slow upon the wet brain rime' is driven by a basic fear of annihilation, and its formation by such fear risks damaging the poem's formal edifice. The line scorns its stanzaic matrix through violence on 'rime' – a violence that both summons and turns away from 'war'. For the verb 'wage' is used mostly in contemporary English as part of the compound verb 'wage war', and given Berryman's habitual deferral of syntactical completion, the verb-component 'war' continues to be awaited even while a rhyme for 'time' is expected; moreover, the anticipation of war is reinforced by the powerful stress on 'star' before a colon and the wrenching caesura in the middle of the stanza's fourth line. 'Star' receives more stress than any rhyme word in the stanza, to the point that stanzaic form threatens to buckle about the caesura. 'Reactor piles wage slow upon the wet brain rime' attacks the conventions of syntactical linking; it could be interpreted as a psychotic attack on linking determined to reduce words to lumps, thereby threatening the basis of communication. Berryman is a [water] 'closet' and while 'foxholes hold men', what 'wage slow upon the wet brain' have emerged from foxholes as excremental 'reactor piles'. Dead words, departing from men's speech, or worse yet, intimating men too may be shit – in the next stanza 'those myriads' have become 'fire-ash, fossils, burled'. 'Burled' is a Berryman invention since in earlier usage the verb meant to *remove* burls while Berryman's twist produces the image of fossils floating 'in the open river-drifts' surrounded by water-swirls as though knots in wood. Charming, except that Berryman would have known the obsolete meaning of 'burl' as a pustule; and hence the line passingly recollects an earlier line, 'a manic stench | of pustules snapping'. Closets and foxholes, outraged wombs, fill with the dying in the wake of the murderous necrophiliac orgasm of the previous stanza:

'Moisture shoots. | Hungry throngs collect. They sword into the carcass.' 'Sword' wields the word 'word'.

The attack on linking is an attack on the poem's containment function. No wonder there follows a retreat from dead words and words representing the dead in speechless but textually inscribed reactor piles and headstones. Berryman's future practice would outrage the conception of the poem as aesthetic object, quarrelling insistently with the textuality of words: for Berryman, text was no bulwark against the workings of time, but excremental and deathly. The drama of this stanza from a literary–historical perspective lies in its assault on the poem as object, on the poem as studied by New Criticism. I believe Berryman was disgusted by his own uncontainable Romanticism. The stakes are shown with extraordinary vividness: collapsing the categorical divisions between subjectivity and object, between human, animal and inanimate material produces an overwhelming disgust and terror. Yet it holds the possibility of recovery. The room that this stanza comprises is a closet, not a tomb. Secrets may die in being exposed, but the death of secrecy may lead to life; the tomb slowly transforms into habitable architecture.

In 1953 the people in the United States lived in a state of apprehension, a Cold War nuclear stand-off engendering a 'climate of fear'. Berryman's line 'reactor piles wage slow upon the wet brain rime' is at once explosive and insidious, an explosion that would go on slowly without stopping. The rime that coats the wet brain is cracking up, but held in place as rhyme. In the event the line is a stopped explosion, beyond which lies return to ordinary life, 'the rain of pain and departure' – as though ordinary life were being necessarily propitiated, since it continues under the threat of annihilation. Following the 'time | rime' insult, the penultimate stanza 56 simply abandons rhyming its first and last lines for the offensive anti-rhyme 'draw off | nothing', and the last stanza, trying to ingratiate, to head off retaliation with the self-cancelling 'love | love', reduces sexual love to a cynical jingle. John Berryman was writing 'Homage to Mistress Bradstreet' as Willem de Kooning was painting the first versions of 'Woman', the greatest depiction of the nurturing and persecutory muse in American art of this or any period.

At last we encounter the Medusa face to face. Petrarch feared that to pour his vitality into a poem would reduce him to a husk.[20] When a poet contemplates female beauty, he courts the Medusa and so faces a double penalty. If his poem's beauty does justice to his beloved, he betrays her through his narcissistic investment in the poem. Its admirable polish encapsulates and stills feeling, while its beauty delivers the coup de grâce to whatever is left of the poet. 'The instituting act – the artisan boast of the poet, perpetualization – illustrates the Horatian logic in which human value is produced by human sacrifice – no middle term.'[21] But the logic summarized by Allen Grossman was unacceptable to Shelley and repellent after the First World War; the more so after disclosure of Nazi death camps, the disclosure of what Stalinist sacrifice entailed, and after the Korean and Vietnam Wars justified as sustaining human value. A vital development from sacrificial 'instituting', linked by Shelley to authoritarianism, lies in rhythm – rhythm that is historical, social, generative and embodying. This is poetry's central task, 'as the site where language is linked not only to structures of identification and displacement before the consolidation of subject positions but especially to rhythm and the bodily experience of temporality, on the one hand, and to the formative dwelling in a particular language, on the other' (in Jonathan Culler's words).[22] The relationship of rhythm with embodiment derives from the baby suckling. In its origins rhythm is dyadic, preceding and managing the infant's individual embodiment during a transition from the dyadic to the formation of joint attention, the baby emerging as a subject through rhythm while protected from separation anxiety by rhythm's familiar rupture and resumption. Therefore the rhythmic 'we' precedes 'I'. Rhythm is not mechanical; there must be 'an element of transition in its periodicity', a continuous adjustment as with the feeding dyad.[23] From the start rhythm entails a kind of dressage, somehow you've got to get into it, and if you can't, you become vulnerable to feelings of abandonment, rage, or superiority. This applies not only to dance, music and poetry, but to intimacy including sex, and to joining a conversation. Rhythm has the potential then to re-embody responsively, or to spark reaction into defensive rigidity and impasse. Neither sneer of cold command nor obsessional workmanship can animate; neither the syllable uttered into emptiness, nor the jewelled casket. In Frank O'Hara's poem 'In Memory of My Feelings', Medusa is Unbound as a bucket of writhing snakes.[24] It took a different serpent to bring God's creation to life, as the close of O'Hara's poem reminds us – a serpent whose characteristic method is poetic rhythm: 'When you turn your head | can you feel your heels, undulating?' As these articulating heels show, step-by-step does not necessitate the fiction of uncontaminated encounter; the event of the poem mobilizes a plurality. Even the lone and level sands can be sculpted by wind into waves.

For rhythm can be joined in stone. Consider this passage of prose and of architecture:

> Footfalls remark the tomb. Architecture reigns also in utter silence. The Redentore interior by Palladio, supreme architectural attainment, magnifies the poignancy of cut-into surfaces. Engaged columns, apertures in those significant walls, the run of the drum, the cupola, the semi-circle of disengaged columns at the end of the nave, the heavy creamy lines above the knotted capitals, the corners with both rectangular and cylindrical engaged shafts, all these and any other volumes or any section of details even without the chapels, can be read in terms of the smoothness of shafts and the rough sprouting of capitals; in terms of the smooth tribune archivolt and the deeply cut archivolt behind, over the altar; or even more simply, in terms of the smooth square feet of the cornice with dark rough gaps.[25]

Can you feel your heels, undulating? This writing by the art critic Adrian Stokes rebuffs the Medusa. Architectural writing from as long ago as Vitruvius's first book finds rhythm in stone, but Stokes's peculiar animation helps to link Ruskin and Pound in a Romantic lineage. For these writers, stone lives – but as we shall later see, its life is confined in a peculiar stasis, a shimmer.

Treading a *via negativa* I want briefly to draw attention to a dissenting aesthetic which insists on the Cartesian mind–body duality. Here the *cogito* is celebrated as the founding moment of revolutionary violence productive of a truly modern art, whereby alienated subjectivity can stand before objects of human artifice unashamedly repudiating the natural world. No event can supervene on the archetypal situations this art commemorates. I refer to the art of Ian Hamilton Finlay, identified on his tombstone as Poet, in an act of intractable, unnegotiable naming. Finlay's art assents to Bruno Latour's proclamation that we have never been modern, and insists on correcting that failure, albeit in a remote Scottish garden and in works of humorously domestic scale appropriate to the human diminution following the Jacobin Terror. Correcting that failure would entail separating the work of translation and the work of purification, and this is precisely Finlay's strategy – to translate the classical era or the French revolutionary era into objects reminiscent of a military board game, while ensuring that categories remain rigorously distinct. Finlay's stone battleships, birdbaths from which little flocks take off to dump their lime bombs, belong in a garden acknowledging the violence of enlightenment reason, amid a collection of weaponry that might be fall-out from the Medusa's counter-attack. In a virtuoso reading of Homer's Shield of Achilles passage, Bill Brown commandeers the shield for the Western cultural prototype of Latour's hybrid object, or what Brown calls a thing – alive, organic, metal, indissociable and rhythmic.[26] Finlay's weaponry clatters to the ground when the Medusa stares at the Shield of Achilles, rendering it useless for war. Nothing to do but contemplate the shield and crossed swords on the wall and the military glory for which they serve as metonyms. Installed in Finlay's garden, named Little Sparta in antipathy to the democratic mess of Athens, is his sculpture-poem 'The Present Order':

Figure 1 Ian Hamilton Finlay, 'The Present Order'. The text reads 'THE | PRESENT | ORDER || IS | THE | DISORDER || OF | THE | FUTURE|| SAINT- | JUST'.

'Nothing beside remains.' The disorder of the future turns out to be artfully displayed, lent to contemplation: Why is this phrase here? Where does it come from? How did it get here? Is it a metonym? – responses thoroughly alienated from the aesthetics of the event.[27] In contemplating this work Gray's elegiac verses may resound, and visiting through the seasons would allow its setting's trained natural cycles to be appreciated. Loss however is prevalent, the breakdown of Enlightenment rationalism against the horizon of the Pentland hills, the struggle to make a garden behave despite pests, drought, canker and exhaustion. The point of this work is that nothing eventuates, and a visitor walks about and through its sepulchral arrangement, relishing what Drew Milne calls 'the elegiac pathos of distance', enjoying her own path even as the stones keep their fixed order.[28] Stokes's passage also relies on ambulation, as its opening phrase 'footfalls remark the tomb' declares: but 'footfalls remark the tomb' denotes the opening of an event, architectural rhythms reshaping the subject as they are launched by the sonic rhythm of the subject's footfalls. Walking about Ian Hamilton Finlay's 'The Present Order' the subject is correctly referred to her own resources.

Contemplating 'The Present Order' engages an experience familiar from curatorial labels, the urge to formulate situational questions about conceptualist art, except where accidental sublimity overwhelms its programme. Granted, fascination and becoming engrossed, or being amused and 'getting it' are all potential in conceptualist art, but where my sympathies lie must now be clear, for all the integrity and logic of Finlay's work. Experience of a poetic event can imagine the real, or as Winnicott suggests more strongly, hallucinates the real, by way of its continuous destruction: 'The object is always being destroyed. This destruction becomes the unconscious backcloth for love of a real object; that is, an object outside the area of the subject's omnipotent control.'[29] The object being destroyed here is an internal object, crossing the barrier between an unconscious inner world and the external world in an hallucinatory migration, it being understood that 'hallucinations are dream phenomena that have come forward into the waking life and that hallucinating is no more of an illness in itself than the corresponding fact that the day's events and the memories of real happenings are drawn across the barrier into sleep and into dream-formation'. Reality therefore requires the continuous cancellation of the hallucinatory ego-investments and also the social preconceptions fabricating its solid-seeming simulacrum. As Shelley wrote in *A Defence of Poetry*, 'we want the creative faculty to imagine what we know'; the real lies inaccessible behind its simulacra which must be strongly imagined and destroyed, making the real compelling, densifying it through re-eventuation so that relations with other human beings, with other species and with the earth can be felt rather than conceived or asserted. Densifying and then dissipating, binding and unbinding: such is lyric's main work. Reality needs to be eventuated time and again. Considering this, look at another work by Finlay, quite properly situated in a museum. Why so? Because the French Revolution was born in blood, and marble so asserts. More radically, Finlay celebrates the death-dealing of art: he was a singularly honest artist and thinker. Clay reduces the body to a corpse. Plaster shapes a death mask. Marble ends all human activity.

Figure 2 Ian Hamilton Finlay, 'Marble the Revolution'.

However, this marble is spectacularly veined. Against Finlay's memorial stone I wish to launch a contra-Medusan attack, the Galatean event of Frank O'Hara's 'Ode on Causality'.[30] The Ode's opening passage offers the lines: 'suddenly everyone's supposed to be veined, like marble | it isn't that simple but it's simple enough | the rock is the least living of the forms man has fucked'. Rock may be the least living, but it is living at least, as differentiated from stone polished to a mirror finish. O'Hara's poem was inspired by his visiting a memorial consisting of a hunk of rock, not a marble cenotaph; its association with living rock proclaims a rough-hewn architecture that holds life, and poetry breaks it out, 'seizing a grave by throat'. Such is the rock's irregularity that the name of the deceased has to be mounted on an unpolished bronze plate. That name is Jackson Pollock, an artist round whose works an influential discourse of eventuation was to accrue. The veined marble of the Ode's opening lines has returned to rock and rock is brought to life in art's event. This is a bit solemn for O'Hara, so rock becomes a phallus which is also 'the pillar of our deaths' and ends the poem in a vast orgasm, a *jouissance* which could never be thought to 'sword into the carcass'. Be stone no more![31] Quite an event to end on, and it must be left up in the air – if only to return in the next chapter.

Chapter 3

ANTI-MEMORIAL ELEGY

Elegy is the lyric sub-genre having the strongest association with stone, and particularly with carved and inscribed memorialization. The first section of this chapter examines elegies by Frank O'Hara, W. S. Graham and James Schuyler that employ strategies for surreptitiously keeping alive the poet or artist commemorated, and for making the elegy itself breathe. The second section focuses on an elegy to his earlier self by Dylan Thomas, revealing a poet obsessed by the horror of birth and death, and whose poetry struggles to suspend the biological in an ever-present by means of the metrical cages it imposes.

1

Frank O'Hara's 'Ode on Causality' is, like his 'The Day Lady Died', an elegy, and the two paramount poets in the modern English language elegiac idiom, however greatly their poetic diction differs, are Frank O'Hara and W. S. Graham; each of them drawn to elegize not fellow poets but composers and musicians, or painters who were their friends, Jackson Pollock and Billie Holiday for O'Hara and Peter Lanyon and Bryan Wynter for Graham. It is no coincidence that their most famous elegies allude to bar (New York) and pub (St Ives) life. These elegies cannot be reproached as a competitive appropriation of shared social discourse, but on the contrary inhabit a shared language, perception, social milieu and place; they are situated between poet and painter or musician, or triangulated between poet and painter or musician and audience, between the living and the dead. Frank O'Hara would himself be elegized by a more reticent poet, James Schuyler, who had felt intensely competitive with him but in his elegy managed this complication with evasive delicacy.

For a generic problem of elegy is how to keep faith with the mourned 'you' so that it is your fame and continuing life that the poem serves rather than mine. Perhaps the foundational poetic elegy of English poetical tradition, John Milton's 'Lycidas', was in part an exhibition piece designed to advertise the young poet's skills. The genre's longest-influential English model, Thomas Gray's 'Elegy in a Country Churchyard', displaces the poet's own fear of eternal obscurity onto the nameless dead; it is Gray's own futurity which is the poem's successful issue. The self-serving nature of elegy cannot be negated, since an elegy unworthy of fame must fail to serve the elegized well. Furthermore, there is frequently a suspicion that the elegist mourns an aspect of himself projected, as Geoffrey Hill's 'September Song' admits with an edge of moral narcissism while mourning the victims of Nazi death camps: '(I have made | an elegy for myself it | is true)'.[1] But neither is ambition for the poem necessarily exploitative; nowhere do ambition and mourning unite, both simultaneously restrained and affirmed, to such devastating effect as in Ben Jonson's 'On My First Son' which finishes:

> Rest in soft peace, and, ask'd, say, 'Here doth lie
> Ben Jonson his best piece of poetry.'
> For whose sake henceforth all his vows be such,
> As what he loves may never like too much.[2]

The problem of elegy is a special instance of a larger problem of lyric address when readers have become touchily aware of a lyric's pronominal identifications, resenting both absorption into a poem's presumptuous 'we' and location in an interpellating 'you'. Who are you to speak? Or, to allude to another great English elegy, who are you to reckon God's purpose as in 'The Wreck of the Deutschland'? And the poem done, 'who would I show it to?'– according to Diana Fuss 'the unspoken challenge of our times', but answered unhesitatingly by 'myself!' in thousands of students' elegies for their own soon-to-be-lost youth, the prevalent selfie elegy.[3] This phenomenon takes another step beyond David Kennedy's contention that 'poetry itself and wider attitudes to experience have become overwhelmingly elegiac' and that 'national identity has become synonymous with remembrance'; or Jahan Ramazani's claim that 'the genre is central to the history and development of twentieth-century lyric. Broadly defined, the elegy permeates a wide range of poems about war, love, race, gender, meditation, the self, the family, and the poet'.[4]

While I agree with Fuss in discovering 'in the elegy not a moribund genre in historical decline but a vital form in aesthetic transformation', I find this vitality elsewhere than in those dying words, reviving corpses and surviving lovers which provide the titles of her book chapters, conducive (by her account) to a social role for poetry as consolation in cultures queasy about facing death. Instead this chapter attends chiefly to the surreptitious elegy, to instances of what Sam Ladkin calls 'the non-heroic elegiac mode', poems so reluctant to admit their generic status as elegy that none dares use the name.[5] Some are non-heroic to the extent that elegiac intent can go undiscerned by a reader until a poignant twist or a breach in the surface, escaping what Fuss recognizes as the inveterate banality of grief and pious hope alike, and capable of surprising with grief – indeed, W. S. Graham's 'Dear Bryan Wynter' appears in the anthology *Poems That Make Grown Men Cry*.[6]

No post-war elegy in English has been more influential on subsequent poetry than Frank O'Hara's 'The Day Lady Died', discussed in the previous chapter. Generally assigned to a sub-genre invented by O'Hara, the 'I do this, I do that' poem of busy distraction, its influence has been marked more in the 'overwhelmingly elegiac' tone of poems mourning the passage of time than in elegy strictly conceived. O'Hara's poem is certainly an elegy, even if this dawns on a first-time reader only through a gradual unease. Its originality becomes clear by comparison with W. H. Auden's two immediately pre-war elegies, 'In Memory of Sigmund Freud' and 'In Memory of W.B. Yeats', a high water mark of the Anglo-American public elegy – memorializing great men in full-on address to a mourned 'you' embodying a set of contributions to civilized values (at a time when insurgent barbarism would have made irony in that regard sound casuistical). In poems whose dominant tone is instructive, accounts are drawn up of what Freud and Yeats taught humanity, while human failings are acknowledged so 'you' might fitfully be humanized when prosopopoeia starts to sound too sermonizing. Writing that Yeats was 'silly, like us', writing of Freud 'if often he was wrong and, at times, absurd' softens a voice that strives to do justice to achievements in terms that can match them. And match them the poet undoubtedly feels competent to do; the final three stanzas of 'In Memory of W.B. Yeats' clearly assume the earlier poet's mantle, starting with the ambiguous apostrophe:

Follow, poet, follow right
To the bottom of the night,
With your unconstraining voice
Still persuade us to rejoice[7]

The patriarchal tone of Auden's elegies is apt enough in the elegy to Freud; there are few elegies which more decidedly

> recall Freud's suggestion that the superego is made up of 'the illustrious dead', a sort of cultural reservoir, or rather cemetery, in which one may also inter one's renounced love-objects and in which the ruling monument is that internalized figure of the father.[8]

This tone would soon become unsustainable, with the presumption of speaking for 'a people' echoing Fascist and Stalinist authoritarianism, wartime solidarity or Cold War professions of patriotism. And not long afterwards the question of who exactly 'the people' are would make it problematic to adopt a spokesman's stance. But from the perspective of the 1940s it would surely have been unimaginable that a great elegy would commemorate a great black female artist, Billie Holiday, include the line 'it is 1959 and I go get a shoeshine' and consist largely of a record of an afternoon's scurrying about Manhattan, while shying away from the likely blackness of a shoeshine, black poetry, Genet's play *Les Nègres* and anything that might trigger distress through reminding the poet of a loss he cannot face. 'The Day Lady Died' does not aim to account for Holiday's greatness; rather, it evidences the effect of her greatness.

Yet for all its seeming casualness and intimacy in 'the non-heroic elegiac mode' of his earlier elegies to James Dean, O'Hara's poem like Auden's is a public elegy. In O'Hara's 'Ode on Causality', linked to 'The Day Lady Died' through its earlier title 'Ode on Causality (in the Five Spot Cafe)', he had written an elegy for a friend, the painter Jackson Pollock. This poem is closer to Fuss's 'reviving corpses' elegiac category, spun out of Pollock's young daughter's insistence at his graveside that 'he isn't under there, he's out in the woods' for a wild version rather than a repudiation of Wordsworth's 'Lucy poems'.[9] Wordsworth's return to nature is converted by O'Hara into a rampant phallicism that refuses to allow the dead artist 'to be layed at all! romanticized, elaborated, fucked, sung, put to "rest"'.[10] 'Lay' unites 'laid to rest' with poetic 'lays' in an abrupt break from the previous stanza's ending in 'the tender subjects of their future lays'. O'Hara's distraction here is breached by the word 'lays', for Pollock's cock becomes a metonym for his living; his death means the end of Pollock's lays as he is himself laid and liable to be 'fucked'. The poem culminates in the re-erecting of Pollock's penis followed by its enormous orgasm; a revived corpse indeed. Although the over-the-top rhetoric of this poem greatly differs from 'The Day Lady Died', the quality of distraction in space is shared. The 'Ode on Causality' scampers from Pollock's memorial at Springs Cemetery through surrounding forest and through cultures, historical periods, music, painting, theatre and religion, before inevitably making its way to the legendary space of distraction, 'standing still and walking in New York'. Here the avoidance is of the penis that the poem shies away from seeing directly – 'everyone's supposed to be veined, like marble', 'then swell like pythons', before lays emerge from ballads and the poem accedes fully to the preposterous phallicism it has been resisting.

The shortcoming of 'Ode on Causality' as an elegy lies in its rhetorical abstraction. The poem could be written only by someone deeply versed in Pollock's art, and at the time of writing this would probably be a friend of the painter. But it gives little sense of personal friendship and loss; rather it offers a general (although strongly gendered) meditation on death which is as tendentious (and as magnificent) as Hopkins's 'Wreck of the Deutschland' – and has the disadvantage of playing into an already well-developed caricature of Pollock as emblematic of the virile heterosexual artist. Since the poem does not advertise itself as an elegy, criticism of its shortcomings in these terms may seem unfair; but it is legitimate to ask to what end Pollock's corpse (his penis) is being revived. And the answer to that question is broadly, 'in the service of art' affirmed in the final lines as organism sublimates transcendently into a work of art: 'love-propelled and tangled glitteringly | has earned himself the title Bird in Flight'.

The distractions of 'standing still and walking in New York' correspond to 'meanders' across a more abstract terrain in W. S. Graham's poems, but Graham's meanders follow tracks rather than distractions. It is tempting to hear 'Dear Bryan Wynter' as Sydney Graham (the name by which his friends knew him) talking to his dead and dear friend, the painter Bryan Wynter (1915–75), but the poem's idiom is explicitly that of a letter.[11] A letter to an intimate, but an intimate to whom he wrote few letters when alive because their near proximity meant there was no distance to be bridged. The letters Graham did write to Wynter are mainly dunning letters, resorted to as a distancing device, in embarrassment. A letter to an intimate belongs to a now-rare genre, letter writing having become an awkward task, marked by a struggle with the desire or the necessity to express deep feeling, as in a letter of condolence. An intimate letter must strive for a voice truer than words said could sound, in their haltingness or inconsiderateness. So a love letter might be addressed to a person working in the next office booth or met frequently, to deliver what could only be stuttered in encounter. But Graham's poems often show frustration with the gap between the abstraction of the lyric voice and the incarnate poet's voice, and with the separation from a reader whom the poet wishes to join or re-join through unified movement. That said, the voice of Sydney Graham's published letters is remarkably close to the poems – and several poems emerge out of first formulations in letters, benefitting from the subtle modulations of tone registered in Fiona Green's sensitive survey of Graham's elegiac practice.[12] Notes become notes of a different kind, for 'This is only a note' is an ambiguous formulation. While a note is a brief letter, it is also a musical note that sets the tone for a lyric poem whose first stanza follows:

DEAR BRYAN WYNTER

1

This is only a note
To say how sorry I am
You died. You will realise
What a position it puts
Me in. I couldn't really
Have died for you if so
I were inclined. The carn
Foxglove here on the wall
Outside your first house
Leans with me standing
In the Zennor wind.[13]

The musical note leads to the prosody of this work. Although the poem's idiom is epistolary, the need to insist on that testifies to the poem's voice effect. The decisions made in reading can oscillate between the voices of a letter, intimate speech and a lyric poem. These voices are subtly distinct, since a lyric poem's voice demands attention to its prosodic make-up, whereas a letter's voice rides on semantic stresses. Decisions are required from the very beginning; and how the first line is sounded (the second line if including the poem's run-on title) will influence the way the whole poem is spoken and heard – as indeed does the echo of William Carlos Williams's 'This is Just to Say', another poem whose title runs on into what might be a note. In an astute reading, Angela Leighton cites the many poems by Graham cast in epistolary form and explains:

> The idea of a letter, as an address to someone who cannot (yet) answer for themselves, involves a knotty contradiction which Graham loves to exploit.

Someone is there, yet not there; the poem becomes an obstacle, not a way through. His playful, informal, loving, ragging tone invokes a reader who ought to be the intimate recipient, but who is, like the writer himself, an invented anyone.[14]

But in a poem entitled 'Dear Bryan Wynter' this cannot be 'an invented anyone' even if Graham's poem is anxious lest it be 'greedy to make you up'. The title announces a specific address. The writtenness of talking (as in a letter) and the talking of writtenness (as in a poem) have to be dealt with throughout, from that first line break 'a note | To say'. How can a note say? Well, in sending a letter to an intimate that's what is presumed, sending a voice as much or more than information. And a lyric note might introduce anything, but chiefly alerts the ear so that the mournful and guilty balance across the line break of the simple pronouncement 'I am | You died' can be registered. This is a break that must be healed, and can only be healed prosodically. Reparation begins with proposing other things that might be sent by the same lyric service – 'Rice wine, meanders' – and this poem will indeed deliver a meander formally, so Wynter can continue to paint in the beyond, having available to him the gestural repertoire, the meanders, of his late canvases. As for rice wine, that may pertain to some fantasy of Wynter as a Zen monk, since The Tinners Arms in Zennor wouldn't have served anything half so exotic. And not knowing allows an assumption, oddly enough, that we do know along with Bryan Wynter. Graham's generous offer of provisions knowingly echoes Guillaume Apollinaire's epitaph on Le Douanier Rousseau's tombstone, inscribed by Brancusi and including the lines: 'Laisse passer nos bagages en franchise à la porte du ciel | Nous t'apporterons des pinceaux des couleurs des toiles' ('Let our luggage pass duty free through the gates of heaven | We will bring you brushes paints and canvas'). There at Modernism's portals, an elegy.

'Dear Bryan Wynter' is a poem which it feels clumsy to interpret pertinaciously, but you'd have to be obtuse to not grasp what the poem is saying and doing. There are however a few things that aren't obvious. Before Derek Attridge's revisionist work, English prosody was conventionally understood in terms of feet, and 'Dear Bryan Wynter' like 'The Day Lady Died' is a walking poem, but troubled by the disconcerting unreliability of once-familiar landmarks, and by interruption. Here is the West Penwith Cornish landscape which Sydney Graham and Bryan Wynter walked habitually, to the pub and elsewhere, and one which they could have walked, as the saying goes, with their eyes shut. So many paces in this direction or that. The oddities of the poem cluster around dislocations, and difficulties in setting out:

You will realise
What a position it puts
Me in. I couldn't really
Have died for you if so
I were inclined.

The line breaks dislodge 'Me' from its position, so that it stands against the left margin with peculiar assertiveness and then might be inclined. This subtle effect is characteristic of late Graham, and the poem's colloquialism should not induce us to take its performance for granted. As Hannah Brooks-Motl notes, Graham came to eschew the rich vocabulary of his early poetry in favour of language that tends to colourlessness.[15] This puts greater pressure on stresses and internal echoes, especially as there is little in the way of sound patterning asserting itself. In this poem the work of attention must train on line breaks, caesuras, modifications in cadence rather than nests of consonants or stretches of vowels. The poem is almost wilfully self-effacing. But within its unobtrusive sonic world, 'Me' comes to be recognized exactly as positioned, while 'I' also standing against the margin might be so 'inclined'. It takes a while to tune in to such delicate dispositions, but when we do we can notice that 'The carn | Foxglove' also stands against the wall of the left margin, and leans. 'If so | I were inclined' shifts spoken word order fractionally to achieve its positioning, its effect. One might pass over the unfamiliar word 'carn', for the enjambment gives the ordinary non-botanist the idea that a 'carn foxglove' may be a particular variety of foxglove. It isn't, and there's a reason for declining to stress the unusual word which is a Scottish form of 'cairn', a heap of stones. Arriving in Cornwall Wynter first lived in a house named The Carn, and it belongs to the texture of intimacy that he would recognize the allusion but we wouldn't – but should not be halted in our reading as though this were the kind of poem that demands frequent recourse to the *OED*. Hesitation and resumption become a shared rhythm. True, not much could mitigate the specificity of the place-name Zennor, but the peculiar name is made a qualifier so it's the wind that seems significant even as 'Zennor' signals to Wynter that this is their familiar landscape. We might now look back and notice how the word 'died' before a caesura avoids portentousness owing to the repeated address to 'you'. If you're still there, you who are able to realize this or that, death can't be so categorical. 'I am' and 'You died' can therefore be enjambed.

But the 'position | It puts me in' is more complicated yet. In day-to-day usage it means you've put me in a fix, a jam, a place I can't get out of. The dilemma is of standing outside The Carn and being unable to move away because Wynter isn't there to walk beside as he leaves his old home. There is only the 'carn foxglove' which stands in for him (Wynter was tall and skinny too). Writing the note and striking a note, again puts Graham in the position of being the poet who is alive, and the third part removes to the poet's own house. So 'here on the wall' identifies a shared world which can continue to be shared only through this poem's intimate voice, a poem whose geography is not so much a map as lines of prosody, lines traced in familiar walks that accompany and rhythmically organize two people's way of talking to each other and laughing together, only one of them now surviving and left with his words unanswered, repeatedly broken off, since there is no-one with whom to walk in step, except an unknown reader whose pace may fail to fall in. The salient performance of this interrupted walking is the instance of a single iamb followed by a strong caesura and then a two or three beat stumble. Thus the inclination to the rhythm of walking is frustrated time and again: 'if so | I were inclined' 'The carn | foxglove here', 'Outside your first house'. The enforcement of a pause after 'outside' in reading the line, separating the iamb from the following three syllables, is felt powerfully. Along with its multiple interrogatives, this prosodic signature influences the curious sense of always starting out in this poem.

The second stanza of this first part begins with a brisk reference to how things are, but this ordinary phrase is perceived as shifting through rhythmic stress to a question about the status of 'things' in Wynter's distanced world, things which in the second part recede into the vagueness of 'anything' and 'something', overcome by mist. The stanza introduces a problem arising unmistakably from dislocation:

> your long legs
> And twitching smile under
> Your blue hat walking
> Across a place?

Across 'a place'? What place? How does an articulation walk over an abstraction, a 'somewhere'? How can you 'still' be 'somewhere' as against being located? Only if the question is ontological, but 'somewhere' pales against 'Zennor'. As for these things, legs and smile and hat, they belong to an attempt to make you up from which the poem recoils back into inclining – inclining across a distance to a you that isn't so much made up, as subject to attempted reanimation by way of apostrophe and prosody, through shared walking, shared too by us as readers if not so presently and surely. The poem seeks to make Wynter up from the requirements of setting forth – he needs his legs, he must put on his hat, his twitching smile is the sign of his companionship. Fiona Green discerns an allusion to 'Lycidas': 'At last he rose, and twitched his mantle blue.'[16] But the re-creation fails, and the inclining solitary poet can make up Wynter only as solitary and walking across 'a place', somewhere not traversed by paths of shared experience. Abandoning this attempt to make you up, the poem strives to restore 'you' not in a landscape abstracted by your absence, but more compellingly remembered through shared relationships, including Wynter's wife Monica, 'you' becoming so close as to join in an intersubjectivity resisting collapse into 'things': you live in the memories of those who love you. 'Place' further dissolves into the question 'Are you there at all?' from which Wynter is summoned back, as it were from the caesura after 'place' and the characteristic iamb before the line break, a moment of doubt followed by lines seeking comfort in imagining Wynter separated from his family by distance rather than death and preoccupied with thoughts of them; even if 'all right' might signal the aftermath of a failed work of restoration – and nobody and nothing in this poem is 'all right', but 'inclined' at best.

Is this speech or a letter? Part 2 of the poem re-stages the question:

> Speaking to you and not
> Knowing if you are there
> Is not too difficult.
> My words are used to that.

> Do you want anything?
> Where shall I send something?
> Rice-wine, meanders, paintings
> By your contemporaries?
> Or shall I send a kind
> Of news of no time
> Leaning against the wall
> Outside your old house.
>
> The house and the whole moor
> Is flying in the mist.

The notoriously disorientating quality of moorland mists unmoors Wynter's old house and every landmark. The dissolution is intolerable, since the landscape cannot be crossed by Graham and Wynter but more especially, it cannot be crossed by language as shared, and threatens to become as abstract as 'a place', unspecified. Part 3 reverts decisively to the poet in present solitude, beginning with a striking displacement into a mirror, or so I imagine, for the phrase 'The front of my face' cannot be found by online search except in this poem:

> I am up. I've washed
> The front of my face
> And here I stand looking
> Out over the top
> Half of my bedroom window.

Furthermore, the phrase confronts the collapse of intersubjectivity into a reflective solitude that relinquishes the joshing tone of shared speech and no longer expects to be joined in response. There is a suggestion of putting on a front for the day, making oneself up, which we know from attempts to make up Bryan Wynter, is liable to fail. The phrase also catches attention because it's a rare unambiguously two-beat line and oddly assertive. The immediate effect lies in contrast with 'The house and the whole moor | Is flying in the mist'.

The blunt opening 'I am up' clashes with 'flying in the mist'. The embodied grief into which the landscape dissolves, now needs the reaffirmed 'I am' passed over at the start of the poem. Such assertion, such a recovery, is as positional as St Buryan's church tower – that's how directions are given in Cornwall, in relation to churches and pubs, not points of the compass, characteristic of a landscape experienced through paths rather than roads, worn by walking between gathering places. But in bereavement the poem has recourse to a world of mapping, not of prosodic lines. The face is being touched as a kind of trigonometrical point, from which a flying landscape may now be mapped in sure coordinates, not necessarily visible, resituating Wynter in a nameable place, although in the past. The three vertical assertions with which part 3 continues, a 'dark rise' alongside 'I am up' and a church tower, map a relationship between the living and dead with remarkable subtlety, almost beneath notice:

> There almost as far
> As I can see I see
> St Buryan's church tower.
> An inch to the left, behind
> That dark rise of woods,
> Is where you used to lurk.

The dark rise conjures the burial mounds prolific in Cornwall; since Wynter used to lurk in the woods, and since the verb 'lurk' implies a continuous presence out of sight, possibly he is there still, a persistence of a different order from the abstraction proposed by a church tower as metonymic of eternal life. That I take it is why part 4 refers to Housman's starlit fences, found in an elegiac poem ('Far in a western brookland' from *A Shropshire Lad*) tracing the soul's persistence in a well-loved landscape, even if that soul is A. E. Housman's rather than a loved friend's, and its distancing is from his own body asleep in the city.[17]

Housman's poem sounds confident in its ascription of 'here' and 'there', in 'pools I used to know' and 'fields where I was known', although they are drawn together by a wanderer in 'brookland', a place of watery meanderings. Yet this confident prosody is that of a confirmed solitary while Graham is mourning the impossibility of shared walking. We are returned to the poet against the wall, unable to move away but striving to find the prosody he needs – not making it up with the feet and hat of Bryan Wynter, but starting forward and falling back into standstills.

The knowing at the end of Graham's poem is difficult to parse. The apology in 'I know I make a symbol | Of the foxglove on the wall' could refer to the public debates on aesthetics in which Graham and Wynter jousted; as an abstract artist in his maturity, even if his abstraction derived from the Cornish landscape, Wynter would have disdained symbolism. He probably wouldn't have approved of making things up either, in the sense of a fiction or a lie; Graham's recording of 'Dear Bryan Wynter' lays an insatiable child's quality of stress on 'again' in the first part's 'Or am | I greedy to make you up | Again out of memory?' as though to bring a deceased Bryan Wynter into a poem as a living presence, again, were greedy.[18] But Wynter's presence is formal too; the poem's meanders around a shared landscape constitute a tribute to Wynter procedurally, a set of meanders or curves where things are very sparingly referenced, and inclining takes the place of representing or making up. The word 'meander', as the *OED* advises, is a transferred use of the name of the river Maeander in Caria (now western Turkey), noted for its winding course. The meanders of Bryan Wynter's paintings are true to this derivation, based on the close study of riverine behaviour, both the meanders of river courses and the meandering and eddies of currents in a river's flow. 'Dear Bryan Wynter' is a poem of obstructed fluency, which must meander, or proceed according to a set of curves, in order to make its way. How then does the foxglove know Bryan Wynter? He must have passed it every day, for it's a perennial. But perhaps there's a shared joke, since Wynter suffered heart problems for some time before his fatal heart attack, possibly treated with digitalis, derived from foxgloves. The second of the 'Two Poems in Zennor Hill' comes closer to making this explicit:

> O foxglove on the wall
> You meet me nicely today
> Leaning your digitalis
> Bells toward the house
> Bryan Wynterless.[19]

All the knowing then becomes quite *knowing*, but as with the reference to carn, could pass without troubling the companionate reader. This quality of reference in Graham's poetry has been noted by Peter Riley, who qualifies Graham's particular obscurity by noting that 'all items of vocabulary remain Graham's [either] local or not; they derive entirely from his life, the where and when of him'.[20]

It's a commonplace to say that a poem makes us feel more alive. An elegy might, disgracefully, make one feel more alive through contemplating the deadness of the dead. But what does it mean for a poem deliberately set out to make a dead person live? If a poem makes us more alive, does it mean that deprived of animation by prosody we are dead ourselves or as good as dead? Ceasing to walk is certainly bad for us:

> Or shall I send a kind
> Of news of no time
> Leaning against the wall
> Outside your old house.

There is a leaning, an inclining, a distance from the event of the poem, which is simply not enough for life. If there are no steps, no feet, there is no time. There is no setting out again in Bryan Wynter's company – that cannot be denied: 'I am aware | You are not here.' 'I am | You died'. Only the anaclisis persists, Graham's dependence on Wynter transferred to his house. But in its fifth part the poem accompanies Wynter walking in his other world, in parallel, where he can 'scout things out' and still be addressed, wearing his blue hat. He is in motion again because he is walking proleptically, for Graham. They will walk these paths together. We too, proleptically, in our parallel world. The foxglove 'knows you' in the sense of 'it knows the kind of person you are', the inclining person who walks again, and the single inclining foxglove resembles the departed Wynter standing again next to Graham; because of that symbolic resemblance one might even say the foxglove wants to start out too, to follow its semblable. Shall we all go unified in time? But foxgloves are frequently pulled apart in Graham's poetry, for instance in 'His Companions Buried Him' ('I see Earth's operator within his glade | Gloved in the fox of his gigantic hour'), and 'Approaches to How They Behave' ('Shines the red | Fox in the digitalis grove' and 'If you can't fit me in | To lying down here among the fox | Glove towers of the moment').[21] The foxglove in 'Dear Bryan Wynter' might then also be a linguistic joke about putting the thing back together as a symbol, having pulled it apart so often.

But the seeming confidence of 'It is because it knows you' disgorges as it must into the unknowable. This is true of every part of the poem, each brought up against a break that cannot be gainsaid, unless a vertiginous 'flying in the mist' erases both letter-writer and addressee, unendurably. 'This is only a note' is repeated and then echoed in 'Although I am not', hastily negated. This poet is still alive. Is he? Where? In these lines and their movement. And why are the final three lines so haunting, apparently careless lines? Maybe because that redoubled knowing, echoing Housman, is ours too as readers, out of this note, out of the knowledge that now this poem is not Graham's alone but is the path we have followed and in so doing have joined in a walk to bring back a news of no time we are bound to share – for if Graham can no longer walk in time with Wynter, and is reduced to 'news of no time | Leaning against the wall', inclined towards the impossibility of lyric unjoined, any of us can join in reading and make such inclination, across time and place, into lyric prosody and so walk with Graham and Wynter along these paths.

If Frank O'Hara walks under the pressure of distraction and W. S. Graham walks shared tracks in a summoning of the departed (a euphemism made poignant at the opening of 'The Thermal Stair' in the quiet phrase 'you were away'), James Schuyler's response to grief in 'Buried at Springs' is simply to sit and stare out of the window on a Maine island, declining 'to go | out the window into the late | August midafternoon sun'. This poem is linked intimately to 'Ode on Causality' since it is Frank O'Hara who now is 'buried at Springs', but it has little in common with O'Hara's poem in its rhetoric of understatement – of which Schuyler is a master. Schuyler was a lover of eighteenth-century diarists and naturalists, and it is the exactitude of his attention to the natural world, the wandering and training of his eye that govern the poem's fluent but exactly stitched syntax. Pulling back from the distance where 'two lines of wake' are visible, attention arrives at a near point where precise description leads to:

> Rocks with rags
> of shadow, washed dust clouds
> that will never bleach.
> It is not like this at all.

The title 'Buried at Springs' has hovered above this poem and tints a phrase like 'two lines of wake' with a funereal wash, but it is recourse to simile that produces a crisis in the poem, however subdued – a crisis comparable to those in the O'Hara poems, precipitated in one by the word 'lays' and in the other by a glimpse of a newspaper photograph. When rocks appear like 'washed dust clouds' the simile alludes to classical Chinese landscape painting; perdurable rocks become transient through this simile and vulnerable to light—and rocks may turn to dust. The simile is tersely rejected, but the breach cannot be caulked; the poem continues:

> The rapid running of the
> lapping water a hollow knock
> of someone shipping oars:
> it's eleven years since

> Frank sat at this desk and
> heard and saw it all
> the incessant water the
> immutable crickets only
> not the same[22]

The immutable now is seasonal, the incessant is changeable, and the meticulously described landscape depends upon a present consciousness. Rocks give way to the muted metaphor of running water for the transience of life, an oarsman's resignation from strife and yielding to the current. The first part of the poem ends with a granite boulder which 'quite | literally is not the same' not only because rocks turn to dust, but because the consciousness in which it is held has been altered by the loss of Frank's coextensive attention. It is this delicate apprehension which brings Schuyler's poem close to Graham's. O'Hara and Schuyler were not striders across rough terrain like Graham, Wynter, Hilton or Lanyon, but the loss of shared experience of a place alters a place for both poets and recalls the lost sharer. What Peter Riley notes in Graham is as true of Schuyler; the second part of 'Buried at Springs' offers further meticulous description that time and again breaches the even surface to reveal fleetingly the pain of loss, in 'the thin scream | of mosquitoes' and in pine cones with their 'gum, pungent, clear as a tear' leading to a final view of the scene 'like wet silk | stained by one dead branch | the harsh russet of dried blood'. The earliest Chinese painting (and writing) was on silk, using pigment made from pine soot. While strict convention governs Chinese landscape painting, the brush strokes of the particular artist can be identified; the scene is mediated by the subtlest distinguishing marks of attention. To know how a scene looks through someone else's eyes is to know them exceptionally well; both Frank O'Hara and James Schuyler used their eyes professionally as art critics, and the 'one dead branch' on wet silk would have united them in recognizing its calligraphic style even as now it suggests that Schuyler has lost a limb with the loss of his friend.

'Buried at Springs' elegizes a poet whom Schuyler envied for his published achievements and his charisma. It is remarkable that the poem makes no allusion to O'Hara's vocation; Frank 'saw and heard' but is not remembered as a poet. As much as a surreptitious elegy this might be thought a suppressive elegy; grief is admitted through bracketing O'Hara's public persona, allowing love to be expressed for a man unrecognizable as the Frank O'Hara of his poems and of others' memoirs. It is telling that Schuyler translates O'Hara from the Manhattan where he so influentially walked and stood still, to a Maine he visited only briefly. There is something of a levelling of the scales here, for Great Spruce Head Island where Schuyler lodged for years with the painter Fairfield Porter and his family was as familiar to him and present to his poems as Manhattan to O'Hara.

A return will be made to this poem in the next chapter, for no poem discussed in this book has completed its work in life. Even the stones in 'Buried at Springs' change and return.

2

Few poets so feared and resisted entombment as Dylan Thomas, and his shade might be gratified that his poems have so successfully resisted attempts to bury them by critics and by writers such as Philip Larkin, ashamed of their early partiality. Nonetheless, declaring an interest, poetic or scholarly, in Dylan Thomas, often brings a response which runs along the lines: 'I used to love Dylan Thomas when I was young but I haven't read him for years.' It is commonplace that Dylan Thomas is an obscure poet with a popular readership, a technically disciplined poet who is also a byword for indiscipline and self-indulgence, and that his poems are loved by adolescents, a love frequently renounced in middle age. An example of such abjuring is the psychoanalyst Adam Phillips's shudderingly middle-aged revulsion from Thomas's 'slap-dash, slapstick, and apparently naively sophisticated Celtic fluency', renouncing the person Phillips was when he loved Thomas because, Phillips remembers or believes he remembers, Thomas 'seemed to be the apotheosis of "having a voice"'.[23] To renounce your first love seems ungrateful. Behind Phillips's repudiation lies the charge that Thomas's writing is masturbatory, and not far behind either in the light of the adjectives 'slap-dash, slapstick', otherwise so oddly applied to a poet of stringent technique; Thomas remained stuck with his stick, while Phillips grew into the adult world where intercourse and literature emerge as regulated practice out of the adolescent enjoyment of voice. Thomas is a writer who troubles us once we become literary, and Thomas's poetry may be popular in part because it disregards the bounds of propriety and the literary. His lyric practice dissents from lyric as intimate address overheard – a now-trite formulation investing poetry with a weird shame, as though eavesdropping were the foundation of generic individuality – and inclines rather to a lyric of a physical sonority made perceptible, almost palpable, through silent reading as well as listening. Thomas is not so much in love with his own voice as stroked into corporeal presence by his poetry's sonority, shamelessly.

Such thoughts are provoked by a submerged history of unrespectable poetry traced by Daniel Tiffany in his book *My Silver Planet*, but Tiffany's wide-ranging diagnosis of poetic kitsch does not quite apply to Thomas, as it would to the gaudier British surrealist and apocalyptic verse contemporary with Thomas's.[24] This is because the plasticity of Thomas's poetry remains motivated, strongly attached to the actuality of a sea-scoured bay as well as the symbolic order of sea and land, and attached to a Welsh social and religious rhetoric; and although Thomas's poems may first sound nostalgic, a significant strain in kitsch, they fight nostalgia in reconstructing memory spatially and collapsing time. At his work's most formally radical – the poems in syllabics – extension of time into space presents a problem for vocal performance, especially for Thomas whose performance can transmute verses into ham; but these poems' inherent voicing and tone amass a wave power independent of performance. This discussion does not intend to set up a voice–text dichotomy in order to adjudicate for voice as opposed to the literary text, although it is clear that Thomas's work fell sharply from favour once New Criticism mandated a focus on the poem as isolated textual entity. But voice–text introduces a dichotomy challenged by Thomas's poetry, and a caesura it would deny. And the meaning of 'voice' in Phillips's dismissal needs specifying; if Thomas's recital manner has become embarrassing, yet it corresponds to a style conventional for its time, and by comparison with George Barker, for instance, and with his own practice elsewhere, Thomas is notably restrained in reading the syllabic 'Poem in October', distinguishing its syllables with a near-mimsy precision as though struggling against a rhythmic counter-force. But a poet's speaking voice has no priority over the internal voicings a poem proposes to a reader. That is to say, the sound of a poem is encoded phonemically, and a different performance can be heard pressing against the reader's restraint – both out of Thomas's oratorical propensity for strongly stressed rhythm and the poem's wave power as it arises from the rhythmic ground of Thomas's poetry as a whole.

In describing the wave power of Thomas's verse, this section of the chapter will explore the term caesura and what it might mean for thinking about Dylan Thomas, and it will return often to 'Poem in October' (1945).[25] Caesura might be understood as *aporia* – that is, a gap out of which something might emerge, or which might cleave an entity violently and productively, while bearing in mind what it signifies more technically in metrics; but this translation would strip the term caesura of a range of meaning rising about it like proud flesh about a wound. Moreover, the aim here is to advance a claim that Dylan Thomas's poetry is driven by a compulsion to efface the caesura and that this effacement is a poetic project which also goes well beyond the making of poems. Poetry is not merely an archive of literary texts and vocal performances. The story of Thomas's war on the caesura is the story of his refusal to be born, to acknowledge what Freud called the birth caesura, his refusal to submit his masturbatory delirium to heterosexual regulation, his refusal to submit his verse to drawing-room mannerliness, to a modest demeanour, and his refusal to die – death temporized from an ending to a caesura through a somewhat inchoate conception of an afterlife, resembling a return to the womb. This defiance of mortality has to be the more strenuous because rhythmic temporality is so insistent, so hard for Thomas to curb. His war on the caesura is the story of the riddled sea – the interminable sea riddled through its enigmatic sound, riddled in the sense of sieved through the latticework of waves which by metonymy catches bounty in its nets, riddled in the sense of multiply penetrated by the 'star-flanked seed' reflected in the sea's even and ever-surging surface.[26] Sky, sea and ground are as one. At their horizon there can be no caesura.

What, then, is a caesura, metrically? Caesura introduces variable in-line breaks to avoid monotony in extended regular lines. As a syntactical pause, caesura differs from a performative pause which reading aloud might introduce at any point (however perversely). Then how does a caesura differ from a line-ending? A line-ending is a type of caesura, complicated by the fact that an enjambed line can work against expectations, refusing a syntactical pause; it might also bring rhyme into accordance or discordance with syntactical pause or not-pause. Internal rhyme and assonance can complicate in-line caesura too. Granted these qualifications, the importance of caesura is that it represents both break and continuity, modifying what comes before and what comes after. 'Caesura. An event that simultaneously unites and disunites."[27] Assuming, that is, a thread which can be picked up again does indeed follow: the fear for Dylan Thomas, to cite the final phrase of a horrifying early poem, is that the conclusion of the poem itself coincides with a temporally collapsed orgasm and birth as a 'gross catastrophe'.[28] But leaving aside line-endings and the special case of poem endings, shifts in regular stress introduced by caesuras increase tension and so enhance one's experience of the poem as an event. In her lecture 'The Caesura', Isobel Armstrong waxes rhapsodic; she asserts that the caesura

> rather than the beat of ictus, creates the poem's temporal self-awareness, its felt time, by holding up, often for a breath, the momentum of rhythm. [...] The gap sets the sensoria in motion. The gap sets desire in motion. Yet the caesura does not represent anything.[29]

Effacement of such syntactical pauses therefore might throw emphasis on the formal contours of the poem; it might contribute to a sense of a poem as an object rather than event, should the poem be regular in meter and lineation. Such, however, is not the effect of suppression of the caesura in Thomas's poetry, and particularly not in the limit case of his poems written in syllabics, despite their reified textual appearance. Thomas's reading of 'Poem in October' dramatizes the contradiction that results.[30] His determination to find a reading style that holds to syllabics is sustained against an irrepressible rhythmic urgency. The poem's formal structure – its elaborate and closed-off stanzas, its mathematically determined lines, its rhyme scheme – seeks to defeat the experience of temporality concomitant on following a poem from start to finish, a poem in this case obsessed with the passage of time from its title forward. If suppressing the caesura is one strategy in a war against mortality, the beat of time in 'Poem in October' is audibly undefeated, pulsing within the poem's constraints. What this evidences is that rhythm is entered into; it does not begin, nor does it end. The caesura of birth is always already effaced; as Derrida writes of rhythm, 'it therefore begins before beginning. That is the incalculable origin of a rhythm'.[31]

Nonetheless, Thomas's attraction to verse syllabics partakes of a compulsion to obliterate the caesura manifest in his repeatedly expressed disgust at parturition, as well as comprising a stage in his struggle to contain his rhetoric formally; as Édouard Glissant writes of the baroque, 'it recognizes only the rigors of form, precisely because it is confronting excessiveness'.[32] The confrontation works at every level – affective excess and rhetorical excess as well as rhythmic – all engrained in the organ voice that causes Adam Phillips to recoil. This is despite the tendency of Thomas's syllabics described by John Goodby in *The Poetry of Dylan Thomas: Under the Spelling Wall*, where he writes of the late syllabic verse: 'These poems (and despite Thomas's own recorded performance of them) eschew emphatic, regular rhythms and distribute meaning more equally among their words, giving a levelling effect, both at the level of signification and the sonic web'.[33] This levelling effect, as Goodby implies, tends to a merger of text and voice which Thomas's vocal performance struggles to sustain while resisting alike both rhythmic impetus and the seduction of expressive stress which would redirect voice towards an audience open to passive reception.

Equal distribution is indeed the salient characteristic of syllabic verse in English, exemplified by Marianne Moore and the formal ability of her verse to incorporate passages of quasi-scientific prose. Although stylistically Thomas's 'Poem in October' lies a country mile from Moore's zoological domain, both poets replicate stanzas of lines varying in length and use insets or tabs to make replication unmistakable, whereas French syllabic verse demands linear regularity and has adopted conventions enabling the incorporation of caesuras in longer lines. If French syllabics are all about temporal regulation, with every line theoretically occupying the same time in performance, Moore and Thomas alike seem bent on averting any danger that the ear might recognize a recurrent syllabic count.[34] Syllabic composition becomes apparent only to a reader viewing the textual pattern, and both poets are drawn to figuratively shaped stanzas that advertise an artifice hard for the ear to discern. Elaborately shaped stanzas insist on a textuality that would immure voice and rhythm in typography aspiring to assign a poem to the condition of objecthood. Objecthood would extricate a poem from time, allowing it to be approached as though a sculptural mobile. Isobel Armstrong's reading of Marianne Moore's syllabic poem 'The Fish' draws out this quality and links it explicitly to visual caesuras – that is, to line breaks enforced by a syllabic patterning regardless of semantic logic or rhythmic diktat, and contriving a prismatic textual object.[35]

When reading as well as hearing 'Poem in October', one is struck by the poem's resistance to punctuation other than pauses enjoined by line breaks. Punctuation is punctilious in Moore and obstructs any possibility that her poems might concede to emergent cadence; although John Hollander writes charmingly that 'her unrolling, idiosyncratically periodic syntax overflows the frequently tightly syllabic cups and basins of her stanzas', his identification of her particulate poetry's 'lepidoptery' better conveys its odd meticulousness.[36] Thomas's suppression of punctuation departs also from its usual association in late-Modernist American poetry with parataxis and optional syntax; the device encourages multiplicity in linking, and asks the reader to distribute stress in relation to what William Carlos Williams called the variable foot. Make your own rhythm is the offer, according to individual breath and ear, but tentatively, mindful at every juncture that this is a choice. Moore's syllabics and Williams's variable foot therefore point in markedly different directions, in the one case towards Language writing, and in the other towards the poetics of banter in the New York School and the poetics of breath formulated by Charles Olson and subsequently acknowledged by Williams. The acme of breath poetics can be found in poems by Robert Creeley where scarcely a syllable passes unstressed, each rotating in a virtual space and throwing out a line to every other syllable. Thomas's poetry, however, is far more syntactically complex, its skeining made harder to untangle by an absence of punctuation which in verse both marks stresses and acts as a guide to semantic relations. Abjuring diacritical enforcement does not thereby extend permission to the reader (or from another angle, demand choice) in the manner of breath poetics; rather it strives against the always-incipient pressure of cadence. Here are the poem's two opening stanzas:

> It was my thirtieth year to heaven
> Woke to my hearing from harbour and neighbour wood
> And the mussel pooled and the heron
> Priested shore
> The morning beckon
> With water praying and call of seagull and rook
> And the knock of sailing boats on the net webbed wall
> Myself to set foot
> That second
> In the still sleeping town and set forth.
>
> My birthday began with the water-
> Birds and the birds of the winged trees flying my name
> Above the farms and the white horses
> And I rose
> In rainy autumn
> And walked abroad in a shower of all my days.
> High tide and the heron dived when I took the road
> Over the border
> And the gates
> Of the town closed as the town awoke.[37]

The first stanza of 'Poem in October' withholds punctuation, to the extent of suppressing hyphens where they would be called on in regular usage; word formations which beg for hyphens proliferate here. The suppression of hyphens is assertive. It enables a pun like 'mussel pooled', which anticipates as it were through physical stimulus the morning and its beckoning, where if hyphenated the phrase would be pinned down as adjectival. But the main consequence of de-hyphenating is the equitable distribution Goodby refers to, rendering this stanza's tangled but conventional syntax, spatial rather than temporal. The spine of its long unfolding sentence can be tracked in the phrases 'woke to my hearing [...] The morning beckon [...] Myself to set foot', but the verbs do not make for a brisk walk; indeed, what this poem strives to bring about and 'set forth' is a personal history about a revolving axis, a history written upon the landscape.

Such an account might seem paradoxical, for a hyphen, contrary to a caesura, is a mark whose Greek origin announces that it yokes two elements together 'under one'. But a hyphen thereby asserts a distinction from the unhyphenated words surrounding it; the at-oneness of the hyphenated expression would break from the semantically defined relatedness of words in the ordinary course, to be yoked in its assertive unity to the noun or verb it modifies. Poetry, however, is not an ordinary course of words, and the effect of suppressing hyphens along with this poem's befuddling syntax is to hyphenate every word in the stanza, to distribute hyphenation equally across the would-be stressless landscape. This effect is exaggerated by the divorce of ordinarily compound words (for instance, 'sun light'), by the reactivation of compound words (such as 'singingbirds' for 'songbirds'), and by a practice of enjambment often carried forward by 'and', the weakest and least stress-bearing of conjunctions, here equivalent to a hyphen. Linkage in 'Poem in October' is persistent, multiple, open to disentanglement, unemphatic and horizontal. It might be described as chained. Further, it would scarcely be an exaggeration to assert that the process of linkage is more important than what is linked – that poetic thinking here reverts to intra-uterine proto-mental processes marked by the dominance of rhythm whose encounter with separate mentality, across the caesura of birth, can be felt to threaten catastrophe. Rhythmic voice produces an intoxicating restoration, which Thomas resists so as to spare his developed sense of self even while inventing elaborate, quasi-mechanical verse instruments for overcoming the caesura between two systems of thinking.

'Poem in October' connects its words in quite a regular way, grammatically, but makes syntax hard to follow through real time – syntax has to be mapped on the page. If every word is implicitly hyphenated, it follows that caesura must be impossible: indeed, theoretically, caesura *is* impossible in English syllabic verse, which is why syllabics are most often used in a compromise formation with accentual verse, as in Thomas's own earlier practice. The *Princeton Encyclopedia of Poetry and Poetics* comments:

> When poets of other langs. tried to adopt Fr. Syllabic metrics, they faced the problem of word stresses in midline, which interfered with the reader's perception of the syllabic pattern. Hispanic and It. poets used these midline stresses to produce a variety of rhythms in their lines, but Eng. poets used them to create regular patterns – that is, accentual-syllabic verse.[38]

Thomas, however, wishes to level out word stresses while mystifying the syllabic pattern unless in sight of the text, so that its control feels integral to its vocal production rather than an imposition on it; he incorporates the poem as a sustainable event, he makes it audibly substantial, through what Goodby felicitously calls its sonic web or Simon Jarvis calls its 'phonotextual clusters' (thus distinguishing textual phonemes from performed phonetics).

De-hyphenating in order to hyphenate is only one paradoxical strategy Thomas uses to restore proto-mental linkages without dissolving identity into primordial rhythm. Thomas's poetry is obsessed by the interrupted and broken, but through negation; it would heal or at least suppress or disguise fractures even if it risks creating monstrosities in the process. Although sharing with late-Modernist disjunctive verse a sensitivity to the oppressive coherences which determine our conscious lives, Thomas's would not challenge the mind-forged manacles with scrap. Instead of arranging fragments of a shattered linguistic armature, freeing the mind to sport and sharpen its political–critical consciousness, Thomas's poetry aspires to produce novel coherences, universes. Or, more specifically, it creates and populates a single universe, instantiated in each poem, although verse techniques are brought ever more firmly under conscious control. In Heideggerian terms, 'world worlds', but its upsurging becomes less dependent on 'having a voice'.[39]

From the start, Thomas was never able to tolerate discontinuity, a catastrophe beginning for him with expulsion from the womb and recurring throughout his life, life experienced as a sequence of losses. Consider the first poem in the Buffalo notebook, dated 3 November 1930, when Thomas had just turned sixteen, which begins 'I know this vicious minute's hour'.[40] 'You have offended, periodic heart', the poem proclaims, going on to anticipate 'Poem in October' in describing 'reality, whose voice I know | To be the circle not the stair of sound'. A stair is periodic, as are the heart's periodics destined either to ascend to glory or descend to the loam, 'each silver moment chimes | in steps of sound'. This draft falls apart after asserting the circularity of the real: How will the poem end if there is no place at which to arrive, no teleology? How will the last caesura be overcome? The young Thomas had no answer; but the circle of sound is what his poems will later convene rather than merely describe. Yet the contradiction in writing poetry, a lineated art, so as to overcome periodicity cannot be disregarded. How might the fateful stair of sound be flattened? The sonic reality of 'Poem in October' is distributed through the lamination of sea, earth and sky; the boy's infant whisper 'to the trees and the stones and the fish in the tide' percolates through the universe which 'sang alive | Still in the water and singingbirds', and must continue to do so. The pun on 'still' is precise; activity remains still and unsuperseded, it persists in time like a wave. But this whispering and singing occurs descriptively; we still need to understand how the poem extends sonic reality to its limits and beyond.

Universing poetry, worlding poetry, is to be distinguished from fictive, science fiction, narrative or surrealist poetry because the poem's binding principle does not depend on temporal progress or external allusion. It can go nowhere, but to go nowhere may be the poem's mission. Such poetry does not need to be intellectual in tenor or rhetorically gorgeous; it can be as brilliant as John Ashbery's, as erudite as J. H. Prynne's or as sensuous as Édouard Glissant's, but often can be recognized through its uncanny mood, something pre-conscious sensed as the determining undertow of a poem's surface reticulation. Universing *poesis* creates a possible place whose interconnectedness incorporates readers within its linguistic field, not explicitly but as participant in its articulations. A reader does not overhear but is invoked. Psychic interiority becomes identical with an elaborated world structured as a domain of being, thinking and feeling, and especially through the poem's rhythm and its phonotext, a thick sonic reality which overcomes any tendency towards commentary, towards the parade of self and its views, for the poem does not depend on externalities even if individual and political forces call on the shaping poem. The interchangeability of elements within Dylan Thomas's verse, a feature ridiculed by Thomas's contemporary Geoffrey Grigson, and the re-assignability of phrases within a complete poetical universe, accords with this poetic logic.[41] Rhythm and phonotext may be primary modes of access to a poem's universe, but Thomas pointed the way to a poet as different as J. H. Prynne in seeking, against his own astonishing facility, to make a poetic universe through different contrivances – even if the worlding of his syllabic poems continues to be sustained by the voice from which a new autonomy for the poem is sought.

'Poem in October' hovers about the present participle sonically, as in its peculiar past-in-present tense, irresistibly turning to singing; although the phonotext is a tightly implicated web, its dominant feature is a chime around the word 'sing'. 'Sing' could imagine performance while not itself a performance, for performance must cease in time, and end in silence. In its singing this poem unifies air, earth and sea to achieve a singularity structured as phallic in the first three stanzas. In the first, birds perform a weaving through the elements (the echoing near-rhymes of 'wood', 'rook' and 'foot' associate 'rook', a most unethereal bird, with the terrestrial) and likewise through hearing, in order then to settle in 'myself to set foot' – a movement performed in a densifying flock of short *e* sounds. A fourth element, fire, stays in reserve for the last stanza of the poem. Alongside, present participles continue to sing, together with the noun 'morning' masquerading as a participle. This movement repeats in the second stanza but in a more overtly sexualized landscape. Again, birds weave between the elements in the first two lines, as does the pun on 'white horses', at once farm animals and breakers in the bay. The name of the previous stanza is scattered in the air visibly, in phonemes, falling to fertilize the earth through the erection and ejaculation indexed in the lines, 'and I rose | In rainy autumn | And walked abroad in a shower of all my days.' 'Shower', here, has its premonition in 'water praying' now audible as 'spraying'. Detumescence follows: 'high tide and the heron dived when I took the road', and again the poem returns to the settled 'I'.

The script is less blatant in the third stanza, but visible and audible nonetheless:

> A springful of larks in a rolling
> Cloud and the roadside bushes brimming with whistling
> Blackbirds and the sun of October
> Summery
> On the hill's shoulder,
> Here were fond climates and sweet singers suddenly
> Come in the morning where I wandered and listened
> To the rain wringing
> Wind blow cold
> In the wood faraway under me.[42]

Once more, birds swerve between air and earth, not so watery this time; they are 'sweet singers' whose singing runs through the first two lines in 'springful', 'rolling', 'brimming' and 'whistling'. While 'the rain wringing' parallels 'a shower of all my days' in a more depressive tone, here the descent falls tellingly on the ear, audible in the short *u* sounds of 'sun', 'summery' 'suddenly' and 'under', a thread that ends in the resolution of the dominant past-in-present tense of the poem (a past tense modified by insistent present participles) with that terminal simple past of 'sung'. What subsequently merges into and must modify the phallic rise and fall, subsuming its repetition into a various continuity, into the stillness of ocean self-expressed as a wave, here is brought about through synchronic meteorological and seasonal change. 'My birthday', as a definite point of temporal punctuation, can be marvelled away as 'the weather turned around' instead of the self turning in its surveying, and this shift governs the further reaches of the poem. The dialectic of this poem brings penis and womb into universe making without the catastrophe of birth. The universe is already-created, has already survived its unliving.

After three further stanzas, fire is reserved to the last, with that element's association with dead autumnal leaves and blood earlier consecrated by Shelley's 'Ode to the West Wind' and Hopkins's 'The Windhover', in a tradition of Lucretian poetry re-shaping the womb of life out of rot and physical damage. The poem's end falls and rises in fire and youth: 'And the true | Joy of the long dead child sang burning | in the sun.' A bloody sunset lies underfoot at the same time, the same place, in fallen leaves – also the leaves of this poem itself, from which 'my heart's truth' will 'still be sung', rising anew from dead words, at once level with the streets of the town and surmounting 'this high hill':

> And there could I marvel my birthday
>   Away but the weather turned around. And the true
>   Joy of the long dead child sand burning
>   In the sun.
>   It was my thirtieth
>   Year to heaven stood there then in the summer noon
> Though the town below lay leaved with October blood.
>   O may my heart's truth
>   Still be sung
> On this high hill in a year's turning.[43]

There is no interruption by death; there is no interruption by birth. The poem would eradicate the caesura identified by Freud in *Inhibitions, Symptoms and Anxiety* when he speculates that 'there is much more continuity between intra-uterine life and earliest infancy than the impressive caesura of the act of birth allows us to believe'.[44] The end-caesura or 'gross catastrophe' of death is challenged in some of Thomas's most celebrated poems, 'And death shall have no dominion' and 'Do not go gentle into that good night' – a gross catastrophe which is the key to Thomas's Christ obsession, defended by William Empson in a splendid riposte to a critic who 'works up his denunciations […] to the point […] of accusing the jealous Thomas of telling Jesus to get back into the womb because he wants to be the Messiah himself. The idea that any man can become Christ, who is a universal, was a major sixteenth-century heresy and has been kept up among the poets'.[45] In keeping with this heresy and Thomas's Unitarian background, Christ's incarnation represents the general catastrophe of birth in the early 'Before I knocked', a poem written in metronomic, knocking four-beat sexains.[46] Catastrophe is both performed and countered by powerful rhythm, and the poem's delirious orality both expels and revels through language's forming, breaking waves. The swing of the poem between castration anxiety and assertive phallicism, between phallicism and the oceanic womb, anticipates resumption on the far side of any break. The poem imagines the protoplasm of incarnation entering the womb as well as suffering its expulsion, and puts immaculate conception under blasphemous pressure: conception has no ovular and spermatozoic origin, but shapes the poetic embryo out of a life-span physical to the extent that it includes its own ordure, while ghostly evoking what precedes life and follows it in a 'last | Long breath' that might carry this poem towards its reader. Even 'before I knocked and flesh let enter, | With liquid hands tapped on the womb', intra-uterine life has compounded a full ontogenesis:

> I knew the message of the winter,
> The darted hail, the childish snow,
> And the wind was my sister suitor;
> Wind in me leaped, the hellborn dew;
> My veins flowed with the Eastern weather;
> Ungotten I knew night and day.[47]

This is followed by two and a half stanzas of premonitory decay and mortality before the staggering final line, 'and doublecrossed my mother's womb'. Both birth and death do violence to the pre-parturient 'molten form', neither internalized nor expelled by the mother. Here is the creation, victim and expression of a Blakeian Godhead swinging the exemplary caesura of 'the leaden stars, the rainy hammer', knocking Christ and himself into shape (theologically they are one). Sonically, God's hammer swings relentlessly across the heavily stressed line breaks. So, also, the double-crossing violence of sexual intercourse is enjoined on the male position in order to defeat the caesura of birth as well as the male–female caesura – for beyond male is female and beyond female, male. As W. R. Bion expresses it in his brief, late text 'Caesura' (1975):

> How is one to penetrate this obstacle, this caesura of birth? Can any method of communication be sufficiently 'penetrating' to pass that caesura in the direction from post-natal conscious thought back to the pre-mental in which thoughts and ideas have their counterpart in 'times' or 'levels' of mind where they are not thoughts or ideas? That penetration has to be effective in either direction. It is easy to put it in pictorial terms by saying it is like penetrating into the woman's inside either from inside out, as at birth, or from outside in, as in sexual intercourse.[48]

But when intercourse in Thomas's poem repeatedly double-crosses the threshold, it knocks against it time and again, an intolerable periodicity. How shall the threshold be crossed without this insistent encounter with the break – without this encounter with the male–female caesura? The poem is saturated with disgust at the flesh, flesh phallically alone in the universe or womb-like in comprising the universe, and intercourse might fill the missing middle between such phallicism and fecundity: but that is not the path taken, a path that would recognize prior and future generations and, by extension, sociality. On such a path, the caesura of birth would continue to mortify. So the one overtly celebratory stanza in 'Before I knocked' instead permits 'my mortal creature' to drown in uterine oceanic feelings, 'the salt adventure | Of tides that never touch the shores'.[49] A rare enjambment hints at the levelling of thresholds to follow in the later syllabics.

The enjambment prepares, then, for 'Poem in October', where flesh dissolves into a sensorium of delight, notwithstanding the caesura of birth and the social world beyond 'the gates | Of the town that still threatens to breach the poem's sphere, obtruding checkpoints which must be trespassed across, before, and after, or made nugatory. The poem dreams that 'all the gardens | Of spring and summer were blooming in the tall tales | Beyond the border' – beyond, rather than before – so that 'my birthday' can be marvelled away and time organized prosodically across space. Lest such protraction be reckoned abstract, part of the poem's force comes from its undergirding by a specific and precisely observed place, Laugharne in Carmarthenshire; indeed in a letter of 26 August 1944, to Vernon Watkins, Thomas refers to 'Poem in October' as 'the first place poem I've written', despite giving it a calendrical title.[50] To anyone who knows how Thomas's poems had been nourished by Swansea and its bay, this sounds disingenuous, but the comment signifies a new ability to tolerate what syllabics perform, secure in simultaneous rise and fall so that dispersal 'in the water and the singingbirds' can coexist with 'it was my thirtieth | Year to heaven stood there then in summer noon | Though the town below lay leaved with October blood'. It is possible now to survive the labial stasis of 'below lay leaved' and to cast out upon the waves. Swansea Bay may be audible and discernible in earlier poems such as 'Before I knocked', but there landscape was internalized; this new universal erases the caesura between internal and external. The psyche and the landscape become identical, not through the one-way vector of pathetic fallacy, but through the coincidence of rise and fall, the exchange of continuous breathing. So the restored middle is breath. The threshold-levelling device of syllabics conforms with the prevalence of mood as opposed to distinct and violent emotions of desire, rage and ecstasy; the pre-separation affective formation of mood, common to mother and infant, suffuses the world and acknowledges no boundaries between self and other. It changes like the weather – 'the weather turned around'.

Crossing and re-crossing the caesura threatens to accomplish only its thickening into a barrier; to overcome it is unintentionally to reassert it. Thomas's irregular rhymes as well as the irregular line-lengths of this poem contrive to satisfy and deny expectations of pause and stress at once. Rhyme cannot be allowed to sign off a sonic completion; Thomas's rhymes are leaky even for assonantal rhyme, leaking between 'wall' and 'forth', to take a telling example from the poem's first stanza. Thomas's running stitch of birds mediates between sea, sky and earth without reaffirming the elements' separation in so doing. Barriers fade into wave patterns, each stanza a wave-form as waves conform to a bay. Rhyme does its stitching job without calling attention to itself; this is invisible mending, inaudible mending within a prosody whose regularity is imperceptible. Neither, despite his frequently religious diction, could Thomas be a poet of transcendence. What Hölderlin calls the 'utterly unbound', the transport of the tragic and the mystical, paradoxically would require caesura:

> In the rhythmic sequence of representations, in which the tragic transport exhibits itself, that which one calls the caesura in poetic metre, the pure word, the counter-rhythmic interruption, is necessary; precisely in order to counter the raging change of representations at its summit so that it is no longer the change of representations but the representation itself which appears.[51]

But Thomas's job is one of universing, where the raging change of representations rotates and unifies to comprise his poetry's sphere. Sexual compulsion and disgust, but also his poems' seasonal synchrony, are alike driven by a pressure to efface that must itself confront the reiteration of difference on the way to effacement. Historical time, marked by birth and death, must yield to repetition: But how to repeat without starting again? Through such universing. Each stanza must suture time and times musically in its waves, an expansive present, an unceasing present. Lyric poetry is the one literary form which dreams of simultaneity, although haunted by the fate of becoming its own memorial; it must resist capturing and freezing, in its artifice it must live illuminated within the sphere it creates. Hence Thomas's elegy 'A Refusal to Mourn the Death, By Fire, of a Child in London': more than a meditation on the inadequacy of elegy, it surges affectively as another negation of endings, a memorial that dissolves itself.[52]

W. R. Bion ends his paper on 'Caesura' with a rephrasing of Freud's reference to the birth caesura as follows:

> There is much more continuity between autonomically appropriate quanta and the waves of conscious thought and feeling than the impressive caesura of transference and counter-transference would have us believe.[53]

What can Bion mean by 'autonomically appropriate quanta', and indeed, what is the relationship between Freud's comment and Bion's rephrasing, including a translation from birth to transference and counter-transference? A further exegetical rephrasing might read: 'There is much more continuity between mobile and clustering phonemes and suprasegmentals of speech (in other words, prosody) and the waves of time, space, mood and a poet's linguistic reservoir, than the impressive caesuras of the poem's beginning and ending would have us believe.' And this leads to another claim to which this chapter has already gestured. That is, each poem by Thomas rises as a wave just as Heidegger describes it in his lecture on 'Language in the Poem'. David Nowell Smith provides a commentary in his book on Heidegger's poetics, *Sounding/Silence*, thereby explaining the sense of resumption that attends a Thomas poem:

> The 'veiled essence' of rhythm lies in the 'source' of the wave – in, that is, the very impetus into movement through which the poetic site articulates itself in

an individual poem; in this, it echoes the movedness [...] that, in 'The Origin of the Work of Art', characterized the artwork's engagement with the limits of its medium.[54]

With Bion and Heidegger in mind, it may be said of 'Poem in October' that it rises from a poetic site that feels familiar to anyone even slightly acquainted with Thomas's poetry. For all its recognizable matrix, it seems less divorced from the material world and the independently memoried poet, than previous poems by Thomas. All signs are motivated: 'And the mystery | Sang alive'. This poet's song, human song and the song of the earth are one, but the achievement encompasses an outward orientation. Listen to the weather:

It turned away from the blithe country
And down the other air and the blue altered sky
Streamed again a wonder of summer[55]

The long vowel sweep of 'blithe' and 'streamed' snatches up the short *u* sounds, rushing the particles forward until calmly suspended at the end of 'forgotten mornings when he walked with his mother'. The particles become visible and audible in 'parables | Of sun light', parabolas of sunlight audible in language as 'wonder of summer' and 'walked with his mother'. Here is the '"veiled essence" of rhythm' as the poem gathers itself rhythmically out of the song of the earth in its wave, in its parabola, in its parable. The poem's singing is visible too – particularly in the last stanza where it is leaved, spread out in text as summer's passing lies displayed in the fallen leaves. Such unsurpassed intensity of sound and vision are reminiscent of Bion's speculations on foetal mental life, starting embryologically with the early development of optic and auditory pits.[56]

'Though I sang in my chains like the sea'. Everything in this discussion seems to lead to the celebrated last line of 'Fern Hill', written in 1945, a year later than 'Poem in October'.[57] The movedness of the poem, to use a Heideggerian term, meaning a kind of buckling against the limits of language marked in rhythm, produces a further magnificent wave out of the same site as 'Poem in October'. It would be easy to point to apples and owls and the rest of the stock shared between the poems, but the wave gathers phonemically, more than in the things it sweeps up, and more powerfully through its linkages than the things linked. 'Parables | Of sun light' in the earlier poem lead to 'legends of green chapels' in another *reading* of the natural world, and audible again in 'Fern Hill' as 'the sabbath rang slowly | In the pebbles of the holy streams' at the end of its second stanza, paralleling the first stanza's 'daisies and barley | Down the rivers of the windfall light'.[58] 'Windfall' falls out of apples – apples and pebbles, apples and parables. 'Fern Hill' too gathers in syllabics, and like 'Poem in October' is notable for its lexical simplicity, eschewing Latinate words, its lines stretching longer than in the earlier poem, but with few commas and only eight full stops in fifty-four lines. These are the chains in which the poem sings a continuous song, each song identical and a variation, precedented and unprecedented. Thomas's off-rhymes chain or stitch through his poems while skirting repetition. The signifying chains lap like waves. Signifying waves, however, are shaped by the geography of a particular coast, much as an infant's language is shaped by her mother's gestural and linguistic embrace. A coast is land and sea both, a place of exchange, of outerness and innerness; so the waves sound like the land and like its people's speech (the word 'lovely' sounds as delectable in a Welsh accent as it sounds complacent in an English one), and the waves shape like verse against its line-endings. After the rivers and streams at the start of 'Fern Hill', the sea is reached only in its last line, opening out and curtailing at once; yet reaching the sea feels inevitable, for we were hearing it all along, beyond Fern Hill and the farm, moving through the poetic site of Dylan Thomas, bringing each poem into hearing and vision, and stretching past the caesura of the poem's ending – which also precedes its beginning.

Such is the wave power of Dylan Thomas's verse. Every poem's semantic and affective wave participates in Thomas's obliteration of the caesura. Owing to the trauma of birth, things have gone to smash already, and the amelioration Thomas imagines is for breaks and resumptions to succumb to waves, in a prosody without end stops or caesuras, pulling back and forth in its chains like the sea. Such a description harkens back to Adam Phillips's charge against Thomas, re-staging the routine condemnation of Thomas's poetry as masturbatory. The shame of lyric poetry which others would overcome, would efface, through proclamations of political and ethical solidarity and sympathy is flaunted, on the contrary, by Dylan Thomas time and again:

> The seed-at-zero shall not storm
> That town of ghosts, the trodden womb
> With her rampart to his tapping

Rather, the seed-at-zero will spill across the universe:

> Through the rampart of the sky
> Shall the star-flanked seed be riddled,
> Manna for the rumbling ground,
> Quickening for the riddled sea[59]

– the sin of Onan seeds the phonemic universe, across sky, ground and sea. What is effaced is not lyric shame, as by a conventional resort to social acceptance and identification with a self-conscious subject, but the caesura. Recall, however, how Bion shifts from the caesura of birth to the caesura of transference and counter-transference. Where might this poem eventuate again in relation to the reading presented here? Is it possible, after the exchange of a reading, even to refer to 'this' poem, using an untroubled deictic? The 'autonomically appropriate quanta' criss-cross between Thomas's poetic universe and a reader's ingestion and exposition.

But there is something to be said in favour of Adam Phillips too. The containment of wave power within the maternal bay is a limitation Thomas could not overcome, using his resources of technical detachment. Universing has to be open to influx, not restricted to the shape of one bay. Dylan Thomas was a poet of London and New York City as well as of Laugharne and Swansea, but you would scarcely know it, with the exception of the wartime London poems collected in *Deaths and Entrances* (1946). Indeed, you would scarcely know that Swansea was a port, open to other worlds; Laugharne, too, up to the sixteenth century. A bay is a mouth, language as abstraction shaped through individual corporeality. But a mouth takes in as well as gives forth. Thomas's universe may have been too small. But in a universe that has indeed become limited, limited in a deadly irony by the illimitability of human aspirations, limitation proposes the stakes. The impulse to epic must be contained, not only in poetic practice, but also confounding the totalizing figures of the local, the national, the racial, while still taking in, still breathing. Universing within limits must be the poetic and human imperative, and reading Thomas suggests as much, even as it affords a shameless pleasure.

Chapter 4

LAPIDARY

This chapter explores the performance of objectification through glass, including the photographic lens, and the affinities between glass and rock. It starts by showing the prevalence in George Oppen's early poetry of windows and windscreens before Oppen abjured humanity for a landscape of rock, crystal and fire. Muriel Rukeyser's *The Book of the Dead* is then shown to advance a powerful indictment of the economic and literal objectification of tunnellers whose silicosis she links to glass and photography.

1

Near the start of his short book of meditations entitled *The Writing of Stones* Roger Caillois declares: 'The fact is that there is no creature or thing, no monster or monument, no happening or sight in nature, history, fable, or dream whose image the predisposed eye cannot read in the markings, patterns, and outlines found in stones.'[1] The predisposition of the eye is crucial here, as is the contrast between the obduracy of stone and its mutative suggestiveness in the eye; while the cloud reconfiguring in Polonius's eye and in his tractable imagination would have appeared no less restless to a steadier view, to Caillois stone can assert its formal finality and simultaneously offer the most fantastic organic visions, such as

> kneecaps and knuckle bones softened by acid to a cloudy, wobbling jelly; intestinal worms glistening with the biles and juices digesting them; a jumble of passages, rumbling innards, excited vulvas, striated tendons; pale partial globes jointed like the knees and elbows and hips of celluloid dolls.[2]

The predisposition of the eye here is historically and culturally specific, trained by the texts and images of Georges Bataille's journal *Documents* to which Caillois contributed, and by the images of awkwardly articulated dolls by Hans Bellmer published in *Le Minotaure*. Contrast Caillois's visceral stony riot with the behaviour of stone in Pound's *Cantos*, influenced by Adrian Stokes's writing on limestone in *The Quattro Cento* and *The Stones of Rimini*. Limestone and its marble variant are there represented as a concretion of oceanic sediment and deeply akin to water; the stone surface also holds light, yellow tonalities evoking amber and hence the historical record captured and visible. For Pound limestone becomes the privileged transactional agent between water, architecture, air, light and history, and definitively so in their Venetian interpenetrations which also produce the clarity of glass. Jennifer Scappettone offers a compelling reading of the intricacies of Pound's and Stokes's revising of the marmoreal as a living tradition, quoting Stokes's *Stones of Rimini* with its vision of stone sharing water's fluidity and of water sharing carved stone's exactitude:

> The water and architecture check and complement each other: 'Water and builded stone vivify the one the other; they are at peace.' Venetian glass, as artifact, literalizes this harmony, generating a new, hybrid material from water and sand, which also permitted heightened light effects in mosaic works.[3]

Pound though abjures Stokes's discovery of primal rhythm in Quattro Cento architecture (to be invested with an enveloping, maternal capacity after Stokes's analysis with Melanie Klein) for an emphasis on perpendicularity, horizontality and linear clarity, so reconciled with his adherence to the hard-edged and classical aesthetics of T. E. Hulme. There is transaction here but no blurring; and keeping faith with both Stokes and Hulme, carving but no modelling:

> Flat water before me,
>   and the trees growing in water,
> Marble trunks out of stillness,
> On past the palazzi,
>   in the stillness,
> The light now, not of the sun.
>   Chrysophrase, [sic]
> And the water green clear, and blue clear;
> On, to the great cliffs of amber.
>
>   (XVII, 14–22)[4]

Even water retains horizontality and clarity, and continues to keep to its schematic 90° axis throughout the long-extended *Cantos*, where water springing from a rock can be at once perpendicular and horizontal, analogous to the perpendicularity of reeds and their song (papyri) and the horizontality of the page and its writing (papyri):

> but the light perpendicular, upward
> and to Castalia,
>   water jets from the rock
> and in the flat pool as Arethusa's
>   a hush in papyri.
>
>   (XC, 61–5)[5]

No 'cloudy, wobbling jelly' here, whether in content, syntax or rhythm. Pound's lines are rhythmically and for the most part syntactically end-stopped, thus averting the 'rhythm-building' he both admired and resisted in Swinburne, narcotic and too yieldingly feminine.[6] When Caillois looks at a stone he sees polymorphously perverse sexual activity and writes vermicular prose; Pound sees hard, phallic evidence to be mortared in lines of verse, words glittering like glass tesserae.

Stone and glass are central to this chapter as is the relationship between flat truth and a fixed position on the one hand, and on the other the fantasized or actual interiority of stone and its epidermal textures with their discharge into rhythm and other expressions of life. Caillois may give fantasy altogether too much play when looking into a piece of jasper he sees

> lopped-off breasts, the mutilation twisting the raspberry nipples aside; there are the bodies of frogs, crucified by the galvanic current, their limbs splayed out by the shock, their skin turned blue and flabby by the violence of the spasm.[7]

But the core of *The Writing of Stones* comprises photographic plates of the interiors of stones revealed by section, and thus the visual exposure of rhythmic patterning. Flat truth as discussed in this chapter is represented by the objectivist poetry of George Oppen with its resistance to rhythm; and in the following chapter by the photography of Aaron Siskind which takes flat surfaces as its primary subject matter, paradoxically negating flatness through flat reproduction. The snapshot and glassed-in distancing of Oppen's early poetry points towards his late obsession with rock and crystal, as though formal capture of an instant in a poem itself objectified were insufficient hedge against time's claim, its snatching back, but also as though the flat truth of representation insufficiently acknowledged the creative force of the mimetic act – the importance of angle of view in the refractive release of light from crystal. Much of the power of Oppen's poetry derives from its poetic resistance to poetry and especially to rhythm, a resistance so sustained that rhythm's push-back develops a strong presence. At the same time, the refractive structure of a serial poem like *Of Being Numerous* does facilitate the play of thought off and about its facets. Siskind's intentions and antipathies are less overtly articulated; but the flattening effect of photography is counteracted by the selection of flat subjects pressing against the print's suave surface, sometimes violently, eschewing the illusionism of depth in the print, as well as by his adoption of serial composition, different from Oppen's in being more about temporal change than angles of view.

If for Pound glass was annealed from sand as an agent of light, and for Oppen glass was a window and a screen, for Muriel Rukeyser glass was first a lens. The limitations of photography and its flattening of the human universe (as well as photography's potential) are a surprising preoccupation of her *The Book of the Dead* – surprising because this work is often cited as an exemplary Depression-era documentary project, whose poetic text was intended to be published alongside photographs by Rukeyser's travelling companion, Nancy Naumburg. A member of the Photo League, an organization to which the young Aaron Siskind also belonged, originally named The Worker's Camera League and destined to be banned as a communist front organization following the Second World War, Naumburg shared a political motivation with Rukeyser; while never a member of the Communist Party, she was friendly with major American Soviet-leaning and Trotskyite intellectuals, journal editors and activists.[8] Their politics pervade Rukeyser's documentary poetic sequence on the death by silicosis of miners hired to construct a 3¾-mile tunnel for a hydroelectric project in the small West Virginia community of Gauley Bridge, a work bent on exposing the cover-ups and denials of the Union Carbide company and its hired doctors. 'Exposure' is what her documentary aims for and employs, but Rukeyser's ambivalence towards photography, despite and because of her training as a film editor and extensive experience with documentary film, will be used as a bridge between the discussions of Oppen and Siskind.[9] It is enough here to note briefly a passage in *The Book of the Dead* on water and colonnades of rock which can be interpreted as a critique of Pound's and Stokes's fantasy of Western civilization's emergence through the Renaissance carving of limestone deposits and into the realms of light:

> Water celebrates, yielding continually
> sheeted and fast in its overfall
> slips down the rock, evades the pillars
> building its colonnades, repairs
> in stream and standing wave
> retains its seaward green
> broken by obstacle rock; falling, the water sheet
> spouts, and the mind dances, excess of white.
> White, brilliant function of the land's disease.[10]

Much work is done in this passage by the final word 'disease' as well as by the suppression of commas. Although at this point in Rukeyser's documentary poetic sequence the primary referent for disease would be understood as silicosis, her verse can be heard to parody Pound, the more so because it ventures into free verse in a book dominated by stanzaic forms.[11] In Rukeyser's lines the land is diseased in a literal sense of being deprived of the ease of natural rhythms of growth and decay, through its creative utilization and the imposed rhythms of human labour and transport. Exploitation is both creative and virulent. Specifically, water flow is harnessed for energy in Rukeyser's poem, not through a surrealist and idiosyncratic plunge into the psychic depths like Caillois's sexual intercourse with stone, but through radically reshaping the landscape. Water far from finding its destiny in 'pillars' and 'colonnades' of limestone, slips over pillars and colonnades of poured concrete, evading them through its sluices and spillways, crossing the verse lines unobstructed by punctuation, then after breaking in its encounter with rock, 'spouts' with renewed force, stimulating the responsive mind to dance instead of reflecting stillness and light in its own tranquillity. What though motivates the disturbing association of an 'excess of white' with 'disease'? The white may be a froth of irresponsible fantasy, with 'brilliant' rendering light meretricious as well as describing the splendour of a cascade; an 'excess of white' then presents a valueless aesthetic surplus. 'The Dam' opens with the declaration 'All power is saved, having no end', and celebrates power 'kinetic and controlled' – power to a purpose. What in this passage water evidently is not is *flat* like a photograph or a printed page; neither for Rukeyser is contemplation the apt human response to water or stone, or a page or photograph. Nor is human labour exemplified by the artisan carving stone to reveal light, but by the social labour of channelling, controlling, diverting, damming and most significantly, *shaping* the motion of water to supply electric power. Such human labour has its specific historical, economic, class and racial organization, central to Rukeyser's investigation.

But how will this be shown in photographs, given, according to Charles Altieri:

> All that photography had come to represent: the authority of the scientific method; the empiricist concentration on conditions of practical life that excluded all spiritual concerns; and the rejection of all values based on historical inquiry, because they seemed incompatible with the ideal of progress?[12]

Altieri reads a response to this question in first-generation American Modernist poetry, in both its explicit affinities and readable analogies with abstract visual art. In particular he studies the cubism and constructivism influencing Pound, Williams and Stevens, a strand of abstraction influencing Aaron Siskind in his early photo documentary work and during his later Bauhaus affiliations. The discussion here tracks American poetry and visual art from the Poundian Modernism of George Oppen's first book up to the mid-century New York painters and poets associated with Abstract Expressionism, and attends to a developing aesthetic strongly marked by Surrealism as well as Constructivism. Siskind was an important figure in pulling together these two strands, along with his interest in hieroglyphics and other non-alphabetical signifying systems developed from contact at Black Mountain College with Charles Olson; and he tied them in the medium which would seem least amenable to the opacity, the crypticity and the incarnating force to which he directed it.

Stone, rock and glass preoccupy the different artworks discussed here, a focus forced forward because these materials are those of art making as well as of representation and reproduction, and their involvement in making and representation also raises persistent questions about temporality and truth. The discussion ends in the next chapter with a response to the Scottish poet Hugh MacDiarmid's poem 'On a Raised Beach', a hymn to the adamant which subordinates stone to a rhythm both impersonal and individually willed.

2

Imagine yourself a poet for whom all writing – a letter or diary even – must be approached with trepidation because to write constitutes exposure, exposure of whatever succumbs to the promiscuous scope of writing. Imagine that your mentor, the poet you judge the master of your language, and for whom verbal accuracy is a prime civic responsibility for poets, turns in the name of truth to quack social and economic nostrums and then to a murderous racial hatred bearing directly on you and your family's disguised name.

Imagine that you had belonged to a political party committed to unveiling the deceptions of capitalism, opening the eyes of the proletariat to its exploitation, that you had worked for a united front to free the oppressed, and then one day learnt you had been entered into a pact with Nazism, the force you understood as a logical extension of the most brutal tendencies in the economic and social arrangements you had fought to overthrow. And that mendacity in the service of cynical brutality became visibly the very mode of being of the leadership and the organization you had championed.

Imagine that you went to war and killed people for a cause you knew would be manipulated by the interests you had sought to overthrow, that in fighting for freedom you were necessarily also fighting for big business, for advertising, for racial segregation and for exploiting the poor. And that you were almost killed and your comrades did die beside you, and you crawled out of a dugout as a hero for whatever freedom might prove to mean.

Imagine that, returning to freedom, you were forced into exile and lived in the shadow world of fellow exiles, none of you able to say an honest word about your deepest convictions or even the simple facts of your personal history for fear of violence or deportation and that your language and the language of your friends were structured around continuous lies of omission, such that even your own child was not permitted to share your thoughts and memories. Imagine you were George Oppen, for whom such omissions were permanent; his two letters to Louis Zukofsky from Mexico might as well have been written under military censorship for all they betray of his location, and in his wife Mary Oppen's memoir *Meaning a Life*, five pages dismiss eight years of Mexican residence.

So imagine that to be creative in language had come to mean collusion in organized lies that have the potential to kill people. So imagine then that to seek to represent reality accurately in language would be to work in a medium that history and personal experience had demonstrated to be treacherously unreliable, that in speaking the truth as you saw it what belatedly became disclosed to you was that you had been induced to lie. Repeatedly.

Then imagine you wanted to write a poem. Why should you want to write a poem? What could poetry do for you or for anybody? What is poetry? A harmless, pretty thing? Or a fabrication? Not a mere fabrication but a fabrication like *The Protocols of the Elders of Zion* or like the Doctors' Plot perhaps. That's how consequential linguistic fabrication can be. Imagine then that disclosure of truth became your central ambition for poetry. How improbable!

Following a famously lengthy break, George Oppen's poetry reused the techniques of his first book for a morally reaffirmed purpose: an all-out assault on the betrayals of language, dedicated to linguistic rectitude. Oppen's poetry was driven by his animus; on the first page of his newly published daybooks, he declares, 'words are a constant enemy: the thing seems to exist because the word does', a conviction earlier and later poets have found liberating but that surrounds poetry with dangers in no way theoretical for Oppen.[13] He set out to oblige poetry to tell the truth, directing this special use of language to combat a linguistic world of runaway corruption. His poetry came to eschew the production of poems as entities detachable from truth telling, the playthings of whimsical or creative reading; as Oren Izenberg writes of Oppen with a note of exasperation, 'the persistent production of non-poems asks that we must entertain the hypothesis that what the poet intends is not, or not always, the poem'.[14] The Objectivist mistrusted his objects because they were linguistic. The poem once released could not be held to truth.

The record of Oppen's attempts to restrict poetic waywardness shows that language survived his strictures to glitter strangely; in the narrow straits where he hammered language according to his will, it showed a resilient tendency to exact its own truths. This was despite Oppen's efforts to oblige language to find him out, to use it as a tool for self-evidence. Subsequently he found permission in writings by Jacques Maritain and Martin Heidegger to let poetry edge forward into what he did not find himself to have known already, opening into the curved horizon of the needle's eye and risking dissolution into the glitter and shimmer that his poetry produced. Hostility to language placed language under such stress that its elements warped and refracted, opening up space beyond its surfaces.

The history then is one of extreme and principled reductiveness. When Robert Duncan wrote dismissively of Oppen to Denise Levertov in 1963 he was seeking to reassure her after Oppen had assailed her work in print, but nonetheless was half-right in his judgement that 'George Oppen [...] may have strong feeling and nervous subtlety but damn it he has a tin ear and slow foot. I suspect he has with the above a narrow mind'.[15] What this discussion seeks to describe is how George Oppen, following an unfeasible programme and with little evidence of lyric talent as Duncan would understand and exemplify it, came to write poetry resonating powerfully within its own structures, resonating through the poetry of successive generations of the American avant-garde. Here such resonances are understood as separate, even contradictory, achievements.

Oppen is an unlikely mentor for an ambitious poet, even if the avant-garde in American poetry has been an accommodating category. There is a cultural shape to this avant-garde that embraces artists – as long as no point of doctrine is examined seriously. Ezra Pound may seem salient when Oppen commends clarity as the prime poetic virtue, as he does tirelessly in letters, daybooks and poems, for repetition is one of Oppen's fortes. However, Peter Nicholls argues convincingly that clarity was not primarily a representational quality for Oppen or indeed a quality of thought but a condition that his earlier poems, up to *Of Being Numerous* (1968), seek to attain in their own status as objects. Nicholls then interprets Oppen's intellectual development as comparable to Sartre's, reading Oppen's interest in Catholic theology and in Heidegger as complimentary, not opposed to, his Marxism. In this way Nicholls accounts for Oppen's shift from the poem as object to poetry as tracking notes, reconciling a sustained materialism with a poetics of emergence and disclosure.

But from the start Oppen's aesthetics were indistinguishable from the Thomist prescription that artworks should be marked by integrity, proportion and clarity. Hence Maritain and Heidegger were Oppen's discoveries rather than his progenitors; their texts enabled him to acknowledge and allow aspects of his poetry that previously had to be attributed, quietly and indirectly, to the distortions incurred by the inevitably mediated nature of seeing and of writing.

For Aquinas *claritas* was 'the objective basis of our own perception of the beautiful'.[16] *Claritas* is that which makes a thing clearly seen for what it is. This helps to distinguish Objectivism from Imagism along the lines Oppen specified, for claritas and Objectivism are effectively synonyms in Oppen's usage. As he puts it in one letter, objectivism is 'derived from an insistence on "objectification," on form, a matter worth mentioning in the wake of the Amy Lowells'.[17] Later he expatiates on this distinction – 'not the falsity of ingenuity, of the posed tableau, in which the poet also, by implication, poses'.[18]

In the same letter Oppen notes that 'Zukofsky wrote also of "sincerity" as the "epic quality"'.[19] Sincerity here is close to Thomist integrity; *integritas* is that which makes a work whole, perfect and complete, and underlies the impersonal quality of epic. Integrity is required for a work to attain clarity in the eyes of the beholder. *Sincerity, integrity*: these are terms of self-sustaining.

Proportion is what Oppen means when he talks in further letters of how 'the line sense, the line breaks, and the syntax are intended to control the order of disclosure upon which the poem depends – And the tone, the intention, is often conveyed, of course, by the prosody'. And, 'more simply: the need to be able to shift focus, depth of focus, with precision, to control distance, real distance, I mean visual distance and audible distance and get at the crucial moments right on top of the thing, an inch from the thing: at that moment, no quotes, no references – at that moment, something near transparence after all'.[20] Proportion in Thomist aesthetics refers to the internal relationships of a work of art, which here Oppen figures in terms of control, of restriction; prosody determines a particular reading, steps towards the revelation of the impenetrable *thing*, and the non-semantic elements of prosody seek to lock poetic language into 'something near transparence'. This insistence on linguistic 'transparence' and 'no quotes', a kind of falling away of the linguistic material, reveals Oppen's great distance from Pound and from Olsonian field poetics, but also entails a contradiction with the values of objectification and obduracy, registered in that phrase 'near transparence *after all* –'. *After all*, it seems the aesthetic object can only be its own kind of truth, and what kind of truth is that? Where is its test, where is its confirmation? Oppen will find in Heidegger a vocabulary enabling him to sidestep the contradiction between object truth and representational truth, by transfiguring the object into the blaze of its standing-forth, in truth's objectified self-disclosure. But what substitutes for the Thomist God as guarantor of this higher truth?

The values of both objectivity and transparency set Oppen's poetics decisively apart from the major American Modernist poetic tradition which derives from the French, with Mallarmé its founder and developed in different ways by Wallace Stevens, John Ashbery and Barbara Guest. During his shift from a poetry of objectified poems to a poetry that 'opens its dazzling whispering hands', Oppen remains consistent in restricting words to the service, not the creation, of truth.[21]

Oppen then was unvarying in his determination to counter linguistic corruption – another term with a Poundian ring, but a theological history. Objectivist poetry was, for Oppen, 'a realist art, in that the poem is concerned with a fact which it did not create'.[22] But Andrea Brady is right too to question Oppen's averred realism: 'If art is meant to honour the world, rather than its own representational power, why does his poetry keep reiterating its own principles?'[23] The answer again lies in Oppen's linguaphobia since reiteration of purpose is one among many devices Oppen resorts to so as to hold words to their right, sincere course.

Putting it schematically, in Oppen's writing poetic *clarity* can be identified with light, typically flat light, and with glass; *proportion* with carpentry, with construction; and *integrity* with the poem's acknowledgement and respect for stone, that is, the stuff of the world from which the artwork emerges but on which it depends, what Heidegger meant by *ground*. These materials are the familiar stuff of preindustrial nostalgia. Such craft might be reliable, even if obsolescent, were not poetic language so disruptively at work. To examine this vital confounding, it would help to focus on the fate of an important 'little word' in Oppen's poetry: *glass*.

While Nicholls's association of Oppen's 'little words' with the thinking of Yves Bonnefoy is misleading, it is misleading in a way that provokes a further revision of Oppen's achievement. Nicholls writes of Bonnefoy's poetics of 'disclosure':

> Such moments of 'disclosure' allegedly show the potential of language to escape the order of the concept, and Bonnefoy even suggests that 'some words – home, fire, bread, wine – are not entirely concepts, can never be taken quite as 'pure notions', for they are bound to potential presences'. Again, we may note the proximity of this view to Oppen's account of his 'faith in the little words' as deriving from their being 'in immediate touch with reality, with unthought or directly perceived reality'.[24]

The quotation from Oppen is disingenuous; Oppen cannot be taken at his word because his poetry constantly belies what he professes. Nowhere is this more marked than in the shape-changing of glass and stone. Oppen's relentless effort to nail down his little words seems motivated by anxiety at the ineluctably mediated nature of seeing and the conditions for seeing, as well as the shiftiness of language. How else to explain, in the work of a poet who scrutinizes every word, that the first poem in each of his first three books, along with the first poem in the first draft of his fourth, presents the act of seeing as from behind a window? The first poem in *Discrete Series* revolves about a quotation from Henry James, 'approached the window as if to see | what really was going on', and in that very short book we have a poem beginning 'Closed car – closed in glass –' while the poem beginning 'This land' concludes with the line 'And the glass of windows'.[25] Typically *Discrete Series* sees from within a car, through its glass windows and while traveling, and this will be a continuing characteristic of Oppen's verse. Partly this is because, as Oppen puts it somewhat defensively in an early letter, 'I like cars and such. I like them when they're handled beautifully'.[26] But while George Oppen was a pioneering American poet of car travel, the car figures in his poems as a restrictive pod like the observing subject himself, whereas for a woman like Edith Wharton it promised emancipation, and for the Beats it would be associated with narrative sweep, freedom and the open road.

Cars and houses are not the only glassed-in mediators in *Discrete Series*. 'Party on Shipboard' contemplates the sea through 'the round of the port-hole' ('Party on Shipboard', Oppen *NCP*, p. 15), and the poem starting 'Civil war photo' (p. 21) introduces the camera lens; this is a posed and historically distant photo, posed like the women in these poems, whether in a painting by Fragonard or perused by a detached lover.[27] Indeed George Oppen's seeing is often mediated doubly; for instance, the tiny poem starting 'Bad times' finishes 'A man sells post-cards' (p. 30) – a nice reflexive touch.

Oppen's anxiety about the mediation of perception is not confined to seeing. In *Discrete Series* paving, asphalt, decks, cobbles and a stage intervene between observer and earth, while the final stanza of the book runs 'Successive | Happenings | (the telephone)' (p. 35). Is that parenthesized telephone rueful, bathetic, or dismissive? Its parentheses apply retrospectively to the entire book. Such complex tonality is lost in Oppen's later poems, where he is less inclined to trust the reader's decisions. This final poem in *Discrete Series* starts confidently, as though something properly obdurate has been achieved: 'Written structure, | Shape of art | More formal | Than a field would be', but runs into trouble with its first parenthesized line, '(existing in it)'. Well, where is the field? Does adducing 'a field' for the purposes of comparison refer to a field, a real field? Or does a field arise within the poem? Or is the field a mere convention, a counter, a wretched word? Collapse ensues with the next lines: 'Her pleasure's | Looser'. What does the poet know about *her* pleasure? Only what she tells him, and what she tells him is '"O –"'. There's a little word alright, but what a word to have faith in. Is this an 'O' of pleasure? Or an 'O' of indifference? Or just a hole? Evidently the poet can't judge because the next line, separated by a stanza break, reads simply 'Tomorrow?' as a question. Who is speaking? If it's the poet, he sounds unsure of his lover. If it's his lover, his feelings must be opaque to *her*. And the poem ends with the parenthetical telephone, so even this doubtful exchange is mechanically mediated.

So much for 'directly perceived reality'. After Oppen's long silence, the Maritain epigraph at the head of *The Materials*, 'we awake in the same moment to ourselves and to things', proposed a new start in direct light. But the first poem, 'Eclogue', immediately belies the epigraph: 'Beyond the window | Flesh and rock and hunger' (p. 39). Not only does glass mediate vision, but here it signifies emotional alienation. And 'Technologies', the first poem of Oppen's next book *This in Which*, also has the poet looking out: 'Tho I distract | Windows that look out | On the business | Of the days' (p. 93).[28] The phenomenology of the Maritain epigraph is particularly misleading because the technique distinguishing Oppen's poems from imagism is his conduct of prosody as the order of disclosure – not a revelatory awakening but a highly controlled sequence of steps. 'A new syntax is a new cadence of disclosure', Oppen writes in 1964, and later, 'it tests the relations of things: it carries the sequence of disclosure'.[29] But this is a disclosure that starts behind windows every time.

'A city of the corporations ‖ Glassed | In dreams': so begins 'A Language of New York' in *This in Which* (p. 114). These lines are transposed into the second section of the expanded book-length work *Of Being Numerous*. Here 'corporations' figure ambiguously in a tense stand-off between 'things' that may be 'absolute' 'but they say | Arid', and those things the body desires and dreams of. 'Corporations' signify not only the skyscrapers of the despised advertising industry exploiting people's dreams, but also the corporeal nature of humans. This section of *Of Being Numerous* (pp. 163–164) feels notably uncomfortable with its own propositions and with their mediated nature. It starts:

> So spoke of the existence of things,
> An unmanageable pantheon

where the verb 'spoke' issues a warning against the contingent, compromised status of 'the existence of things'. The word 'pantheon' is a curious choice that registers a fetishistic quality to these 'things'. Although as things they may be arid, how can things be accessible if undesired and unrepresented: 'Glassed | In dreams ‖ And images –'? Oppen returns to 'the mineral fact' while acknowledging its aridity, 'Tho it is impenetrable', before wobbling back into the conditional: 'As the world, if it is matter, | Is impenetrable.' 'If it is matter'! This is a fundamental doubt in a poet insistent on the stony materiality of the world, who restricts his art to disclosing impenetrable things. If the world is not matter, what is this poetry doing, besides directing with ever more implacable rigour the order of disclosure of what may be then found illusory or mendacious?

In a 2003 letter to his niece, Oppen cites from Simone Weil what would become a talismanic passage:

> When we hit a nail with a hammer, the whole of the shock received by the large head of the nail passes into the point without any of it being lost, although it is only a point. [...]
>
> Affliction, which means physical pain, distress of soul and social degradation [...] is a nail whose point is applied at the center of the soul, and whose head is all necessity spreading throughout space and time.[30]

Oppen worries away at this idea in the daybook contemporaneous with the composition of *Seascape: The Needle's Eye*:

> *Hidden from the image of the needle*
> *image of the [ ], has died [*
> *   ] pounds again and again*
> *on the one nail*

> *post*
> *spike*
>   *Drill*[31]

– and the passage returns in a synoptic version at the head of the poem 'Of Hours' in *Seascape: The Needle's Eye*:

> ' ... as if a nail whose wide head
> were time and space.... '
>
> at the nail's point the hammer-blow
> undiminished
>   (p. 217)

This poem is central to Nicholls's discussion of the distinction between Pound's poetics and Oppen's. Pound's poetics lead to 'reified identity' whereby subject and predicate are joined tautologically by the copula, particularly in the more didactic *Cantos*, while Oppen's later poems 'might be read as a search for ever more extreme ways of recovering that "is" of being by freeing language from the closure of predication and from the pitfalls of "political generalisation"'.[32] Oppen's daybook entry can then be read as registering anxiously just where 'pounds again and again' might lead, that is, to the poetics of *Rock Drill* (hence a capitalized initial for 'Drill') as opposed to the vast maritime horizon of the needle's eye. A tiny aperture and precise vision hail the infinite through this paradoxical figure. Oppen's synoptic quotation from Weil complements the needle's eye by a reverse or rebound causality bringing 'time and space' to bear on a single point – which may be a little word. But to belabour the point, if you hit the same nail on the head often enough, the head spreads and the point distorts or blunts, and this is very true of little words.

For what does the word *glass* designate? So far, house and car windows, along with a ship's portholes; to this might be added the airplane porthole of the first line in 'Flight' (p. 146). Windows recur, right up to 'Semite' in the late book *Myth of the Blaze* (p. 251). If time and space are focused, they are focused through an estranging medium that draws attention to its own material density, that is to say language and especially the language of poems.[33] Thus poetically, if looking through a window is the rule for seeing, so stepping out from behind glass becomes momentous and hints at transcendence, most vividly in 'The Forms of Love'. This love poem for Mary Oppen recalls the first of the three defining crises of Oppen's adult life, with college and a privileged family background abandoned for automotive and sexual freedom. A break between the first two stanzas divides the lovers looking out of their car at lake and moon from the moment of their 'Leaving that ancient car | Together'. Unenclosed by glass they walk into a confusion of night sky, fog, ground and water so they seem to be walking on water in that conditional transcendence acknowledged by the final line, 'Had it been water' (p. 106). Leaving the car associates the start of Oppen's life with Mary with his two other adult crises: crawling alive out of an overturned car and emerging alive from a foxhole.

Glass recurs also in lenses, as late as 'The Book of Job and a Draft of a Poem to Praise the Paths of the Living': 'lonely as the shutter closing | over the glass lens weathered mountains', and here he acknowledges the influence of the observer on the impenetrable and intractable stoniness of things (p. 243). Indeed, Monique Claire Vescia's book *Depression Glass* reads *Discrete Series* as a set of 'lyrical apertures' evoking the contemporary flourishing of documentary photography, and it would be possible to imagine the landscapes of the late poems through the etched and sublime forms of Ansel Adams.[34] Seeing always has its lens, even when not reliant on eyeglasses (as it is in 'Philai Te Kou Philai', p. 97). Not only can seeing be frustrated by the semi-opacity of windows, 'the glass | With the ripple in it', but seeing can distort and abrade as well as glamorize what is seen ('Image of the Engine', p. 41). Glass in the form of reflective windows and of mirrors presents Oppen with an ever-present danger, from *Discrete Series*, where 'a false light' plays 'between glasses' (p. 13), to the troubling San Francisco poem 'But so as by Fire':

First life, rotting life
Hidden starry life it is not yet

A mirror
Like our lives

We have gone
As far as is possible

Whose lives reflect light
Like mirrors

One had not thought
To be afraid

Not of shadow but of light
Summon one's powers
           (p. 233)

Such fearsome light may be the light of truth, but this is far removed from the material world and its 'rotting life'; not all things are adamant, and their impenetrability may mark a subjective or dream life or history ('Hidden starry light'). And if our lives are mirrors, what exactly do we see? The mirror that sees would see seeing. How fearful to pursue clarity and end in this mirror trap of solipsism.

The lines 'The evening, water in a glass | Thru which our car runs on a higher road' in *Discrete Series* announce a more enigmatic glassy recurrence. Glass as a container haunts Oppen's poems, evolving out of the glassy enclosures of car windows and the windows of high-rise office blocks dominating human beings in *The Materials*, as in the poems 'Tourist Eye' – 'A thousand lives || Within that glass' (p. 64) – and 'Antique' – 'Against the glass | Towers' (p. 72). Frail domestic survival is pitched against massive constructions, hand tools and human labour against the occlusive transparency of high capitalism. But glass containers on the smaller scale of 'water in a glass' return in Oppen's late poems to imply that words themselves are in some way glassed in; not only is the visible, phenomenal world mediated through glass panes, except in rare moments of crisis and transcendence, but words that are to construct exemplary disclosures of truth by virtue of their clarity, integrity and proportion cannot permanently subserve the imposed will to truth. Poems become messages in a bottle; and the poem 'Latitude, Longitude' goes so far as to suggest that words' refusal to speak a message may itself be the basis of poetry. Poems are matter-of-fact and therefore can supply no message. They simply are. If so, the requirement that words should disclose the impenetrability of things in the world seems merely tendentious. Rather, poems might be mimetic of the coming-into-being, the self-disclosure of things. Poems would have no call to respond to an external world except by such analogy; poems themselves should attain impenetrability, or at least their prehensile and signifying power should be contained within a non-semantic envelope securing their integration.

But this would be a vertiginous prospect. Oppen had striven to hew words to unambiguous signifying. 'The writers [*sic*] first concern is to be sure that he means anything, and for this he must preserve and restore the meaning of words. The dictionary merely records every possible mis-use of every word in the language.'[35] That way lies the end of poetry, with Laura (Riding) Jackson devoting herself to dictionary making.

Oppen advances words' tautologous self-disclosure for a poetic fulfilment beyond the exigencies of mere use; but even words ensphered in their own lustre threaten the poet. In his poem 'Populist' the social world viewed ambivalently in *Of Being Numerous* is left in the dust; 'other lives' are seen 'in the rear-view mirror' while he pursues the romance of disclosure, a cleansed world of pure emergence, tacking close to sentimentality in the poem's repeated reference to 'magic | infants'; for this poem was written at the height of flower power in San Francisco. Here

>   a word like a glass
> sphere encloses
> the word opening
> and opening
>
> myself and I am sick
>
> for a moment
> with fear

The injunction follows that 'word must speak | and speak the magic | infants' speech'. The self-disclosure of words within their own glassy sphere induces the sickness of vertigo, and the antidote entails language being restored to an act of pure origination in the mouths of infants, in turn restoring the earth. The poem's closing lines support such a reading:

>   birthlight
> savage
>
> light of the landscape magic
>
> page the magic
> infants speak
> (p. 276)

This magical landscape page differs sharply from the composition of the world through discourse mapped in the early poetry of the New York school – for example, in Barbara Guest's elaborate play in 'A Way of Being' with its literary old manse looking out over 'twenty volumes | of farmland' or in John Ashbery's 'The Instruction Manual'.[36] Oppen's poem thinks the word as logos as against discourse and in particular against the eliciting of the lyric self out of dialogue, polylogue; he writes contemptuously in a daybook of 'The New Yorker, who knows nothing and never can know anything. The shopper, the chooser, *the talker*'.[37] Here is the deep fault line in twentieth-century American poetry: both Oppen and Frank O'Hara can admire, in Oppen's case through more-or-less gritted teeth, *Four Quartets* and *Howl*, but their poetics are inimical. In Oppen's last book, the glass through which the world is beheld becomes the world itself, an autonomous sphere of language lifted out of the social and categorically non-creative; it discloses itself as the objects of the world disclose themselves, that is, as long as they're not commercial or tacky. What Guest, Ashbery and O'Hara variously celebrate and embody is what Oppen fears and despises: a creative sociality. Mary Oppen noted, 'We have always felt that our writing required distance from the politics of experience.'[38]

If glass is compromised and so comprising a word, what then of rock? Rather than conduct an inventory of stone and rock, it is enough now to note that the abundant loose gravel, chips and sand dunes in the *New Collected Poems* represent different forms of stone; once again a foundational term for Oppen's poetic turns out to be troubled. What I want to discuss now is what shines where glass, rock, light and water meet – that is, crystal and the glitter, refraction and resonance crystal admits into an intensely restricted body of work.

One contradiction central to Oppen's poetics: a flat light presents a clear, integrated and proportional object, eschewing the temptations of artifice and of fiction. The model is of a poem as a tool or implement. However, the aspiration to mimetic autonomy disallows usefulness in the recognizable sense characterizing an implement. Hence Oppen's discomfort with politically instrumental verse and his annoyance with Levertov. For Oppen the implement must reveal itself to the witness in its full ipseity, a stipulation reminiscent of nothing so much as Heidegger's tendentious reading of a painting by Van Gogh:

> Van Gogh's painting is the disclosure of what the equipment, the pair of peasant shoes, in truth *is*. This being steps forward into the unconcealment of its being. The unconcealment of beings is what the Greeks called ἀλήθεια [...]
>
> In the work of art, the truth of the being has set itself to work. 'Set' means here: to bring to stand. In the work, a being, a pair of peasant shoes, comes to stand in the light of its being. The being of the being comes into the constancy of its shining.[39]

For Heidegger, Van Gogh's painting seems to need nothing as vulgar as a viewer for its 'presencing'. The shining of Van Gogh's peasant shoes corresponds to the light bursting from the crystalline structure locked into the heart and surface of rock, the heart and surface of water in Oppen's poems. Glitter, refraction and resonance increase in power through the limits on their free play, while rocky and oceanic masses counter-posed against and supporting the poem's edging forward are themselves the precondition for the act of seeing; stone and sea transform into glass time and again. Oppen calls this disclosure, and Heidegger calls it a bringing forth out of concealment.

Heidegger legitimated Oppen's hankering after an unwarranted light, poignantly recorded in the recently published daybooks. First hints appear as epiphenomena as early as *The Materials* with 'the sea's glitter' and 'the glint of flesh' in the poem 'O Western Wind' (p. 74), and as 'the gleam' of a woman's body in 'The Source' (p. 76). However, 'the glint of flesh' is referred to a flash of blue eyes, and 'the gleam' of a woman's body in a slum depends on a trope familiar from Victorian genre painting. Before reading Heidegger, Oppen found it difficult to reconcile such tentative metaphysics with the proclamation that 'ultimately the air | Is bare sunlight where must be found | The lyric valuables' ("From Disaster," p. 50). Worse, the glimpsed numinousness that suspends time had become the lyric centre of Pound's late *Cantos*, where a dazzling transhistorical compact was deeply compromised by Pound's contemporary instantiation. As Oppen wrote in a letter to the British scholar-poet Donald Davie, he wanted 'a metaphysic ... which does not deny historicity'.[40] And Oppen's poems were always truthful enough to show there is no unmediated seeing. 'O Western Wind' forms a riposte to the imagistic tableau poem, registering a multiplicity of mediators – the distance of memory, the obsessional desire of the viewer, reflection in eyes and in water, the partiality of 'my vision' – as well as deploying the artifice of a refrain and echoing the language of the medieval lyric that names the poem (decidedly not Shelley's *Ode*):

Beautiful and wide
Blue eyes
Across all my vision but the glint of flesh

Blue eyes
In the subway routes, in the small rains
The profiles.
             (p. 74)

But it is much later with 'To the Poets: To Make Much of Life' in *Myth of the Blaze* that glint and glitter, which had become ubiquitous in *Seascape: Needle's Eye*, now concentrate as crystal: 'the poem || discovered || in the crystal | center of the rock image' (p. 260).

Oppen's habitual gloss on the needle's eye represents the term as a synonym for declination, the arc of the horizon contained between the vertical plane and the prime vertical circle; it is difficult visually to conceive of the relationship between a needle's eye and the horizon otherwise. However, crystal in the rock recalls the widespread naming of rock chimneys as 'The Needle's Eye', surely familiar to a sailor like George Oppen. Oppen's 'Daybook V' offers the various possibilities of 'eye of the needle | image of the horizon', 'needle's eye ... center ... center of the mandala ... shadowless water, shadow of water', and 'What does a needle symbolise? Phallus, I asked? but obviously a needle is a symbol of femininity!!'[41] 'Needle's Eye' turns out to be as mutable as glass and stone; but horizon, mandala, crystal, phallus and vagina offer a nice array of archetypes, simultaneously reductive and transcendent.

'To the Poets: To Make Much of Life' gets expanded into the poem 'To Make Much' in *Primitive* and preserves 'the crystal | center of the rock image' (p. 271), while crystal reappears in 'Disasters': 'verse with its rough || beach-light crystal extreme | sands dazzling under the near | and not less brutal feet journey | in.. light' (pp. 267–268). Crystal then is associated in these late poems with 'the poem' itself, with what concentrates 'Glass world || Glass heaven' and makes to shine ('Inlet', p. 250).

Crystallization is an apt analogy for Oppen's poetry, where a temporal art, through echo and repetition, resolves into one multifaceted structure. Oppen's perverse poetic, according to moral stricture, would have turned upside down the common understanding of one distinction between prose and poetry. Where Pound demanded that poetry should be at least as well written as prose, Oppen in his central poetic statement, 'The Mind's Own Place', went further: 'It is possible to say anything in abstract prose, but a great many things one believes or would like to believe or thinks he believes will not substantiate themselves in the concrete materials of the poem.' The art of liars is thus reformed as a test of truth more rigorous than any philosophy: 'It is a part of the function of poetry to serve as a test of truth', and Oppen dismisses poetic performativity as mere histrionics.[42]

But taking Oppen at his word and scrutinizing a word – *glass* – that belongs among the handholds of his poetry reveals a different poet. 'If we can hold the word to its meaning', he writes in 'The Mind's Own Place', and that is one big if. The act of seeing and the basic materials of glass and stone offer unreliable places for crampons, and words wobble. This failure was the making of Oppen's poetry. Norma Cole remarks aptly in her essay 'The Poetics of Vertigo': 'I had been thinking about the limits he set for himself, for writing, the limits a writer sets and struggles with and against and sometimes through.'[43] Thinking about George Oppen's poems necessitates thinking about their limits and how their limits reconfigure into lyric. Oppen was suspicious of lyric cadence, both tempted and resistant, fearing that cadence runs away into rhetoric, envious and troubled by Duncan's conceptual and musical leaps. When Duncan wrote of Oppen's 'tin ear and slow foot', he considered the poetry line by line and could not have anticipated the ringing of the repeatedly struck little words, the simultaneous compaction and refraction.

Oppen's poetry refracts through and about its entire and increasingly internally referent structure. Internally, recurrences work as structural rhyme. Seemingly fixed entities mobilize. The little words resonate. Oppen's poems stress the hard physical, not the maternal or the social, and under stress they crystallize; rebuking his intention that they should stand in a neutral, flat light, the poems shimmer, glance, mirror, dazzle, obstruct, diffract, distort. They are stronger owing to the apparitions conjured in the light they cast than when demanding respect for authenticity, as in late poems like 'Myth of the Blaze' and 'Semite', too dependent on the self-mythologizing of the poet.

Jacques Rancière has pointed out, 'the ordinary becomes a trace of the true if it is torn from its obviousness in order to become a hieroglyph, a mythological or phantasmagoric figure'.[44] It is odd that even in Oppen's earliest work the suggestion of the meretricious rarely attends 'glitter' and 'gleam'; these arise from the ordinary, whether isolated details or the masses of ocean and rock. The phantasmagoric apparitions that light summons and projects rely on the boundaries of the poetic act being clearly delimited. A more mythopoeic poetry would need greater exploitation of poetic artifice so as not to scatter into spurious truth-claims of a non-poetic register. Oppen's poetry aspires to the consolidation of objecthood by scrupulous mimesis of seen objects undertaken in concrete and restricted language. It is the internal resonance of this language, as it extends through time and doubles back on itself and answers itself, that permits Oppen to be reconciled in a late prose fragment to the centrality for lyric poetry of 'music and cadence and therefore … the force of events'.[45] In what was, according to Stephen Cope, 'among the last writings Oppen is known to have produced',[46] Oppen found his way from an insistence on object status to the lyric poem as an event curving time in cadence, as his poetry had itself come to demonstrate.

It is ironical that Oppen's reception has worked to expiate the sins of Modernism, especially those of Pound. George Oppen's twenty-five years in the desert allowed a connection to be drawn between the great first-generation Modernists and socialism, between sixties counterculture and spirituality. Meanwhile Oppen is identified increasingly as a poet of a Jewish spiritual identity. The shibboleths of contemporary American progressivism, with the signal exception of a sexual politics, are thereby read back through the exemplary figure of Oppen so as to redeem a conservative, even authoritarian, even racist strain in Modernism. The connections are spurious, but they have been important to the invention of an unbroken progressive American poetic lineage. Such a Whig history underpins the influential anthology *Poems for the Millennium*, Ron Silliman's blog, and a gamut of publications from historical summaries to avant-garde manifestos and pronouncements.[47] This is ironical to the pitch of violation; imagine yourself a poet committed to truthfulness and disclosure, whose work has been fated to serve such a false narrative.

George Oppen fought and worked for democratic freedom. His poetry was separate from this fully felt necessity. It was a conservative poetry, avowing a realist programme and insisting on the second-order nature of language. His poetry's finest qualities are traditional. Its resonance and glimmer imagine a reanimated world. But Oppen's is an unpeopled world, a strange vision for a lifelong socialist. The animation belongs to stone, sea, sun and crystal as they respond to the isolated self or the self and his wife. Oppen's sense of humanity was abstract and separate; he perceived Americans as unrelated to their land. In a letter of 1964 to an English poet he likens this American alienation, which he shares, to a pane of glass and acknowledges that only the non-semantic properties of poetry have restrained him from claiming an integration he does not feel:

> I think of the people – I think there is such a thing as humanity, and moreover that no one could exist without it. And I think also of the land, Of the people and the land. And they seem to be standing on a pane of glass. And I would so very much rather say otherwise. I keep dreaming of a poem of final affirmation. Can't, probably, be done. The ear itself knows better, and rebels.[48]

This is moving and deeply truthful. George Oppen's silence has been accepted as the evidence of an integrity confirming his poetry. But while his integrity was great, Oppen's integration was fragile. Was it intellectually and poetically true that socialist art must mean a cooked-up social realism? Was there no alternative for Oppen besides his isolation of poetry to protect its integrity and avoid a crisis in his own integration?

Barrett Watten identifies an American 'constructivist moment', imaginatively enlisting William Carlos Williams and Vladimir Mayakovsky as dialectically linked forefathers for Language Poetry. The two poets met in an apartment on East Fourteenth Street in Greenwich Village on 19 September 1925, and Mayakovsky's reading then was a profound experience for Williams, according to his biographer – a touchstone for epic revolutionary art exposing the bombast of Carl Sandburg, even if its influence cannot be discerned directly in Williams's poetry.[49] But Williams continued to publish both poetry and prose through the Depression and the period of the Cultural Front in Communist Party-affiliated journals and in the press of the broader Left. Not only was his writing uncompromised by this company, but historians of the Cultural Front record that Williams's short stories exercised a powerful influence on the proletarian writing movement.

Strangely it was the poetry of the shopping boulevardier Frank O'Hara that would exploit Mayakovsky's idiom in developing its subtle and radical assault on the pieties of Cold War United States; and it was O'Hara who introduced Allen Ginsberg to Mayakovsky's poetry, thus providing the poetic and activist model for Ginsberg's career as a public revolutionary. By contrast with Oppen's workshop, artisanship and his natural materials, O'Hara inhabited concrete and steel and commerce, and his poetry emerged from the rhythms of social exchange. During this same period, did the protective hygiene in which Oppen sought to quarantine his lyric practice constitute the greatest of the glass enclosures he inhabited, from which his writing is forever stepping out or breaking out in those crises, those flaws that allow it to glitter?

3

The relationship between car travel and photography not only enabled the rise of politically committed documentary photography in 1930s United States, but was strongly represented in American poetry of the period beyond Oppen's. Published in her second collection, *U.S. 1* (1938), Muriel Rukeyser's *The Book of the Dead* is the most compelling example, by a poet and film editor who understood that photography could become a glass enclosure shielding the poet's interiority, as well as rendering more opaque the interior of those things and people it seemed to capture. This was unacceptable: for Rukeyser rock's interiority was a resource to be quarried, and hidden forces (mainly economic) had to be exposed. In an online lecture Cary Nelson notes that 'car travel deliverers the quintessential Modernist gaze that presides over a new regime of looking that hails the entire body to energize itself with the eye's energy', an observation more pertinent to Rukeyser than the relatively detached George Oppen, before summarizing the journey of Rukeyser's 1938 *The Book of the Dead* as follows:

> At the outset references to local sites and scenic overviews give way to urgency as Rukeyser and a photographer companion, Nancy Naumburg, though not identified in the work, descend into a strange and even forbidding area, tracking a scandal and a mystery. The glass plates used by documentary photographers now figure as products whose origins in usually invisible labor will be unavoidably present as they record industrial crime in this journey.[50]

There is much more to be said about the multiple valence of glass in *The Book of the Dead*. The sequence's first poem, 'The Road', opens with strikingly Audenesque rhetoric, but Auden's tropes will turn to literal, practical purpose in an insistence on flat truth asserted by interposition of the definite articles suppressed in Auden's verse of this period:

> These are roads to take when you think of your country
> and interested bring down the maps again,
> phoning the statistician, asking the dear friend,

reading the papers with morning inquiry.
Or when you sit at the wheel and your small light
chooses gas gauge and clock; and the headlights

indicate future of road, your wish pursuing
past the junction, the fork, the suburban stations,
well-travelled six-lane highway planned for safety.[51]

When a decade earlier the young Auden announced:

We made all possible preparations,
Drew up a list of firms,
Constantly revised our calculations
and allotted the farms

– it would have been a naïve reader indeed who imagined Auden and his chums making such practical plans for revolutionary action, any more than the injunction 'Leave for Cape Wrath tonight' would have induced revolutionary leaders to buy railway tickets and hiking boots to assemble at that bleak northernmost promontory.[52] But in reading *The Book of the Dead* it becomes clear that Rukeyser did indeed consult statisticians in its writing, and that her travel routes were planned to forward her inquiry into the 1931 industrial crime of the Hawks Nest Tunnel. A major hydroelectric project was the epicentre of an outbreak of occupational silicosis among miners, resulting in an estimated '764 workers [dying] from silicosis within five years of completion of the tunnel'.[53] Auden's abstraction is countermanded both by Rukeyser's literalism and by a more exact political intention. 'These are roads' introduces *The Book of the Dead* and the particular road is selected from several possibilities, each promising to reveal a different aspect of the nation's baleful state. Rukeyser checks her equipment for surveying the world, including the car and its instrumentation and her companion's camera: 'Now the photographer unpacks camera and case.' In these opening verses no windscreen divorces the poet-traveller from encounter, and the poem ends with a strong assertion of the road's unambiguous delivery of meanings, through a zooming shot performing a telescope's shockingly rapid annulment of distance:

Here is your road, tying
you to its meanings: gorge, boulder, precipice.
Telescoped down, the hard and stone-green river
cutting fast and direct into the town.

'Telescoped down, the hard and stone-green river' merges with car travel and with the act of seeing; but rather than telescoping, Rukeyser's line collapses the major forces of *The Book of the Dead*, stone, water, seeing and the automobile, into one fell swoop which the remainder of the book will investigate. But there is no incompatibility between her telescoping and panning shots, and the ineluctable 'fast and direct' meanings or their rock-like solidity. For Rukeyser, movement whether on the road or in prosody, always must subserve communicable meaning.

Muriel Rukeyser travelled to West Virginia with Nancy Naumburg in March 1936 and 'began serious work on *The Book of the Dead* in the early summer of 1937' after a trip to Spain in summer 1936 as correspondent covering the People's Olympics, an antifascist alternative to the notorious Berlin Olympics.[54] Once thought lost, two of Naumburg's photographs have resurfaced and are reproduced in Catherine Venable Moore's moving introduction to a new edition of *The Book of the Dead*. Captioned 'Shacks and Railroad Tracks in Vanetta', one shows the shockingly rudimentary housing for black workers employed on the tunnel, and the second the kitchen of George Robinson, their spokesman.[55] The poetic sequence's ambition to map American social fault lines is not unusual in the 1930s literature of ethnographic class and racial investigative travel. What is remarkable is its linkage of capitalism's abuse of its workers with activities depending on glass, a product whose manufacture requires the mining of silica, and with a mimetic poetics presented as needing a lens-like eye and a prepared glass plate. Not only must the photographic surface be prepared, but the mind too prepared to receive images, information and ideas through, for example, 'reading the papers with morning inquiry' and consulting maps. *The Book of the Dead* might as well be titled 'The Book of Glass', for glass is both discovered and found to be an agent of discovery throughout. As Michael Davidson summarizes:

> The ocularcentric world of modernist commodity culture is literally 'ground down' to its basic component, silicon dioxide, this reversing the process of industrial production to show its effects on workers. The windows, lenses, X-ray machines, and glasses that become metaphors of unmediated access to truth suddenly become clouded, obscured by a fine white powder that chokes the lungs.[56]

Only at the end of the sequence does glass solidify to wrap as a protective shield about the motorist-poet. Until then her observations are never mediated – as Oppen's invariably are – through windscreen or windows. Immediacy is for Rukeyser a defining quality of poetry, and far from objectifying must deliver 'a moment of proof'.[57] For this, 'we need all our implements', a contradiction which will receive an attempted reconciliation in the book's final poem. But at the start it is striking that 'The Road' and the entire sequence begins with the poet gathering her tools for work, one more labourer amid silica and glass. In the town survey poem 'Gauley Bridge' which begins 'Camera at the crossing sees the city', a camera becomes an investigator independent of its operator; but what it can see is limited by the incapacity of a still camera to pan, hence the movement of a little boy 'blurs the camera-glass'. The town becomes a glass construction, 'many panes of glass | tin under light', tinning being the process that makes of glass a mirror, as well as an effect of light that obstructs scrutiny of the buildings' interiors. Meanwhile 'the owner is keeping his books behind the public glass' where glass acts as a disguise (as the rhetoric of 'transparency' does in contemporary business-speak). 'Public glass' turns immediately to 'Postoffice window, a hive of private boxes' paralleling the previous line. Time is captured as a 'coast-to-coast schedule on the plateglass window', and by the end of the poem even a beer glass signifies the oppressive presence of 'harsh night eyes'.[58] Surfaces are scanned, and while the boy's blurring shows Rukeyser's awareness that a still camera cannot keep time, her glass citadels share much with Oppen's, symbolic for both of financial capitalism.

But human interiors are more important to Rukeyser, even if the technology for depicting them produces something as flat as an X-ray plate or the court testimony of a physician. The breath of this poetic sequence is choked with silica filaments. Glass is deathly in *The Book of the Dead* not only as emblematic of congealed labour for the extraction of its ingredients, as Cary Nelson makes explicit, but as a penetrative toxin; while car travel may spur 'the entire body to energize itself with the eye's energy', the silica miner's body petrifies with glass until in death silica overwhelms his lungs. In these poems silica figures from the beginning as 'white glass' – 'precious in the rock the white glass showed' – and although only one ingredient in glass manufacture, sponsors a powerful poetic opposition between breath (lungs) and represented visibility (glass), whose confounding through extraction for profit halts breath: 'hundreds breathed value, filled their lungs full of glass'.[59] The apparent redundancy of 'filled'/ 'full' enacts the capture of the very breath of miners for profit while waste sediment clogs breath's corporeal mechanism.

Rukeyser's attitude to glass and to seeing is ambivalent. Visibility is important to her and her *The Book of the Dead* imagines breath defeated by technologies of seeing – using some poetic licence, since the poem 'Statement: Philippa Allen' identifies the actual use of the tunnelled silica 'in the electro-processing of steel'.[60] At the same time Rukeyser is invested in a documentary project that depends on exposing evidence, not only what a photograph or set of documents can reveal at first sight, but whatever technologies disclose:

> He stood against the rock
> facing the river
> grey river grey face
> the rock mottled behind him
> like X-ray plate enlarged
> diffuse and stony
> his face against the stone.[61]

Here glass and stone become co-substantial, the X-ray view of the miner Mearl Blanksenship flattening him (as a photographic image flattens, whether silver halide or X-ray) against the rock-face; his face and the rock face merge as 'grey face'. But his physical interior, lungs with their bronchioles, has been confused with the enclosing tunnel earlier in the poem, in Mearl's dream: 'the tunnel choked | the dark wall coughing dust'. Not only confused, but flattened into the wall. In a later poem 'The Disease' the words 'mottled' and 'diffuse and stony' are applied to lungs in medical diagnostics, explicating the evidence of an X-ray: 'Now, this lung's mottled., and 'More numerous nodules', 'streaked fibrous tissue–'. The poem itself becomes a technology of disclosure in reporting Mearl's own speech: 'J C Dunbar said that I was the very picture of health | when I went to Work at that tunnel.' Seldom has 'picture of health' been so bitterly exposed as a false, superficial image, belied by both X-ray and dream: the picture revealed by the X-ray is one of progressive petrification – or vitrifying. This no more respects the worker's interior than the rock does the tunnel's; what comes to light is evidence of exploitation. In Caillois's words, 'Wounded flesh shows how this monstrous realm works, idly limned by imperturbable stone which neither feels nor knows.'[62] Rukeyser finds a way into the damaged interior using implements capable of tracking the disease process.

The final and eponymous poem of *The Book of the Dead* asserts the power of the photographical and written documentary record:

> Are known as strikers, soldiers, pioneers,
> fight on all new frontiers, are set in solid
>   lines of defense.
>
> Defense is sight; widen the lens and see
> standing over the land myths of identity,
>   new signals, processes:

'Defense is sight' is a stirring proclamation, but widening the lens foreshortens processes that are seen to be *standing* 'over the land'; 'myths of identity' are by no means self-evident (setting aside Rukeyser's seeming approval), and 'new signals, processes' demand the corollary of active interpretation beyond the view a flat photograph affords. What is required is the combined power of lens and voice, although voice must be accorded priority since not only can it 'speak to us directly' as a photograph is able to, at least figuratively, but crucially, it can be roused into a chorus of solidarity:

> Carry abroad the urgent need, the scene,
> to photograph and to extend the voice,
>   to speak this meaning.
>
> Voices to speak to us directly. As we move.
> As we enrich, growing in larger motion,
>   this word, this power.[63]

At the time Rukeyser wrote these lines, the exemplary way to 'carry abroad' and to extend both photograph and voice was through documentary film. Film's 'larger motion' could track the opening assertion of 'The Dam' that 'All power is saved, having no end' and its closing hyperstrophe: 'Nothing is lost, even among the wars, | imperfect flow, confusion of force.' In the course of this poem, water's force and gleam are visibly translated in silver halide photography, but the inadequacy of a still photograph to convey the energy damming converts into electricity, demands a new medium:

> Rivers are turning inside their mountains,
> streams line the stone, rest at the overflow
> lake and in lanes of pliant color lie.
> Blessing of this innumerable silver,
> printed in silver, images of stone
> walk on a screen of falling water
> in film-silver in continual change
> recurring colored, plunging with the wave.

This complex passage not only celebrates film within a broader celebration of electricity generation, but it rewrites the Romantic sublime of Shelley's 'Mont Blanc' by celebrating the physical and imaginative taming of both mountain and torrent with a technology equal to their force, so challenging Pound's and Stokes's pre-industrial visions of order, balance and equity. If 'Blessing of this innumerable silver' might sound kitsch, 'printed in silver' and 'film-silver' perform a twist as bold as 'walk on [a screen of falling] water' which re-materializes a transformative miracle as a feat of technology. The flat truth divulged by an X-ray imprints the miner on the stone he quarries, but the miracle lies in mastery of 'continual change'. Mountains are penetrated by rivers 'turning inside' tunnels and conduits, while 'images of stone' are in motion and their 'continual change' is registered, having been traced in film-silver capable of colour projection (1936 marks the date when Technicolor pictures became a standard). Recurrence does not diminish force; even when repeated, 'images of stone' are felt to be 'plunging with wave'. This plunge, a managed sublimity heralded by the telescopic verses of 'The Road', differs essentially from Pound's perpendiculars, its force channelled to drive the poem as well as the hydropower of the dam illuminating cities downstream. Mountain and torrent play the parts of both 'creator and destroyer' as 'Mont Blanc' apostrophizes. Whenever Rukeyser seems tempted by the still image and the iambic pentameter, her poem fights back:

> This is a perfect fluid, having no age nor hours,
> surviving scarless, unaltered, loving rest,
> willing to run forever to find its peace
> in equal seas in currents of still glass.
> Effects of friction: to fight and pass again,
> learning its power, conquering boundaries,
> able to rise blind on revolts of tide,
> broken and sacrificed to flow resumed.

It is impossible, given Rukeyser's politics and this poem's date, to be deaf to the rhetoric these lines draw on – summoning the 'inexorable tide of history', the 'discovery by the masses of their power and their historical destiny', the 'willingness of the revolutionary vanguard to sacrifice their lives', the inevitability of struggle resumed after each revolt is broken. Under pressure of contemporary events Rukeyser abandons the British-style documentary realism she admired, for the stock metaphors of Soviet-style heroic propaganda. Nonetheless, a moment of reflexive scrutiny occurs a few lines later when the poem reflects on this 'perfect fluid', 'these are the phases of its face'; in leading up to the outburst of revolutionary rhetoric, the poem has worked through first, a brief verse history of the dam's construction and its financial beneficiaries, secondly a passage from the proceedings of a Union Carbide stockholder meeting, and thirdly, statistics on the firm's stock performance. The poetics of such a sequence would be advocated explicitly in an essay Rukeyser contributed to *Poetry* in 1941, 'The Usable Truth', arguing passionately against the failure of teachers to explain the use of the poetry children were obliged to memorize. Rukeyser had no hesitation in justifying poetry instrumentally, and she clearly articulates the specific use of poetry evidenced by 'The Dam':

> What strength we have must be developed with all our imagination and equipment. And here, as equipment, enters that attitude which has been given us, which we have been told we are not to use. The attitude of poetry, capable of facing the tragic, the complex, the fantastic, capable of meeting the process of reason that works, not in the single-track a, b, c, d of logic, but rather in the cluster-to-cluster progress of an emotional sequence moving from group to group of idea and feeling.[64]

The word 'sequence' evokes film technique while 'cluster-by-cluster' suggests Rukeyser's mixed-media work with magazine photo-texts as well as with montage in the cutting-room. 'Equipment' sounds belligerently anti-Heideggerian, emphasizing the gulf that separates Oppen and Rukeyser both philosophically and poetically. If human labour turns the natural world into what Heidegger derides as a 'fund', *The Book of the Dead* deploys all available materials to arraign United Carbide and its apologists for its crimes.

Discussing *The Book of the Dead* in a 1938 radio interview Rukeyser denied it was a narrative poem, asserting, 'I have tried to write a series of poems which are linked together as the sequences of a movie are linked together' and likening her poetic practice of shots and cut-aways to Hart Crane's *The Bridge*.[65] While it would be a stretch to describe *The Bridge* as documentary despite its historical scope, both poems can be associated with the development of American Studies which Catherine Gander's study *Muriel Rukeyser and Documentary* links to the rise of documentary, and in particular with the Melville revival that read *Moby Dick* as proto-documentary. This moment stands at the fount of an influential stream of American poetics running through William Carlos Williams's *In the American Grain* (1925) and Charles Olson's *Call Me Ishmael* (1947), embodied in William Carlos Williams's *Patterson* as well as Olson's *Maximus Poems*, and still strong in the work of Susan Howe and M. NourbeSe Philip, poets of documentary-based witness in the present.⁶⁶ The emphasis on the film technique does however distinguish Rukeyser's work from these last, influenced by *The Cantos* and hewing closer to practices of assemblage in static visual art. One ready way of registering this distinction is to consider the page as a spatial unit of composition from Olson to Howe, compared with Rukeyser's page-to-page reel of poetry.

Consistent with this film analogy, 'The Usable Truth' and Rukeyser's subsequent major statement on her poetics, *The Life of Poetry*, are preoccupied with movement that challenges both the objectivist aesthetic and the objectification of the poem performed by New Criticism. In *The Life of Poetry* she takes issue with 'the conviction that "poetry is words"' on the grounds that it involves 'thinking in terms of static mechanics. [...] The treatment of correspondence (metaphor, analogy) is always that of a two-part equilibrium in which the parts are self-contained'. She argues for a dynamism of 'motion and relationship' and tellingly refers to poetry and science as rolling together in a 'watercourse', recommending dismissal of 'every verdict which treats poetry as static'.⁶⁷ No wonder she was ambivalent with regard to photography unless images were juxtaposed and accompanied by text to produce 'the cluster-to-cluster progress of an emotional sequence'. Neither did Rukeyser consider motion valuable in itself. Unlike Oppen she made full use of the non-semantic armamentarium of poetry, and was susceptible to primitivism in relation to rhythm (a pervasive tendency in Western art and art criticism); but rhythm had to be allied to interpretative if not didactic communication. She approved the British documentary film-maker Paul Rotha's disdain for the aestheticizing of film:

> They shot, these aesthetes, the rhythms of a rotary-press or the parade of a milk-bottling machine and rested content with the visual effects of movement. They did not, for a moment, realize that these repetitive rhythms, beautiful to watch in themselves, raised important materialist issues of the men at the machine, of the social and economic problems lying behind modern machinery and transport.⁶⁸

Rhythm needs to be disrupted periodically lest it lull the dialectical intelligence: 'The selection and ordering are a work of preparation and equilibrium, of the breaking of the balance and the further growth.'⁶⁹

After the extraordinary achievement of *The Book of the Dead* its final poem arrives as a disappointing concession, a full-throated re-broadcast of the then prevalent American frontier myth, celebrating both miners under monopoly capitalism and European fighters against fascism for keeping the broad frontier of the future open, for their sacrifice to the dynamic of progress. Characteristically of such frontier rhetoric, the future is perceived as ready for exploitation by analogy with the colonizing push viewing land to the West as empty. Rukeyser's assent to the myth is troublingly evident in her resort to a photographic still to reveal boundless potential:

> this land was planted home-land that we know.
>   Ridge of discovery

> until we walk to windows, seeing America
> lie in a photograph of power, widened
>   before our forehead[70]

– verse that introduces a panorama directly in the Whitman idiom unfolding America from coast to coast, following a glance back to Europe, and troubled only passingly by 'this fact and this disease', progress's collateral damage. The dynamism of contemporary capitalism is reduced to 'a photograph of power' lying before the viewer, available if not for rape, for commandeering every step of the way by a 'frontier pushed back like river | controlled and dammed'. To add to the sense of back-sliding in this poem, such a vision is available only through windows, and not from the open 'ridge of discovery'; America is 'widened | before our forehead', which in the wake of the imperative to 'widen the lens and see' suggests strongly a driver's-seat perspective. Rukeyser in this last stretch succumbs to an imperative for communication that freezes motion to propound a message. Motion as such becomes the message to be conveyed; similarly by the close of *The Life of Poetry* Rukeyser can see and embrace progress everywhere, from 'Einstein, Picasso, Joyce' to 'the Hippodrome girls', Lindbergh and Roosevelt – even Proust: 'The nature of motion reached us from Proust as from the second-run movie'.[71]

In the light of this collapse into progressivism, it is remarkable that when Rukeyser publishes, following the appearance of *U.S. 1*, a film treatment of 'the story of the tunnel drilled at Gauley Bridge, West Virginia, where the suffering and death of hundreds of men who had worked in a silica hill was incidental to the building of a power plant by a great monopoly', most of the reference to glass, transparency and the film medium itself (other than instructions on camera angles and movements) gives way to a subversive preoccupation with masks.[72] From one point of view this looks like a creative use of the black-and-white film medium, with strongly dramatic chiaroscuro adopted as an aesthetic matching the darkness of tunnelling and whiteness of silica. Black-and-white serves also to bring forward as *The Book of the Dead* did not so forcefully, the racial composition of the workforce, dwelling on faces 'from the broad black faces to the bony, lengthened, French-English face of the mountaineer'.[73] In fact 'the majority (around 75 percent) of workers inside the tunnel were black', and the disdain of the companies involved, followed by the West Virginia legal and political establishments' efforts to deny and cover up the crime, were deeply racist.[74] Rukeyser's film treatment shows black workers cheated by a disembodied white hand passing into a black hand a company check for three dollars, then another white hand cashing it for $2.80 after a compulsory service charge.

Immediately afterwards, however, the black miner Robinson is heard to say, 'As dark as I am, when I came out of the tunnel, if you had been in the tunnel too and had come out at my side, nobody could have told which was the white man. The dust had covered us both, and the dust was white.' Illustrating equality under economic exploitation, 'as he says this, the screen has gone black'.[75] But while white and black miners' faces reach a visual identity, company agents can be identified by their masks. The first masks encountered belong to members of the surveying crew; 'the masks resemble gas masks, they are visible as second faces for the two men, the faces of the Company'. Their masks are utilitarian, protecting them from the fate to be visited on the miners, as well of signs of their two-faced nature as company stooges. The white engineers wear black leather jackets. Disturbingly, the script suggests that dead black miners provide the engineers with masks, their eyes turned to glass:

> Close-up of a gas-mask hung around the engineer's neck. The face very black, very earnest, the glass eyes not reflecting anything, not even shining, but dead satin black.[76]

A sequence follows drawing on the verbal evidence to the House Investigative Committee that Rukeyser used in 'The Disease' in *The Book of the Dead*; thereafter the film script takes a strikingly surreal turn. The Chief Engineer drives 'a wealthy, furred delicate woman' (and 'furred' surely has to be visualized as white) to 'the power-house' of the hydroelectric dam. The power-house is depicted as a sexually saturated Modernist edifice: 'The whole tone of this passage is lyric, the narrow-waisted towers lift a protective network, straight, accurate, distinguished. The power-house is rich skin-white'. Contrasting with dead black skin cured as a leather mask and in the context of the script's black-and-white dynamics, the last sentence is truly shocking. The power-house skin can be white owing to wealth extracted from silica whose white dust encrusts the miners' skin; and the building and journey within it symbolize the white woman's body and its sexual exploration by the Engineer. The Engineer, boastful of his ability to quote Milton, leads the woman on an interior tour where they encounter 'a masked man', a welder with an oxy-acetylene torch 'which throws points of dazzling light'. Soon 'the welder pushes up his mask, showing the tender face of a young boy'. Black and white, darkness and night, alternate rapidly, and the production of light is shown to have darkness as its by-product: 'He finds a switch, and another uncovered bulb throws long oval shadows, parabolas of darkness along the tube.' The distinction is between the light the welder brings, a spark, a torch and a technology that welds, a young boy behind the protective mask symbolizing such human advance; and the light the Engineer commands which depends on abstracting power from nature and from the proletariat. As the Engineer and his companion approach the wall of the dam, a sexual apotheosis is approached but not achieved, for she resists him 'in horror of the place', the force held back by the retaining wall and embodied in its Engineer who in turn embodies the Company, owner of nature and labour. 'He turns to her. "That wall up there," he says with terrible exhilaration, "the river's behind it," and starts kissing her, possessively, in conquest'.

The generic demands of film, including a compelling visual design and the need to sustain motion, exploiting its opportunity for rapid cutting and juxtaposition, militate against 'Gauley Bridge' repeating the failure of the final poem of *The Book of the Dead*. While the film script's concluding scene may be heavy handed, the camera lens continues restless to the last and will not dwell on anything so abstract as 'a photograph of power'. Rather, the final sequence of shots establishes the power relations disposed across horizontals, verticals and diagonals and importantly left unresolved:

> As he climbs the last rungs, the camera sees his feet moving more slowly. He is out. She rises after him.
> The light on the ground is very sharp.
> She sees his back.
> Facing him are the ten men and women of the Committee.

Compare this sequence to the end of *The Book of the Dead*:

> and this our region,
>
> desire, field, beginning. Name and road,
> communication to these many men,
> as epilogue, seeds of unending love.[77]

Here possession is *ours*, and here is 'desire, field, beginning' as though finding virgin territory in every road and act of naming (or rather, re-naming what had been named by Native Americans). This verse then could be thought 'a photograph of power', and in a collapse to the first person plural that belies the poem's conflicts, these 'many men' have been identified as a 'we' exercising *power* 'down coasts of taken countries, mastery, | discovery'. This triumphal, imperial Americanism, 'widened | before our forehead' and unashamed to boast 'taken countries' is absolutely the wrong note on which to end a poetic sequence that has investigated the depredations of capitalist power with precision and passion. This triumphalism is hardly mitigated by the sappiness of 'seeds of unending love' (if seeds they become plants, plants die and so on).

For all the failure of the sequence's last poem it hardly accounts for the relative neglect of Rukeyser's work next to Oppen's. One explanation would be that this reflects a general neglect of women's poetry of the mid-century, applying as much (for instance) to Gwendolyn Brooks. A subtler version of this argument would note the importance of patrilineage to American Modernist poetry, where the genealogy from Pound to Objectivism to Black Mountain is secured by patriarchal benediction (New York poets receiving a benediction from Auden in an alternative queer patriarchal line). Another factor may be Rukeyser's overt Marxist politics; activist commitments in female poets – Adrienne Rich's feminism, Gwendolyn Brooks's black power politics – are derogated as devaluing the special attributes of poetry. Each of these poets was insistent that her work should be of use politically, not merely make her political position legible. And finally there is the aesthetic restlessness of all three poets, their refusal, connected with their sense of poetry's social value, to adhere to a set of formal principles. Avant-garde art in the twentieth century has tended to be identified, catalogued and set into the historical record according to formal innovations. The rethinking of *The Book of the Dead* performed in 'Gauley Bridge' is an excellent example of poetic process in Rukeyser's work, lacking interest in the issue of branded products. She was closer to American pragmatism for all her Marxism than to Objectivism. The objects of her attention were social forces; her poems sought to represent forces in motion, in rhythm, in documentary evidence. When Rukeyser looked at rock, she checked her equipment and then examined how humans were making something of it, creating and despoiling, profiting and exploiting. Rather than drawing up a list of firms, she set out to record in verse. *The Book of the Dead* succeeds in overcoming the scepticism about poetic language's capacity to be truthful that so troubled George Oppen, and which she shared; in a poetry that saw seeing, reflected on reflection, voiced what it found and made voicing extend through verse.

Chapter 5

ON A RAISED BEACH

This chapter considers Muriel Rukeyser's film script based on *The Book of the Dead* and her photographic captioning, before turning directly to photography. The photographs of Aaron Siskind interrogate temporality, bringing the instantaneity of the medium to bear on rock and stones and revealing their mutability. The chapter advances to a rocky landscape with the poetry of Hugh MacDiarmid, in which Marxist dialectic compels the emergence of life from rock while keeping it within stony limits.

*

Flatness and the freezing of motion are basic creative constraints of the photographer's art, and in a period when much ambitious American painting and art criticism repudiated the conjuring of depth from paint and canvas, photography could be regarded by artists as exemplary less for presentational truth than for flatness. Thus Josef Albers, relocating to Black Mountain College in North Carolina in 1933 after closure of the Bauhaus, saw the flatness of the photograph as a positive attribute where the textural invariance of its printed surface limited but also sponsored ingenuity in representing texture:

> In his only known writing on the subject of photography, a lecture entitled 'Photos as Photography and Photos as Art' delivered at Black Mountain College in the spring of 1943, Josef Albers writes that 'photos represent the flattest type of picture.' Although he made this statement in relation to the illusion of spatial depth, Albers could just have easily have applied it to the inability of photography to render texture in a way equivalent to its ability to render form and line.
>
> Photography cannot record the haptic with any degree of verisimilitude. It therefore translates *materière* characteristics into its own vocabulary, turning texture, facture, and structure into light and shadow (or pattern).[1]

In the eyes of this rigorously formalist painter, photographs dissolve important characteristics of verisimilitude into pattern; this is by no means to be counted against the medium's artistic potential, since it allows a demotion of the representational function of photography, including claims made for its transparency, in favour of exploiting the medium's properties. This thinking about photography is consistent with an aesthetics valuing most highly what is unique in the medium's material substance.

By contrast, for Muriel Rukeyser photography's capacity to take in more than could the naked eye, although in a clearly defined frame, risked sponsoring an uncritical assent to what it reproduces; and just as bad, its freezing of motion and tendency to pattern-making could license a connoisseur's detached appreciation. Rukeyser's ambiguous attitude to the medium, strongly marked in *The Book of the Dead*, was also troubled that a legitimate aim to convey flat truth could coexist with semantic indeterminacy. She therefore sought to overcome these drawbacks with a practice of juxtaposition demonstrated and theorized in two photo-essays for the mass circulation journal *Coronet*. Both her first 'portfolio of photographs', 'Adventures of Children', and the second, the more tendentiously titled and laid-out 'Worlds Alongside', centre on dance as emblematic of directed movement: a photograph of girls practising ballet in their tutus is juxtaposed with the dirty face and dirty shift of a young girl posed immobile in the kitchen of a tar-paper shack, interior walls lined with newspaper. Rukeyser's caption to the latter image reads: 'Or she backs against the wall, she is lost in her past and her family; against this kind of decoration, she is hardly distinguishable from the furniture.' But a girl in the juxtaposed picture waiting to be called to the dance floor is declared to entertain 'plans of grace'; invested by Rukeyser with an imagined future, she 'becomes a dancer of great art'.[2] The verbal supplement is necessary for the pictorial contrast to go beyond extreme deprivation and relative class advantage. The 'plans of grace' ascribed to the girl against the wall waiting for the authoritarian ballet instructor to call her, might just as well be plans to escape; and describing the impoverished girl as 'part of the furniture' seems even more tendentious when no furniture is visible – unless a broken-down stove and basin count. As for 'her past and her family', where are they to be seen? They are a 'kind of decoration', captured perhaps in the girl's face. Is it poverty or the girl's immobile pose or the photograph or Rukeyser's commentary that reduces all that is visible and inferred to furniture? The potential for sprung movement offered the girl awaiting her turn in ballet practice makes it possible for the caption to entertain on her behalf the 'plans of grace'.

But it is 'Worlds Alongside' that displays Rukeyser's more explicit thinking about artistic media: 'We freeze into placeless art the shadows and bright waves' runs one caption. A photographed wooden plaque of a boat breasting high-relief waves among yet more prominent fish, filled with warriors facing the spears of a defensive band fending them off from a rocky shore, some falling transfixed into the water, is divided by this caption from a second photograph taken on a sailing boat at a dramatic angle, its tilted horizon and spray contriving an effect of motion.[3] 'Alongside' is the operative principle of the portfolio, and here the relationship is left undetermined. One might ask which image is freezing 'into placeless art'. The carving (as seen in its photograph) does not merely render texture; it delights in texture, fish in high relief against the boat's sides seeming to leap from the carved surface, and the battling groups setting about each other. The energy of the carving transcends its flattening in a magazine and becomes an actual if nameless place, actual in engaging the senses of the viewer. If the photograph of a yacht yawing dramatically is supposed only to contrast with 'placeless art' and demonstrate the medium's ability to represent motion, it would be banal: the image looks like countless technically assured photographs where plumes of spray signify the thrill of sailing. Are the two images meant to show the affinity of carving and photography as arts capable of freezing 'the shadows and bright waves', rather than contrasting them – ambivalent whether this is a common achievement or shortcoming?

The use of dance in this portfolio is less of a puzzle and more problematic. A studio portrait photograph of a young African woman, carefully lit to enhance the part-face and shaved skull's sculpted planes, is juxtaposed with a three-quarter profile of the dancer and choreographer Martha Graham printed en face. The caption reads:

> These worlds alongside bring together faces; the primitive waiting face that is ready to receive history onto itself, a dark genesis for us all. It lies beautiful and receptive, a living rock ...

and the finished face of the dancer turning to her audience.[4]

The relationship therefore is complementary. A summary page at the end of the portfolio cites 'the basic African face while Martha Graham dances'.[5] In this progressive variant of racism, the beauty of the 'primitive waiting face' lies in being unmarked by history; full of potential, it is a rock-like form ready to be carved or shaped by time and to receive the imprint of 'us all'. It is 'beautiful and receptive' but has no interior, no history of its own. Because 'primitive' the African face is not conscious of itself, unlike the 'finished' dancer who knows herself through her audience – what she has *bestowed on them*. The African head (for in fact it is a head, nor a face) is a fund, an available resource, and evidently 'receptive' to the projections of the caption-writer. And in what sense is Martha Graham's face to be understood as 'finished'? There is an almost comical hint of the finishing school; a face that has been *civilized*. Perhaps too after the dance Martha Graham is finished, spent, having given her all to the audience; and that being so, it could be inferred that the present civilization has given its all (rather than taken its all), and must now renew itself on the 'living rock' of the black body. Facial angles are telling. Tilted up and slightly away, the black head is denied its own expression; while Martha Graham's face is all expression, full lips parted, eyes hooded, head tilted as if to receive a kiss. It is patently untrue to tag this picture as 'Martha Graham dances'. She awaits the kiss or the music that will animate, just like the girl awaiting the call to the dance floor in 'Adventures of Children', while the black face awaits a history (denied by the very word 'primitive') and a futurity which is not her own.

Formally, the distinction between the two photographs returns to the problem of what Albers calls 'the inability of photography to render texture in a way equivalent to its ability to render form and line'. What makes Martha Graham appear most *finished* is the cascade of hair contrasting with her chiselled cheekbones; it is this range of represented texture that allows her to emerge as a woman rather than a mask. The African woman is nothing but a mask, nothing behind it. Rukeyser fears that 'the flattest type of picture' will send its subjects' 'backs against the wall' – or even as in 'Mearl Blankenship' in *The Book of the Dead*, might pinion the subject as a ghostly X-ray, a miner reduced to a shadow cast against the rock face. How can the still image be animated so as to communicate? How can life be seen in the 'living rock', except through fantasy projected by a caption, where the projected are those who exploit the rock even if themselves exploited?

Rukeyser's gauche captioning responds to the deficiencies as she perceived them of photography as reportage on the one hand and as art form on the other. These two aspects of photography are usually regarded as contrary, with realism opposed to abstraction. But Walter Benjamin remarked as early as 1934:

> [Photography] has become more and more subtle, more and more modern, and the result is that it is now incapable of photographing a tenement or a rubbish-heap without transfiguring it. Not to mention a river dam or an electric cable factory: in front of these, photography can now only say, 'How beautiful'.[6]

And how authoritative! The authority of black-and-white photography in particular, its ascription of edges and definition of forms, asserts that whether a photograph is spontaneous or long prepared, its exposure is rapid or slow, its lighting is natural or rigged, this is indeed the shape of things – and the shape of things is their reality. To select an angle, an aperture and an exposure time is therefore to perform an act of abstraction; and by the same token, Western perspectival painting depends upon abstraction. This is implied in Maurice Merleau-Ponty's description of Cézanne's painting where 'perspectival distortions are no longer visible in their own right but rather contribute, as they do in natural vision, to the impression of an emerging order, an order in the act of appearing, organizing itself before our eyes'.[7] Cézanne's painting resists the abstractions that are the armature of mimesis. Such resistance is exceedingly difficult to achieve in photography, as Rukeyser intuited, because of the transfigurations even a snapshot performs.

The technological change from silver halide film and physical prints to more easily manipulable digital images and their screen display has made the falsifiability of flat truth a byword and a political peril. Photography in the mid-twentieth century was however vulnerable to Benjamin's strictures against aestheticism. Art photographers reluctant to abandon the still image for movies or to editorialize their work had to work within their medium's limits to generate a resistance that was more than a technical problem to be overcome with superior equipment. A compelling response to Benjamin is found in the work of Aaron Siskind, a photographer often linked to Abstract Expressionism. Given his work's usual identification as abstract, it is ironical that it came to resist what Josef Albers described as the formal necessity of photography to translate '*materière* characteristics into its own vocabulary, turning texture, facture, and structure into light and shadow (or pattern)'; by putting such translation under stress, and by compromising the flat surface of photography and its perspectivism through training the camera on flat subjects. Siskind's resistance might be pertinent to re-thinking the abstraction of some of the painters who were his friends and to an extent his collaborators. The term 'abstraction' is too easily applied to a range of quite various practices in painting – and in poetry – in mid-century New York and elsewhere.

Asked to imagine a photographic analogue to Frank O'Hara's 'Poem ["Lana Turner has collapsed!"]' or any of his so-called 'I Do This, I Do That' poems, some might cite the laureate of the decisive moment, Henri Cartier-Bresson, whose street photography was contemporary with O'Hara's poems. The strongly rhythmic, spiral composition of the Magnum photographer Burt Glinn's 'Back Table at the Five Spot' (1957) shows Cartier-Bresson's influence, although its depth of field and the animation of the group makes it resemble a film-still. This photograph often accompanies poems by O'Hara online, as indexical of them, poems likewise imagined to capture the decisive (or indecisive) moment. Glinn's photograph also is iconic of The New York School as a coterie centred on O'Hara, and an artistic practice disseminating from his conversation. But O'Hara's poems, even when most seemingly improvised, are temporally complex as the first chapter of this book seeks to show, and a decisive moment is exactly what they won't or can't entertain.

The use of Glinn's photograph, staged or snatched, exemplifies a tendency of the indexical to shape the reality to which it refers. It isn't arbitrary – it refers to something we intuit about O'Hara's poems, but may mislead in designing to make improvisation their defining quality through analogy with barroom badinage. This caution should extend to the so-called Abstract Expressionist photography of Aaron Siskind, since improvisation has been a key word in describing Abstract Expressionism, ever since Harold Rosenberg's advocacy of action painting with its promise of immersive experience. When a viewer's aesthetic experience is presumed to dissolve the object status of a work of art, semiotic theory falters. For a sign, whether symbolic, indexical or iconic, is divisive by its nature, and the desire of poets and painters to heal such division in a presencing that transcends signifying, devolves from semiotics into philosophical aesthetics. Nonetheless the indexical function of photography in the mid-twentieth century in testifying to the joys of happenstance, does have affinities with musical improvisation swerving off the structures of tin pan alley songs, and with painting responsive to accident; even as the iconic sign continues to exercise authority, with action paintings interpreted, by painters as well as by critics, as inner psychological chaos, a higher rationality, auguries of communist revolution etc..

Reading the indexical signs of abstract paintings calls on hermeneutic ingenuity: the link between Barnett Newman's zip paintings and his anarchist politics is obscure, even if Newman remarked: 'Harold Rosenberg challenged me to explain what one of my paintings could possibly mean to the world. My answer was that if he and others could read it properly, it would mean the end of all state capitalism and totalitarianism.'[8] Although Newman entreats a response to his paintings in political action, it is hard to descry here a set of precepts or instructions or even a mobilizing vision of a liberated future. The US State Department surely did not read Newman's paintings in this way when deciding to subvent their international exposure, but as indexical of actual and present American freedoms. A Newman painting could also be read as divine light emerging from primordial darkness, or symbolically in relation to the entire archive of Newman zip paintings – reference to a painter's *language* at once suggests work amenable to symbolic interpretation.

Abstract Expressionism is a capacious term, so it is important to specify the more exact idiom. Siskind advertised his photography's affinities with Franz Kline's painting, and he was friendly with Willem de Kooning. In paintings by both de Kooning and Kline, the coexistence of different types of sign in the same painting, even in the same mark, stimulates thinking about relations between the media of painting and photography. Can photography achieve such semiotic ambiguity, without reduction to a mere riddle about what it represents? Barbara Savedoff is emphatic on how Siskind's work signifies:

> In the case of Siskind's photograph, it is identification which is crucial. In looking at *Chicago* we quickly recognize that it shows part of a sign, perhaps a segment of lettering turned on its side, so that the image has a dual nature or identity: cropped sign/abstract form. We have the scraped and punctured, but primarily flat, surface of the presented sign contrasting with the shallow depth and smooth surface of the photograph. If Siskind had created his images without a camera, there would not be these contrasts and tensions. And there would not be the joy of discovering compelling abstract composition in the world of the everyday object.[9]

Note the contrasts and tensions here. Sign and form. Rough and smooth. Chance and composition. This sounds uncannily like an Abstract Expressionist painting – 'scraped and punctured, but primarily flat, surface'. Is that what Siskind did, go on safari to find abstract expressionist paintings in the wild and transfix them with a single shot, embalming each behind a photographic surface that is 'matte and somehow stupid' in Roland Barthes's words?[10] And such 'compelling abstract composition' must first inhere in the eye of the photographer, hardly 'the world of the everyday object' inhabited by a user of signs, sidewalks and so on. When Siskind remarks in a 1963 interview 'I didn't push photography [...] photography, in a sense, led me', he sounds abstracted, but he goes on to express the complex tension whereby different types of sign can coexist in a photograph as well as a painting:

> In the pictures you have the object, but you have in the object or superimposed on it, a thing I would call the 'image' which contains my idea. And these things are present at one and the same time. And there's a conflict, a tension. The object is there, and yet it's not an object. It's something else. It has meaning, and the meaning is partly the object's meaning, but mostly my meaning.[11]

The contrasts in Savedoff's account are between the rough, showing time's passage, and the smooth and perfected representation; and between two kinds of significance, signs that would guide the urban pedestrian to do this or that, associated with rough, and the abstract form, associated with smooth. Siskind's photograph is read as lining up rough, symbolic and temporal on one side; smooth, abstract and stilled, the dead, on the other. But Siskind's comments suggest rather that these signs co-exist, and the depicted object is released into active communication through its encounter with the photographer's eye. He goes so far as to suggest that the object is superseded by 'my meaning' although 'my meaning' depends on the prior existence of the object. Identification in that case would not be crucial, nor would it be quite accurate to speak of 'the presented sign' as 'primarily flat' since the act of presentation actually results in the primacy of 'my meaning'. Siskind's gallery presentation of his photographs was prominent in striking contrast to the reticence of the standard window mount and frame; he 'mounted his prints carefully on blocky Masonite boards, as assertive of 'my meaning' as canvas stretched prominently over a timber frame.[12]

But where is Siskind's meaning in the eye of the photograph's viewer? It depends on the viewer, evidently, since meaning is transactional – first between the object and the photographer, and then between the photograph and the viewer. 'We quickly recognize': How true is this? It depends who 'we' are. Recent lyric studies show how readers orientate to a text as lyric; and likewise people who look at quite a lot of abstract art respond to cues that a work is abstract, and put themselves in the appropriate receptive stance. More, the adept of abstraction can recognize – although there will be liminal cases – what *kind* of abstraction she faces. Even more specifically, a particular photographer's imagistic vocabulary can be learnt – an archive of photographs or of poems trains us in their desired reception – so the photographer's or poet's meaning may indeed be communicated above and beyond ordinary expectations of a photograph or poem. Identifying the represented, which may be an expectation for photographs, can be blocked or deferred or even transcended through an abstract attitude and more particularly in the present case, a Siskind attitude.

As a student at City University, New York, Siskind belonged to a poetry club with the painters Barnett Newman and Adolph Gottlieb. His long life linked Black Mountain College (where he taught photography to Cy Twombly, Ray Johnson and Robert Rauschenberg among others during a 1951 summer school), New York School Abstract Expressionism, and the Bauhaus via Moholy-Nagy's Institute of Design in Chicago.[13] Is his work Documentary? Experimental? Expressionist? Constructivist? to cite the defining adjectives of these institutions. The visual arts of New York and Black Mountain are so strongly associated with painting and its investigations that artists in other visual fields tend to be seen as secondary. So it needs stressing that a Siskind photograph was not merely *like* de Kooning's paintings but actually *guided* de Kooning in his painting, and anticipated as well as responding to Kline; as James Rhem writes of Siskind's relationship with his painter contemporaries, 'the records show that Siskind's photographs had as much influence on their work as theirs had on his'.[14] For an example of influence, one of the twentieth century's most iconic paintings can serve: Thomas Hess describes the importance of Siskind's 1950 photograph 'New York' for de Kooning's 'Woman I':

In 1950, while Willem de Kooning was struggling with the first of his series of monumental 'Women', he kept by his work area a print that Siskind had given him. 'I learned a lot from it, Aaron', he told the photographer who was visiting the painter's Fourth Avenue studio one afternoon. [...] The image confronts you, head on, with an old sheet of waste paper–trash, lying on a sidewalk; it is crumpled, stained with oil. Siskind transformed it into a lyrical meditation on the possibilities of shallow 'virtual' space caught on a flat 'actual' plane – that is, of dented bulges and valleys, an inch or two deep, projected on the flat svelte surface of a photographic print. A photograph of de Kooning's *Woman I* (which wasn't finished until 1953), taken in the summer of 1950 by Rudolph Burchhardt, indicates how near Siskind was to de Kooning's train of thought.[15]

On the visual evidence it looks possible Siskind's photograph may itself have responded to de Kooning's earlier 'Gotham News' and 'Excavation'. But leaving aside the cross-currents of influence, a strange and indicative move is made in Hess's passage. We are informed that the image confronts us, head on, with an old sheet of waste paper, and that it has been transformed into a lyric meditation. What is going on? Can a viewer at once be confronted by a symbol and swept up into a quite different experience, a lyric meditation? This is exactly the transcendence Barthes claims a photograph cannot achieve. The small intertextual reproduction in Hess's essay shows a photograph plainly enough of a crumpled sheet of paper, but the magnificent full-scale tritone reproduction in the volume *Aaron Siskind 100*, given the fuller title 'New York, West Street 14' invites lyric meditation because the scale and the rich blacks and greys entice into the 'dented bulges and valleys', a difference showing the central importance of tonal values to black-and-white photography and the difficulty of distinguishing value from texture; only *afterwards* does the question arise from what basis in reality this abstraction has arisen.

For it is, unmistakably, a photograph and what it captures probably gets to be asked, *eventually* – although as this example shows, the question of where 'the photograph' is to be found, in its negative, in which of its reproductions, disturbs the very idea of indexicality.[16] But identifying what it represents cannot be the *answer* to the photograph, which maintains its lyric integrity and resists resolving into a riddle. It may not be absurd to follow Jonathan Culler's theory of lyric in talking of Siskind's photograph as apostrophizing its object, the address of the photographer to the object assuming the overlooking presence of a third-party viewer. Much as in front of *Woman I* the observer may see a portrait and an abstraction and an urban landscape and a department store makeup counter explosion all at once, 'New York, West Street 14' offers a documentary, a still-life and an abstraction. Hess's description of Siskind's photograph in relation to de Kooning's painting may be close to Barbara Savedoff's, but 'the possibilities of shallow "virtual" space caught on a flat "actual" plane' were evidently not regarded by de Kooning as peculiar to photography, more as a cue for non-perspectival painting.

Figure 3 Aaron Siskind, 'New York, West Street 14'.

One difference however is that 'Woman 1' took three years to paint, and shows it. Yet Siskind sounds like de Kooning in saying:

> I think a picture [that is, a photograph] is a kind of a result of a conjunction of circumstances of which you are one. A picture is basically not a statement of

what you believe but rather a kind of indication of what you might believe, or what you might be believing, or what you didn't know you believed.[17]

But it is the contingent nature of 'the indication of what you might believe' that distinguishes the photograph. It is in the moment, even if recognizably depicting a rock, even if the print is on the way to a belief. Such an emphasis on contingency needs however to be tempered by recognition of the influence of Bauhaus, particularly of Josef Albers, on Siskind's development as a photographer, even if his stay at Black Mountain College followed Albers's departure. A useful distinction can be proposed between taking a photograph and making a photograph. To take a photograph suggests that the photograph exists already out there, that any object is attended by its potential photograph which the camera as prosthesis merely reaches out to secure. Making a photograph requires an acknowledgement that the manipulation of light to fall on a plate, a film, or a sensor is a work of artifice. Even if the technology incorporated in a smartphone allows the production of a reproducible image to be largely automated, the act of selection can if founded in a discipline of seeing (starting from the first principle that what is seen through the eye and seen through a lens differ in many respects – the existence of an edge to the lens image for example) and also in the discipline of an emotional and intellectual project, serve the making as opposed to the taking of a photograph. The immediacy of taking exists in relation to the recording function of a snapshot or a lengthy preparation, which need not entail elaborate lighting and camera rigs, but the development of a disposition to make.

Temporal disparity produces tension in an image, and this is by no means unique to the disparity between pressing a button and what might be lifelong preparation. The disparity between the photograph of a moment, however long the preparation, and what it represents if that is a rock, can give rise to at least an intellectual tension. But of particular interest for this discussion is disparity in rhythm, in temporal pattern rather than duration – and pattern, as appreciable recurrence, is fundamental to visual abstraction. Compare Siskind's photographs abstracting the seashore rocks of Gloucester, MA with Fairfield Porter's studies of the Maine seashore, and James Schuyler's poem 'Buried at Springs', an elegy for Frank O'Hara which meditates on transience and persistence:

>   Rocks with rags
> of shadow, washed dust clouts
> that will never bleach.
> It is not like this at all.
> The rapid running of the
> lapping water a hollow knock
> of someone shipping oars:
> it's eleven years since
> Frank sat at this desk and
> saw and heard it all
> the incessant water the

> immutable crickets only
> not the same: new needles
> on the spruce, new seaweed
> on the low-tide rocks
> other grass and other water
> even the great gold lichen
> on a granite boulder
> even the boulder quite
> literally is not the same[18]

Rocks photographed by Siskind consolidate from sand, or emphasize the sandy texture of sedimentary rock, or balance perilously, or focus on a living surface of lichen; they are so trained on the present state of things that a granite boulder would quite literally not be the same re-photographed a year later, and its shadows would be otherwise cast. The pressure of the instant on the immutable is felt as a challenge that enlivens. These photographs are at an opposite pole from Ansel Adams's mountainous sublimity, and resist associating rock with eternal laws, whether in fascist architecture or the marble-clad and glassy facades of banks.

Siskind's prints whose rich tonalities connect seeing to the finger-pads, whether velvety or rough and peeling, ridged or glassy, work with and against the immiscible photographic surface at a time when painters were introducing into oil foreign objects to compromise the slick of the medium, and building oil paint into forceful, impasto presence. Siskind focuses so tightly that rough surfaces want to burst forward from the flat, svelte print, but those textured surfaces derived from rough parts of town, from derelict sites, present forms of beauty which, even if the reproduced rocks and walls are quite literally not the same, the photographs capture in an instant. But how far is that so? Siskind canvassed his subjects for a considerable period before photographing them, and between the pressing of the button, the developing of the film, the selection of the image to be printed, the printing and the framing, is interposed a sequence of analogies – even before exhibition, reproduction in a catalogue, in an essay. There may be a 'substratum of instantaneity' in a photograph, but in Siskind's rock pictures this encounters a substratum of eternity; and the instantaneity and the eternity of the captured image reveal their kinship even as they defer to the emergent haptics of a warm, rough rock surface.[19]

In this regard Siskind's rock pictures have their homologues in the hayrick-like rocks of Fairfield Porter's 'The Bay' (1964) or 'Flowers by the Sea' (1965), either of them possibly the painting James Schuyler was thinking about. One obvious difference lies in Porter's use of colour, although colour is by no means the dominant aspect of his paintings – there is nothing eye-popping about them, and indeed colour is muted sometimes to the point of tentativeness. Rather, Porter's aesthetic privileges tonal values and texture, and his use of Maroger's Medium, allowing rapid drying of oil-paint and therefore necessitating its rapid application, allows 'the local color [to be] transparent and porous, letting the dark light of space show through' – by which I think John Ashbery means that negative space is always involved with shape and pressing into and against it, so contour becomes rather friable.[20] Porter wrote that 'one of the discoveries of Impressionism was that the contour was unimportant relative to the interior light, substance and weight of what it contains' but his own painting puts even this unemphatic containment into question.[21] Although he admired Balthus because 'his paintings have the materiality of stone' the stone and rocks in a Porter painting are as much like 'washed dust clouts' as their 'rags of shadow', and not impermeable. The 'materiality of stone' is more about texture and tonal value than contour and line, and Porter's kinship as a painter with de Kooning or Helen Frankenthaler lies exactly in this emphasis on texture and tonal value, irrespective of representation or abstraction.[22] It would be implausible to claim Siskind's photographs of rocks dissolve their stoniness to the extent of Porter's translucent brushwork, which in reproduction could easily be mistaken for watercolour. Nonetheless Siskind's attention to texture and tonal values can make rocks appear fleshly, as in 'Martha's Vineyard, 1950', a composition with uncanny affinities to his earlier photographs of human feet, exploratory of skin creases and whorls as his pictures of rocks explore their rough texture; and in describing the rock pictures as 'about the business of contiguity' Siskind shifts emphasis from boundaries to dynamic interlocking that evokes sexual activity (see 'Martha's Vineyard Rock 108, 1954').[23] This after all is 'the business of contiguity', not its settled fact.

Figure 4 Aaron Siskind, 'Martha's Vineyard 1954'.

The assertive and appreciable rhythm established by such interlocking depends, to be sure, on visible boundaries and abstraction into rhythm is often a compelling quality of black-and-white photography. Abstraction is a unsatisfactory term however, when facing a Siskind photograph of seaweed, rock or sand, with its powerful analogical force. To take an example, 'Seaweed 8' (1947) shows a strand of seaweed curling about the right side of two forms in sand and then running to the centre of the bottom edge of the print, in a shape roughly like a question mark – and at the bottom edge there is a small and doubling curl now wholly separate.[24] The more prominent strand anticipates Jasper Johns's catenary paintings, drawings and prints of fifty years later, and the questions it proposes are comparable to those of Johns, in relation to their flat surfaces. The strand is doubled along its extent, showing a variable but always close separation between the two. For some stretches one strand appears like a shadow cast by the other; elsewhere one strand might have been displaced fractionally to leave its trace as a depression; and elsewhere the primacy between what might be termed the 'positive' strand and the 'negative' is undecidable. Or perhaps the strands have simply been laid on light-sensitive paper. Further complication is introduced by the two sand forms. Although the print's lighting is perceived as flat, there seems to be a strong and deep shadow to the top left aspect of the upper form, identifying it as a relief, with the bottom left edge then resembling a miniature cliff face. However, the lower form cannot readily be accommodated to a revised idea of a light source falling from the lower right to create shadows on upper left aspects – variation in the tonal value of the sand does not correspond to such a hypothesis. Once the top form is perceived as a bulge, and the disappearance of the catenary around its highest point confirms that perception, the lower form starts to oscillate between a depression and a relief, and the upper form is again compromised even if study returns it to its prominence. This print does not only make a point about flat surface and depth, but pushes back the flat surface of sand (a precursor of glass) to background, and obtrudes its tumescent forms. The flat surface cannot switch to foreground in the same way because the catenaries decidedly lie above.

The movement experienced in this 'abstract' print generates analogies. The print subjects the viewer to its incessant presencing. The resemblance to a profile face in cameo or intaglio references such a presence but does not contribute to it as strongly as the primary and sexualized rhythm of the two forms in rise and fall posed against the appreciable rhythm of the catenary as it mediates between the sand surface and the print surface.

What does the almost tangible texture of the rock introduce? A sensual quality apparent at once when looking at Siskind's photographs of rocks is warmth – their texture evokes the warmth of flesh, as his photographs of feet in their turn etch appreciable rhythm. The earliest rock images, which represent a turning point in Siskind's work, were made in Gloucester in 1944 – a decade before he came into contact with Charles Olson, author of an epic poem on Gloucester's history, a later influence at Black Mountain on Siskind's photographs of texts and hieroglyphs.[25] In these early photographs the analogies can seem over-intrusive. Take for example

'Gloucester Rocks 1' (1944), an image so obsessionally focused on texture that to describe it as 'abstract' is as misleading as to describe Dubuffet's heavily encrusted images as abstract.[26] The first impression is of skin, or more specifically elephant hide, with folds and creases warmly proposing a body's folds and apertures. A small sprig of vegetation at bottom centre confirms the rock face as in relief from a narrow wedge of flatness extending from top left to bottom centre. A second view resists the fascination of the rock's or hide's variable texture – variable in composition, weathering and lichen cover – and takes in the dominant form as a hieratic head frowning down to the lower right in profile. Eyes and a ridge above a nose can be distinguished. What first appeared as sexual openings and folds now resolves into facial features. So this second look becomes an encounter with a vast head which does not return the gaze. Primal rhythm lies instead in response to the warm skin textures and investigation of the less-resolved apertures. But there is a further distancing possible, where a question of scale arises. The extreme closeness of skin texture flips back into a distant aerial view, as the smooth wedge evokes the sea. A shoreline shelf of rock acquires vegetation when the eye travels to the right into a landscape that might be splotched with small copses and the creases of river beds.

Appreciable rhythm and primal rhythm engage with greater enigmatic force in the Martha's Vineyard prints of the 1950s. One reason these are so much more compelling is that the rhythm of formal abstraction clinches tightly with primary rhythm without the blatant analogies of 'Gloucester Rocks 1' offering rapid resolutions. 'Martha's Vineyard 4' of 1950 has particular art–historical importance, as it was selected by Robert Motherwell and his co-editors for the frontispiece to a volume on contemporary art, *Modern Artists in America*. The picture is therefore not only enigmatic but was seen by the editors as emblematic of current work in painting – Siskind was the only photographer represented, making their choice of frontispiece all the more striking.[27] Balanced rocks are photographed against a pure white background, making scale indeterminate and irrelevant.[28] The composition is dominated by a cradle or sled-shaped rock balanced at either end on formations extending out of the frame, and upon which rests a round rock with flat base. In the aperture between the two plinth rocks are stacked two sets of smaller rocks, the top rock on the right echoing the shape of the cradled rounded rock. This photograph's poise between the perilously balanced and the safely cradled is truly remarkable. My use of the word 'cradle' does immediately reach for an analogy difficult to resist, but makes the point that even purely formal relations will summon likeness if they achieve any potentially palpable presence. Some 'pure' abstraction may indeed aim for the numinous or spiritual, a theological abstraction that is a negation of the carnal Catholic Christ. What 'Martha's Vineyard 4' offers is abstraction in the process of incarnating – that is, exactly the negation of Oppen's stony negation.

The incarnation achieved here plays with and against the warm and chill textures of rock, between forms reminiscent not only of cradles but of Neolithic tombs and balanced quoits, of a phallus entering the vagina of the lower aperture, of a sled that wants to slip away and a massive weight. Here play with the print's flat surface activates the background, as though the rocks had been disposed on

Figure 5 Aaron Siskind, 'Martha's Vineyard 4'.

light-sensitive paper like early photography of algae or ferns. Eventually what the rocks are like is *like rocks*. Looking at these rocks can change the sense of what rock is to something more capacious – what rocks happen to be at a particular time in a particular place. This differs from Fairfield Porter's rocks in that a representational painting allows the escape clause of 'the artist's vision' which need not disturb adherence to rock as an identity, an affixed noun.

Abstraction can be understood as transitive: abstraction *from*, although that would not apply, for example, to Jackson Pollock's drip paintings, any more than to Siskind's later Martha's Vineyard photographs which even more strongly emerge as abstraction *to* the corporeal, rocks turning organic as the reversal of coprolite or coal, and developing surfaces which can uncannily become velvety or furry (as in 'Martha's Vineyard Rocks 124A, 1954').[29] Such negation of the negation, a confrontation with the tomb, may look oddly calm and rested in these images. But as Lesley Stonebridge explains, following Ella Freeman Sharpe:

> Art then does not, as in other accounts of sublimation, *stand in* for a missing object. Far from being vicarious in respect of something lacking, art is essentially an *affirmative* space. Just as primary processes know no negation, so too for Sharpe pure perception belongs to a period in psychic life in which 'anxiety is absent'. The figure that marks the absence of anxiety is rhythm.[30]

Sharpe's position here may be too absolute; elsewhere she asserts that an artist can be identified in infancy by her 'natural' grasp of perspective.[31] Art involves both primary process *and* sublimation, and their contention. Such combat urges to resolution and to make works of art compelling. Abstraction *from* coexists with abstraction *as* – as what is unnamable, unrecognized, compelled and primal. The affinity of abstraction *as* with flesh and with bodily shapes and processes is therefore unremarkable. But flesh can be turned into *living* rock in a photograph instead of finished stone so long as primal rhythm remains strongly in contention; primal rhythm was, after all, Siskind's motivation in photographing feet: "'I think," he said to a group of students, "that it has something to do with my kind of wallowing in something, because feet to us, culturally, are something we try to forget about".[32]

Benjamin's charge that photography severs the aesthetic surface from political reality and his disdain for the aestheticizing of a river dam echo Muriel Rukeyser's critique of the art. 'Camera at the crossing sees the city' she writes, but what it sees is stopped in time, superficial, and in the general case impersonal – an impersonality carrying the spurious authority of flat truth, as distinct from 'placeless art' with its ambition for a truth unconfined to representation of the object, attentive to the medium as interface between the individual artist and the world. Documentary photography is problematic in disguising the act of selection which Rukeyser's line succinctly expresses – how can the camera see 'the city' from its fixed angle, at its fixed distance, at its moment? Taking the camera into the human hand does not itself solve the problem. A politically committed photographer may eschew a display of technique, to convey violence directed against him as a political activist. But the resulting grainy immediacy is vulnerable to abstraction in the eye of the viewer and to aestheticism; see, for instance, the great Japanese photographer Tomatsu Shomei's 'Protest, Shinjuku, Tokyo 1969'.[33] Involvement in the thick of the action smears – such trace of event shares in the paradox of action painting, where the action held in view has always already been completed. Reception complicates: a shot taken in extreme conditions and a much worked-over canvas alike fall under the appreciative gaze – whatever the production schedule, in reception an immediate impact is followed by the controlled temporality of taking in.

How does Siskind's photography answer Benjamin? First, through the tension between photography's instantaneity – and Siskind took photographs rapidly, although often after a long-developed acquaintance with the object – and the complex temporality of weathered stone and of walls covered with graffiti and the shreds of old posters. Second, as with the poetry as well as painting of Siskind's contemporaries, through serial composition developing a symbolic repertoire, sequencing the marks of attention evidenced in the photographic moments, and training attention away from likeness towards the symbolic set and its mutations and permutations. Thereby it is possible to say in front of a photograph 'It is not like this at all', rather 'a kind of indication', as Schuyler can through the technically unmediated experience of looking at the same scene year after year. But Schuyler's phrase also points to the fact that the original is an already-existing analogy, something seen through the eyes of an observer at a particular time; and that the painting or the photograph or verbal description, however precise, introduces one more analogy. A third way in which Siskind answers Benjamin is through the co-presence, mutual interference and alignment of appreciable and primal rhythm in his best photographs.

These three characteristics can be grasped by a brief look at photographs by Aaron Siskind specifically in homage to Franz Klein and a painting by Kline that accompanied the Art Institute of Chicago 2016 *Aaron Siskind: Abstractions* exhibition, 'Painting' (1952), and by considering their differences and similarities.[34] Discussing Siskind and Kline, Phillip Barcio points out:

> Graffiti originates in passion, and demands speed and stealth. Kline achieved the same aesthetic over time, in a deliberate, careful manner. His process was exacting and laborious, not quick and dirty. The fact he was consistently able to convey the same energy, passion and grit in his studio as would be seen in a furious spray of paint on an alley wall is astonishing.[35]

Siskind's 'Homages to Franz Kline' followed closely on his high-speed photographs of divers and athletes; and while Kline was painstakingly and slowly reproducing graffiti effects, Siskind was capturing graffiti through instantaneous technology – with a particular emphasis on marks of weathering, not evidence, as on Kline's canvas, of a duration mimicking urban decay, but of defacement stopped. Aestheticizing of decay may be betrayed in the titles of the Homage to Franz Kline photographs after the places where taken, Jalapa, Lima or Rome. None of these names, not even Rome as epitome of dilapidation, has much bearing on the associated image. Rather than recording, Siskind's achievement with these photographs is identifiable as a peculiar coming into being – a freezing that releases. Although attention to texture can lead to fetishism of the original print, can the bonding of the surface provoke the high-contrast image to push out? Apparently so.

But this relationship between surface bonding and the emergence of texture corresponds to the relationship between appreciable and primary rhythm, central to Siskind's own understanding of his photographs, and encapsulated in the key term 'conversation'. Often this entails a containment of violence. In the most extensive work on Siskind to date, *Aaron Siskind: Pleasures and Terrors*, Carl Chiarenza refers throughout to Siskind's principle of 'conversation' as assuming a stress not usually associated with so civil a word. Thus:

> The *conversations* here are the dialogues a mind has with itself. In one, the light shapes seem caught in violent action; still, the emotion insists on being graceful, and the tones and their relationships remain appealing. Formal order carries metaphorical chaos: one sees the terror and pleasure of levitation in another form.[36]

But 'metaphorical' is wrong here; the chaos is pre-metaphorical. Siskind's own words when discussing the 'Homage to Franz Kline' photographs are less metaphysical too: 'I think that on these walls I photographed, there is a lot of violence. The feeling is much more raw [...] the very act of selecting and arranging gives order to the violence, tempers it.'³⁷ The rawness of feeling is what demands the photograph; the photograph tempers it but does not tame it.

Imagine walking along an anonymous street in an anonymous quarter of some town one day. You scan the walls and see graffiti and the scars of time and events. A rhythm of specificity and abstraction. A rhythm of speed and fixity. A rhythm of index, logo almost, flag almost, revolutionary commemoration almost, railroad tracks almost, construction almost: A rhythm between index, icon and symbol. Time and place are nailed by any photographic shot, but in Siskind's images struggle to resurrect as unfixed. There is a rhythm of violence and serenity, and the more you look the more you recognize this violence struggling to break surface. Discussion of New York painting has emphasized surface or shallow layering as a push-back against illusionism. But what if there is an equal force in the powerful abstraction that struggles to break surface to emerge into time – time as we receive it, as our eyes move across the surfaces and we feel not only in our eyes and fingers but in our responsive bodies an emergence from the painting which is also our emergence. As painting breaks surface we re-apprehend our physical thickness and our bodily rhythms. De Kooning's painted slather may look like mineral salt deposits *at the same time as* swift strokes, and even Helen Frankenthaler's thin staining may slowly suffuse the canvas from behind *at the same time as* looking like a sudden spill. The written surface of Schuyler's poem is ruffled by time. Maybe lyric poems want to never bleach, to become boulders (or chestnuts in anthologies), but they are freaked by the running of time, and the way things are in a poem depends on the quality of attention in and on them, just as the seemingly unchangeable world of a Maine island is influenced by the way it's taken in. The loss of Frank O'Hara from Great Spruce Island means everything changes; looked at differently it, well, looks different.

It isn't a statement, this picture, this photograph, because it's not a final and mortified thing. It isn't a depiction but an indication, with something behind it that pushes to come forward but may keep its enigma, its primal rhythm that may be violent but whose violence is acceptable. In series the rhythmic evidence shifts to the symbolic domain, where it might start to reveal what you believe, because belief connects moments in time consistently and appreciably but is susceptible to change. Just like our self-presence. Moments lithify. Rocks in the stream. A rivulet in the *corsa*. Roger Caillois concludes his study of analogies in insect behaviour to human by making this distinction: 'Man's freedom implies an imprecise, ambiguous language, which invites misunderstanding, not an exact system of unequivocal signals, such as make up the limited code of inexorable turns and choreography which is incorrectly labelled the "language" of bees'.³⁸

Nor is this picture 'an abstract'. Rather, in resigning from representation Siskind's photographs also resign from abstraction. It would be more accurate to say that his photographs can achieve the force of incarnating; and incarnating would also describe better the non-figurative painting of Willem de Kooning (for example) than 'abstraction'. Looking at an exemplary work by either of these artists, is it not that it develops 'in response to external solicitation, which is both tactile and visual, and it solicits a similar response from other perceivers'?[39] Silverman here is echoing Merleau-Ponty who insists

> distinctions between touch and sight are unknown in primordial perception. [...] The lived object is not rediscovered or constructed on the basis of the contributions of the senses; rather, it presents itself to us from the start as the center from which these contributions radiate. We *see* the depth, the smoothness, the softness, the hardness of objects; Cézanne even claimed that we see their odor.[40]

If Siskind could photograph rocks and stones as 'lived objects' in the sense used here by Merleau-Ponty, photographing them to activate and incorporate all the senses Merleau-Ponty invokes, such an achievement precisely counters Albers's approval of photography's translation of all sensory properties into patterns of light. For photography to do this it must lock horns with the drive to abstraction Albers sees as ineluctable: the rhythms of primal incarnation Merleau-Ponty celebrates Cézanne for restoring in paint, and the force of abstracting block and reinforce each other powerfully in Siskind's photographs. Abstracting itself is released in Siskind's work from its usual photographic subservience to representation and from its linguistic subservience to signification; an irresolvable movement between these poles is what keeps the abstract alert, as Charles Olson wrote of Mayan glyphs, and in the present participle.[41]

While such abstracting and appreciable rhythm requires arrangements to be made or recognized, and the viewer's aesthetic detachment, by training or by an effort or sudden pleasure, traces the rhythm to be appreciated, time and again, what is stepped back from at the same time draws forward as primal and unspeakable. These are not exclusive rhythmic modalities; rocks and stones may also present, in their apparent obduracy, a challenge to an ego-driven determination to enforce a totalitarian rhythm, one that seeks to claim stones' obduracy for its own virtue or for the virtue of an impersonal historical force which ego is invested in heralding and joining. The supreme example must be Hugh MacDiarmid's 'On a Raised Beach', published in 1934 and written on the island of Whalsay in the Shetlands. Although relatively fertile, Whalsay offers ample material for meditation on rocks and stones, and the poem is vocalized 'on the stones forming the raised beach at Croo Wick, on the uninhabited island of West Linga, which was visible from MacDiarmid's cottage'.[42] But no raised beach or marine terrace could offer the geological diversity obtruded at once by the stony vocabulary of MacDiarmid's opening lines:

> All is lithogenesis – or lochia,
> Carpolite fruit of the forbidden tree,
> Stones blacker than any in the Caaba,
> Cream-coloured caen-stone, chatoyant pieces,
> Celadon and corbeau, bistre and beinge,
> Glaucous, hoar, enfouldered, cyathiform,[43]

The stoniness here is predominantly verbal, with the poem's continuous torrent of hard-edged nouns and adjectives forced into a fairly regular four-beat line and a conventional syntax giving the impression of a writer formidably conversant with these recondite terms. David Trotter identifies in the poem a synthetic English developed in the wake of Scottish Modernism, an idiom it deploys and simultaneously undermines when native primitivism (as found in Charles Doughty's synthetic prose) is invaded by a string of French terms.[44] This opening passage heightens and crowds together scientific, biblical, ultra-literary ('Glaucous, hoar, enfouldered') and sonic usages and properties of language. It is easy to mock MacDiarmid's orotundity, but 'On a Raised Beach' is serious in several ways – relentlessly solemn yes, and also fearless and repellent as the unapologetic elitist MacDiarmid surely intended. A lexicon necessitating recourse to a scholarly dictionary (a real obstacle to most readers in days before the online *OED*) must still be rebarbative to a casual reader; although MacDiarmid's lucidly didactic passages may be more provocative politically.

The first two lines encapsulate the poet's ambition – for this poem is written in an aggressive first person singular hard to avoid identifying with Hugh MacDiarmid – which is to assert his own stoniness and where insufficiently adamant, to turn into stone (lithogenesis). The apple picked in the Garden of Eden and condemning humankind to sex, sin and guilt was itself stone ('carpolite'), for it was a stony world that truly was born in God's Creation; 'lochia' is post-childbirth vaginal discharge, so presumably the birth of humankind was a stillbirth. The Christian mythology in these lines recurs throughout 'On a Raised Beach', coupled with a Nietzschian disdain for Christ as saviour of the weak. Christ is compared unfavourably with the implacably stony Lenin, not named here but identifiable from MacDiarmid's earlier 'First Hymn to Lenin'. Lenin figures as the Great Man, pure expression of 'the real will that bides its time and kens | The benmaist resolve is the poo'er in which we exult'.[45] MacDiarmid's membership of the Communist Party did not mitigate his contempt for the masses and their lack of stony resolve, allied to an individualism dismissing most individuals as incapable of true individualism – 'I have in my grip […] my own self, and as before I never saw | The empty hand of my brother man, | The humanity no culture has reached, the mob' (p. 432). It is remarkable to invest 'brother' with such scorn, and at times this version of communism feels indistinguishable from fascism; at around this time MacDiarmid briefly found fascism attractive, hoping it might reconcile socialism and Scottish nationalism. His commitment to dialectic fortunately proved irreconcilable with blood primitivism. Stones for MacDiarmid stand uncompromised by Christian charity or fallible human instincts and desires, and their 'detachment' exemplifies the qualities the vanguard needs to blaze its revolutionary trail:

> This is the road leading to certainty,
> Reasoned planning for the time when reason can no longer avail.
> It is essential to know the chill of all the objections

That come creeping into the mind, the battle between opposing ideas
Which gives the victory to the strongest and most universal
Over all others, and to wage it to the end
With increasing freedom, precision, and detachment,
A detachment that shocks our instincts and ridicules our desires.
        (p. 426)

While early in the poem MacDiarmid vows to 'turn again | From optik to haptik and like a blind man run | My fingers over you', the poem remains strikingly lacking in sensory detail both optically and haptically; what MacDiarmid sees and feels is rhetorical and theoretical, and the actual stony beach offers little more than grist to his mill and words to roll about the mouth.[46] His revealing demand is for 'bare stones', and when lichen makes an appearance it is appositely fenced off in parentheses with an allusion to 'the dual nature of lichens, the partnership, | Symbiosis, of a particular fungus and particular alga' (p. 432). The life of lichen ('partnership' indeed!) would blur the dialectic of rock and void driving the poem's historical vision, and a surface that invites touch might stir unstony instincts. Disdaining, in a sideswipe at T.S. Eliot's cultural nostalgia, to mourn 'a heap of broken images', MacDiarmid pursues a truth that will crush, and 'gorgonises all else into itself'. Stone and truth are one hard fact, but truth is stone motivated to turn all else to stone. 'Truth has no trouble in knowing itself. | This is it. The hard fact' (p. 430). This is a frankly totalitarian version of Marxist dialectic that regards dialectic as precedent to humanity, as embodied in the very stones, and human beings, far from making their own history, as determined entirely by an implacable force which it is humanity's destiny to realize, and the man of destiny's mission to enforce. Such a totalitarianism will not reappear in English language poetry until J. H. Prynne's *Kazoo Dreamboats* (2011) which draws on a combination of Mao Zedong's essay 'On Contradiction' and the physics of Van der Waals Forces to advance a comparable argument for inhuman dialectics.[47]

Rhythm organizes MacDiarmid's totalizing stony force, sweeping up poetry and stone into historical necessity:

    my Muse is, with this ampler scope
This more divine rhythm, wholly at one
With the earth, riding the Heavens with it, as the stones do
And all soon must.
        (p. 429)

MacDiarmid pushes back at once against these lines for being illustrative and dragging stones down 'to the futile imaginings of men' rather than 'just accepting the stones'; but the threat carried in 'all soon must' goes well beyond acceptance. The danger of uninterrupted, unparalleled, and inexorable rhythm is evident here, with its demand that all (all human beings? all creatures great and small?) fall into line with a force that engulfs heaven and earth –

> By what immense exercise of will,
> Inconceivable discipline, courage, and endurance,
> Self-purification and anti-humanity,
> Be ourselves without interruption,
> Adamantine and inexorable?
> (p. 429)

Once reason finds its terminus in a dialectic of being and non-being 'where by death's logic everything is re-composed', 'reason can no longer avail' and a virile, stony acceptance of the inevitable is the only option open. To name this philosophy dialectical may be too generous; 'without interruption' its single object oscillates between two positions, stony and weakly human, stone and non-being, stone and death, but not between life and death because life that is not stone is an aberration to be discounted or expunged from reckoning. At least Prynne's version (and Mao's) finds the seed of life in internal contradiction in its relation to external contradiction, where the on/off switch of negation is complicated by the cross-rhythm of *actual* history. For MacDiarmid any such external influence is reduced to the effects of 'a fever passing over my vision' troubling his view of what 'is necessarily a desert' (only a desert landscape can be sufficiently uncontaminated by humanity to support his 'anti-humanity') – a fever which does however allow him to see 'a brightness through a burning crystal' (p. 431). The appearance of crystal has a certain inevitability; Oppen's crystal shines as a brilliant and obdurate externality but MacDiarmid exceeds all restraint by casting his own mind as the medium to illuminate the desert world. Notorious though MacDiarmid may have been for inconsistent affiliations, his fascism, Stalinism, monarchical nationalism and traditionalist Roman Catholicism share a consistent authoritarianism and disgust at democracy, and an identification with dictator, Pope or monarch as the Platonic philosopher-king bringing enlightenment: 'Intelligentsia, our impossible and imperative job!' (p. 432)[48]

Danger lies in submission to any single rhythm, primal, appreciative or totalitarian, and where the last arrives at collective bondage, the former can in different ways harm both individual and collective. Rhythmic discrepancy is needed to actuate both bondage and freedom, primary process and intellectual grip, detached admiration and submission; and in their co-existence, contradiction, convergence and their variable polyrhythms, to enliven. MacDiarmid's clangorous prosody becomes wearisome in its lack of creative and critical attention to line-endings or internal caesurae, its acceptance of a rhetorically monotonous syntax, its dependence on the grammatical and doctrinal authority of the first person singular, and in its fitful adoption of rhyming so inconsequential to the poem's semantic and constructive emergence as often to pass unnoticed, and in its strings of statements supported only by the copula:

> I am enamoured of the desert at last,
> The abode of supreme serenity is necessarily a desert.
> My disposition is towards spiritual issue

> Made inhumanly clear: I will have nothing interposed
> Between my sensitiveness and the barren but beautiful reality
> (p. 431)

This passage is itself a desert poetically; there is little to feel, to contemplate or to decipher. If nothing interposes between 'my disposition' and the desert, a disposition whose 'sensitiveness' must be taken on trust since it is exercised only on nothing by 'the reflection | Of brightness through a burning crystal', there is no space for art or indeed for creative human activity of any kind. The desert is political also, conforming to what Walter Benjamin meant by left-wing melancholy, despite MacDiarmid's compensatory rhetoric. At the end of his poem, MacDiarmid returns to the synthetic idiom of its opening strophe, 'Diallage of the world's debate, end of the long auxesis' (p. 433). The fact of stone in the end is revealed as no more than rhetoric, or in Trotter's detailed and more sympathetic exegesis:

> Tutored by lithogenesis ('apprentice endocrinite'), dialectical materialist song replaces one rhetorical form (auxesis, or Romantic hyperbole) by another: diallage. Diallage is a rhetorical figure by means of which various arguments, each having been considered fully in its own terms, are brought to bear on a single point. It is also a kind of rock: grass-green pyroxene. Tutored by the dictionary, synthetic English could be said to enact song's lesson from stone[49]

Like George Oppen, MacDiarmid started his working life as a socialist organizer, in his case in the Welsh valleys, and despite the two poets' very different poetical and political trajectories, the poetry of both suffers from left-wing melancholy. In both bodies of work there is a striving for the monumental tending towards inertia, contested in Oppen's case by adoption of a serial form designed to refract its objects, and in MacDiarmid's by sheer volubility. Rukeyser's interrogation of her medium and of the other media with which she engaged means her poetry wears a less consistently recognizable countenance, but one which keeps the reader alert, even if her work sometimes falls short of its own ambitions. Rukeyser's poems generally feel more alive than Oppen's or MacDiarmid's as they negotiate glass and stone, representation, event, objects and their own object status.

Chapter 6

STONE THRESHOLDS

This chapter characterizes three kinds of aesthetic experience: the 'frozen and marmoreal', the 'voracious and totalizing' and what is called here the 'threshold experience', the mode of poetic or aesthetic apprehension that does not settle into any human commonality or graven form, but vibrates and shifts, engendering an hermeneutic enlivening. The space of this threshold is first approached by a reading of Veronese's paintings, *Hermes, Herse and Aglauros* and *Mars and Venus United by Love*. The chapter then proceeds through readings of poems by Trakl and Hölderlin by way of Heidegger, Blake and Shelley, and closes by reading an aubade by Andrew Crozier that teeters between wild life and bomb-site dilapidation.

1

The Western poetic and visual arts traditions have been haunted by transformations from human to stone, tree, plant or animal, performed by vindictive Gods in stories which collated in Ovid's *Metamorphoses* radiate through these arts – music and dance also – even to the present. At moments of transformation the human, the divine, the animal and the inanimate engage in reattributions; indulging their petty spites the gods and goddesses acknowledge human feelings and disengage from them, while the supplication of animals reaffirms a human kinship and the reeds sigh out a human song, suffering human feeling while remaining irremediably separate from humanity. This chapter meditates on such transformation, and instances how stone and the disengaged, finished lyric can bring life to an aesthetic encounter through a haunting from beyond the stone threshold, which calls for a hermeneutic response. Haunting is produced by a discrepancy, interference with a dominant rhythm by a coexistent rhythm that will not be suppressed. Across the threshold arrives a message from the Gods, with exegesis required for the sake of sanity, but not at the cost of resolving all discrepancy. Another way of putting this, taking a cue from the poet Lisa Robertson who follows Auerbach, is that such discrepancy produces a figure that goes on figuring, rather than settling into a symbol.[1] This chapter distinguishes such art works from those laying claim to human commonality, whose humanistic force is directed to dissolving the aesthetic threshold. Hence three varieties of aesthetic experience are identified:

the frozen and marmoreal artwork demands reflection, although reflection can confuse radically the source and the receiver; the voracious and totalizing artwork demands submission; and the threshold artwork, where the threat of petrification is countermanded by a discrepant rhythm of life, engenders an hermeneutic enlivening. The term 'hermeneutic' is used throughout the chapter in its Platonic sense, as a force which commands attachment, engendering in the recipient the unity of a sensation of direct transmission with a critical reshaping. A strenuous version of this would be 'interpretation' as performed by great musicians, including singers, when inspired. Such interpretation is never settled. Here I start by comparing two Renaissance paintings, one figuring through interruption and the other extending an invitation into an embracing, total and human rhythm.

Figure 6 Paulo Veronese, *Hermes, Herse and Aglauros*.

In the Fitzwilliam Museum, Cambridge, hangs a late painting by Paulo Veronese, dated after 1576. *Hermes, Herse and Aglauros* depicts the moment when Hermes strikes with his wand the envious Aglauros, the god's sexual choice having lit on her sister Herse. Spectators familiar with the story in Ovid know she will be turned into a statue stained dark with her literally deep-died jealousy. The painting presents a gallery of frozen poses; flaunting a naked but alabaster breast a rather satisfied-looking Herse along with her judgemental spaniel stare directly at Aglauros from the right, as does an insufferably cool Hermes from above, tapping his wand on Aglauros's back. At the centre rear stands a gold statue in a niche, gazing sightlessly out of the picture frame to the right and anticipating Aglauros's fate while also, in her cold and garmented nobility, standing in as a *Venus Pudica* for Herse's chastity.[2] Especially intriguing is what the caption in *Treasures of the Fitzwilliam Museum* describes as 'a sensually painted female satyr, clearly a bedpost, backing the pillow and sheet glimpsed behind Hermes' cloak'.[3] 'Clearly' does considerable work here; if anything is 'clear' about this chaotic passage of yellowish terracotta paint emerging from behind a drape in a painting otherwise of luminous clarity and detail, it is that a sensually painted bedpost demands some interpretation. So does the bland identification of a 'female satyr', unknown to classical art and on its rare appearances in the Renaissance, found cavorting in humorous sexual play with male counterparts or doing suckling duty for baby satyrs. The Veronese scholar Richard Cocke also is unpersuasively categorical, identifying 'Aglauros' envy, embodied in the statue of a satyress, hidden behind the rich curtain, where 'hidden' is every bit as questionable as 'clear' – leave aside the contradiction between Ovid's description of Envy as a disgusting crone and the almost coquettish poise of the figure pulling aside 'the rich curtain'.[4]

Where all else in the painting offers itself as finished to a fault, the 'female satyr' is positioned so not only is she uniquely active in whisking the curtain open, but she is blurred with urgency. Mortals and animals meanwhile tremble on the threshold of petrifaction – even the lovers who should be on the verge of consummating their passion. This painting is at least in part an allegory of the work of art as representation, a point emphasized by the viol on the table at centre and the musical score on which Herse's hand rests, as though physically stilling music. Next to the viol stands a small spray of flower-heads in a table vase, an apt symbol of transience overcome by art. The transfixed and transfixing spaniel holds the balance. It follows that Hermes could be imagined as a portrait of Paulo Veronese himself, the wand representing his artist's brush; the contrarian female satyr in the colour of living clay is emerging to preside over an envisaged but undepicted conjugal bed. The satyr might be described as emerging in her effacement, since the facial structure visible behind the clayey daub has its outlines almost obliterated.[5] The painting sports this centre of imperfection; Hermes is about to complete his artist's work, but the artist at the threshold of fixation daubs a bedpost which he invests with more energy than all the living creatures disposed so statuesquely. Indeed Cocke asserts that 'the *paragone* with sculpture is one of the keys to the *Hermes, Herse and Aglauros*' (p. 28), where *paragone* denotes a competition between the arts: 'Mercury and Aglauros are the painterly equivalent of the interlocking two-or three-figure sculptural group' (p. 31). The female satyr is determinedly travelling in the opposite direction from Aglauros, out of the inorganic. Art can animate the dead as well as petrify the living. Even if his human and divine figures are destined to be frozen under his gaze and wand-like brush, Veronese spares the painting's spectator from sharing their fate by detonating an erotic power defying representation, a sensuality so concentrated in its uncanny emergence that it exerts a supernatural force – supernatural in the sense that Eros frankly challenges death.

But here is a very unusual eroticism. The sex of the satyr denies the creature the engorged phallus prominent in classical satyric depiction – and indeed, Hermes's wand is laid on flat in what seems a studied restraint from phallicism. Such a phallus would signify lust and procreation, whereas the female sex introduces a puzzling disturbance. If there is a lack here, it lies in a lack of finish troubling the threshold between painting and spectator. There had been a fresh-hued gaiety in Ovid's *Metamorphoses*, a flicker between categories, lost in Veronese's perspectival world. When looking at this picture there seems to be a threshold before the pictorial space; and at this threshold a world of stone threatens to extend on either side, the spectator frozen in place as a counterpart to the gold statue where perspectival lines converge in the blocked depth of the painting. The statue averts her eyes, and one arm crosses her breast while the other keeps the folds of her garment stretched tightly across her belly and thighs, in immediate contrast with the disorder of drapery before her and out of which the satyr peers. There is a drama of drapery in this picture, with Herse, Hermes and even Aglauros attired as becomingly as models, while restricted to its niche the statue is tightly bound in a cerement-like robe and the satyr emerges from a flurry she generates in stiff brocade.

Happily the female satyr *dislodges* the viewer from the place assigned perspectively. Once I discovered her, and she needs to be discovered since her colouration sets her back in a blur, my eyes darted about the painting and I found myself walking from side to side and to and fro, looking for the proper place to resolve the satyr's lineaments. Failure made me restless, even as I developed a kind of composite view of this daub, this imp of the perverse. I was involved in an eventuation of this picture that freed me from the frozen position that its perspective sought me out to enforce. Through its entirety the painting exercises a Medusa effect rather than through a particular figure, and it freezes the spectator as the spectator freezes the scene. Or would, were it not for his or her satirically induced pacing, responding to a hermeneutic injunction. It is such agitation that prompts attention to small details like the sprig of white fallen roses dropped on the floor tiles in the right foreground, next to Herse. The sprig might be viewed as a sardonically equivocal comment on Herse's willingness to relinquish her chastity to the god, since while two blossoms are tightly closed, one is openly in display; but also it lies immediately in front of the painter's inscription, depicted as carved into the base of a large floor-standing jardinière: 'PAULO CALIARI | VERONESE FECIT'. Here in the rumpled bloom before the reproduced lettering is expounded one theme of the painting in little. The sky against which Herse and the jardinière are silhouetted is a painting of a painting. The evanescent flower is consigned to paint as Herse is consigned to Hermes and Aglauros is sacrificed, all brought under the sway of inscription. The hermeneutic agitation provoked by this painting obliges me to consult the literature. How apt that Paolo Veronese's original family name 'at his birth in Verona in 1528 was "spezapreda" – literally translated as stonecutter'.[6]

But another text interferes with this inscription. The passage in the *Metamorphoses* on which this scene draws, devotes more time to a back-story accounting for Aglauros's envy than to the scene of petrifaction. The staginess of Veronese's 'classical' interior, associated with Palladio's contemporary Teatro Olimpico in Vicenza, contrasts with the architecture of Envy's lair as Ovid describes it. Ovid's 'The Envy of Aglauros' is a tale of two thresholds. Seeking means from Envy herself to inoculate Aglauros with her poison, Minerva strikes with her spear the door to Envy's lair, 'a filthy slimy shack', and pausing on the threshold she cannot cross, beholds Envy: 'black decay | Befouls her teeth, her bosom's green with bile, | And venom coats her tongue'.[7] When Hermes approaches Herse's door, Aglauros forbids him to cross the threshold, vowing never to budge while he still continues to press his suit on Herse. Hermes uses his wand to open the door as Minerva used her spear; doors fly open when a god or goddess points. It is Hermes's opening the door that turns Aglauros to stone; so in Ovid Aglauros herself personifies the uncrossable threshold. Veronese brings Hermes into the frame, across the threshold, where he becomes attached to the sculpted group; meanwhile the painting's spectator remains stranded at its threshold, compelled by Herse's loveliness and her artfully arranged garments, and troubled by the satyress's inchoate lure.

Veronese's *Mars and Venus United by Love* now in the Metropolitan Museum of Art of New York, is presided over by a male satyr, sexual organs decently obscured by Mars's shoulder. By contrast with the *Hermes, Herse and Aglauros* and painted a little earlier, this painting is redolent with animation and sensuality. If reproductions of the paintings are viewed side-by-side, Hermes and Herse appear to be thrown apart, while *Mars and Venus United by Love* pulls the viewer into the vortex of an all-gathering embrace. Here a benevolent satyr, shown in carved three-quarter profile but with pronounced belly advertising a navel, inclines towards a domestic scene comprising: Mars in leathern armour seating himself; a naked Venus seemingly expressing milk from the swollen nipple of her right breast, her sex obscured by a drape Mars gallantly situates; a Cupid tying a fillet around Venus and Mars's ankles; a sportive cherub playing with Mars's sword; and a peculiarly ingratiating horse. I see an analogue to depictions of Christ in the Manger: a humanistic convergence has been achieved between the Classical and Christian. There is nothing statuesque in these gods or their surroundings; if Veronese's two canvases were hung together, as they were until the Orleans Collection was dispersed at the end of the eighteenth century, the contrast in treatment of flesh would have displayed the painter's flexible virtuosity. Furthermore, stone in *Mars and Venus United by Love* is treated quite differently from the marble halls of *Hermes, Herse and Aglauros* which infect the flesh disposed in them; here outdoors, the satyr supports a broken entablature, while a pediment inscribed

Figure 7 Paulo Veronese, *Mars and Venus United by Love*.

with Veronese's name provides Mars with a seat where he is settling himself for love-making, left arm shifting his robe for greater comfort. In other words, the broken threshold is absorbed into the painting's totalizing affective rhythm. In *Mars and Venus United by Love* all is sensual ease, mutual pleasure, responsiveness and amusement; the scene framed by this picture is one anyone might wish to cross into, since over and above the attractive figures and their mutual activity, the painting is suffused with an atmosphere of joyful integration joining gods, their human presentation and beasts. Here curvature and inclining preside; the fluid continuity in the main group invites use of a poetic term made literally true: Mars and Venus are enjambed, with a pink ribbon. The curve of the horse's neck echoes Mars's shoulder and redirects a spectator's straying eyes to pull the figures together more strongly yet, and with the reverse curve of Venus's body, creates a force field of inviting enclosure. The tug of the horse's rein and the parallel restraining sword across the horse's front legs at right foreground, answer the left Cupid's tug on the ribbon; but this horse needs no restraint beyond the compulsion of the animate space encircled by enjambment.

How strongly this contrasts with the two figure groups pulling apart from the vacant centre of *Hermes, Herse and Aglauros*, bridged only by the petrifying look of Herse and her spaniel. The verticality of Hermes, who hasn't yet struck Aglauros, is emphasized by the standing columns and central statue. Strong verticals separate rather than attract the human figures on either side. The female satyr does not compensate for the absence of action in the centre but calls attention to it. In one painting a spectator is invited into the congress of flesh; everything conspires to collapse and unite interiorities. The broken threshold succumbs to human love. In the other, beholding a scene frozen into statuary less by Hermes than the gaze of the observer observed (Herse, seconded by her spaniel), the spectator is left to pace before the threshold. But the spectator's pacing, her affective and intellectual restlessness, are produced by a discrepancy: this is the agitation occasioned by irreducible, irresolvable aesthetic experience.

For Hermes and Herse can enjoy no concupiscent pleasures. Ovid never suggests that Hermes crosses the threshold or can have his way with Herse; once he has opened the door but end-stopped the threshold in Aglauros's petrified person, he flies back to heaven. Gods and goddesses may not countermand each other; if Minerva has arranged for Aglauros's envy to block access to Herse, Hermes's response is to punish Aglauros, but this cannot free him to enjoy the desired woman, presented both as sexually receptive and as marmoreally chaste in a striking visual ambiguity. So Ovid relates a story of inaccessible interiors, two female spaces. The one is a world of putrefaction (i.e. Envy's shack) and the other of impenetrability, chastity guarded by stone. With his transfixing art Veronese cannot move between these interiors, but must deal in a discrepancy, in the two interiors' overlay. Although Herse may be destined to stay chaste, she awaits ravishment as though she has made up her mind to it. The female satyr disturbs the drape, metonym for a veil across the entire sculpted group which her tug reveals as frozen on the threshold of sexual disorder and physical mutability. All this while the spectator must stay behind the threshold. Through being held back, we may be protected from Hermes turning us too to stone thanks to a permission from visual hermeneutics; hermeneutics (which this god has named) can be received as tidings from a discrepancy in aesthetic experience, demanding our full liveliness.[8]

To conclude this lengthy preamble, *Mars and Venus United by Love* is a voracious work, demanding that a spectator yield to its vortex, whereas *Hermes, Herse and Aglauros* in its frozenness plays between transfixing and humorously detached acts of looking, and in place of a human vortex (for Mars and Venus are unequivocally human) offers an enigmatic figure both emergent and self-cancelling. The painting therefore compels hermeneutic activity.

The threshold of lyric can also cast a witch's spell on the wanderer who approaches its cave or circle. Where groundsel grows, a weed named after the threshold it infests, an interior totality might beckon and that seductive call lead into a trap.

Ein Winterabend

Window with falling snow is arrayed,
Long tolls the vesper bell,
The house is provided well,
The table is for many laid.

Wandering ones, more than a few,
Come to the door on darksome courses.
Golden blooms the tree of graces
Drawing up the earth's cool dew.

Wanderer quietly steps within;
Pain has turned the threshold to stone.
There lie, in limpid brightness shown,
Upon the table bread and wine.[9]

What is this threshold and why should pain turn it to stone? Trakl's poem has attracted extensive commentary since Martin Heidegger singled it out as exemplary of language speaking (in, from and to itself); as has the poetry of Georg Trakl in its entirety, read by Heidegger as a single poem manifested in variants. Along with Hölderlin's body of work, Trakl's becomes a *topos* for discussions of Heidegger's theories of language by Jacques Derrida and less celebrated expositors, and a bone which Trakl scholars seek to snatch back from Heideggerians.[10]

'Ein Winterabend' is a nocturne and it sounds a curfew in its 'vesper bell', foretelling a death – or even the deaths of all the 'wandering ones'. However, not much wanders in this poem; rather, 'Ein Winterabend' might be found exemplary in its creative deictics, in its firm and uncompromising naming of objects into essentials. In reading this poem I imagine each object to emerge as the language pronounces; and for these objects to emerge I must greet them, since I am one of the 'wandering ones' arriving at the sill of what is to be my home, a wanderer no more. The table laid for me and others lies beyond pain, but relief from pain is not the promise that lures the wanderer. Far from it: without pain the threshold could not be named, and Heidegger claims that for Trakl 'everything that is alive in the sense in which the soul is alive, is imbued with pain [...] Everything that is alive, is painful'.[11] Pain is valued for bringing the object world into ensouled presence. This presence has no particularity; every noun here except 'graces' takes a material entity necessary and common to human thriving, and waves over it the wand of

Hermes so that it stands forth independently of sociality and commerce. Bread and wine become stony abstractions, through acts of representation calcifying them in numinous objecthood. The transfiguration is deadly, with the stuff of daily life recreated as it were ex nihilo and related only to nothingness, stillness and the blank sheet. The glowing tokens of physical life and the unattended table of fellowship only will nourish me if I step over the threshold into the frame. That I can do only in dying or through not having yet been born.

What nourishment is available to me as I live and breathe? Is it enough to name bread and wine? It is not. I discern in this poem a mood abstracting what I would put in my mouth, offering and withholding bread and wine in an aestheticizing of the death-wish. This is a haunting, compelling invitation and its call must be resisted. I must ask what has happened to the many, the more than a few? The poem insists from the start on separate arrangements, with the window of the first line (although the pursuit of a rhyme in English exaggerates the objectification of the weather – in literal translation Trakl writes 'When the snow falls at the window' and it was the translator's decision to 'array' it). The poem approaches repeatedly, window to door to threshold. The transfigured objects the wanderer is called on to witness are central to the Christian Eucharist, but obdurately resist transubstantiation since they lie beyond the threshold of death, beyond the flesh's domain. 'The subject-matter of poetry is not that "collection of solid, static objects extended in space" but the life that is lived in the scene it composes; and so reality is not that external scene but the life that is lived in it', Wallace Stevens admonishes.[12] But to cross this threshold will mean entering a world of unchanging light, oneself to be cast as an object, a statue. Outside it is snowy and dark, a world of veils; whereas across the threshold an exact placing of objects will be recognized. Heidegger makes much of such placing, *Erörterung*, and indulges his etymological passion in recovering the root 'ort' as 'the point of a lance' where all is gathered. Thinking back to *Hermes, Herse and Aglauros,* there the transfixing effect of the situating lance in Hermes's hand is vividly apposite. In a way it is self-denying, transformation presented as flat truth. To cross the threshold is to secure visibility, as with the lance of our succeeding and more pointed spectator's scrutiny. In Veronese's painting though, the threshold has been compromised; the veil lies within as though a macula on 'limpid brightness'.

But is there no macula here, in Trakl's poem? How can I have been stayed at its threshold, pacing there? Why do I have to ask what has become of the many? The poem sends me its hermeneutic demand through a discrepancy, the lines 'Golden blooms the tree of graces | Drawing up the earth's cool dew'. It is at this position on the threshold, drawn forward by the rhythm of setting a table, putting in place, that the discrepancy of these lines interferes with the beckoning spell. Is this not a coincident threshold, the dewy threshold between day and night, between life and death; the dew of fertility but also the cold dew of a death agony, sustaining a tree – which is where? This threshold lies between the tree and the tree represented, between the tree elsewhere or nowhere at all but within this poem, between the tree as a golden artifice and the tree which abstracts water. It is vital that readers continue to wander among the many at the stony threshold of this poem and do not cross into death's domain. But is death's domain not also salvific, the end of death promised in the Eucharist? The rhythms of total love and of death are indistinguishable; both lay an absolute claim. Everything has been set.

'Blood and wine', the final phrase of 'Ein Winterabend', evokes Friedrich Hölderlin's major ode 'Brod und Wein', also a nocturne but starting assertively in the contemporary marketplace before it modulates into a lament for the Greek gods, then amplifies into a magnificent apostrophic unravelling in the idiom of *ubi sunt*: 'where are the temples, the vessels, | Where, to delight the gods, brim-full with nectar, the songs?' (strophe 4).[13] Heidegger opens his essay 'Words' by discussing comparable lines from strophe 6 of Hölderlin's poem, 'Why are they silent too, the theatres, ancient and hallowed? | Why not now does the dance celebrate, consecrate joy?' It seems perverse for Heidegger to take these lines and this particular poem as a pretext for a dissertation on 'the word', when the poem expresses a desire so urgent for hollowed-out monuments to be filled again with life – a life as communally and rhythmically full as the marketplace before the curfew marks the close of day and of commerce. Now Bacchic joy will transfigure the twilight world and leave the watchman with no threshold to patrol. Even in the lines Heidegger quotes, the striving is towards physical expression, just as the temple 'vessels' await a Keatsian replenishment with *songs*, not 'the word'. When in the final strophe Bacchus 'reconciles Day with our Night-time' his gladness is compared to 'the living boughs of the evergreen pine-tree', and most splendidly, when 'Father Aether' concerns himself with naming, 'Now for it words like flowers leaping alive he must find'. Even the clumsiness of this line's English rendering cannot disguise a naming that rebels against the fixity a golden tree compromises in Trakl's later lyric, a naming whose performance in Hölderlin's verse generates a dizzying ecstasy from rhetorical and rhythmical accumulation. There are no flowering annuals there: the perennials perish and do not perish; they persist in their mutability, they renew, while evergreens still flourish. Hölderlin's choice of Bacchus as the deity capable of erasing the threshold between day and night, life and death, is a gesture as strident as the noontide marketplace, and provides a striking poetic analogy to Veronese's introduction of a female satyr within his pseudo-classical scene of theatrical architecture. Bacchus and the satyr alike trouble thresholds with their force of life.

When in his talk 'Words' Heidegger pronounces with odd inconsequentiality that 'Rhythm, *rhusmus*, does not mean flux and flowing, but rather form. Rhythm bestows rest' his categorical negation betrays unease at the truth of Hölderlin's poem, which would explode Heidegger's 'way to language' and confound the detached reflection which Heidegger wishes lyric to serve.[14]

The reflective posture demands that stillness has first been achieved. In his paper 'Marginalia to Geschlecht III: Derrida on Heidegger on Trakl' David Farrell Krell discusses 'one of Heidegger's favorite phrases [...] *das Ge-läut der Stille*, "ringing stillness"'.[15] For Heidegger the poem points towards and strikes stillness, making stillness resound. 'The poem' is that absolute song to which Trakl's poem supposedly points, as a spear or a wand, a song lying beyond sound. 'Surely, the rhythm of a poem has something to do with its sounding', Krell expostulates. This opens the way to a distinction between enunciation and singing:

The transition from saying to singing occurs, according to Heidegger, in and as pain [*Schmerz*]. Reminiscent of the *suffering* that Hölderlin says offers us our most intimate experience of *time*, pain is, in Heidegger's view, of the utmost importance in poeticizing. Heidegger's *carmen* is bound up with the language of rapture, seizure, enchantment and ecstasy, the very temporality of the spiriting year. The gathering of saying in the spiriting year is song [μελος]. Such enchantment, however, breaking into song, arises always and everywhere out of agony.

Enunciation is social, communicative and technical, whereas song is linked to seasonal change in Heidegger's idealized pre-technical world whose inhabitants have yet to turn against the Earth supporting them. They suffer time, rather than seeking to grind it into segments, but their painful submission attunes them to the earth. For Heidegger, rhythm and song concentrate the suffering of recurrence, presenting a portal to enchantment, to a unity in stillness. Song would carry each one separately over the threshold. But as we have seen, rhythm and song shed any physical embodiment on the way to the ringing stillness serving reflection; and 'the language of rapture, seizure, enchantment and ecstasy' is one of the subjects transfixed or transcendent, exactly the ringing of stillness wherein the earth's goods arise as it were miraculously.

What kind of suffering is this? The terrible bereftness which Hölderlin summons the Gods of antiquity to repair will not be satisfied by the earth's appearance of plenitude. Whereas 'Brod und Wein' starts with market stalls and with bourgeois tradesmen drawing up their balance sheets of the day's profit and loss, Heidegger's language evokes a world of spontaneous wealth and beholding, a world of beautiful timepieces and polished fruit, rather than the time of labour or of capital investment. This fairy tale stands in opposition to a more plausible story of song's relation to soil and to physical pain through the rhythmic collectivity of work song, a history spun out of a gloss on Wordsworth in J. H. Prynne's *Field Notes*.[16] Troublingly this entails a story of song exploiting the rhythm of others' labour, with the laments of slavery and serfdom forming the rhythmic substrate to delicate inventions and the chants of fraternities alike:

> How different far the fat fed hireling with hollow drum;
> Who buys whole corn fields into wastes, and sings upon the heath
> (ll. 125–126)[17]

This hireling's song is taken up in the polite parlours of the eighteenth century and swells into the present-day lyric crescendo. Their progenitor – our progenitor – is Theotormon who sings paralyzed upon a threshold in William Blake's *Visions of the Daughters of Albion*:

> At entrance Theotormon sits wearing the threshold hard
> With secret tears; beneath him sound like waves on a desart shore
> The voice of slaves beneath the sun, and children bought with money.
> (ll. 29–31)

Blake is no sentimentalist; this is how things are, despite the clunky mythologizing. Theotormon sits at the threshold of Bromion's cave where Oothoon lies after Bromion has ravished her. The cave's threshold divides not the twin domains of eternity and of life in its brevity, but the climates of liberty and tyranny. The seasons and even night and day offer no natural recourse, having fallen under the aegis of Bromion, personifying perverted desire, authoritarianism, organized religion and the exploitation of labour. On the one side the 'spiriting year' perhaps; on the other grinding oppression. But the 'spiriting year' was not Blake's idea of liberty; he would not have recognized a liberty born of painful submission, whether Christian or subject to reason.

The paralyzed Theotormon cannot rouse himself to challenge Bromion's sway, despite the urgings of the raped Oothoon who loves him, since Bromion's rape of Oothoon has reduced Theotormon to impotent jealousy of Bromion's patriarchal power. The combined 'terror & meekness' which results, forms the perfect medium for self-absorbed lyric performance. Theotormon gives way to those 'secret tears' which in Trakl's poem have 'turned the threshold to stone' and here too are 'wearing the threshold hard'; while unperceived by Theotormon in his sullenness, his watery effusions resonate with 'the voice of slaves', with 'waves on a desert shore' breaking in a collective rhythm compelled by pain and misery. The 'desert shore' is desert by reason of Bromion's brutality, but also signifies Oothoon's desolation, unrelieved by her erstwhile lover's whining and windy lamentation. Theotormon's self-pity cannot respond to the true lyric of Oothoon, a lyric lament arising from a pain Hölderlin might recognize, and challenging Theotormon's passive complicity with Bromion's sway:

> Why does my Theotormon sit weeping upon the threshold;
> And Oothoon hovers by his side, perswading him in vain:
> I cry arise O Theotormon for the village dog
> Barks at the breaking day. The nightingale has done lamenting.
> The lark does rustle in the ripe corn, and the Eagle returns
> From nightly prey, and lifts his golden beak to the pure east;
> Shaking the dust from his immortal pinions to awake
> The sun that sleeps too long. Arise my Theotormon I am pure
> Because the night is gone that clos'd me in its deadly black.
> They told me that the night & day were all that I could see;
> They told me that I had five senses to inclose me up.
> And they inclos'd my infinite brain into a narrow circle,
> And sunk my heart into the Abyss, a red round globe hot burning
> Till all from life I was obliterated and erased.
> Instead of morn arises a bright shadow, like an eye
> In the eastern cloud: instead of night a sickly charnel house;
> That Theotormon hears me not! to him the night and morn
> Are both alike: a night of sighs, a morning of fresh tears
>   (ll. 44–61)

While the world of liberty is Edenic in its open commons and free attachments, the world of tyranny encloses, physically and mentally, in a kind of negative Platonic cave. Bromion is not spared as a henchman of tyrannical forces, painfully aware of the denial he endures in service of a religion consigning all to 'eternal fire, and eternal chains' (l. 109). He laments the shutting off of his 'senses unknown' and subordination to a science whose 'infinite microscope' (l. 102) and exploratory zeal are put in service to exploitative interests and 'wars of sword and fire' (l. 105). In Blake's design for this passage, Theotormon lies clawing the ground in a despairing attitude with mattock abandoned, neither fully in thrall to rationalism and lust nor participant in the living world. Oothoon craves release by Theotormon from the distorted nature enveloping her, daylight deployed as a means of surveillance ('like an eye | In the eastern cloud'), while night, the medium of the eagle's hunt as well as of human love and refreshment, has been lithified in Bromion's cave. This 'sickly charnel house' recalls Envy's dwelling in Ovid and the lumber room of the unforgotten crawling with worms in Baudelaire's 'Spleen II'. Throughout *Visions of the Daughters of Albion* envy's curdling of vision and carnal experience into surveillance is a recurrent theme: 'his eyes sicken at the fruit that hangs before his sight. | Such is self-love that envies all! a creeping skeleton | With lamplike eyes watching around the frozen marriage bed' (ll. 195–198). All fruitfulness has become repellent. This is the dominion Oothoon challenges in her song and asks Theotormon to challenge. Ecstatically she apostrophizes the matutinal animal world, ready to return across the threshold to newly dawning life. She must secure Theotormon's aid since crossing the threshold requires free sexual congress; her repeated cry to him to 'arise' sounds frankly phallic, demanding he wield his pick. She knows her prison to be both physical and mental, imposed through rote teaching of mendacities ('They told me .... They told me') and suppressing her agency to that radically negative point where 'all from life I was obliterated and erased'.

The surpassing affirmation in this passage is Oothoon's 'I am pure'. This follows her rape and Bromion's dismissal of her as 'this harlot', taunting Theotormon with his contemptuous refusal of responsibility for her pregnancy: 'Now thou maiest marry Bromions harlot, and protect the child | Of Bromions rage' (ll. 24–25). Nonetheless Oothoon asserts unequivocally 'I am pure', an assertion of renewal crucial to Blake's romantic poetics as well as his radical sexual politics. *Visions of the Daughters of Albion* prepares for Oothoon's great affirmation with a little foreplay around a flower:

> For the soft soul of America, Oothoon wanderd in woe,
> Along the vales of Leutha seeking flowers to comfort her;
> And thus she spoke to the bright Marygold of Leutha's vale
> Art thou a flower! art thou a nymph! I see thee now a flower;
> Now a nymph! I dare not pluck thee from thy dewy bed!
> The golden nymph replied; pluck thou my flower Oothoon the mild
> Another flower shall spring, because the soul of sweet delight

> Can never pass away. she ceas'd & closd her golden shrine.
> Then Oothoon pluck'd the flower saying, I pluck thee from thy bed
> Sweet flower. and put thee here to glow between my breasts
> And thus I turn my face to where my whole soul seeks.
> (ll. 3–13)

Plucked and plucked again, Blake's marigold is without guilt, without stain, and offers itself as the emblem of repeatable evanescence, a virginal nymph. In William Blake's time a 'Mary's Gold' would have designated the flower *calendula*, the modern Pot Marigold, a member of the daisy family whose petals open and close diurnally, adjusting for changes in daylight hours. Hence when the marigold 'closd her golden shrine' she is preparing for the night, not for death. When glowing between Oothoon's breasts the flower exhibits its property of heliotropism, the sun her 'whole soul seeks' being glossed in a later passage where Oothoon is described as

> a virgin fill'd with virgin fancies
> Open to joy and to delight where ever beauty appears
> If in the morning sun I find it: there my eyes are fix'd
>
> In happy copulation;
> (ll. 173–176)

Blake's mysticism lies on this side of the threshold, exalting the carnal and material world of an experience ever renewed poetically. His insistence on Oothoon's renewable virginity not only assails the Christianity which would preserve virginity as a shrine to be breached only in marriage, but radically unsettles custom and practice, memory's ossified forms. Recurrence of night and day is perceived by Blake (self-identifying with Oothoon) as renewed occasion for joy and liberation. Theotormon's impotent dreams of freedom, sought in a promised land across the threshold, depend on 'waves on a desert shore' chorusing the doleful song of bondage. The hammer-blow rhythm of 'They told me that the night & day were all that I could see' (l. 53), echoing the anvil's ring and the loom's slamming rather than the 'ringing stillness', contrasts with resurgence time and again in Blake's expostulatory proclamations at the turning of the verse line: "Art thou a flower!" (l. 6) and "Another flower shall spring" (l. 9). Meanwhile Oothoon strives to turn the rhythms of insistence and oppression into weapons of liberation, directing them to rouse Theotormon to action. Their blows are means to an end – a creative destruction that will return the desert shore to fertility. The poem to which we are drawn as a bee to a flower also disposes the world to live or die as we approach it and feed on it time and again. For we would not stand at the threshold and bewail our alienation, nor gaze through the window, gaze across the doorstep, look over the threshold at the Eucharist. The telling *aporia* of Trakl's 'Ein Winterabend' is that when the wanderer 'quietly steps within' the reader is left outside to witness the 'bread and wine' which can offer no more than a promise reverberating in a chain-gang chorus of pain.

Of its nature, poetry tends to objectify against the slippage of discourse, but not through securing referentiality; rather it can conjure up a self-sustaining universe of meaning whose formation through the multiple bracings of quasi-metaphorical dissemination, affective constellation and sonic nodes, then threatens to calcify into the temple 'Ein Winterabend' presents and represents, or into a monument immuring the life it would affirm. Discrepancy must restore life through complicating the disposition to calcify. The paradox is that to achieve its self-sustaining, self-framing entireness, the poem must confuse itself at the very edge of its looming consolidation, for entireness must involve the capacity for more. A complex of shored objectifications submerging and emerging in a continuous 'disobjectification', elicits the poem's fullness in a standing wave, produced by the mutual interference of two rhythms, their discrepancy.[18] Wholly given over to a poem's unifying vortex, its reader might be devoured in a simultaneous cancellation and affirmation; but the tug towards enfoldment or extinction can be countermanded by the rhythmic ground, communal and phylogenic in its shifts, or by a singular rhythmic event.

On rhythm Heidegger is remarkably evasive, declaring 'the site of the poetic statement, source of the movement-giving wave, holds within it the hidden nature of what, for a metaphysical-aesthetic point of view, may at first appear to be rhythm' and then saying no more about it.[19] How tantalizing of Heidegger to hold in reserve here the identity of 'the movement-giving wave' from *his* point of view. His evasiveness may seem less surprising if Heidegger's siting of Trakl's poetry *in toto* as a paean to the persistence of life-in-death, memorialized in stone, is brought further into view. This gloss on Trakl from 'Language in the Poem' exemplifies his 'siting' of Trakl:

> In the poem 'Bright Spring' there is this line:
>
>> And the unborn tends to its own peace
>
> It guards and watches over the stiller childhood for the coming awakening of mankind. Thus at rest, the early dead lives. The departed one is not dead in the sense of being spent. On the contrary. The departed looks forward into the blue of the ghostly night. The white eyelids that protect his vision gleam with the bridal adornment that promises the gentler two-fold of humankind.
>
>> Silent the myrtle blooms over his dead white eyelids.

Contrasted with 'a dead who decays' (p. 175) it is hard to recognize this passage as representing anything except 'a metaphysical-aesthetic point of view' (p. 160) hardened into the appurtenances of a death cult – although this could be charged against Trakl's poetry, populated as it is with dead children and closed eyelids (more usually blue than white). 'Petrifying pain' is celebrated by Heidegger inasmuch as it 'delivers itself into the keeping of the impenetrable rock in whose appearance there shines forth its ancient origin out of the silent glow of the first dawn' (p. 182). What this rhetoric hymns is the immaculate lifelessness of the before-birth, as opposed to 'the troubled, hampered, dismal, and diseased, all the distress of disintegrating' (p. 183). Although responsive to Trakl, such a categorical rejection of the decaying flesh disregards Trakl's explicit linkage of decay with renewed life: for instance, 'Soul sang death, the green decay of the flesh | And it was the rustling sound of the forest' ('To One Who Died Young').[20] 'Springtime of the Soul', the poem from which Heidegger takes 'Silent the myrtle blooms over his dead white eyelids', is a poem that celebrates burgeoning and verdancy, even if shadowed by death.[21] But then, for Heidegger the greatest destiny of the poetic work is to cause its reader to *reflect*, an activity which would be greatly confused were the 'dead white eyelids' of Trakl's poem to open and reflect back.

Imagistically it is impossible they should open, but the rhythmic rocking of 'Springtime of the Soul' attaches to eyelids and unfolds them musically through a pun. As the translator of Trakl's poem, Alexander Stillmark, notes, '"Lidern" ("eyelids") is phonetically identical with "Leidern" ("Songs")'.[22] Heidegger refers to 'bridal adornment' because myrtle is associated in Greek antiquity with weddings; a bridal song might be apposite, but this is a poem and therefore the song is silent. Although Trakl's poetry is death-obsessed, Heidegger's ideologically saturated contention that the poem *looks* to 'the coming awakening of mankind' fails to *hear* the pressure life exerts against death through poetic rhythm. The myrtle does not rest on the eyelids, it blooms in time; while it is 'the rustling *sound* of the forest' (my emphasis) which asserts life's persistence even in decay.

Reflection for Heidegger is an activity of central importance in distinguishing his philosophy from Husserl's; as distinct from ordinary usage of the word, reflection is a form of 'understanding-looking' that can afford access to a pre-theoretical lived experience. Heidegger's lack of attention to rhythm is all the stranger in that rhythm is often held to offer such access. To explore this potential in an English translation of a German poem would make little sense; it is necessary to return to an English poet. An account and a performance of reflection that bridges ordinary usage and a Heideggerian understanding, while also evoking the processes of both petrifaction and dilapidation and making a claim for the animating force of rhythm, can be found in two incomplete poems by Percy Bysshe Shelley, 'On the Medusa of Leonardo da Vinci, in the Florentine Gallery' and 'The Tower of Famine'. The first of these has attracted extensive commentary as exemplary both of complex ekphrasis and of the Romantic conception of beauty. Here it is the dynamics of reflection which will be the focus, especially the first two stanzas of the five-stanza Medusa poem:

> It lieth, gazing on the midnight sky,
>   Upon the cloudy mountain peak supine;
> Below, far lands are seen tremblingly;
>   Its horror and its beauty are divine.
> Upon its lips and eyelids seems to lie
>   Loveliness like a shadow, from which shine,

Fiery and lurid, struggling underneath,
The agonies of anguish and of death.

Yet it is less the horror than the grace
    Which turns the gazer's spirit into stone
Whereon the lineaments of that dead face
    Are graven, till the characters be grown
Into itself, and thought no more can trace;
    'Tis the melodious hues of beauty thrown
Athwart the darkness and the glare of pain,
Which humanize and harmonize the strain.[23]

A hesitation arises in subjecting this poem to pertinacious interpretation, because it is an incomplete draft. Nonetheless the astonishing second stanza does legitimate a return to the radical confusion of lying and gazing in the first, which begs comparison with Trakl's 'Springtime of the Soul'. In Shelley's poem death, although spasmodic and even orgasmic rather than marmoreal, provides the physical substrate to 'loveliness like a shadow', while Trakl's poem overlays the bodies of the dead with a sequence of colours – roseate mists, lingering blue and at last a darkening green. These perhaps conform to 'the melodious hues of beauty' in Shelley's second stanza, a synaesthetic phrase consistent with the earlier reference to 'lips and eyelids' and later expanded in the phrase 'harmonize the strain'. The Medusa is gazing, although the third line complicates point of view, and indeed in the painting that occasioned this poem the Medusa's eyes and lips are open; the emphasis on apertures rather than organs insists on the Medusa's receptivity. To gaze is more passive than to look or even than to see; the passive phrase 'are seen' begins a shift in point of view from the gazing Medusa, to a spectator in the throes of transformation into a 'gazer' indistinguishable from the gazed-upon. If 'it' – a notably de-sexed Medusa all the way until the poem's final stanza where its female sex appears as a superficial 'countenance' stabilizing 'loveliness like a shadow'; if the It-Medusa is 'gazing on the midnight sky', by whom then are far lands 'seen tremblingly', and indeed who or what trembles? Trembling, in any event, seems to be stilled in the 'gazer' through an imprint of the Medusa's face upon his spirit, reflection turning the spirit to stone, a transformative kind of mirror that fully reproduces rather than reflects. An ambiguity is to be found however in 'characters' which as well as referring to the attributes of the Medusa's 'dead face' transferred by 'beauty' as a disembodied life force, suggest also that what is 'graven' might be the very 'characters' of this poem – an equivalent for the image rather than a representation of it. (It is tempting here to allude to lithography – reproduction of characters on the stone – invented about twenty years before Shelley wrote this poem.) The relationship between death and beauty in 'On the Medusa' is therefore uncannily similar to Trakl's line 'Silent the myrtle blooms over his dead white eyelids', and can be mapped around the words 'grace', 'graven', 'gazer' and the grave present in their characters.

It is a striking departure from convention that such petrifaction or lithography should not be produced by the Medusa's gaze, since as Shelley's poem asserts from the beginning, this Medusa (no longer attributed to Leonardo) is gazing upwards, not at the painting's spectator. Rather it is the grace and loveliness of the Medusa that transfix the spirit and cancel mediation; as a result of this process, 'thought no more can trace' – that is, between source and receptor no representational gap exists to be crossed by thought. The closing of this gap is celebrated for its power to 'humanize and harmonize the strain', transfiguring the source which prior to this reflection was overwhelmingly representative of 'darkness and the glare of pain'. Turning to stone, in a profoundly contrary metaphor, is figured as the ultimate capacity to receive beauty and to restore humanity through its reception. But the stone and the face are one by the end of the second stanza, and it is the movement of what is 'thrown' that simultaneously transfigures both reproductive stone and painted image into music; 'harmonize the strain' unmistakably brings forward the emergent claim for music's potential to overcome the mortal and aesthetic schisms in this poem without the further schismatic mediation of thought.

The next two stanzas shift focus from head to vipers, and then to an extraordinary confusion of light and darkness anticipated by the first stanza's transposition of light and dark between the shadow of loveliness and the shining of anguish and death:

> And from its head as from one body grow,
>   As [ ] grass out of a watery rock,
> Hairs which are vipers, and they curl and flow,
>   And their long tangles in each other lock,
> And with unending involutions show
>   Their mailèd radiance, as it were to mock
> The torture and the death within, and saw
> The solid air with many a jagged jaw.
>
> And from a stone beside, a poisonous eft
>   Peeps idly into these Gorgonian eyes;
> Whilst in the air a ghastly bat, bereft
>   Of sense, has flitted with a mad surprise
> Out of the cave this hideous light hath cleft,
>   And he comes hastening like a moth that hies
> After a taper; and the midnight sky
> Flares, a light more dread than obscurity.

It is hard to resist an analogy between these vipers and the extraordinarily tangled syntax of the poem; they grow from the head, they interlock, and their 'unending involutions' penetrate the 'solid air' – air as solid as 'the gazer's spirit' and as mobile as a 'watery rock'. Every stanza in this poem consists of a single serpentine sentence. The solidity of spirit and air might be contrasted with the opening of rock, 'the cave this hideous light hath cleft', and rock's emission of life in the form of a bat 'bereft of sense' which nonetheless in its blindness is compared to 'a moth that hies | After a taper'. Blindness is sight then, and the 'midnight sky | Flares' and light is 'more dread than obscurity'. The rock's life has been prefigured in the grass growing out of it as well as in its wateriness. The bat's flight sutures primordial oppositions. The heavily end-stopped lines of the poem's first stanza have now been succeeded by a writhing fluency – writhing on account of the unpredictability of caesuras, but fluent within the confines of the stanzaic form.

The poem ends with this stanza:

'Tis the tempestuous loveliness of terror;
    For from the serpents gleams a brazen glare
Kindled by that inextricable error
    Which makes a thrilling vapour of the air
Become a [ ] and ever-shifting mirror
    Of all the beauty and the terror there –
A woman's countenance, with serpent locks,
Gazing in death on heaven from those wet rocks.

The central event of the poem, where air, rock and human body join in a single rhythm, reopens to reflection. The observation splitting this stanza from the foregoing is precisely a trace of thought, a schism producing the detachment of a spectator. Air has returned to 'vapour' (albeit 'thrilling' in the event's aftermath), and the insistent 'it' of the first stanza, refusing to locate 'it' as a sexed human body or as painted representation, is now specified as 'a woman's countenance', with 'loveliness like a shadow' and 'melodious hues' returned to their distinct physical substrate. The poem's last phrase, 'these wet rocks', contrasting with the earlier 'watery rock', has a post-coital finality to it – as indeed the painting warrants, evocative of orgasmic satiety as much as of death. The couplet this phrase concludes performs a nailing down of the 'inextricable error' to undeviating representation; these are 'locks' indeed that correct 'error', they are depictions.

Shelley's recent editors draw attention to 'the final two stanzas of *The Tower of Famine* which incorporate the triple rhyme "terror-mirror-error"'.[24] This much more fragmentary poem receives a fantastically detailed gloss (although its kinship with the 1819 fragment 'And like a dying lady lean and pale' is missed) but it is only the final lines that are significant for this discussion:

    As if a spectre, wrapped in shapeless terror,
    Amid a company of ladies fair

Should glide and glow, till it became the mirror
    Of all their beauty, and their hair and hue,
    The life of their sweet eyes, with all its error

Should be absorbed,[25]

– which is where the fragment breaks off entirely. After the lips and eyelids, the definite edges of 'On the Medusa' and their rhythmic confounding, the drawing-room language of 'ladies fair' and 'their sweet eyes' is deployed almost sadistically for its cancellation. The extended simile likens the tower of famine, associated with wreck and ruin, standing amid the elegant and undespoiled towers of Pisa, to a spectre amid a company of beautiful women. The tower of famine cancels its surroundings 'so that the world is bare' as the spectre will absorb and cancel female beauty (and the poem too). The relationship here between beauty and absorbent spectre is more ominous than the earlier poem's performance of a complex dialectic that overcomes mediation before it restores the painting, the depicted and the spectator to their places. The performance of this fragment is sheer negation, and the reader, liable to be involved in the coils of 'On the Medusa', is left here to join or not in the gloating contemplation of the devouring of the privileged and frivolous. 'Error' here surely has a different valency from its appearance in the earlier poem; there its coils have a Miltonic inflection and suggest a Satanic challenge to representational and patriarchal naming, whereas here it points to irresponsible levity. The collapse of the poem bears witness to its author's alienation.

What then of the thresholds of these unfinished poems by Shelley? The opening of 'On the Medusa' seems at first to establish clear coordinates – the sky above, the mountain peak in the foreground, but their complication leaves a reader struggling to establish firm ground and a point of view. The second stanza makes a strong hermeneutic demand. The contemplative spectator behind his threshold, having a mind also to the 'graven' written text, nonetheless is caught up in the 'strain' of the poem's music, winding around the hammered, monosyllabic rhymes. Just so in contemplating Veronese's *Hermes, Herse and Aglauros* a viewer is disturbed from the graven text and marble halls into an hermeneutic agitation resolving into the winding rhythm conjoining flesh, stone, paint and words, the viewer and a painting whose finish is never arrived at.

2

Dilapidation can form a threshold to aesthetic experience, where the rhythmic ground to transfixion pushes up against the broken pillars and slabs of human hope, memorialization and triumphalism. Rhythm, rhyme, linguistic pattern and chromatic passages constitute and are constituted by a dynamic and recursive network in which consciousness recognizes its own formation at a level prior to temporal and consecutive thinking and active still beyond its 'rope of sand'. This network corresponds to what Julia Kristeva, following Plato in the *Timaeus*, calls the domain of the *chora*, which 'precedes evidence, verisimilitude, spatiality, and temporality'. The *chora* is rhythmic; what was magnetic in the *Ion* here denotes 'an essentially mobile and extremely provisional articulation constituted by movements and their ephemeral stases'.[26] A reader falls in with a *chora*. Bringing the *chora* into relation with the pillars and slabs of the symbolic order demands that a spectator or reader turns and paces before the threshold of her standing in the world, surveys that surveying balcony while still governed by its rhythm. Such a demand could scarcely be more exacting than what must be accepted in reading the last poem published by Andrew Crozier, in 2004, and built on the rubble of a post-war cityscape and of post-war political hopes. Here are no temples; but see and hear the reparation achieved by this poem out of stony rubbish:

Blank Misgivings

Our father death speaks through the child our father
the sailor lost beside a dream of immense steppes
perfectly rigged violets inside a sunken bottle
tears condensed beneath the clear glass in the path

O fly you creatures, asiatic cranes and gazelles
slender ribbed of arctic birch and whalebone
air twists into grey sheets of old starlight
the extinct hiss of incendiary in a bombed cellar

This morning's trace of footprints leads back where
sidereal years modelled in spars and struts
thrust from the ground, stumps of brickwork
a broken corner where the sky turns cold

Remember such things under the new city
shadows of ruin swept into unlit night
one bare horizon drawn after another
day into day breaks the calamity of the heart

What to call to out of ignorance and loved best
the abrupt twilight and the unexpected dawn
when brief cries summon falls unanswering voice
pauses between the echoes of the century

Listen to the wagons thunder and the static roar
light outlined burning through the grid
the abandoned garden and the tumbled fence
alike and other unbuilt monuments to hope

The stones rest as they fall, the dying fall
among the dead and I could wish their bones
at rest their day so what there was each find
so be it the unhoped-for be no more than man[27]

An early review compared Crozier's poem at death's threshold with Philip Larkin's 'Aubade', a voracious poem that drags the reader into its death vortex, with its enfolding, ten-line iambic stanzas the nightmare negative of John Donne's erotically embracing secular songs.[28] The pause in the face of emptiness at the three-stress ninth line of Larkin's otherwise pentametric stanzas, corresponds to Donne's breathless appetitive pauses. 'Aubade' exists so as to assert the end of hermeneutics; there can be no news from the other side or remnant of what has passed over the threshold, for the universe consists wholly of the terror-stricken poet's consciousness. If *Mars and Venus United by Love* or Donne's 'The Sun Rising' draws a spectator into its embrace, 'Aubade' drags to the grave. The unknowable other side asserts its blank dominion over this side, even if 'One side will have to go' as the poem pronounces. The only protection against consciousness of death is the occupation that holds back the paralyzing encroachment of 'the anaesthetic from which none come round'.[29] But work is itself an anaesthetic in Larkin's poem, a pointless and repetitive round good only to stave off ultimate vacancy – an anaesthetic against the complete anaesthetic. What can Andrew Crozier's poem offer in its stead?

'Blank Misgivings', a title borrowed from Arthur Hugh Clough, begins with a line that parodies both The Lord's Prayer and Wordsworth's line 'The Child is Father of the Man'. At the start the poem acknowledges the caesura of birth, with individual sentience arising from the death or unbirth that precedes a life, but also from a human history filled with ruin and war, as well as love, yearning, painful isolation and remembrance. Sentience belongs not to the one but to the many; to the present, the foregoing and the following, the proximate and the absent. But such larger human history and geography are attended by inhuman immensities as well as blithe animals. The first stanza mourns death's prevalence in a sailor's foolish dreams of virgin geography, in the 'rigged violets' associated with both Persephone and Venus, death and love, and in the suffering congealed and concealed in transparency. The poem-trap longs to release from its domain 'cranes and gazelles' that leap over a cellar hissing with incendiaries. Since Crozier was born during the Second World War, this cellar feels like his negative womb. 'O fly' – such yearning must surely carry with it the desire for a restored physical and imaginative freedom, as the body decays and the conscious mind faces death.

Larkin's poem slides easily from 'I' to 'we', and total identification is its order. Such is hard to resist; 'Aubade' can indeed induce *timor mortis*. Crozier's poem holds back the first person until the final quatrain and manages to eschew 'we' entirely, a striking achievement in a poem on our common fate. It does this in part through performative language. First, it opens with a prayer, 'Our father', the poem's only first person plural an empty formula; the second stanza begins with poetic apostrophe; other stanzas command 'Remember' and 'Listen'. The 'trace of footprints' in the third stanza negotiates the broken spars, struts and stumps in the poem's progress, and its first three lines are enjambed, after the abruptly end-stopped lines of the two earlier stanzas. Next, while the poem starts with categorical acts of cancellation, the 'extinct hiss of incendiary in a bombed cellar' is sheer poetic show-off. Its hissing insistence sounds especially contrived after strip-like lines, characteristic of Crozier, whose repeated end-stopping is the more jarring for not being signalled by punctuation and initial capitals. The line's self-advertisement draws a reader into a circle haunted by the *chora* that 'precedes and underlies figuration and thus specularization, and it is analogous only to vocal or kinetic rhythm'.[30] After all, this hiss is performatively not extinct, not as read, not as we are reading it; this hiss is Crozier's continuing life as he writes, and beyond, as we read. Now we can notice how 'immense' reduces to 'condensed' in the first stanza, and that the discrepant life in this poem is audible, in this contradictory 'extinct hiss' and more generally in the rhythmic tension between the poem's end-stopping and the frequent choriambic lilt of its lines. Asiatic cranes and gazelles do fly and leap poetically.

In the watches of the night the poem confronts, as Larkin's does, the blank terror of 'one bare horizon drawn after another', but human cries return. The ruined landscape fills with sounds and obstructions as well as 'unbuilt monuments; like the 'extinct hiss' which is still incendiary and the 'static roar' from space, it is haunted by futurity as well as the past. Negated past participles throng in this poem, still hissing and burning. What is performed here and enjoined on a reader is a hermeneutic work of remembrance, reconnection and shaping. 'Grey sheets of old starlight', the extinct hiss and static roar of stars become 'sidereal years modelled in spars and struts' enjambed in the ground. With one person's recent 'trace of footprints', there are three scales of past here, yet 'the unexpected dawn' breaks again, and a reader might feel at peril of being consoled. However what the poem offers is not consolation but 'light outlined burning through the grid'; is this the grid of versification? Or the National Grid that keeps light burning through the dark? And connecting this poem too to J. H. Prynne's 'Die a Millionaire': 'power by the grid, putting | lives into strings of consequence'?[31] I can't settle what this line means and perhaps it won't settle. I do know that a misalignment of rhythmic and temporal grids in this poem makes me feel more alive, burning through the grid of life's measure that seals my fate. 'My heart leaps up'. So what if the poem finishes in a conditional wish bound in a baffling nearly monosyllabic quatrain that somehow reverts to the man to whom the child is father, 'no more than man', an abstraction? The unhoped-for here is what we make of it; it is our hermeneutic charge. Stones fall and rest at once, they are in motion and settled. The simplest words come to rest in motion. It is moving to realize that the words heaped up at the end of this poem had been put under decades of unequalled pressure in the body of work which lay behind it, by the poet who titled his collected poems *All Where Each Is*.

When we talk of feeling more alive in the experience of an art work, that recognition of what we never earlier cognized is what overcomes us, as formal completion captures us to the life, eyes trembling open. What revives us but a female satyr seeking form? 'Golden blooms the tree of graces | Drawing up the earth's cool dew'. Such discrepancies can rouse us to pace in the hermeneutic circle, a circle which aligns our responsive alacrity with magic, with the unthought known. As Blake adjures:

Hear the voice of the Bard!
Who Present, Past, & Future sees
Whose ears have heard,
The Holy Word,
That walk'd among the ancient trees.

Calling the lapsed Soul
And weeping in the evening dew:
That might controll
The starry pile:
And fallen fallen light renew![32]

Chapter 7

DILAPIDATION AND SINGING STONES

This chapter divides into two sections. Beginning in the clouds, the first section discusses a recurrent *topos* in lyric poetry of the stone tower and its overturning, collapse or inversion in a lacustrine reflection, from Shelley to Yeats to Hart Crane to J. H. Prynne. It then further revolves the theme of dilapidation broached at the end of the last chapter, by way of the dilapidated column and font of Barbara Guest's poem 'An Emphasis Falls on Reality'. The second section extends my reading of this exemplary twentieth-century poet of dilapidation and singing stones, concluding with her late sequence *Rocks on a Platter*.

1

It would be hard to identify a poem more foreign to contemporary taste than Percy Bysshe Shelley's 'The Cloud'.[1] How can personification be read now except as appropriative, so banal have become the expectations attached to lyric, and the function in lyric of the first person singular – how to understand 'I' not as grandiose but a position open generously to a reader, and mutative? But not so fast. This poem might overturn expectations in more ways than one: it might turn the world upside down as dizzyingly as later poems whose dislocations are more plainly flaunted. A reading of 'The Cloud' offers an opening to reflections on prosodic contradiction and counter-rhythms, as well as what is here called 'bouleversement' or poetic overturning.

When thinking through poetry and contradiction, the work of line break and caesura may exercise a critical pressure, furthering and interrupting completion and syntactical sentence regulation. These formal features amount to ridges and fault-lines across which mellifluousness and resonance can be stoked up and damped down. Such faults can act as time-signatures and to mark off staves, setting signposts for lyric cadence and phrasal encapsulation. At the same time they can interrupt the impetus of poetry towards shared sentimental song, completed emotion and gestures released from its own orbit, grasping at external supports. So completion can simultaneously be asserted and interrupted through enjambment. Reading is both blocked and hurried on. For this to be so, faults must neither be subsumed to a metric pattern so wholly achieved in its artifice as to strike the ear as natural, nor can their obtrusions be decoded straightaway as effectively onomatopoeic. If these conditions are met, lyric will insist on interpretative attention across its fault-lines. Both line and sentence press against design; and design strives back for their compression when line and sentence would open out to how things are. Just as completion can occur internally by phrasal encapsulation or rely on external relations, 'how things are' can be encapsulated in objects or reach back inside the pale of the poem.

The urgency of a line to extend into space beyond its limits in a prehensile relation to the world, and its simultaneous desire to attain total fluency, lifting and unmooring words from reference – these urges might seem contradictory, but appropriation and radical unmooring betray their delirious affinity when brought up against faults. The earthly counterforce to their disbanding is exercised by line-breaks, caesuras and rhyme, and by sonic thickening which dreams of exceeding the thingness of any referent by incorporating it into a linguistic substance polymerizing consciousness with materiality. More negatively, this counterforce yearns for the narcotic thickness of full song and the reassurance of encapsulations. What imagination entails is strife between these forces, their contradictory working. Such strife, with the full pressure of 'how things are' negating the poem's tendency towards encapsulated autonomy and the poem negating the fiat of 'how things are', might enlarge the definition of 'dialectical lyric'. Where dialectical lyric was held by David Trotter, in a revealing use of Shelleyan language, to 'stage [...] the drama of the "adverting mind" [...] turned toward a "vastness" which reveals it to itself as a lack: disenfranchised, internally riven', and to have been inaugurated by Celan and Jabès, it becomes possible through the 'adverting mind' to see a more formally engineered dialectic at work as early as English romanticism.[2]

What of 'The Cloud', which has hovered over these preliminaries? A quiet but momentous bouleversement occurs in the four lines ending the fourth stanza:

> When I widen the rent in my wind-built tent,
>   Till the calm rivers, lakes, and seas,
> Like strips of the sky fallen through me on high,
>   Are each paved with the moon and these.

'The calm rivers, lakes, and seas' are paved with 'strips of the sky', which they are like, and the 'strips of the sky' are paved with 'the calm rivers, lakes, and seas'. Each is behind the other, undecidably, shifting – that is how such complex reflection works on the gaze. So radical is this layered undecidability in 'The Cloud' that 'the calm rivers, lakes, and seas' appear to have fallen through me from on high, fallen from the air in watery strips. But just so! The circulation of vapours means 'the calm rivers, lakes, and seas' have fallen from the skies, fallen through my cloudy changes. 'These' are as mutative as I am, and indeed as mutative as the reflective moon.

A stratification can be imagined, permitting the stars to filter through the seven lines between their appearance behind the moon and the terminal 'these', to think of these lines as strips through which starlight falls. Verticality is contradicted by strong laterality, time's passage by crisis. Much as the vertical organization of heaven and earth writes down into a horizontal layering, so the temporal delay in syntactical resolution is counteracted by 'broken the woof of my tent's thin roof' and 'the rent in my wind-built tent' by the anapaestic churning of cloud. These lines run without caesura except in the particulate nouns and supererogatory second comma of 'rivers, lakes, and seas'; otherwise their strip-like quality is emphasized at the expense of breaks, even while the phenomena described depend exactly upon breaks in the cloud, upon faults.

What could be more rudely different from a cloud, errant and pervasive, than a stone tower? Raised on earth as a human claim, as the upright animal's self-image, as the lookout dominating the land and ocean beyond, as the defensible regal cell of the expansive clan – massive stone asserts the law against mutability and vapor. Raised in a lyric poem as it will be variously in romantic English and American poetry and subsequently, a tower resists the threat of scatter and vapid dispersal. Trade extends, sons travel overseas and shepherds' transhumant expeditions extend out of sight. About the tower huddle workshops and hovels, and further off the factories and merchants' houses. Colonies will be established, but the poem of Babel and the Babel of the poem construct a city. With Babel, human beings 'come to model heav'n | And calculate the stars, how they will wield | The mighty frame, how build, unbuild, contrive | To save appearances' (Milton, *Paradise Lost* Book VIII, ll. 79–82): 'and now nothing will be restrained from them, which they have imagined to do' (*Genesis* XI:6).

In Hart Crane's poem 'The Broken Tower', the tower's collapse into a hierarchical impasse parodying the ranks of angels and seraphim comes to necessitate acceptance of 'the visionary company of love' as a Christian organization and in its secular version, a vision of communism: horizontality must be completed in equality.[3] A voice is only traced, it is only heard 'an instant in the wind' and is immediately made answerable to a promise of individual salvation dependent upon a revelation that 'strikes crystal Word | In wounds pledged once to hope – cleft to despair'. Thereupon the poem halts and is threatened by accumulation in its fault. What can restore the dynamic potential of its disobedience to a city-hating God, of its fault, and rescue the wounded from despair, including the poet who feels responsible to redeem the world? It is *another* 'through whose pulse I hear', and it is owing to *another* that the tower is not so much demolished as reconstituted horizontally as a 'slip | Of pebbles'. Not merely horizontal but urging down towards a 'quiet lake':

And builds, within, a tower that is not stone
(Not stone can jacket heaven) – but slip
Of pebbles, – visible wings of silence sown
In azure circles, widening as they dip

The matrix of the heart, lift down the eye
That shrines the quiet lake and swells a tower …
The commodious, tall decorum of that sky
Unseals her earth, and lifts love in its shower.

The fault now has become a slip, and a gaping disjunction between stanzas rhymes with this slip; the slipway must be formed across language's fractures, it cannot disavow them in relying on the unifying impetus of lyric and its tendency to encapsulation. The poem dips into the fault of a radical and awkward stanza break, leaving a reader floundering for a preposition whose handhold cannot be located, and everything turns upside down: visible wings 'lift down the eye' and at the last the shower 'lifts', responsive earth impregnating the sky. Such a revolution chimes with 'The Cloud':

> Till the calm rivers, lakes, and seas,
> Like strips of the sky fallen through me on high,
> Are each paved with the moon and these.

Poetically the verb 'shrine' has most frequently been used to mean, as the *OED* has it, 'to enclose, envelop, engird, as a shrine or sanctuary does the body or the image of a saint'. There develops a contouring or Russian doll effect, with the womb (the matrix) shrining the lake in which can be descried a swelling tower held like a penis, a child or a preserved body, shaping an equivalence between enwombing and entombing which echoes the final lines of Shelley's poem:

> I silently laugh at my own cenotaph,
> And out of the caverns of rain,
> Like a child from the womb, like a ghost from the tomb,
> I arise and unbuild it again.

The revolutionary moments of 'The Cloud' and 'The Broken Tower' lead alike to a nesting of earth and sky performed through water (ocean or lake), which in Shelley's poem is mediated through the ledges and layers of cloud and in Crane's through banked and terraced voices. Shelley opens his poem in a mutable first person, whereas the attributable first person of Crane's poem is a stone jacket which must be broken into a slipway, reproached by choirs of poetic accumulation (maybe an equivalent for Shelley's meteorological cumulus). This leads to a contained and revolutionary order; no more merely 'to trace the visionary company of love' but through this poetic act to achieve the consummation that 'lifts love in its shower'. This consummation arises from encounter with the human other who can 'lift down the eye', destroying the tower, while also releasing 'I, their sexton slave', as the poem's third stanza has it, from subordination to the banked choirs of religious and poetic litigation.

Crane's poem contrives a new formal architecture wherein grammatical positions become contingent, and the eye is unlocked from its tower. 'That sky', 'her earth', 'its shower' consort according not to a point of view, a perspective, but according to their contingent occasion within a realm of interconnected possibilities. Poetic contradiction leads to *this here*, where the most basic coordinates of heaven and earth and of life and death shift and flicker.

Crossing the poetry of J. H. Prynne, interpretative manoeuvres produce thickets of more-or-less plausible inference. Such ensnaring is exacerbated by the poems' combination of internal connectedness and extraordinary range of reference. Allusion to major political events and economic activity is caught up in the poems' internal systems, and also implies analogies between this poetic physiology and systems on a macro level in which the poems participate. For instance, in the 1999 sequence *Triodes*, sugar is processed within the poems' internal economy, sustaining and threatening their metabolism, as well as figuring prosodically and rhetorically as a contested sweetness, tracked through trade relations revealing the grammar of brute exploitation and, from what might be called a balcony seat, converted into energy through the supposedly self-regulating physiology of markets. These systems are imbricated in the imaginative domain, not fully aligned, and the admixture of consciousness is meticulous, extending through all the poems' structural levels. System faults can be discerned at single word level as well as between discursive registers and at line-endings exposed as bitten-off – all offences against lyric gorgeousness, efficient interfacing and metaphorical alignment.

A hyper-intentionality governs *Triodes*, with the minutest details of text subject to decisions weighed within several coinciding and contradictory frames of meaning-potential. The poems' character can be summarized thus: a combination of *hyper-intentionality* with a realistic acknowledgement of *the given*, for instance in the recurrent diurnal cycle, or meteorology or geological change; with a *semantic and organizational complexity* so exceeding efforts at apprehension that the work tends towards the status of an internally developing organism (which also entails developing dialectically in its systemic and contingent relations with the circumferential world). Readers striving to apprehend this work's totality devolve rapidly towards a particular sub-system, but as with human physiology soon become sensible of the arbitrariness of systemic taxonomy, and involved in any sub-system's inextricable linkages with other sub-systems and indeed with any number of external systems – such that the division between internal and external becomes unsustainable.

Shelley's poem remains syntactically focalized, with its shifting of relations between astronomical and meteorological entities subject to the governance of a first person singular, even as that assertive singularity changes shape incessantly and can 'pass through the pores of the ocean and shores'. The poem constitutes a circulatory system of the self. Hart Crane's poem offers an open-ended current system lacking even the mutative perspectivism of 'The Cloud' although as a 'stand-alone' poem it is unsealed at its outfall. *Triodes* consists of poems of ambiguous status: linkages must be of critical importance for the working of this poetic organism, since they not merely influence but re-articulate how things are and how things comport internally and across the apparent barriers of form. What is a thing in Prynne's poetry? It is what occurs *between*, a function, as in an experience of translation where a poem's moves can be sensed aside from the specific information they carry and aside from a single language's vocabulary –

indeed regardless of *any* vocabulary. Such an assertion needs testing, and the following page, poem or burst of energy is chosen from *Triodes'* middle circuit:

> You can get the knack of it Pandora said,
>   by measure or proxy get a move on
>   in sedimented mirror-image sets:
>   he wrongs, he is wronged, he advised,
> he deliberated, they seized, they were quarreling,
>   grasping one another, they rage,
>   they went on a rampage,
>   whew, those boys act primitive right at
>   the verbal root with a cap, wind
> spun and flying outwards gibber gibber
>   floored by exposed pavement, Irene,
>   bank on the grammar flowing
>   in piedmont heat across the pediment.
> Among the Romans the pediment was so much
>   respected, it was confined entirely
>   to buildings sacred to their immortal gods.
> Just bring one up on the balcony, she said,
>   radiant divine lunch-time.[4]

Pandora and Irene are twinned throughout *Triodes*, spreading pestilence and bringing peace, respectively – although per contra peacekeeping forces attract a jaundiced eye, and a good argument could be made for opening Pandora's box instead of keeping it for an investment. Capital needs to be put to work. What is unusual here within Prynne's poems is a diction consistent with prose explication that appears to incorporate unmodified clippings from antecedent texts – as does the previous page with its list of partners in a Mozambique sugar enterprise, clipped from *The Times*. (The startling extent of Prynne's mining of *The Times* for poetic resources is revealed in the 2018 annotated edition of *The Oval Window*.[5]) In the present poem a banal piece of information asks to be treated as a powerful assertion of a revolutionary state of things and linkages, the lines beginning 'Among the Romans' sounding authoritative after the posey and pseudo-etymological wordplay of 'in piedmont heat across the pediment'. That is, if the poem's last line does not imply that such pieces of information offer little more than snacks.

By this stage in *Triodes*, a reader will have been prepared for serious play around 'pediment', by way of the lines three pages earlier 'the pediment writes the balcony | with the script of a gap gene code' and on the previous page the less direct allusion 'Meet and make a match on the pedigree as follows' where 'pedigree' makes a match with 'pediment' on the balcony. The balcony here is relayed through *Romeo and Juliet* to *Breakfast at Tiffany's* perhaps and eventually to the decadence of 'divine' in the final line here. The balcony view belongs to the Gods or to today's international rich set, radiantly above it all. As for gap genes, these are segmentation genes specifying subdivisions in an embryo, and a pediment can transcribe as both balcony and pavement/piedmont – that is, superstructure and base – because the gap emerges within the history of the word 'pediment' itself, applicable equally in current usage to a wide, usually triangular structure crowning the front of a classical building and to a base, a foundation; a pavement. So the pediment is a fault in itself, perhaps even a 'sedimented mirror-image set' and in being floored, those boys are sedimented – sedimenting being 'right at | the verbal root', a literal sinking down. Such contradiction is a prerequisite to 'get a move on', making it feasible to 'bank on the grammar flowing'. A river cannot exist without a bank, but the formula also points to a politically irresolvable choice between accumulation (banking) and spending (flowing).

The poem returns to 'the verbal root' where 'those boys' conduct their diplomatic negotiations, and questions of war and peace are weighed and measured at a distance, above events and above the passions, with Pandora and Irene together occupying 'The View | from the Balcony'. The view is sugared over, art mounts to its superstructural pediment and routine decisions on investment – in a Mozambique sugar enterprise for instance – form the piedmont above which rise the sublime heights of capitalism.

The revolution here has been incorporated within the systemic circuits. Whichever way you look at it, from the prophetic first person or the economic base, fault-lines have already been designed into the workings of the triodes, and the conjunctive jumps factored into biological script. Or to be more exact, *they will have been*. Faults are pervasive in these poems, and that is why for all their regular appearance on the page their prosody is relatively inactive. The poems are starting to resign from lyric with its progress across and against overt faults, and to evolve a compages, an organism without edges, leading towards the progressively de-cadenced anti-verse of *Unanswering Rational Shore* (2001) and ensuing works. If all possible faults and all possibility of revolution have been factored in down to the word (pediment) and phrase, and all talk to 'gibber gibber', and if stirring a cup of tea affects the entire world economic order and can start bloody wars in the Congo, what then? That question will hang over late Prynne's poetics of seizure, unmoving block accumulations of metrically inert materials subject to epileptic shudder. Such is the fate of an organism with no freedom: the end of cadence. Maybe a lyric somersaulting produced in hilarity or in love, in burlesque or in obscenity, could supersede the revolutionary potential of contradiction, not only in poetry but in disturbing the seizure that afflicts the social and economic imaginary. A great shudder, a great perturbation may yet turn the world upside down again. If twittering, even for a moment, can call home the exiles to a revolutionary Babel in Tunisia and Egypt, poets must never succumb to what will have been, possibilities blocked in their articulation, but must envisage what will come to be, must still 'gibber gibber' and pace across the descendant heavens – even as the world below collapses into gibber, a term for loose boulders adopted into Australian English from the indigenous Dharuk.

Classical buildings with their pediments advertise their resistance to lawless chaos and to the perils of unlicensed primal rhythm. In the *Introduction to Metaphysics* Heidegger cites the first choral ode of Sophocles' *Antigone* in the interests of establishing "the word" as a pillar against the force of primal rhythm:

> [Man] gives up the place, he heads out – and ventures to enter the superior power of the sea's placeless flood. The word stands like a pillar in the construction of these verses.[6]

What emerges from this amniotic not-place is The Word as patriarchal erection, a much-to-be-admired and unflagging erection. Heidegger's pillar contrasts with Blake's pillar in *Visions of the Daughters of Albion*: 'Does not the worm erect a pillar in the mouldering church yard? | And a palace of eternity in the jaws of the hungry grave' (ll. 152–153). Blake's pillar rises out of organic decay, constructed by the humblest of creatures. The grave supplies the stuff from which a palace is built; only it must be expected that pillar and palace also will prove transient, and their overthrow may unleash revolutionary energy—even if to install a new oppressive authority. While in its content a lyric poem may bow to the authority of the afterlife or a living tyrant, poems that subtend a lyric event must offer a repeatable evanescence, a flowering as of a marigold plucked time and again as Chapter 2 argues. Disease and disintegration await the marigold as they do each human life, but art that aims to stop time sacrifices the possibility of life. The 'placeless flood' lacks even those 'waves on a desart shore' marking the limits of human inhumanity; and a pillar in a flood is merely a something in a nothing before time. Should lyric aim through its animating power to preserve the loved one, it 'hides your life, and shows not half your parts' – although so impossible an ambition may grant you a generative power, if you are Shakespeare's beloved.

Frank O'Hara's pillar in 'Ode on Causality' will of course collapse and rise again, repeatedly, providing Oothoon with the 'happy copulation' she yearns for in Blake's *Visions of the Daughters of Albion*. Disease and disintegration, 'the pillar of our deaths', must be acknowledged even in embracing life, and O'Hara is as weary of 'a Buddhist type caught halfway up | the tea-rose trellis', the representative fashionable poet of his day, as Blake is of the poetaster Theotormon stuck bemoaning on his threshold. Half-way measures will not do. Pressured matter is the source of poetry's energy; in 'Ode on Causality' such pressure becomes palpable even in 'the thickness in a look of lust' and 'the bang of alertness'. 'The bang of alertness' is incumbent on readers of poetry, for poetry is potentiated by the reader whom it potentiates. Frank O'Hara's poetry takes shape from the stuff of human exchange, in the marketplace, in sex, in song, in noise, in mess, in gossip. Badiou shows a deficient understanding of the dialectic of poem and noise when he asserts in 'Language, Thought, Poetry' that the poem stands as 'an exception to the noise that has usurped the place of comprehension'.[7] The dialectic of poetry and noise both as sound and as communicative interference is that of 'the kiss of love meeting the kiss of hatred' ('Ode on Causality'). Silence, emptiness and contemplative time are expensive commodities too often forced into communion with poetry, their 'moon | not our moon' as O'Hara telegraphs; the lyric event arises from sociality, and bread and wine are to be found in the supermarket. Amid the din of machinery, the barking village dog and the eagle's swoop, all these crisscrossing the diurnal rhythm; amid mud, ordure, pustules and under the weight of reactor piles; in the necropolis and on the heath, human beings sing.

This is not a business of rising above conditions, whether weeping or worshipping on the threshold or stuck half-way up the trellis. The poems discussed here and in previous chapters invite us to rouse ourselves that we may approach and pluck Blake's 'Marygold' with its sexual and solar opening and closing, the rhythm of our days and lives, time and again.

What is 'flying outwards gibber gibber | floored by exposed pavement' in *Triodes* is not only trash-talk, but dilapidated stone fallen from the pediment to the pavement, according to the Aboriginal loan-word. Ruination of buildings and cities, and the fate of the vagrants, wanderers and refugees expelled from them, is a pervasive theme of *Triodes*. In his teasing out of another sub-system of the poem, but a sub-system responsible for much of its pathos, Justin Katko begins from the final line of its first stanza-page, 'with the tatter of a homonymous city':

> The city of Wye River, Maryland, site of the October 1998 peace talks between Palestine and Israel, is 'homonymous' with the River Wye of Wordsworth's 'Lines written a few miles above Tintern Abbey' (1798). The homonym liking Wordsworth and Palestine casts up a dual-image of the ruins of Tintern Abbey and the ruination of Palestine. This dyad becomes a triode by the introduction of a third figure: the contemporaneous English ruin caused by IRA bombs.[8]

More details on the Palestinian and Irish sub-systems of the poem are provided in Robin Purves's earlier and extensive essay on the political context for the poem. Of particular interest here is his discussion of the cover art of the original pamphlet publication of *Triodes* with its 'post-Augustan rendering of an authentically classical building's frontage' and his tracking of the defacements and dilapidations visited in the poem on a generic 'neo-classical public building'.[9] Such a stony edifice, often marble-clad, asserts either the reality or the ambition for established and enduring authority, whether governmental, financial, religious or cultural. It diminishes the spectator into impotence, with its classicism evoking imperial Rome or the inflated pretensions of fascism. The poems discussed here manifestly belong to a Western Romantic tradition, even if 'Ode on Causality' mocks the bric-a-brac of 'Old Romance' and balladry, as well as the deference to power of Marvell's pre-Romantic lauding of Cromwell. The poetic gibber or glitter O'Hara treads over is a more systematic concern of his contemporary Barbara Guest, explored in the third section of this chapter as it disposes in her book-length work *Rocks on a Platter*. A more closely tessellated lyric pavement is offered by Guest's complex short poem 'An Emphasis Falls on Reality', a paean to 'fair realism' (l.8) and 'The necessary idealizing of you reality' (l.36).[10] The poem opens with the characteristically enigmatic line 'Cloud fields change into furniture' (is 'fields' a noun or a verb?) before tracing 'the face of lilies' and 'two fountains' as it thinks through the activity of mimesis, rendering reality in all its fairness whether 'real' or bestowed through the mimetic act. The 'furniture' into which 'cloud fields change' in turn 'metamorphizes into fields' (l.2), but the fields are an abstraction requiring that 'an emphasis falls on reality' so they may be perceptible as lines of poetry, a song, or flowers. Any interpretation of this poem must be tentative, since it is inexhaustibly rich in the power of analogy, but the orderly world it reproduces or the world it sets in order is threatened by the natural world:

> willows are not real trees
> they entangle us in looseness,
> the natural world spins in green.
> (ll. 28–30)

The natural world then is not real; reality requires an emphasis, a frame, for even the diurnal cycle cannot be apprehended as real unless distanced in focal range:

> I desired sunrise to revise itself
> as apparition, majestic in evocativeness,
> two fountains trace nearby on a lawn …
> (ll. 9–11)

Sunrise is perceptible when pictorial, when the shadow cast by a fountain moves ('illuminations apt | to appear from variable directions' (ll. 14–15) as the next stanza glosses), and when the cast of the fountain cannot be distinguished from the 'original' except through its greater reality – especially when 'composed of calligraphy' as this poem is. The first three parts of this four-part poem finish in ellipses, but it is only the third part that ends by sensing a threat to the classical world which mimesis designs:

> A column chosen from distance
> mounts into the sky while the font
> is classical,
>
> they will destroy the disturbed font
> as it enters modernity and is rare …
> (ll. 31–35)

'Font' here plays on typography as well as referring to the classical source for the mimetic principles governing the poem's moves until entangled in looseness effected by its metaphors– metaphors which cross the mimetic divide and 'have brought their dogs and cats' (l. 26). I read 'they will destroy' as alluding to the looseness of metaphors and the confusion they bring about. The classical column and font claim the world as its phallic surveyor and orderer, its maternal source and its linguistic inscriber; but on entering modernity the font in some sense becomes 'rare'. How can the font be destroyed and yet discoverable, if rarely? Maybe the broken font can be discovered as relic, but it seems possible Guest is drawing on an older range of meanings current in 'rare gas' and in 'rarefied', that is, 'having the constituent material or particles loose or not closely packed together; not dense or compact; attenuated' (*OED*). The column (also a typographical feature) may have been brought low and the font dilapidated, but they remain dispersed through a world now represented for humanity's usage, a world which along with the two figures moving into what 'looks like a real house' at the end of the poem, we inhabit in modernity. Accordingly there is no real to be distinguished and we live in a forest composed of 'The darkened copies of all trees' as the final line states ('copies' may be intended to echo 'coppice' which is a sort of copy of 'natural' woodland created for chopping). This reality is far from fair realism – it shares in the sinister realism of a fairy tale and also reduces the natural world to a fund. In time both column and font will come to be arranged by Guest as *Rocks on a Platter*.

'What broke the tower?' asks Allen Grossman in his essay 'On Communicative Difficulty in General and "Difficult" Poetry in Particular: The Example of Hart Crane's "The Broken Tower".[11] Inevitably his answer goes straight to Babel, to a babble linked here through *Triodes* to 'gibber gibber' and to gibber linked here to glitter, to stones strewn on a slope. The meteorological circuit of Shelley's 'The Cloud' is translated by Guest into an historical allegory, starting from 'Cloud fields' which after a series of metamorphoses return to a watery and typographical font and a column, perhaps akin to O'Hara's 'pillar of our depths' which becomes rare, dispersed through its destruction:

> I pass through the pores of the ocean and shores;
>   I change, but I cannot die—
> For after the rain, when with never a stain,
>   The pavilion of Heaven is bare,
> And the winds and sunbeams, with their convex gleams,
>   Build up the blue Dome of Air,
> I silently laugh at my own cenotaph,
>   And out of the caverns of rain,
> Like a child from the womb, like a ghost from the tomb,
>   I arise, and unbuild it again.

2

What is the ground of lyric poetry: that is to say, on what basis can a use of language properly be termed poetic, as distinct from literary, philosophical, expressive, descriptive, sententious or informative, although not discounting any of these other characteristics? And how can poetic work be not so much constructed as redisposed out of the rubble of these other discourses, what lies strewn about the linguistic ground? Here Barbara Guest's compositional process is examined through different versions of *The Türler Losses*, and in the 'singing stones' of her late book *Rocks on a Platter*.

The poetry of Barbara Guest (1920–2006) has been the focus of some categorical dispute and position-taking. Educated at Berkeley after a Californian upbringing, Guest moved to New York City where she associated with the poets later to be identified as central to the first-generation New York School – Frank O'Hara, John Ashbery, James Schuyler and Kenneth Koch. Infamously the editors of a groundbreaking early anthology of New York School poetry failed to represent her work, a dereliction which epitomized the sexist prejudice of the 'advanced' poets responsible. Subsequently Guest's poetry has been claimed for an important progenitor of Language poetry, and she has been hailed by women poets associated with Language writing (and their successors) as a pioneer who beyond the example of her own poetry, helped to uncover a lineage for a specifically female avant-garde poetic practice through her biography of the poet H.D.. As well as New York poet, proto-Language poet and feminist poet, Barbara Guest has most often been identified as a painterly poet, more so even than Frank O'Hara, a routine characterization supported by reference to the *Art News* reviewing she shared with O'Hara, Ashbery and Schuyler. Neither Ashbery nor Schuyler is usually read in this way. Such an identification tends to attribute her poetry's oddities to its second-order status as mimetic of the major painting of its time, denigrating it indirectly even if the painters invoked may be Grace Hartigan or Helen Frankenthaler rather than the heroic males of 'action painting'.

Critical categories often obscure the singularity of the positioned, and Guest's poems are no exception. Close reading can unveil unexpected lineaments, but close readings of poems are usually granted only to the securely canonized, unless subordinate to a thesis or a programme. Some existing fine essays on Guest by careful and scholarly readers emphasize either what is held to be a gendered disposition or else a pictorial structuring of her poetry through its radical ekphrasis, and in the main less attention has been paid to the poems' prosody and sound – which Guest identified repeatedly as her work's ground and origin. Furthermore, readings have tended to assert her poetry's distinction from lyric poetry judged to be relatively conservative, rather than to consider properties which make it recognizable as lyric. Nobody would dispute the 'melopoeia' of Ashbery's poems, at least after *Self-Portrait in a Convex Mirror*; but the way in which Guest's poems hold together, their *consonance*, is less readily apparent and therefore invites investigation. How can poetry often so stony, so sharp-edged and seemingly fragmentary generate or tap into such haunting intensities?

Consider these two lines of verse:

> There under the leaves a loaf
> The brick wall on it someone has put bananas

They are the second and third lines of Barbara Guest's poem 'The Hero Leaves His Ship', a poem which occurs early in her first collection, *Poems: The Location of Things; Archaics; The Open Skies*, published in 1962.[12] The poem appeared earlier in her small-edition Tibor de Nagy debut *The Location of Things* published in 1960 – a date and an imprint identifying Guest as a first-generation 'New York School' poet despite her Californian upbringing.

But to stay with the collection: how remarkable that a major trade publisher should issue a book on whose exact title there remains no agreement. Indecision stems from the relationship between the elements of the title, obvious in the typographical layout of the title page but difficult to represent bibliographically. Guest would do something similar with her 1996 small-press book *Quill, Solitary APPARITION*.[13] Her trickiness with titling does not stop at the book's equivocal threshold (the threshold to her body of work). A further difficulty occurs with the title of its first poem, 'The Location of Things' – a poem opening a section of the book titled 'The Location of Things', reprinting the contents of the previously published small edition. What with this book's title and the section's title and the poem's title, the poem might be thought tolerably well located. Not so, for after an opening stanza of a rhetoric at once grandly and absurdly generative, progress is suspended in the isolated line 'Recognitions', followed by no punctuation. What is this line doing? Are we to infer that the poem's title, 'The Location of Things', is actually the title of a poem series, raising the dizzying prospect that in a page or two we might discover the further sub-title 'The Location of Things'? Or does 'Recognitions' operate as a long prosodic pause, amounting to a for-instance? Certainly it signals a major discursive shift, transforming the lordly philosophical 'I' of the first stanza into the raconteur 'I' of 'On Madison Avenue I am having a drink'. If 'Recognitions' is a subtitle, it appears somewhat embarrassed by its status; if it is a stanza it is very deficient. Can one line be a stanza? Can one word be a line?

There is no scene set for 'The Hero Leaves His Ship', although the poem offers quite a lot of green, yellow and blue. Whether 'There' ('There under the leaves') is a deictic pointing to botanical leaves or occupies a reflexive relation to the poem's pages is undecidable, and made the more so by the compressed set of relationships following within these two lines, or subsisting outside them, or negotiating inside and outside. 'There under the leaves a loaf' is a phrase whose impact recalls the line 'The lake a lilac cube' in Ashbery's contemporary poem '"They Dream Only of America"', made the crux of an influential reading by Veronica Forrest-Thomson. The impact derives, as Forrest-Thomson shows, from the non-referential characteristics of the phrase surpassing its referentiality. While here it is possible to think of a bready, crumby loaf under leaves (evoking a garden terrace in Tuscany at lunchtime perhaps), and possible too to think of a literary reference to Wallace Stevens, the phrase 'under the leaves a loaf' is over-determined by the audibly (or inaudibly) missing term 'left'. The loaf that is left is what someone leaves. Maybe he loafed in leaving? Or are these whispers merely bats in the belfry, leaves in the loft? In any case, no light will be shed on the loaf or what it is doing in the garden of this poem, co-existing with scenes recalling the onset of the Trojan War. The important thing is the surface of the poem assumes an intrusive presence through such verbal play, and the deictic 'There' now sounds like a connoisseur pointing out a feature in a painting. Later this poem will produce the line 'I am about to use my voice', in a flagrant tease of the reader. Is this a voice within Barbara Guest's poetic voice? Is she coming into her poetic voice? Or is she about to use her voice somewhere else, to address Agamemnon or to call for a pizza? A sensible, referential reading of 'There under the leaves a loaf' is compromised yet further by enjambment with the following line. Expressly these lines are verse lines, for most of the poem's lines have initial capitals, even where they contribute to a syntactically continuous sentence. There are three haphazard exceptions, hinting that some of this language may have been acquired elsewhere; with texts written before word processors, such decisions look deliberate – that is to say, their arbitrariness appears decided. The slightly stilted elegance of this poem dismisses the idea that inconsistency could signify improvisational haste. The absence of punctuation might be a further decided arbitrariness: What punctuation has been suppressed, and where? A line-break constitutes a punctuation of itself, particularly if enforced by a subsequent initial capital; but what does this pause denote? To understand a comma here would move the brick wall beneath the leaves or even on top of the loaf – maybe both at once. Alternatively, to understand blank space would imply a paratactical relationship. Neither of these choices would allow what is here achieved, the disposition of different elements across a plain, set at tangents. To this extent, then, these lines might be considered ekphrastic, especially if 'There' is taken to direct the reader to a prior, external scene, whether painted or actually present during writing.

There is a tension between the very idea of ekphrasis and an ekphrastic relationship with a visual art eschewing perspectival illusion or even representation (for these objects are so disposed that they may have been conveyed from different places, remembered voluntarily or involuntarily, or perhaps torn from magazines): how could a refusal to represent be performed ekphrasitically without itself succumbing to representation? Given the question, it is important that this poem preceded Grace Hartigan's four black-and-white lithographs of the same name. Hartigan's 'The Hero Leaves His Ship IV' is reproduced en face with the poem in Guest's *Dürer in the Window: Reflexions on Art*, and clearly represents a sail-boat – whose shape is developed from the gull's body shape similarly placed in 'The Hero Leaves His Ship III'.[14] Hartigan commented, 'I was working with poets at the time, and after a week stalking the stones, I plunged in with splatters of tusche, free drawing, rubbing, pounding with hands and with rags and did four lithos based on Barbara Guest's poem 'The Hero Leaves His Ship".[15] Therefore the lithographs are as much literary as the poems are ekphrastic, and may indeed reach for their precedents in Picasso and in Raoul Dufy through the poem, as the poem may have reached back for its Mediterranean and classical allusions through Picasso and Dufy.

The two lines cited from 'The Hero Leaves His Ship' exemplify some abiding qualities of Barbara Guest's poetry. Her lines are hard-edged, and the undecidability of her poetry's syntax is an attribute which tracks both coincidence in its becoming deliberate, and linguistic play in its becoming significant. The multivalent syntax might cause head-scratching, but never the portentousness liable to cling to parataxis. A reader scans a Guest poem in order to get at its internal consonance, rather than to fill in the gaps – a 'democratic' or authorially collaborative reading of a Guest poem would seem presumptuous, since her poems are fleeter-footed than any likely companion. How can a poem's internal consonance be discerned? Phenomenologically, a poem's terms of coherence might be apprehended in an instant through the poem's appearance on the page, whether according to traditional form, showing evidence of intricate patterning, or scattering words and phrases. The performance of that coherence is another matter, and its consonance, its acoustic coherence, can be apprehended only through reading out loud, even if it may be strongly evident in the duration of a few lines and certainly by the end of reading. The basis of such consonance may at this point remain obscure. Indeed, the recognition of coherence at any level, whether acoustic or conceptual, demands an inclination to the poem's designs which exegesis cancels. On the other hand the fragmentary apparitions fleeting through a poem leave merely plaster casts of 'imagery' and 'assonance' when trapped. Thus the present exercise in detailed commentary is perverse necessarily and undoes its own best designs as well as the poem's as it picks its way through. Here is a labour to explain what seizes the ear, quite as unwieldy as a reading of a painting that strikes the eye:

> Technological analysis does not grasp the spirit of a work even when this analysis is more than a crude reduction to elements and also grasps the artwork's context and its coherence as well as its real or putative initial constituents: it requires further reflection to grasp that spirit.[16]

Barbara Guest's poetry insists on its manufacture from linguistic materials. 'There under the leaves a loaf' serves a number of purposes, including a problematic ekphrasis and an emphasis on the poem's verbal construction: once this assertive phrase is encountered, the previous line, the first line of the poem, has to be reviewed: 'I wonder if this new reality is going to destroy me'. This line now looks odd; 'I' becomes disjunct from 'me', and where do we as readers stand relative to 'this new reality'? What may first be read as opening an internal monologue, probably a meditation on a major change in life – a grandparent's demise, a child's drug addiction etc. – now demands reading at the level of microscopic syntactical negotiation. Indeed, 'syntax' in Guest's poems returns to its Greek root as 'arrangement', without its subsequent connotation of regulation: the verbal elements of a Guest poem are assembled more as the materials of collage than as discourse. This characteristic suggests Guest's poetry may be in some sense self-cancelling and self-regenerative; the phenomenology of an encounter with this poem seems to require an impossible simultaneity of total apprehension and minute attention. The effect is not unlike viewing one of Jasper Johns's alphabet paintings, large canvases filled with ranks of typeface, where the viewer cannot take in activity at the level of type 'sorts' (i.e. characters or letters) at the same time as grasping the overall design revealed in the type 'forme' (the body of type) when stepping back to middle distance. Each view aspires to cancel the other; letters are both inscribed into the canvas, and wrested into the symbolic order. Barbara Guest's poetry performs this *agon* of lyric poetry with unusual energy and clarity.

Because of her syntactical arrangements, Guest has been hailed as the pioneer of a feminist strand of 'open field' poetic practice, but that is a partial reading.[17] It is a reading she tended to resist and implies an essentialism her poetry repudiates; for instance, in a 2003 joint interview with Kathleen Fraser, having been asked whether 'there was space for you as women poets in this very rich artistic scene in New York' she responds 'everyone was so close. We were close to the artists, and they were close to the poets' – a response which not only ignores the question of gender, but quietly takes issue with the importance of space and asserts the greater value of 'closeness' and 'exchanging ideas all the time'.[18] The essentialist assertion of an affinity between female sex and open field poetics has been deplored by Jennifer Ashton, writing that 'despite their frequent proclamations of anti-essentialism, the most visible purveyors of women's "innovative" writing end up with an "innovation" that is itself gendered', as though formality were somehow 'male' like T.S. Eliot's penchant for suits, while dispersal about the page resembled flowing, female garments.[19] There is a morality insinuated here too, with egalitarian sociability coded as female. But as a rule Guest's poems – and all of her greatest poems – call more for their progressive disclosure than for readerly collaboration in their making, as open field theory would require. This is in large measure connected with their internal consonance. To hear may lead to active listening, but active listening can only work on already-organized sound (or on noise); its work is primarily to 'tune in' before memory, both involuntary and purposeful, can locate sound according to its cultural and historical resonances.

The linguistic, historical and cultural hinterland is arranged by Barbara Guest strictly to subserve her poems' urge towards internal coherence and autonomy, an urge impossible ultimately to fulfil. The poems demand a deferential work from a reader which has little to do with bringing his or her experience to the poem's aid, even if prior reading might enrich the poem by unattributed echo or located allusion. There exists in a reader a level of consciousness prior to retrievable experience, answering the emergent poem and contributing to its consolidation; but it is the poem's arrangements which elicit this answer. The reader's work is to recognize and greet the lyric body emerging out of its arrangements, a body marked by what Geoffrey Ward nicely calls 'composure'.[20]

'Consonance' will be preferred here to 'composure' because it asserts the primacy of sound in Guest's poems. What Forrest-Thomson calls a 'block-like resistance to empirical contexts' is achieved by Guest in the phrase 'under the leaves a loaf' primarily through the movements of mouth and tongue in producing sound.[21] Having inveigled the reader into the poem through its deceptively friendly first line, Guest deploys the block-like phrase to demand: use your ears! And if you use your ears in attending to the internal voice of poetic reading, you will hear a further injunction to use your mouth. Since this is a very early poem by Guest, 'The Hero Leaves His Ship' does not demand any special vocal agility; indeed, the poem is generally more discursive than the two lines anatomized here would suggest. The lines' great interest lies in what they anticipate of Guest's later procedures, and in their disrupting a poem whose easy movement might otherwise make language reticent, facilitate glossing over, despite the highly reflexive poem being preoccupied throughout by its own architectonic tactics, for instance asserting 'the green turf is made of shells' – that is, I take it, of sound. Towards the poem's close 'I ask if that house is real'; the question is addressed both to the poem and to the questioning voice it houses and which composes it. This sense of the poem as a house (but not a home) is characteristic of Guest's early poems, its finest expression being 'A Way of Being' from her second book, *The Blue Stairs* (1968).[22] There, cabin and manse alike are construed as manifestly literary performances, with their surrounding farmland composed of 'volumes'. Here though, in a more traditional arrangement, the loaf continues to be distinguishable under the leaves.

Block-like resistance and music may sound like contradictory attributes, with blocks evoking not only text but an impermeable, stony text resisting all airs and graces. Stone and air, stone and breath, shells and music nonetheless have close affinities in Guest's poetry. Her characteristic music is unfamiliar in the English lyric tradition, departing as far from Tennysonian mellifluousness as imaginable; it is indicative that while Frank O'Hara loved high romantic orchestral music, Guest's taste led her to serialist, twelve-tone composition. Such a partiality does not preclude extended melodic lines, but demands attention to their ipseity as they carve through space and time, resulting in precise patterning rather than sentimental yielding; so the great long poem 'A Handbook of Surfing' in *The Blue Stairs* is at once an eroticized threnody over the young men killed in Vietnam, a performance of mastery of adolescent and less accessible earlier memory analogous to a surfer's skilful bending and riding in exploitation of the waves' force, and a complex meditation on language and sound.[23] Prosodic thinking remains the generative centre of Barbara Guest's poetry even as its block-like resistance visibly turns to rubble in the major sequences *The Türler Losses* and *Rocks on a Platter*, the latter written about forty years after 'The Hero Leaves His Ship'.

The Türler Losses demonstrates that Barbara Guest's ruses are glimpse, indirection, tangent, linguistic assemblage and prosodic inflections of connective air. This last ruse suggests song, and is intended to; but the cadences of Guest's exploratory verse are always intellectual as well as musical. Intellection is not exhausted by signification, and together Guest's ruses allow her to forestall both signification and the 'mystery' she sometimes espouses. Signification alone might produce an 'off-text' (a fully paraphrasable text) or a 'metatext' (with tactical dabs of knowingness), both reducing Guest's redoubtable language-quiddity to a springboard for what would be consummated elsewhere. In other words, meaning would be produced after the fact. But what matter for Guest are words as sounded. Her knowingness comes with the linguistic territory: it is not contrived or concealed, not mapped-on or realized at the poem's destination.

The history of *The Türler Losses* shows Barbara Guest paring away at too-obtrusive, unincorporated metatext. For the most part, her revisions are successful: she sharpens edges where blur and dissolution threaten. At some points, however, she appears to court enigma through abridgement, to settle on mystery, leaving linguistic outcrops exposed, high and dry. The sonic hum and buzz that shape the ground of her poetry are more apparent in the revised version because this version refers less obviously to the context of its composition. But Guest's discomfort with some autobiographical aspects of the book seems also to have motivated cuts at its beginning and end whose effects are less successful.

The Türler Losses comprises passages of a Swiss travelogue in prose, drawn from Guest's visits to Zurich and to the house H.D. shared with her lover Bryher; some whimsy around the loss of two Türler watches, which Guest associates with importunate and vanishing faces and surfaces; a response to paintings in both prose and verse; and a considerable amount of probably autobiographical material emerging in compressed lyrics. Characteristically of Guest, the most seemingly frivolous passages take on special significance. A bizarre riffing on watch faces, canvas surfaces and poets' noses (for a face must have a nose), puts in doubt the abstract expressionist fetish of surface. If a painting does not have a perspective, does it then have a phallus, does it protrude? Like the dolphin swimming through the important later book *Rocks on a Platter*, the assertive nose or 'knows' of signifying had earlier made its bow in the poem 'Saving Tallow' (an increasingly resonant title, given the material it contributed to later poems and the light it sheds on them):

> the nose of a window
> louvered as coral rock
> where a person walked[24]

Here all representation is understood to be distorted by desire, with even a window's consistent transparency compromised by the dominant sense of early infancy, the olfactory (and rock here is biological because 'coral', and even the rocks are humanly shaped). In *The Türler Losses* the nose 'as it orders the face gives it thrust', and 'the painter uses the nose like a trowel'. 'The nose' refers both to the depicted nose in a male poet's portrait, and to 'the Türler face with its nose' – like the window in the earlier poem, it has a nose because it is looked at and because it signifies, it tells the time.[25] The poem finds its way between protrusions, as winged phalluses establish the circulatory movement of some Cy Twombly paintings. What break the surface in Guest's poems as in the Twombly paintings are not icebergs vaunting hidden depths, but calls of language and line. The medium knows, and the poet and painter attend to it physically, voiced and armed. Significance is not the same as symbolization: 'Türler' is a brand name and a sound, not a horological mechanism and not bearing any special social cachet.

When Guest made a studio recording of excerpts from *The Türler Losses* in May 1984, the text she used had been published as a chapbook in 1979 by the Mansfield Book Mart in Montreal. This text differs significantly from the text published in *Fair Realism* as 'Türler Losses' (1989), reprinted in 1995 in her *Selected Poems* with the definite article restored and thus in *The Collected Poems*.[26] Notably, the final version of *The Türler Losses* loses the four final poems (or poem sections) of the original text, several brief narrative linkages and two clearly metatextual passages. One or two changes may be printing errors retained in Surrealist deference to chance, notably the curious 'Less isn't so important' (from *Fair Realism* onwards) for 'Loss isn't so important': the identical lineation of the prose sections in these two later printings makes it plausible that an error might have been carried over.

The first deleted metatextual passage too unambiguously defines the book as biographical work or as its outgrowth:

> SEE: INDEX, CROSS-FILING, UNIVERSITY,
> CORRESPONDENCE ac-Va
> Yu, post, previous, subsequent, intervening, chronological, summary, additional material, foreign-native, biographical, birth, posthumous ... NB All private papers withheld. Possible prohibition publication. cf. (Libel Laws)[27]

This biographical preoccupation pervades all of Guest's work at the time. The preface to her novel *Seeking Air* notes that it was composed in the 1970s 'in the same apartment in the E. 90s looking over the East River, as *Moscow Mansions* and *The Türler Losses*', and the preface to her H.D. biography *Herself Defined* dates its composition from 1977 to 1982. Stylistically, *Moscow Mansions* (1973) is closer to the work of Frank O'Hara than any other of Guest's books of poetry, and it shares its coterie backchat and discursiveness with *Seeking Air*. By contrast *The Türler Losses* performs dramatically the discursive collapse that threatens *Herself Defined: The Poet H.D. and Her World*, a book whose prose is notably unstable and ungainly.[28] (Biography is problematic for Guest since its meaning-making is extrinsic to its linguistic materials. One kind of fidelity – to the narrative project of a life – proves irreconcilable with another to language's fitful calls.) The classificatory usage in the deleted passage both solicits translation into narrative and (rather contrivingly) enacts the linguistic instrumentality that poetry disdains.

It seems symptomatic that when Guest wrote with a non-poetic ulterior purpose she could prove astoundingly incompetent. Possibly the purposes directing *Herself Defined* were too various and contradictory to allow resolution into consistent prose. A painfully mixed admiration and disgust for her subject; a barely concealed self-interest in approving H.D.'s artistic recalcitrance and independence of paid work; the origins of the biography in Guest's introduction to H.D.'s work by her first husband during their courtship, himself earlier an object of H.D.'s sexual attentions – such mixed feelings would surely induce anxiety. At the same time, this biography stood for 'real work', market-approved, while justifying pleasant trips to Switzerland. (These trips were artistically to be best justified by *The Türler Losses*.[29]) *Herself Defined* is valuable for its research, but welds the reader to Guest's own preferences within its cast-list more successfully than it recommends H.D.'s writing. For to read this book is to learn to love H.D.'s lover Bryher, and Guest's preface comes close to acknowledging it is best read as romance, tracing her own progressive disaffection with H.D. and falling into love with Bryher:

> When I began this book I assumed in my precarious innocence that I would be writing a biography of H.D. After I had reached the first encounter of Bryher and H.D., which was in 1918, I realized that within the chambers of the life I was examining lay another nautilus, Bryher.[30]

Which raises the question – *which* life was Guest examining, and in whose heart were these chambers? An engrossing book could have been made of this in the *Quest for Corvo* tradition, but the prose's malapropisms, grammatical incongruities, startling expostulations and abrupt veering of tone make *Herself Defined* difficult to enjoy except patchily. Only a very problematical 'ulterior purpose' (and a torpid or bedazzled editor) could account for a poet with an ear like Barbara Guest's writing prose as clunky as (opening at random): 'That H.D. was capable of possessiveness and jealousy is illustrated by her reaction to a visit to Kenwin, where H.D. was staying with Bryher, Silvia Dobson made with a friend after the two young women had been hiking in the Black Forest.'[31]

Guest's revisions of *The Türler Losses* represent both an attempt to rescue it from the damage biography had inflicted (by diverting her energies) and a vengeance against Guest's younger self who had betrayed her ambitions by focusing on biography at all. A 1994 interview begins with Guest declaring: 'It was 1975 and I wanted to get away from poetry.' She reveals that she regrets spending five years writing on H.D., that she didn't 'write more *Türler Losses* and less H.D'. She mentions that she was invited subsequently to write Bryher's biography but recoiled: 'I went to the library and just walked out, thinking "I cannot bear to be around those people any longer." And I began writing poetry again, much more intensively.'[32]

The Türler Losses gives the impression of someone researching her own traces while close on the trail of another, and finding that her own story is the more distressingly elusive of the two. The reader experiences frequent confusion between the objects of this biographical search, for at times Guest's personal history and material from the H.D. research are difficult to separate. Fittingly, the confusion recalls the gradual displacement of H.D. by the more compelling Bryher in *Herself Defined*; and indeed, an example of Bryher's history overtaking Guest may inform the second significant metatextual suppression. The lines appear towards the end of a two-page passage of montaged glimpses of one or more recollected love affairs. The whole is introduced by a line from Wordsworth's 'Ode. Intimations of Immortality', 'Though nothing can bring back the hour':

'TAKE'

The rest of us after the filming felt,
        reluctance
        partial joys

        half-minutes
They also continued in the kitchen under the Seth Thomas.

It brought the holidays. A month or so early:
not just a week, not just a day, but always
an hour or so fast. [33]

In the revised text, Guest retains only the central line in the shorn form: 'Continued in the kitchen under the Seth Thomas.' This brief 'take' may draw on research material related to Bryher's professional involvement with the film director Kenneth Macpherson and the production of his movie *Borderline* (starring cinema's most unlikely couple, Paul Robeson and H.D.) or it may refer to Bryher's pioneering cineaste journal *Close-Up*. The lines may have been suppressed because, like the previous cross-indexing lines, they appear too baldly metatextual in concluding a passage of involuntary 'intimations'. Furthermore, the stitching of narrative through 'takes' seems the wrong analogy for work, whether Macpherson's or Guest's, whose lyric style resists temporal logic.

When much later Guest devoted an entire book to film, not only did she write in prose described as 'stories' but the prose was firmly and consistently established in the past tense, as a cultural memoir of Los Angeles.[34] *The Confetti Trees* is a remarkably unfilmic book in its own technique, preoccupied with the nuts and bolts of film-making rather than film effects, consistently with Guest's description of Bryher's attitude to the medium rather than H.D.'s: 'Unlike H.D., who did initiate film into her style, Bryher kept her distance thinking about film in a more or less scientific manner.'[35] The suppressed passages in *The Türler Losses* also occupy the past tense, while the book's general procedure more closely resembles the technique associated with *Borderline* – what H.D. referred to as 'clatter-montage.' This term described rapid montage combinations creating an effect close to superimposition, as demonstrated in the Wordsworth-headed section and then encapsulated in more elegant and apt metatext. In the revised version of *The Türler Losses*, three lines were transposed from the end of the page preceding the Wordsworth-headed section, and isolated on a separate page after it:

> Seemingly realistic codes have pointed to other
> levels of image beyond their limits, ice
> permitting time to decorate a block.

The passing of time superimposes images as in ice, where one temporal period can be frozen on top of another, although here are no mammoths but rather snatches of conversation and glimpses of settings. The final word 'block' is a perfect instance of Guestian ambiguity, operative both on the semantic level and as a wry metatext referring to the previous section's clatter-montage and stopping it in its tracks, freezing it. Through the act of revision, what the first version presents as a fleeting aside become a meditation too on the effects of time on writing; in the first version, the superimposed snatches were, so to speak, still warm and attached to their 'realistic' origins. What may once have been confused emotionally has been consolidated across time, 'ice | permitting time to decorate a block'. But to consolidate is not to resolve; the decorative block also obstructs deciphering.

The somewhat later and much more linguistically consolidated long poem *Biography* offers a delicate gloss on the confusing of its biographical subjects, whose separation for fear of mutual suffocating is seen to render both insubstantial: 'A need to escape so we breathed separately, the air spun into a pact, as wistfully the figures disappeared into – Geneva – as the chairs reassembled themselves, her and mine.'[36] The film term 'TAKE' may signify what is sacrificed to art, leaving behind only 'the rest of us' composed of temporal fragments and traces of emotion; while the filmic 'take', what it fixes, unnervingly suggests the factitiousness of biography, whether autobiography or heterobiography: what is hers? what is mine? are the objects of ownership, whose chairs are whose, more substantial than the selves they evoke? But although the subjects may have lost definition, that the air between them should be 'spun into a pact' attributes an enduring primacy to poetry. The pact remains – the air's compact, the compact air of the poem. So in *Biography* Guest articulates an elegant reconciliation between the claims of poetry and biography beyond the multiple 'takes' of *The Türler Losses*, while her revision of the earlier poem shies away from the cinematic metatext.

The losses Guest inflicts on *The Türler Losses* are certainly not all gain: sometimes less is less. The later version is tighter prosodically, with the prose and verse categorically distinguished. Geographical and autobiographical contexts are less overtly signalled, and the work becomes at once more enigmatic (for a reader unfamiliar with the earlier version) and less turbulent emotionally. Several allusions to the Türler watches are lost, possibly Guest's private joke in 'losing' her watches one more time. In one sense, then, 'the art of losing isn't hard to master', as Elizabeth Bishop wrote, but in another sense, loss may demand acuity and good timing.

The most notable loss occurs in the future tense, and this seems the key to the virtual suppression of the first poem as well as the final four. In the *Collected Poems* the first poem becomes little more than an epigraph:

> Türler patterns
> > distinct as
> > Palmyra ruins

The lines introduce the poem as part rubble, part noble ruin, part unearthed remnant: distinct against the page as 'Palmyra ruins' remain distinct against the sky of the Syrian desert in their scarcely corrupted detail. This epigraphic reduction visited on the remains of an earlier sensibility seems like something of self-critique, an admonition of the revising poet to herself to make her work more distinct, to focus more on its intrinsic pattern than its fidelity to her own biography.

The first poem in its earlier version runs:

> The Türler losses
> exact patterns
> distinct as
> > Palmyra ruins
> Less buzz
> perhaps

in the herbal cups, the bishop spires
sweetness turned
    to say and saw
and telling which is time.

Why would anyone want to lose this? A beautiful prosodic effect chimes 'perhaps' with 'cups', which itself will be picked up in a later poem with the otherwise baffling use of 'decanters'. Saying and seeing are unified in the penultimate line through the word 'saw', which linked in this way to 'say' simultaneously means an adage (a saw) and a thing seen. This unity of saying and seeing is *telling*.

Sound, seeing and significance ('telling') combine in lyric, 'which is time' both traced and figured out in its dipping between past and present. Traces of sound may sing through ruins and remember sexual pleasures and losses, making them more poignant, but 'exact patterns' (patterns exacted painfully) compensate for the fading of the buzz. These patterns are fertile cognitively and affectively, even if 'perhaps' less so than the bees' business, less sexy than the lovers whose bodily gestures still animate this verse – 'sweetness turned'. 'Herbal cups' evokes at once a drink, herbal drink like Pimms or vermouth, and those nectar-filled cups of flowers round which bees buzz. This allows bishop spires' to be read simultaneously as features of the ruins (a 'bishop spire' is 'a tall obelisk in a cemetery with a carving indicating a Bishop is buried there' [*OED*]) and as floral spikes, such as the purple buddleia beloved of bees. Maybe, wickedly and wittily, Elizabeth Bishop too has been buried in this text as a second mother alongside H.D.; Bishop's 'One Art' admits 'I lost my mother's watch'. Guest's sensuous, witty animation of the ruinous scene contrasts strongly with the opening poem of H.D.'s *Trilogy*. That poem, with its mineral bee and its eagerness to visit on wartime London the fate of Pompeii, epitomizes H.D.'s frieze-like and commemorative lyric arrays.[37] Guest's verse animates an incessant figuring out, allowing indecision ('perhaps') and the pauses of thinking rather than its staging.

The bee–cup cluster recurs in *Biography*, 'finding the bee in a cup', this later book in its entirety being a kind of herbal border of bees ('B's) and other initials, specifically 'e's, and most probably H.D.s.[38] There are passages in *Biography* (notably Part 3) whose linguistic materiality courts a Saussurian anagrammatic reading such as Mutlu Konuk Blasing performs on 'Hugh Selwyn Mauberley'.[39] Blasing's hypothesis of an infantile aural substrate to lyric poetry works well with Guest: when in *The Türler Losses* she writes 'That body is a bird | without rhythm or even tied to the old decanters', the word 'decanters' can be considered a magic word basic to the body's subjective composition through sound, and its physical mapping in rhythm.[40] 'Decanters', although retrieved later in the phrase 'wrists reaching for decanters', is spoken out of the pre-semantic sound-map; it is meaningless in itself but fundamental to making meaning, part of the formative linguistic buzz prior to symbolization.

The fate of Guest's 'Palmyra' poem betrays the seesaw between 'losses' and 'less' that makes revision problematic. The epigraphic residue in the later version refers to what will follow as though in retrospect. It sets limits for the book from the start, encapsulating the revisionary act. What was chiefly lost in revising *The Türler Losses* (or had been lost to the heart and therefore could no longer be suffered in the poem) was a *pairing*, to use the word with the fullness of joined love and new birth. The vernal first person plural ended the first version of the book as a sustained note, confirming the opening 'Palmyra' poem in which seasonal time breaks through the ruins. Throughout her revisions Guest proves wary of 'we' and 'us', and even though these pronouns may seem suspect to many contemporary poets, their use in the biographically saturated *The Türler Losses* tends to be particular and intimate, rather than conscriptive.

The suppression of these pronouns, then, seems more personal than ideological, a 'we' that involves a loved 'you':

How wild you frolic red petal
The hour for Krispies we plunged

and

"Where did it vanish this
loss that used to cling
like herbs to our sleeves?"[41]

The stanza in quotation marks (which sounds like H.D. but for the compressed syntax) finishes the first version of the book, with loss dissipating like the scent of rosemary from clothes. The watches may have been lost, but for 'us' mechanical time with its privations has been succeeded by a time beyond the poem. Guest, however, sacrifices this temporal horizon in her revisions of the poem. In the revised version, futurity is sealed with the penultimate poem, which features a bride and groom consigned 'behind' canvas or cellophane, the groom stealing 'a look at his watch'. Although the watches may be replaced, this restoration takes place 'off-text', in a future the poem cannot animate. It implies a future brought to a halt in a conventional tableau. This is a drastically shortened version of the original poem, which tightens the verse and excises the previous concluding stanza with its obtrusively particular 'us':

What an absurd tone is put to our shadows,
pistachio-mint,
It's the last time
We'll repeat our vows in a tent.[42]

The 'us' is now a historical fixture instead of a promise of bliss: 'mystery' resides not in the future ahead of the book or even in the biographical explorations running alongside, but in the touches of Guest's complex negotiations of the words and their reverberations.

These revisions reveal the skill Guest developed managing tentative sequences in the sixteen years between versions, and the agility of her ruses. On the other hand, the dying note of the poem left exposed at the end of the book, after the excision of the four poems which had succeeded it, seems a mistake. 'In the blown haze | a search for crystal || Broken glass' may at one level recapitulate ruefully the end of an affair, the end of a biographical adventure, the end of a self-scrutiny, but in its poetic reflexivity it is too knowing and even banal. Such banal and self-conscious recapitulatory moments will tend to mar Guest's last poems, like several collected in *The Red Gaze*, forgoing the restraint she usually exercises in declining to wrap things up.[43]

The revised third page of *The Türler Losses* allows a recapitulation of the characteristics of Guest's art. The earlier version of three lines in the first stanza reads:

Yes, the sand's ribbon overturning the shell. The mollusc
unable to survive. Such prettiness the shell and its
drip of water, later dryness lent to a shelf.

The revised version reads:

Yes, the sand's ribbon overturning the shell. The mollusc
pause. Such prettiness the shell and drip of water,
later dryness lent to a shelf.

The gain made in revision from the dully editorializing 'The mollusc | unable to survive' to 'The mollusc | pause' is tremendous and quite disproportionate to the semantic change. Guest's touch is perfect. Prosodically, 'pause' demands a strong pause at the enjambment, not just by virtue of syntactical interruption and semantic injunction, but because it is impossible to get the mouth around 'mollusc | pause' without forcing a vocal pause. But 'pause' also obtains a strong pause at the end of the line it opens, by echoing the 'water' now moved into the end-limit position. The first version is flabby by comparison – there enjambment is negated in the run-on of 'mollusc | un'.

What the revised lines perform is a reluctance to let go, to consign a line to its loss. This is done through a kind of suction, with the sounded retention of the twice-said 'shell' obtained in its display on a 'shelf'. Reinforcing these hardened edges, 'The mollusc | pause' functions to change the conditions of reading, and evokes out of 'lent on a shelf' the word 'leans' in the past tense. This was too fleeting to discern in the earlier version, although when Guest recorded the poem, she paused for emphasis before 'lent to a shelf', ignoring the printed lineation. Furthermore, 'lent to a shelf' now proposes itself as the negative of 'left on the shelf': this is what 'The mollusc | pause' is all about.

This revision shows a great lyric poet at work, exploiting matter inaccessible to other uses of language. In a 2003 conversation, Guest was unequivocal when asked 'whether as you write you are following your mind's own jump-cuts, or whether there is a more willed afterthought to that construction'. She responded: 'It's what I call "shuffling mind." I go a great deal by sound, and I mean I can write on sounds.

I guess you can say I write by ear'.⁴⁴ 'On sounds' is a strikingly original formulation, and in Guest's poems there are sounds which remain hauntingly prior to discourse, the kind of magic words and phrases that surface in moments of distraction – 'such prettiness the shell and drip'. It is from this buzz, this irreducible residue, that song rises, and Guest's revisions to *The Türler Losses* help to expose this even if they sometimes lose much that might be regretted.

3

When Barbara Guest died in 2006, some poets were invited to contribute to an online 'Memory Bank', selecting a favourite passage from her writing and offering thoughts and anecdotes. The New York poet and painter Marjorie Welish chose a page from Guest's late book *Rocks on a Platter*, first published in 1999, glossing as follows (and what Welish learnt from Guest is well attested by her decision here to gloss a gloss on 'gloss'): 'Her spacing is primarily of literature and of literariness, as is indicated in the remarkably located "*thee* GLOSS GLOSS" – this being text, intertext and metatext all at once'.⁴⁵ Welish's terminology is structural, describing the characteristics of *text* as a completed artefact rather than poetic writing. For the present purpose, her threefold division might be transliterated into more dynamic terms as substrate, resonance and reflexivity, where 'resonance' refers to the poem's response to the calls it 'takes in' from other poems across time and cultural divisions; also calls from philosophical and other discursive works, and from the daily welter of language.

These terminological triplets would seem applicable to any literary text (begging the question of 'literary') if most appositely to lyric poetry. But Welish wishes the reader to remark the *location* of a phrase – perhaps *locution* in the transliteration suggested; and '*thee* GLOSS GLOSS' certainly looks like a collapsed and technically complicated piece of phrase-making. It is a paradoxically elliptical phrase, countering ellipsis through the machined coincidence of its three plies. In naming and thus spacing the terms so aligned, Welish identifies the phrase as a *point de capiton* for the highly elliptical text surrounding it and characteristic of Guest's late poems.

What lures across ellipsis in Guest's elliptical late poems? There are two intriguing references by Guest to film ellipsis. In a letter to Susan Gevirtz published in 1988, she remarks 'I admire the elipses [*sic*] in *Miami Vice* and I wonder if that program has advanced (or is an advance) scientifically (and metaphorically) from film montage'. In 1994, she talks in connection with 'Japanese movie scenarios' of catching 'the noise that the eye makes when it blinks'.⁴⁶ Film theory refers to gaps between ellipses bridged by 'exorphic reference' supplied by the viewer (referring back to the 'real world') in place of semantic linkages prior to and following the ellipses, while in literature the lapse similarly has to be filled in by a reader drawing on her experience. This does not quite answer the case of *Rocks on a Platter* or indeed of the category of lyric poetry in general, where exorphic reference between ellipses is replaced by endogenous reference – endogenous in that it calls on a sounding substrate. The distinction matters because the invocation of exorphic reference would necessitate either readings which ran the risk of what Veronica Forrest-Thomson termed 'bad naturalisation', reducing poems to attractive commentaries on external events and feelings; or readings oblivious of the text's prior unity on the non-semantic level and the semantic coming-into-being the text insists the reader should reconvene. *Rocks on a Platter* demands working-through on its own terms, a following of the text that restores lyric emergence from the obdurate materials the title advertises almost belligerently.

Such an approach, however, must trust the ear. It must take on trust the unforged signature of the sounding substrate, assigning the concrete a primacy over the cognitive. Such is the poet's voice, as recognizable in a highly faceted passage of Pound or Prynne as in a passage of Tennyson. Acceptance of this primacy, fundamental to post-Romantic Anglo-American lyric poetry and fully exploited by Barbara Guest in her early poems, cannot survive a reading of *Rocks on a Platter* unchallenged. While the sounding substrate may support a reader's apprehension of textual unity prior to a developed understanding of its meanings, the sudden resonances of Guest's text determine that its endogenous echoes and sonic variations, however powerful, cannot comprise a closed circle; a resonant intertextuality puts the emergence of lyric unity constantly in question. The poem's substrate as it comes to be trusted may after all be construed from the textual surface rather than *arise* towards the reader. Incidentally, such tension between a gathering or gathered sonic coherence and this prodigious if fleeting allusiveness induces chronic indecision in designating *Rocks on a Platter* – this book, this suite of poems, this text under consideration.

When talking of ellipsis, Guest does not refer to transitions taking place in the blink of an eye, but rather to the scarcely audible noise an eyelid makes during blinking, marking such transitions. Amplified, this eyelid has the sound of a shutter; the mechanical eye works alongside the sounding vessel of the body. Ellipsis completes the tripartite structure: text, which in Welish's own writing is closely related to a textile's coherence, corresponds to the sounding substrate; intertext corresponds to resonance; and metatext corresponds to the sound of an eye blinking as impersonally as a camera's shutter.[47] But 'all at once' as Welish has it, applies only to exceptional nodes in Guest's performance; it does not propose a consistent coordination between levels. Specifically, this late writing eschews or no longer finds possible the remarkable consonance of Guest's early poems, nosing forward like dolphins by way of their trustworthy sound and its soundings. This distinction in mind, it is possible to read Welish's use of the word 'spacing' as meaning more than disposition of phrases on a page, for all the strikingly exploded appearance of many pages in *Rocks on a Platter*. 'Her spacing is primarily of literature' introduces intervals between 'text, intertext, and metatext' even while asserting their momentary and peculiar tying, and implicitly separates lyric poetry of the kind Guest once wrote from *literature* or 'literariness', which is governed by consciously deployed rhetorical convention and structural contrivance. This conception of literature as rule-bound accords with Welish's own poetry and strongly opposes the conception of lyric emergence. Certainly, both kinds of poetry exploit intervals in space and time for pattern and sound, which high lyric aspires to conflate into sheer presence, albeit presence susceptible to review and to re-staging. Sheer presence entails displacement from the semantic domain into spiritual uplift or a secular and physical equivalent such as the Shelleyan swoon. By contrast, constructivism of Welish's kind substitutes collage and citation for resonance, leaving clearly visible – and audible – the intervals between adjacent elements. But *Rocks on a Platter* is a very different kettle of fish from either high lyric or such constructivism. To read it is to negotiate a dialectical drama, a push into emergence, a falling back onto the page of text, the click of the surveying lens, the dip beneath the surface.

It is difficult to expose the intricate workings of this heteroglossic writing, owing to its sparse and complicated layout over the many pages of the original book – a careful *spacing* hard to re-envisage from the reprint in *The Collected Poems*, where page-breaks in the original are designated by single dots against the right margin.[48] Therefore, my present thinking-through will rely as much on description as on demonstration. For reasons of economy, it will mainly restrict its focus to a particular part of the fifty-one-page *Rocks on a Platter*, Part IV (the last part), and following Welish, even more closely on one single page. The page Welish cites appears as follows:

> Is evanescence the wool beggar?
> strike that simpleton
>
>   'Bafflement'.
>
>   *Thee*   GLOSS GLOSS
>
> point to the Mix, and
>
>   there! it slides into view
>   the Dolphin,
>
> *before* the moment oversteps,
>
>   into
>
>   the *hum* pour his ivory.
>
>   (p. 40)

The '*hum*' might be thought of as the ground of poetry, a sounding substrate able to cross wide and deep spaces and gather them through prosody into the register of the body (a body known in reading, neither hers nor yours or mine). This ground can accept the trace of 'evanescence' both in its sonic ephemerality and in the paradox of its written and still-sounding persistence ('there! it slides into view'). The 'wool beggar' is a good example of what dominates the first few pages of this fourth part of *Rocks on a Platter*: flotsam. 'Flotsam' will inevitably be absorbed by 'hum' because, as the part's epigraph from Adorno's *Aesthetic Theory* has it: 'The Moment a limit is posited it is overstepped, and that against which the limit was established is absorbed'.[49] Flotsam, like rubbish, is the evanescence that will not go away; indeed, it will return in this poem alongside 'a sheepfold' in a passage which may think biblically, which may also think of William Wordsworth – hence memories of Wordsworth may resonate, thinking backwards, with 'wool beggar' (p. 44). An object as unpretentiously material as a sheepfold can also be set adrift as linguistic flotsam and as linguistic flotsam carries deep poetic and historical resonance. The hum is endlessly connotative. And the hum is the ground in quite a literal sense; this part of the poem will also make a line from Ovid consonant:

>   Ovid writes,
>
> 'Earth, painted with flowers, that *shone brightly*',
>
> *Pictaque dissimili flore nitebat humus.*
>
> (p. 43)

Hum being the humus, then the ground here, on the page in question, can be understood as both the ground of sound and the ground of painting (its gesso or, more suggestively, its primer), and also the ground of being. 'Being' puns deliberately in evoking bee-hum and fertility.

Two poems from Barbara Guest's collection *If So, Tell Me*, short lyrics contemporary with *Rocks on a Platter*, make more explicit the musical and prosodic significance of 'hum'. The poem 'Strings' starts ethereally with 'Wing of glass in high up floating', pauses lengthily before 'stave of time', and even longer after the line 'measured, measure of', before resuming with the critical phrase 'pulls own weight'.[50] This tiny, delicate poem ends with the line 'plucked instrument, voiceless hum'. The hum generates the sounding substrate, making possible the lyric poem's (relative) autonomy, a foundation for consonance between all its levels. Strings return later in this collection with the poem 'The Strum', including the lines:

>   Spill of ink not enough
> Lather
>   bottomless
>   passage in the *red strum*.

Ink then is no more than 'lather' or froth with that 'bottomless passage | in the *red strum*', the strong hum felt deep in the blood (a 'red strum' is a downward strum on guitar strings, but here the pun on 'read' is audible).

If hum is the ground onto which pigment is poured, the 'GLOSS', the 'Mix' and the 'ivory' on this page belong across a different angle of incidence to the activity of painting. Specifically, this page brings to mind Cy Twombly, a painter conjoining fine detail, language, mythological allusion, broad-brush gesture and tentative structures. This prompts a line of questioning: Does the dolphin exist *in potentia* in the Mix, the jar of paint, or does the dolphin exist in the mind of the painter or poet before it is stipulated or does the dolphin rise from the hum when the hum is inseminated with this poured ivory? On the next page, '*the hum pouring into another*' is pronounced to be definitive of '*transfuse*'; hum, therefore, is blood as well as semen, as well as earth. Or, should the dolphin be glimpsed as evanescent, an apparition then effaced by the obtrusive presence of the very paint which has summoned it? Although posed as options, the proper answer is: all of these, just as by the end of the book, the 'platter' of the title is at once a palate and a palette, as well as a display of its own antecedents (John the Baptist's head exposed on a platter) – for this is a poem about writing a poem glimpsed in potential, in fragments, recalled and anticipated.

But what makes this text (a word compelling a stepping-back) more than a speculative game of glossing? How delicate and how amusingly applied is what Welish rather off-puttingly calls Guest's metatextuality. A dab of gloss is enough. Fundamental is the working of the hum; voice restores the lost thread to the lyric skein. For instance, there appear to be numerous ur-texts to this poetical commentary (the book is subtitled 'Notes on Literature' in a gesture of combined modesty and devilment and one of several salutes to Theodore Adorno). One such ur-text may be the story of Arion as told by Ovid, where the poet is rescued from avaricious sailors by dolphins; but in Guest's poem-commentary, the poet seems to be rescued instead from her 'intellectual rage' by riding the evanescent dolphin. Another ur-text is a pastoral scene, stocked with wood-nymphs and tomb. A third allows glimpses of a sheepfold, a 'pickled axe', savagery and the *anima*, perhaps evoking the psychopathic Abraham. A fourth fragmentary text features a stately, regular but modern colonnade of palm trees. Here in fits and starts, in the lightest touches, Guest scatters a history of Western lyric: Dionysian, biblical, classical and modern. These allusions contribute to both this poem-commentary and the unseen poem-in-progress (the book cover announces '*Rocks on a Platter* began as an attempt to write about the making of a poem').

In his most accomplished and suggestive account of Guest's poetry, Robert Kaufman addresses a different page of the same book (beginning 'Intimacy of tone') and discovers a comparable historical depth:

> Guest's poem is remarkable for many reasons, not least for the ways it unearths and vivifies – as only an artwork can – the very poetic and aesthetic histories that informed Adorno's theory of Modernist constructivism. Guest discovers and makes visible buried touchstones of the theory, apprehends its foundations in the interanimating tension between Keatsian negative capability and monumental construction. Her poem accomplishes this sheerly by giving itself over to its own imaginative acts of investigatory poesis, pursued via Guest's

formidable erudition and ability to sympathize with her materials, and animated by her ceaseless examination of the literary-historical constituents of her own experiments in musical architectonics.[51]

The work of resonance and recognition performed in *Rocks on a Platter* also draws on Guest's own earlier poems; for instance, the dolphin has been torn out of 'Saving Tallow' and has already recurred in *The Türler Losses*.[52] The line in 'Saving Tallow' 'Take me on your dolphin skin!' is remembered more exactly in 'vulnerable dolphin skin' (p. 48) and in the saturated lines:

Swimming off in the twilight
is the Dolphin, what occurs
absorbed in the skin.

(p. 41)

A dissertation could be written on this dolphin, which pleats and separates Art and Reality through its plunges, leaps and breaking surface, breaking a writing surface by the end of the work: '*The Dolphin God* – does he swim on the page?' (p. 51). A poet writing in English cannot introduce a dolphin without evoking W. B. Yeats. In Barbara Guest's suggestive notes on her own work, subtitled 'Byzantine Proposals of Poetry', she succeeds in acknowledging numerous writers and painters while neglecting the author of 'Byzantium'; but she places 'Tradition || tantamount to theory' 'near Trebizond' early in *Rocks on a Platter* (p. 8), deftly laying claim to a later Byzantine Empire. In Yeats's 'Byzantium', 'That dolphin-torn, that gong-tormented sea' lies underfoot in marble tesserae, but the dolphin skin in 'Saving Tallow' is allied rather with painting, either the roughness of canvas or a piece of fabric to be affixed to a collage. The distinction from the keyed and formal artifice of Yeats's later manner is thus exactly drawn.

When it comes to *Rocks on a Platter*, the Dolphin's markable and sensitive surface suffers a further transformation into an intersubjective integument, a pierced and written boundary – what Guest rides vocally is what has scribbled, splattered, hurt and pleased at special, intimate points in her own historied body. The dolphin 'slides into view' '*before* the moment oversteps' and therefore can be conceived as pre-literary. Navigating by echolocation, visibly stitching the levels of sea and air, interface's creature and the most sensitive skin, always potential but breaking surface, and in a common imaginary the very image and expression of joy in movement, how can the dolphin be fixed symbolically? For it is the precursor to meaning, the stitcher of the *point de capiton* that spaces out along its wake, visually and audibly.

While the poem-in-progress alongside or behind *Rocks on a Platter* remains unseen as a whole, it may be *heard*. The 'wool beggar' page reveals in one small area how Guest's prosodic 'overstepping' works. On first sight, the page appears like stepped or exploded prose; a tension (at best) or an inconsequence seems to join a prose syntax which is complicated but readily parsed; and a spatial disposition proposes non-sequential relationships between discrete phrases. The detachment of these phrases, given the poem's complicated dependence on prior texts and invocation of a future text and given the history of twentieth-century American Modernist verse, evokes palimpsest, fragment and erasure. All this is true (all at once) but the line '*before* the moment oversteps' points to more, for 'The Moment a limit is posited it is overstepped, and that against which the limit was established is absorbed'. Guest makes Adorno's adage her prosodic watchword.

Imagine the line 'Before the moment oversteps', blandly swinging and iambic, preparing for the kind of effortless continuity that routinely posits a limit and overstepping it. By contrast, the line '*before* the moment oversteps' stops short at a redundant comma (the three blank lines following do the necessary syntactical work) and throws attention back to the limit: the limit *before*. This poem may feature urns, tombs and other bric-a-brac of a *memento mori* akin to the vases, decanters and cups of Guest's earlier verse, but here and elsewhere the poem is as much preoccupied with what precedes consciousness, and what may not have given rise to consciousness, and may yet fail to do so. Every line on this page points back prosodically to what precedes it and does this through disproportionate weight on its first stressed syllable – even if this needs to be secured by the typographical device of italicization against the 'natural' cadence. Nothing is *bound* to happen, but must be put in motion by breath. The consonance of this page, therefore, voices simultaneously its anterior (being its contrapunctal 'intertexts', being the intentional mind, being amniotic fluid), its prospect (being limitless and being limited), its present-constituting syntax, glimpses between these temporal dimensions and, as Welish notes, its own reflexive 'metatext' (including the line 'Bafflement'). When voice so attends to anterior body, to vocal production and to its overstepping movements, that definitively is the domain of lyric verse and not of commentary. The voice goes beyond words, even if it cannot escape the reflexivity harrying consciousness; as Susan Stewart puts it pithily, 'sound tends to escape the confines of closure'.[53]

It may appear strange that an enterprise so sophisticated declares itself earlier in this poem to be undertaken 'With no ulterior purpose' (p. 30). Or is it only 'morning' – 'dissident morning! | with no ulterior purpose' – which Guest's lines here apostrophize and mock for dissenting from the inescapability of ultimate purpose once fallen into words, the brightness become black letters, the dolphin nailed to the platter? The progress of *Rocks on a Platter* teaches that rocks whether stumbled across in words or food or paint (on a palate/palette) form the prerequisite for their overstepping. Pockets of substance may be stumbled into, or the airiness surrounding them or eddying beside the path to past or future which rocks mark, may be breathed, must be breathed. A certain rocky awkwardness in the materials and motives promotes a graceful while attentive overstepping, an incessant re-balancing.

Ann Lauterbach reports a conversation with Barbara Guest in the late 1970s or early 1980s when 'She told me she thought mystery was the most important poetic value'.[54] To take this seriously, 'no ulterior purpose' could not mean a lyric voice should proceed without bearing – 'purpose' becomes felt through the prosodic work, regardless of any positive or negative prescription. As Guest allows with breathtaking concision in *Biography*, one of her most beautiful long poems, 'shards decorated into vases where you looked for a winged foot'.[55] The 'winged foot' refers to poetic rhythm, shaping 'shards' into 'vases', vases belonging with the large group of vessels that 'decorate' Guest's poems. 'Ulterior purpose' might therefore be encoded in sound, in a rhythmic intimation: what 'you looked for' shapes the journey as a vessel, even if it does not seek a grail. For striving to generate mystery through suppression of whatever might be read as 'ulterior purpose' would leave only a field of verbal rubble for a reader to pick across and would be an act of lyric abnegation performable once only without becoming routine or pathological. An inert, obstructive materiality of language would go hand in hand with a nebulous, dissolute spirituality. The evident tendency of ambitious poetry to fail in one or the other direction shows how hard it is to attend to material while resisting its obduracy, and to register the multiple courses of words rather than luxuriate in their penumbra. Fortunately, Guest is a philological poet whose work is shaped by lyric necessity. Her awkward grace sustains attention: we neither crash on the rocks nor become stupefied and blissed-out, for there is too much to be missed.

The awkwardness of this writing strengthens the idea that the 'machinations' (Susan Gervitz's word) of Guest's poetry must not be disregarded through seduction by its 'exquisite surface refraction' (Charles Bernstein's phrase).[56] They are one, with machinations signifying complex and mutable intent, and with surface refraction an effect of source material (rocks, inner insistence, serendipitous '"finding', considered research – whatever) within the poems' field of play. Despite Guest's ambivalent disavowal of 'ulterior purpose' in *Rocks on a Platter*, machinations and surface refraction are remarkable features in this work, both of them compellingly overstepped. That is what *Rocks on a Platter* exemplifies repeatedly, from one ditzily alliterative page beginning with 'Tradition' and ending in a sardonic but fully meant 'tra-la-la', to this following page comprising a compact and entertaining 'gloss' on imagism:

> pumpkin glazed in the sun
> no alphabet, no grief.
>
> Overstepping the farmstead to make way
> in the underbrush for a faun-like portrait,
>   sweet pumpkin.[57]

Sara Lunquist has written well on Guest's abundant and errant humour, and both pages are outright funny and reflexively wry.[58] Somewhere the pumpkin may be 'glazed' in its tendentious ipseity, but once it is 'glossed' and alphabetized, this most material and actual pumpkin becomes teasingly elusive 'in the underbrush', it becomes absurdly 'faun-like'; and it is teasingly allusive too, since such is the effect of alphabetizing, that to place a pumpkin in a farmstead in a poem so plumply is to summon William Carlos Williams, plus shed-loads of folk sentiment – 'sweet pumpkin' indeed. Perhaps an overstepped intention had been to acknowledge a prior world of 'no alphabet, no grief' (the usually disregarded initial limit is never taken for granted by Guest) or to dream it into being, but this pumpkin steps into the alphabet already glazed and the poem must do what it can with that.

Throughout *Rocks on the Platter*, the movement is of feline investigation and responsiveness: to *touch* on something – a phrase, an idea, a sound – chooses it and sets it to work in simultaneous semantic systems as well as a unifying lyric. Everything chimes. Moreover, such a procedure redeems Guest's awkwardness; or rather, the intricate threading through time and space conducted in a text like *Rocks on a Platter* defines a disposition unlikely to accommodate to conventional prose. Guest starts with her rocks, her pebbles, and arranges them so that what first appears discrepant, disconnected, arbitrary, slowly reveals itself as marvellously deft and complex. Part of the pleasure offered by Guest's 'metatext' is to participate in the poem's phenomenological emergence – it encourages an identification with the poem's shaping intelligence, its voice. By contrast, the prose of the H.D. biography *Herself Defined* cannot find the syntactical resources necessary to map connections and events clearly, and Guest's statements on writing collected in *Forces of Imagination* rarely rise above brief notes, sets of references to be followed up, notions and assertions falling short of argument.[59]

The exception to this difficulty with prose is Guest's one novel *Seeking Air* (1978). Here Guest often comes close to the impossible – warping linear narrative so as to produce a recognizable kinship with her long poems. In *Seeking Air*, the permission, even the *intention* to release thoughts and feelings from their ascription to particular characters produces sensational effects – and characteristically these are *glossed*:

> And so instinctively he, Morgan, left her and his feet took him out into the snow while she, Miriam, waited at the door, her hat on her head. Wasn't it her turn to leave? But no, even the farewell must belong to Morgan. The hello at the doorway, the how are you, once inside the house, and then the goodbye, all, all belonged to Morgan Flew. There was her soul which once even she had thought chastely bound to herself. But now she was not sure. Even it had begun to feel tears and threads at its seams, gradual thinnings in the garment, and of course out at the elbows.[60]

This passage may recall John Ashbery and James Schuyler's collaborative novels, drawing in turn on the English comedies of manners of E.F. Benson and Ivy Compton-Burnett. But while funny it not camp, because these events and objects searching for their protagonists, these floating farewells and hats, comprise a somewhat frightening emotional world: 'It was useful to carry a mantle; to be thin; to think; he still remembered his phrases. They would often rise in the night to curse him. Yet in the day they rested beside his wheelchair, ready if he signalled.'[61] Only art (or psychoanalysis) can possibly hold such a world of part-objects together, and it is an extremely difficult thing to do in art, always provisional.

It remains to gloss 'gloss' and to think about its relationship both to its etymological origin in γλωσσα, tongue, and in this text to painting, the visual world and the word 'glitter'. The poem 'Deception' in *If So, Tell Me* made it conditional that

> instinct develops   coveted and heard,   allowed to develop, even
>   to deploy or wander   if *glitter* is not abolished[62]

– and the plying of 'gloss' brings together three main components of this 'instinct' poetry. First, the sense of 'tongue' alludes to the sounding substrate of language. Secondly, the fleeting, glittering apparitions and gestures reminiscent in Guest's poems of the classical gods and goddesses revenant in Pound's *Cantos* and scratched cursorily into and onto the humus, the primer of Cy Twombly's canvases, are evoked by the flickering light of 'gloss'; but this too can be understood as fixed, through the curdling of apparition into image, a stabilizing slather of paint. Thirdly, 'glossing' happens in the reflexive sense; and reflexivity too can be fixed as metatext, although fixity in this regard is deleterious to lyric poetry since it represents a special case of 'bad naturalisation'. The relationship between these three plies tends to buckle; for each component can itself be regarded ambivalently, and although closely interconnected, they exist in constant tension. As listening forward and thinking back always directs when following a poem by Barbara Guest, the moment when the thought occurs is the moment when the poem seemingly decides to confirm the thought in a new event. Across pages 42 and 43 and immediately above the line from Ovid which position the *humus* at the bottom of page 43, this gloss on glitter is performed:

Grandeur oversteps,
artificial and strange, lifting

a leg above glitter…

… … … … … … … … … …. [page break]

The rule of thumb under *glitter*
is that *glitter* disturbs, and

paled, finds painting

a wild grape loosens

glitter
from the *rock platter*.

The word 'oversteps' goes back to the epigraph and its assertion that 'the Moment a limit is posited it is overstepped'. On the previous page, 'grandeur' had itself been 'overstepped' by 'intellectual rage', which then died away and was again 'absorbed in the skin'. Now in turn 'grandeur' oversteps 'glitter' and under glitter is found the 'rule of thumb' which pales the glitter in painting (one might think of the thumb supporting the painter's palette); but the painting in turn here 'brings out' the 'rock platter' so that it glitters as an instance of the earth shining brightly, as the line from Ovid then confirms. Earth is the ground of paint and paint is manufactured from earth: in representing 'a wild grape' earth glitters. But it also seems more than likely, given these lines, that Guest knew the dialect usage of 'glitter' recorded by the *OED* and meaning a loose boulder, with the wonderful cited example (1882) 'A craggy and glitter-faced hill'. The lines 'glitter | from the *rock platter*' thus achieve a further resonance.

This brief *glossary* helps to make a point about Guest's syntax. Ellipsis is not the same as parataxis, as the discussion of the 'wool beggar' page has intimated; a signal difference being that parataxis creates one temporal space, an endlessly extensive *durée*, where Guest's syntax characteristically sets up knight's moves, reconsiders, revises, thinks back and listens ahead. The passage here glossed hews closer to the rhetoric of argument, ever anticipatory, ever checking its tracks, than to the juxtaposition that leaves it to a reader to infer connections more intricate than a weak 'and'. The gaps between lines resemble *stages* in an argument rather than implying a kinship between discrete elements. Quite evidently here translation into an empirically consistent scene can make no sense; 'grandeur 'lifting a leg' might in a different context recall, say, Elizabeth I stepping across the mud on Sir Walter Raleigh's cape, but objects here consort on equal terms with abstractions and properties in such a way as to thwart visual reproduction.[63] In fact, the manner of connection, 'the noise that the eye makes when it blinks', is at least as important as what is connected, so before the page break overstepping is carried out syntactically, but the final ellipsis of '*glitter* … ' makes it clear that glitter is not absorbed, that it will remain active under the 'Grandeur' that 'oversteps' it. 'Glitter' might be understood as the process of which 'grandeur' is one product, 'artificial and strange', but the process is not stopped. Artifice is apparent in the whole, glitter in the becoming.

But the relationships of syntax and those determined by consonance are also intermarried, and argument can be carried forward acoustically, as happens after the page break. The stage where the reader arrives with the phrase '*rock platter*' is rock-solid not principally on account of the italicization and subsequent full point, but because the puzzling term has been prepared by a bevy of 'p's and 'l's and 'a's that combine with 'glitter' to give '*rock platter*' its settled and unsettling inevitability. Prosodically, this is reinforced by the satisfying sense of arriving at the end of a complex sentence, one which has almost fallen apart with the possibly parenthetical, possibly dependent clause 'a wild grape loosens'. The final 'glitter' could be a noun, or could have been transformed through this syntax into a verb. It is because Guest thinks prosodically through her poems at so detailed a level, that they can sound awkward beside those of her contemporaries – the poems edge forward by sound and syntax. In thinking back, a poem such as this short piece looks brilliantly adept, but when listening forward, following the poem becomes a perilous enterprise of keeping eyes peeled and ears open, feeling for hand-holds. Reading Barbara Guest strengthens the impression that the syntax of much contemporary American verse suffers from paratactical extension, a narrative goal-directedness or the preconditions of a project. Such implicit metaphors of boundless space and progress through time have become anachronistic, and Guest's verse may point towards a more ecologically situated lyric mode. 'Strictures tightening down there in the bite section lip gloss etc.', glosses the English poet Ian Patterson in a sequence of poems afflicted with glossitis, again nailing down the point made by Marjorie Welish – '*thee* GLOSS GLOSS' need not unravel tiresomely, but can advance the basis for a compact, to be undone by further pertinacious glossing.[64] Because the strictures are vocal in the first instance, that three-ply compact has here been named 'consonance'. But over the terrain of *Rocks on a Platter* the shifting laminar relationship, stitched and pinned haphazardly, opportunistically, or contrivingly, is not consistently or reliably consonant. Tapping down his crampons, the glossator feels the scree shift, and walking on the rocky level fears to stumble and fall flat on his face. This poetry insists you know exactly where you are.

Chapter 8

A SHOWER OF NEEDLES

This chapter deals with catastrophe, nuclear, environmental and cultural, as negotiated in the poems of Drew Milne and Layli Long Soldier and in works of eco-poetics. It is concerned with dissolution, de-materializing and vaporizing; and with lyric poetry's resistance to the passage of event into accelerated montage and of objects into fetishes behind which their substance withdraws. What poetic gabble could survive catastrophe as anything other than a stony beach? Far from envisaging a restoration of nature and relying on art's reparation of the undamaged human figure, the chapter discovers a pulse of dissolution and reformation in lyric 'set to decay' but growing again in strange forms – 'life as it would be if it had had existence', in Winnicott's formulation.

1

Lying restless in the night I was visited by two lines formed out of the remains of the day:

> Friends speak of the dying;
> a sharp shower of needles bursts from the pines.

Satisfied with this false haiku and hardly anxious to remember it, I returned to sleep. But not for long. I found myself restless and disturbed by my satisfaction, with a growing suspicion that what I had formed was no more than a mental coprolite. Do all poetic lines consist of hardened faecal matter? Well, that wasn't a just self-reproach because poetry is where my thinking happens, such as it is; poetry isn't merely a residue of mental activity occurring in a prior state, even if 'my thinking' receives directions from various quarters through the language I work in, the hardened crust I seek to disturb or that seeks to disturb me. So why did I remain wakeful and unhappy? After a while I associated this discomfort with a BBC programme I heard through internet radio while cooking the evening meal, one of a late-night poetry series. I had caught a few episodes previously, and all seemed reliant on poets' response to landscape, either natal or long familiar. This time I grew repelled by what I was hearing owing not so much to the content of the poet's commentary or verse, as to a way of speaking which I realized had been shared by the poets I heard in this series, a lascivious orality around the articulated words as though every phrase was being fellated. I suspect this kind of speech was contrived by the programme director, with close miking to push forward the mouth's workings. What disgusted me was a linguistic connoisseurship audible especially in the savoured lists of dialect and childhood turns of phrase, and I recognized how alienated I had become from the proposition that poetry is entirely a practice in language – a once-animating proposition now decayed into a performance of language appreciation. A kinship with landscape appreciation was strong here, with quaintness, localism, and a retrospective view from a distance (following exile into higher education) held in common. The assertion was the persisting vitality of language in connection with a special locale, issuing from deep within – these loved turns of phrase and scenic beauties treasured in the poet as comprising her inner self. More than half a century ago this sort of thing occasioned the far-sighted Jack Spicer's disgust: 'Others pick up words from the street, from their bars, from their offices and display them proudly in their poems [...] What does one do with all this crap?'[1] Listening to the programme I wanted more than these stroked words which offered nothing to resist the unreal streaming world and drifting consciousness – but then what?

Most poets think within identifiable registers which at some points their thinking exceeds, should they be lucky and resolute. For the poet herself and sometimes for her readers such excess is gratifying, as the language is felt to achieve a life of its own which also charges the calcified sense of self with liveliness and weakens its boundaries. It becomes hard to distinguish between self and linguistic activity. Like dependence on a drug, a sense of being real can depend on such rarely-eventuating language acts. Poets may struggle against this linguistic dependency through strong assertion of their connection to the earth, whether politically or as too-much-feeling human beings or as questing spiritually, or indeed be led in these directions by their linguistic usage. If issuing assertions of authentic being, such connections may strike a reader as little more than conventional parades. Their truth can be tested against Frank O'Hara's poetry, whose emergence out of a rich individual and social liveliness is palpable and which a reader is invited to share, as I argue in the first chapter. I imagine most poets and readers of poetry discover a similar attachment to poetry they sense to open onto a reality beyond what the poem achieves in accountable ways – work that if sometimes messy and 'uneven' yet yields a bounty beyond what the poem's tactics evidently contrive. One question that urges itself is whether this liveliness is now anachronistic because of its relation to a world of bounty; to ask with O'Hara, 'But is the | earth as full as life was full, of them?'[2] A feeling of universal depletion and despoliation unoccasioned by war or famine is a historically new condition for Western humanity, and must affect what we can stomach, however enriched any individual might be through love, faith or material plenitude. This 'we' is very blowsy and will need pinning down and qualifying; for instance, while sharply felt scarcity is the lot of most of the world's people, an economy of limitless expenditure makes a novel pact with hoarding as billionaire survivalists excavate shelters in New Zealand.

Dependency on what language can do for me may be a drug that not only redeems me from a world of just existing, but might act as a barrier against a sense of reality located elsewhere than in poetic work – I might have hoped to find this reality in myself, if 'myself' is understood as a familial and social formation exceeding individual embodiment. Without such a constitutive sense of liveliness, poetic feeling becomes abstract even if it can generate an almost overwhelming aesthetic–erotic charge – 'rainbow blown plumes' of futurity to cite the poet Drew Milne; and the absence of a real, living matrix can be disguised by a parade of reach-me-down emotions. Trust in that living matrix may be ill-founded. Liveliness in individual developmental terms requires experience of a world of bounty, its near-destruction, and its survival of that near-destruction; and its failure to develop can leave a space to be filled by fanaticism, compulsive consumerism or wanton rage in the endeavour to feel alive at all – individual pathology merging with collective ailing. Indifference and helplessness are the more general disorders. The reality afforded by art differs structurally in developing on the border between inside and outside, recognized as external loci of liveliness and able to produce substitute formations for the True Self. Finding such temporary addresses can be at once ecstatic and desolating; but can aesthetic experience mean anything for the damaged earth and self beyond a projection that prevents giving way to despair, to test and be assured of the survivability of what is loved?

My fears are not unusual, nor particular to poets. They are apprehensive of the earth as streaming scrim ('an emulsion of blank nothingness and tiny particles') threatening to turn the religious theory of world-as-illusion into the most actual material – material drained of substance.[3] For our material here and now is always in the process of transmission, it is always streaming, felt as depleting. The Heideggerian idea of the 'fund', of the material earth as merely stuff available for human exploitation, can sound poignantly concrete. No surface, no touch, no resistance. There is much talk of the poisoning of and by media, referring to cable TV and social media; but poisoned media include the media of life itself, air, water, earth. The scrim-like unreality of media induces the chilling reflection that my death might coincide with the death of the earth, and that envisaging this disaster is no narcissistic fantasy but bears on a real possibility as the exhausted fund of this earth (what once was a world) streams into oblivious space. Humans' infantile greed controlled and intensified through the triumph of unkind reason and highly developed technologies in a place of no resistance, evokes a justified fear that the earth cannot survive such a combination of aggression and management. This fear leads to empty compliance, words and images that warp insubstantially around knots of behaviour (human units) deferent to the instruction of power. Aggression continues as an automated power system for whose agency individual humans feel little responsibility; human fear of the catastrophic effects of their own aggression cuts off at the root all affects, joy and love included. I see in my daily course, enviable lovers bound up in each other, truly alive, and almost visibly dissolving as they part: how can their erotics, how can aesthetic pleasure re-substantiate the earth, so human beings and earth alike be restored to common clay from which life and its copies have formed? The clay tablets of the earliest written poem, *Gilgamesh*, have survived for four millennia, and Gilgamesh's inconsolable mourning for the reduction of his friend Enkidu to lifeless clay continues in our time the millennial work of restoring Enkidu through the tablets' clay; their clay has proved more durable than the obsolete digital records of writing three decades old, but even those floppy records have a physical memorial unlikely to be left by digital clouds as they vaporize. We need the resistance of clay to take our imprint. Gilgamesh's clay tablets are a magic writing-pad – so many recoveries from the dump, so many errors, so many translations sedimented into thick but nonlocal text whose deposition, whose exclusion still goes to shape the human form.

Drew Milne's abstract to his poem 'Nuclear Song' asks: 'What future-proof forms of memory stewardship and signage can survive the ruins of nuclear wastelands? What happens to the lyric stanza when it is irradiated, its very atoms split and fused in new compounds?'[4] He intends his poem's cookie-cutter stanzas, tessellated or lichened with diverse vernaculars and political and ecological discourses (having a Scottish sonic edge), to respond to the second question, not so much in coprolites as in Trinitite or Alamogordo glass. Where though can 'Nuclear Song' be inscribed so it outlasts the end of institutional access? To seek the substantial in the grains of the stanza and to invest memory there makes the fund rich and strange, fuses it in a dense medium allowing 'Nuclear Song' to end thus:

> Even the nuclear song is
> set to decay come debris
> in the fungal harp clasp
> bards on fire that gloam
> to behold some greatness
> in a question of gravity
> to scale with martyrs as
> wild boars rooting ruins

Gloam: greatness: gravity – to gloam is a Scottish verb meaning to darken, to turn towards dusk; and 'martyrs' etymologically are *witnesses*, so bards here earn the name of martyr through rooting about for evidentiary memory in the irradiated post-nuclear landscape, through their beholding. 'Gravity' and 'scale' are important words for this poem that begins in the scrim of 'fine print' and 'rainbow blown plumes' and with art as a small-scale luxury, 'truffle art scar' and 'made to measure nothings' – 'made to measure' since it is characteristic of scrim that it must be measured for output, for transparency, for tolerance, for impact, for citation, for approval, for conformity to standards. There is a troubling residual hope in this last verse and elsewhere in the poem that what remains after nuclear explosion may re-substantiate as shit, as debris, and that would be at least not nothing – shit might be preferable to streaming.

Humans now occupy a strange space between an imperilled material habitat and its withdrawal behind a scrim of representations that afflicts us with a toxic indifference to the habitat's contamination and our own routinely denied agency. I startle at this sentence's evidence of a structure of exploitation and oppression, and at what it exposes in earlier paragraphs: that is, when writing 'human' and using the first person plural I am writing about business transacted in the white world, where 'our' agency is more than ample to motivate denial. I shall return repeatedly to this point, the existence of connected asymmetrical worlds that reference to 'earth' can obfuscate. Reverting to the matter in hand, some poets (as ever) seek a substantiation which would forfend death and total shit. Milne seems to make this aim explicit in a stanza that situates poetic memory as 'touch screen savers' offering 'throw backs to the world' the touch screen has 'factured', 'factured' being a word that attention must light on or it reads as 'fractured':

> Helter what the computer
> says huh but factured in
> touch screen savers slap
> crackling like withdrawn
> but ever so tenderly the
> throw backs to the world
> before nuclear pens draw
> said pain across the sky

Does skin turn to crackling, and are poets, those wild boars roaming the environs of Chernobyl, 'throw backs to the world' at points where they touch it, tenderly and effortfully? What is the 'said pain' that would destroy the earth when human beings are thrown back onto an earth refusing any longer to nourish, exhausted as it is? Or is the fear of destruction an attempt to figure the unimaginable? Pens keep turning to pain because pain can be located and also it localizes.

In his book on Winnicott, Adam Phillips writes: 'Winnicott even suggests, in a characteristically oblique sentence, that "it may even be possible for the child to act a special role, that of the True Self *as it would be if it had had existence*". Is it possible to enact an idea of authenticity, and where would the idea come from if it was possible?'[5] Yes, it is possible, and 'enact' is a notably neutral word, without pathological connotations. 'An ideal of authenticity' is what poets can enact, either deprived of True Self development and fearful of destroying an earth whose reality is tenuous, a mere screen, a scrim, 'neither existing nor non-existing' as Buddhist wisdom literature formulates it, or cringing at the vulnerability to destruction of the True Self which a False Self imitates but as it were elsewhere – 'a defence against that which is unthinkable, the exploitation of the True Self, which would result in its annihilation.'[6] This As-it-were True Self is a good thing, potentiated in otherness, because the creator or receiver in this 'special role' knows it can be upheld only briefly during the art work, whereas to further call to what is evoked through art to exist authentically, not as-it-were and just-for-now, and in another, would make an impossible demand. Winnicott identifies in the artist 'the co-existence of two trends, the urgent need to communicate and the still more urgent need not to be found'.[7] Therefore the conditional-subjective self is the artist's actuality, or more accurately, her actuality derives from constitutive part-selves. Interior life exists only in contact with a substantial outside – or perhaps there is no such thing as interior life but at best a series of life-investments in the vicarious. The poetic enactment can stage life *as it would be if it had had existence*; and to make life in this way, through art's alchemical transformation of material into liveliness, is not to trump-up but to awaken the As-it-were True Self lost behind layers of compliant behaviour and yet worse, compliant feelings, in the shape of part-selves arriving at feeling substance in common with the earth and with others felt to be true. It cannot be necessary to go nuclear, re-substantiating the earth in corpses, in an act of narcissistic rage like a domestic abuser machine-gunning a church full of worshippers, on a scale commensurate with an absolute, infantile, unbounded narcissism. But hang on – the more prevalent style of falsity is compliance, Winnicott's False Self, accepting that things go on as they are, in a succumbing to unreality. Instead let's make lives, every now and then.

In his late writing where he elaborated the idea of the True Self, Winnicott was drawing on Coleridge's conception of creation as a continuous activity of the earth and its poets, poets being Coleridge's capacious term for the earth's inhabitants. Creation does not preclude a sense of loss. Drew Milne's preoccupation with witnessing and memory, reduced to tiny truffles hunted among ruins, speaks volumes about the foreclosure of the future for which art can offer a seductive substitute in its 'rainbow blown plumes' (these 'plumes' are punningly pens but not 'nuclear pens'). Should we for memory's sake write on clay that some unimaginable future life-form will disinter and painstakingly translate? Milne's stanzas look like tablets 'factured' to be interred before the libraries upload their material texts into the stream, into the cloud. The cherishable displacement of aliveness into the As-it-were Self animated by art can become an aesthetic fix, an insatiable need for rapture simulating a futurity disconnected from the substantial, suffering environment and its (non-)creatures – although in times of despair, even this simulated future is preferable to slurping over mollusc phrases moist with nostalgia, offered for delectation and slipping down the throat effortlessly. Maybe the True Self is too infected by idealism to survive; from infancy the self is contested by objects. If its best products are more like coprolites after all, they are the tailings of an animal strange to itself.

The most intimate is impenetrable. In her remarkable book *Whereas*, the Native American poet Layli Long Soldier writes 'I have always wanted *opaque* to mean see-through, transparent' and this is not quite the oxymoron it sounds, for she goes on to specify that 'I and you can be things, standing understood, among each other'.[8] Trust in the opaque is the basis of love; and what you see through is your own obstructions and opacities, not the other's. Who wants to see through the loved? The impenetrable is distinct from the merely incomprehensible, often comprehended easily enough by retreating from real engagement and finding a context or theory amenable to coat it with a neutralizing polymer. For Winnicott the True Self must remain impenetrable and non-communicative – 'at the centre of each person there is an incommunicado element' – so as to resist the destructive intrusions of an unsustainable and unsustaining environment, as our mother earth feels to be.[9] (The relation between the maternal and the earth-environment is too plain for the stock epithet to be resisted.) Winnicott's paradox is that communication depends on a non-communicative core being preserved. This paradox can be negotiated through art, where as-it-were part-selves form in the medium of communication, whether linguistic, musical, visual or any other elaboration of play; these are neither inside not outside, but located at the border, in exchange. The stymied True Self is found there in yearned-for analogues, the impenetrable art works that resist destruction and consumption and survive through millennia. Is that what we must come to, trust in what defies our best efforts to exhaust it in interpretation, depositing clusters of stuff, coprolites and clay tablets with some chance of their resisting dissolution?

What Winnicott asserts of the True Self may equally be applicable to the vicarious selves invested in art works, and therefore consistent with the property of 'withdrawal' articulated by Husserl and now central to Object Orientated Ontology: 'Entities must exist in a relatively *flat ontology* in which there is hardly any difference between a person and a pincushion. And relationships between them, including causal ones, must be *vicarious* and hence *aesthetic* in nature.'[10] Likeness to a pincushion is a dangerous state, and the likening irresponsible; but could vicarious, as-it-were selves be as actual, even more actual than a True Self?

How can the thrilling excess of the aesthetic experience that touches on life *as it would be if it had had existence* resist becoming a mere drug, a mysterious pill made in who knows what back-street lab? Perhaps in the convulsive edge domain where art mediates between the aborted True Self and a depleted unsustaining environment, loss on both sides can be felt even in fabricating and responding to the works of resistance – felt in the extinct plants, penned animals and tormented humans crying to be restored. And in the very stones. Can trust in the aesthetic preserve at the same time break its saturated horizon, throwing us back to an earth made substance, that demands reciprocal care and sustains the force to make such a demand bite through still being there, however damaged, in active deposits behind the shifts and feints of scrim? Might we grow up? If instead of taking the streaming channel for the real, its unstable, always disintegrating inner analogue could be touched through this complicated pluperfect conditional-subjunctive – *would be if it had had* – and thereby activated; if such moments of truth threw forward and outward to extort the reparations demanded by the losses a drifting sense of unreality continues to connive in:

Friends speak of the dying;
a sharp shower of needles bursts from the pines.

2

Drew Milne's stanzas in 'Nuclear Song' comprise a kind of compacted ballad, English-language poetry's most socially consecrated form, and the balladry of nuclear song is what sings the singer, much as life's daily demands put everybody through their paces. How authentic does a person need to be to do the washing-up? The question troubles the adage, conventional in advanced poetics since the 1970s, that language speaks or even constructs its would-be author. Milne's animating inquiry 'What happens to the lyric stanza when it is irradiated, its very atoms split and fused in new compounds?' evacuates the poet from agency in the poem, from determining what might happen. This move entails too great a denial; it parlays the white avant-garde's escape clause. What is speaking the poet – some linguistic admixture from the deep history of balladry, the permeation of nuclear radiation, the discourses of the day? The shaping of Milne's stanzas and their diction are identifiable as Milne's by anyone familiar with ambitious British poetry of the past quarter century; Milne's poetry is substantial and trustworthy, more than most, in responding to language's cross-currents and shaping them, but does not escape situatedness and nor should it try. It is not 'the lyric stanza' which betrays irradiation, but this poet's crushed and glittering lyric stanzas.

A poet must submit to being used by language; but it is also necessary to shape language intentionally, even if only to censor what would be disgraceful, and further to consider what shapes your intentions. Which requires acknowledging an identity, however sketchy; and if your (possible) identity has not been disparaged or even stolen it is easy to decry identity and 'identity politics'. Identity signals a texture of lived experience, a history, and specific kinds of precarity more immediate than apprehension of slow catastrophe; or those sharp and immediate premonitions of 'our' slow catastrophe experienced in a poisoned well or hurricane-raked settlement. By contrast the present-day bourgeois self is like a patrolled gated community, fearful of an earth no longer his for the taking – and fearful too of those exploited and looking to exploit in turn. Meanwhile objects of pleasurable consumption fade before the unpacking video ends or eating spoils the expensively plated collation and its innutritious social media 'shares'. The Ferrari stays in the garage to appreciate in 'value'. It's difficult to write without quotation marks that signify words needing to be wrested back to mean something real. In language and in figure, unlike his nineteenth-century caricature, the present-day bourgeois loses weight – he *wants* to lose weight, and everything he owns wants to join the digital stream along with his investments. The hungry still value substance.

'Substance' prompts a question of solidarity, a word arriving in English, tellingly, in 1848; does substantiality need to be consolidated in the self and its relations with the circumambient earth, or might it evolve through mutual action? Confronting thin abstraction and promoting solidarity has proved difficult for socialist parties seeking an effective response to consumer capitalism; and an abstraction forever dreaming up new goods exercises a sorcery which reference to 'concrete' conditions has proved powerless to counteract. Even more than by police formations and the impulses of an armed citizenry, for affluent Westerners existential threat is characterized by insidious dispersal through the very basis of sustained life – the air, the water supply, the food chain – virally, radioactively, meteorologically, financially, poisonously and weightlessly; apocalypse bodes in different temporalities and scales, from large-scale climate catastrophe to plastic beads in fish gullets. In his essay 'Poetry after Hiroshima?' Milne coins the term 'nuclear implicature', adopting 'implicature' from linguistics where 'what is suggested in a conversation – although not explicitly expressed, strictly implied or entailed – is nevertheless implied'.[11] Implicature can be imagined in the ground water seepage of nuclear waste, as distinct from the formal and symbolic shape of a nuclear bomb's mushroom cloud, with seepage extending into the food chain – even as dread of a universal extinction event continues to exercise its own slow disintegration, and insidious decay and decline can always accelerate to tipping points. 'Implicate order' is also a term in quantum theory, where 'particles are manifestations of some deeper process, like waves on the ocean' or waves are manifestations of particles.[12]

Microbeads in the ocean are harder to get to grips with even than virtual reality owing to the interests enforcing their reality's denial as well as their invisible dispersal, and their implicature is hard to detect without the most sensitive gauges. A sense of *slow* and tissue-level dissolution and collapse is so pervasive in the developed world that many cannot bear facts but seek refuge in a determinedly blind faith in cyclical recurrence, transformative rapture or failed nostrums of economic renewal. 'Growth' is the second and third and ad infinitum supplicated and salvific coming. Milne's essay, whose title flags its engagement with Adorno, identifies spots of nuclear implicature in a range of poetic texts, claiming that '[detecting] nuclear implicature works more obliquely to suggest critical niches, ways of registering and assessing the violence of the nuclear without reproducing it'. Is that all poetry can do? Does the value of poetry consist only in witness and critique? The symptomatology Milne finds in his chosen texts is overt rather implied; and when he concludes by noting of E. P. Thompson (in an unfamiliar guise as poet) that 'his framing of the question of agency amid the ruins of the nuclear imagination has its own poetic necessity', is the phrase 'its own' limited to 'the framing of the question' in Thompson's poem or to Thompson's wider political thought, or might it have something to say beyond 'framing the question' about agency and poetic necessity for Milne, for poets, for readers of poetry?

The problem of summoning the agency, individual or collective, to confront systemic collapse is a theme of Amitav Ghosh's book, *The Great Derangement*, which claims that consciously literary writing, even literary writing that confronts and disputes the category of the literary, has proved unwilling or incompetent to imagine either the insidious or the catastrophic effects of global warming. The same unwillingness or incompetence applies to 'the nuclear threat', a phrase suffering from its very persistence, its weightlessness in the present. For Ghosh, writing as a novelist, fiction is constrained by 'the grid of literary forms and conventions that came to shape the narrative imagination in precisely that period when the accumulation of carbon in the atmosphere was rewriting the destiny of the earth'.[13] What he envisages for fiction is something of a technocratic solution, abandoning logocentrism and print technology for hybrids of language and image including, presumably, non-alphabetical language:

> With the Internet we were suddenly back in a time when text and image could be twinned with as much facility as in an illuminated manuscript. It is no

coincidence that images too began to seep back into the textual world of the novel; then came the rise of the graphic novel – and it soon began to be taken seriously.

So if it is the case that the last, but perhaps the most intransigent way the Anthropocene resists literary fiction lies ultimately in its resistance to language itself, then it would seem to follow that new, hybrid forms will emerge and the act of reading itself will change again, as it has many times before.[14]

This prospect of new narrative forms and media tends to smuggle in a hope for technological remedies for global warming itself. The idea that the decline of the literary should be helped on its way, conceding to the 'resistance to language itself' the responsibility to challenge, even forfend, the systemic corruptions and imminent collapse of the Anthropocene, investing hopes for the planet and its inhabitants in comics and undefined 'new, hybrid forms' presumably emerging from digital media, is reminiscent of the phenomenon Milne describes in 'Poetry after Hiroshima?' whereby 'claims for nuclear energy, whether in the forms of fission or fusion, have somehow re-emerged as "realistic" anthropogenic solutions to fossil fuel capitalism'. The digitalization of what is to be *preserved* is actually complicit in its erosion – unless you believe the earth will be saved by playing games in its digital archive. Ghosh's Pollyanna-ish and vague gesture towards changes in the act of reading does little to reassure if your model for the act of reading is not so much following a narrative as engaging with language use that resists and is resistant.

Layli Long Soldier and a remarkable generation of African American poets including Danez Smith, Shane McCrae and Tyehimba Jess differ from Drew Milne in confronting past, present and future devastation through their communitarian vision and the localization of their outrage. Their worlds of the palpable concentrate a force of resistance, at the expense of bracketing universal threats since these poets inherit and inhabit places deeply mistrustful of universals. McCrae's *In the Language of My Captor* and Jess's *Olio* host a range of historical and imagined African American voices focused to work into racial problematics and contradictions.[15] That description does these books less than half-justice; for instance, *Olio* goes well beyond a plurality of voices to embody plenitude in a jubilant collective voice mutative and transcendent in its creativity. Jess can rely on the saturation of American popular music and popular culture by the ballads and songs on which he brilliantly improvises and as brilliantly juxtaposes, to resonate with a large readership. Layli Long Soldier faces the difficulty that little or nothing can be assumed regarding her readers' knowledge about the desolate and abraded historical record her book tracks, and she therefore must do more didactic work than McCrae and Jess, notably in the revelatory (to this reader) poem '38' on the hanging of thirty-eight Dakota Nation people ordered by President Lincoln in the same week that he signed the Emancipation Proclamation. Long Soldier's work does feel like a prolegomenon to the articulation of an 'indigenous' self where indigeneity has no present home – she writes poignantly of 'Indian emptiness' as a psychological state. Although her poems are studded with Lakota words

Long Soldier must rely on others' language, archives and laws, serving often as metatext to the extra-linguistic abraded earth she tracks, and accompanied by her mockery of her own recourse to metatext (since she knows there is no such thing as metatext). *Whereas* could be read analogically in relation to existential threat of different kinds, rather than implicative evidence of the damage of nuclear regime or global warming; and crucially it is also a seismographic trace of past catastrophe in its continuing disturbed harmonics. To read *Whereas* as allegory, however, would be disrespectful – a work that struggles to establish its language in its territory should not be re-abstracted for 'a veneer of connection and respect hijacked to validate one's own presence and disturbance of land'.[16]

Amitav Ghosh associates global warming as much with imperialism as with capitalism – more so indeed, if defensively.[17] Therefore when turning to Franco 'Bifo' Berardi's *Uprising: Poetry and Finance* with its indictment of the earth's abstraction through the specifically capitalist technologies of financialization and digitalization, it is remarkable to discover a comparable Polyanna-ish gesture to Ghosh's, but wholly invested in the capacity for resistance of poetic language and resorting to rhetoric the most overheated LANGUAGE manifesto can scarcely match:

> Digital financial capitalism has created a closed reality which cannot be overcome with the techniques of politics, of conscious organized voluntary action, and of government.
> Only an act of language can give us the ability to see and to create a new human condition, where we now only see barbarianism and violence.
> Only an act of language escaping the technical automatisms of financial capitalism will make possible the emergence of a new life form.
> [...]
> Poetry is the reopening of the indefinite, the ironic act of exceeding the established meaning of words.[18]

Here is the rhetoric of revelation, returning with a passion to a shop-soiled belief in poetry as secular religion but accompanied by a technological fantasy akin to Ghosh's 'hybrid forms'; bizarrely it is poetry (taking the place of Ghosh's mutant comics) rather than biotech industries that are believed to 'make possible the emergence of a new life form'. Would it be worth demanding *whose* act of language will make this possible, bearing in mind the political role of Serbian epic or of poetry among ISIS fighters? It is not difficult to see how Berardi's rhetoric could be turned to right-wing extreme nationalism as a counter to 'digital finance capitalism'. And if we do indeed inhabit 'a closed reality' where is such an act of language to come from and how can it be recognized except within a cenacle already detached poetically from 'a closed reality'? A claim like 'poetry is the reopening of the indefinite' must surely be met with questions such as *what* poetry (after all, plenty of poetry has no truck with the indefinite) and *for whom*, and how the 'indefinite' or anything else can succeed against 'closed reality'. A horizon of hope may be necessary psychologically, although far more people secure it through religious faith or political commitment than through reading poetry. To contest its utopianism does not mean reversion to Auden's saw that 'poetry makes nothing happen', which Joshua Kotin observes sharply is 'made ridiculous by Akhmatova's career'.[19] But if like Berardi you devote a book to asserting the totalitarian power of a closed system, to prophecy its shattering by poetry that will create a new life-form in its midst either grossly inflates the power of poetry or collapses the claims about the totalitarian power of 'digital finance capitalism' or both. If a parity of power between the closed finance (and 'the' representational, communicative) system and poetry were imaginable, the locked-down system of reason would presumably engender a reaction replicating the formal structures of reason even as it rejects the stamp of 'closed reality' – in, most obviously, paranoid structures (conspiracy theories) or, less obviously, a range of 'procedural' poetic techniques. And when it comes to replicating, 'exceeding the established meaning' could almost become a successful investment strategy.

How then can poets and readers of poetry work within and against the pervasive, the dispersed, the near-critical and the totalizing, without laying claim to a sublimity that draws its power from trampled grounds, their exploited peoples, creatures and yields?

3

The techno-fantasies of Ghosh and Berardi would pile Pelion on Ossa, exacerbating the toxic combination of greed and narrow rationalism in late capitalism. It must be past time for a little humility when the Faustian pursuit of mastery, powerfully effective in improving human lives, can so plainly be seen to have brought disastrous threat to life, with the downstream effects of technology bringing humanity and its planetary home to the verge of ruin even while (and because) supporting an ever-increasing human population. A recrudescence of vitalist thinking recognizes that to treat complex systems such as weather or rivers though piecemeal interventions brings incalculable consequences; and that sustainable, productive human relations with any aspect of the environment must entail reciprocity. Andrew Pickering's work is especially suggestive in its explicit connection with poetic thought and activity; following Heidegger he talks of preferred human–environmental interactions in terms of poiesis, glossed as a 'dance of agency':

> Poiesis, to remain with that term, is a form of practice centred not on knowledge but on dances of agency between human and nonhuman elements and entities. Poiesis stages these dances as a way of finding out about complex emergent systems and, when successful, as a cooperative way of steering them. The contrast here is with domination through scientific and engineering knowledge – enframing, in Heidegger's terms. The mystery – the fog obscuring poiesis – has less to do with poiesis itself – there is nothing hard to understand about what

I call the dance of agency – and much more to do with a traditional obsession of academic discourse (and probably western commonsense) with knowledge.[20]

Here Pickering is discussing water and forest management, chiefly in Japan, but his argument for what Deleuze and Guattari call 'nomad science' as opposed to hard science is equally applicable to artistic work – to poetry in its narrower sense. What Pickering's practical idea of poeisis offers is an overcoming of the gap between the inner-real and the outer-real which produces what I want to call, returning to the historical roots of the word, the *actual*; while I would further suggest that the gap or interface where the actual does its work might no longer rely on consolidating the real, on either side of inner and outer, as though hyphenating two secure entities. The actual is that which develops through the work of poeisis, dynamically and in constant reformation of what it mediates. The model here is work in language where a poet tests incessantly the effects of her interventions, correcting, re-shaping, cancelling, improvising, attentive not to what an imagined reader might demand or find acceptable, but responding primarily to language's feedback, its release of energies from under the crust of ordinary usage. This is a process that modifies both the poet and her linguistic matrix, and also the poet–reader dyad. Discussing J. H. Prynne's papers on poetics in relation to his poetry's involvement with biochemistry, Sam Solnick writes 'the figure of that which is neither dead nor alive but which might re-emerge under certain environmental conditions (i.e. in the manner of viral lysogenesis) is resonant of the way past usage codes are "re-activated"'.[21] And in Prynne's own words, 'the focus of poetic composition, as a text takes shape in the struggle of the poet to separate from it, projects into the textual arena an intense energy of conception and differentiation, pressed up against the limits which are discovered and invented by composition itself'.[22] The poet then must separate her (provisional) self from the emergent text so as to respond to the directives discernible as 'past usage codes are re-activated'. Poetry as imaginable with the help of Prynne and Pickering, an activity exemplary of *poeisis*, might model how responsible habitation of the earth could be actualized, in a dance of agency resisting any sentimental 'return to nature' while also resisting the urge to master.

But we are where we are, and even if such an ambition for poetry/*poeisis* eschews the promethean creation of new life-forms envisaged by Berardi, to enter any poetic ambition and practice into the lists against such unboundaried agent-things, such 'hyperobjects' as global warming, nuclear spread and financialization, must sound a bit preposterous. But it may not sound so preposterous when experience of hyperobjects is localized to what is discernibly implicated in the school playground; when a racist jibe is tracked like the bone in *2001 A Space Odyssey* into the global systems that level the insult. Layli Long Soldier writes:

> I think of Plains winds snow drifts ice and limbs the exposure and when I slide my arms into a wool coat and put my hand to the door knob, ready to brave the sub-zero dark, someone says be careful out there always consider the snow your friend. Think badly of it, snow will burn you.[23]

– and the totality of snow, of the endlessness unto abstraction of the American prairies, and of the snow outside the door to be made actual through her footsteps, will become a support in going forward. Facing cultural devastation too and the language of imperial, legal theft and mastery, the Lakota words released by Long Soldier from under the crust of neglect can make deep tracks. In Jonathan Lear's *Radical Hope*, his book on the persistence of the Crow people despite loss of its lands and the impossibility of sustaining its rituals, he writes of the need to neither give way to despair nor to determine to 'go down fighting'. For the Crow this meant a willingness to break with old ways while still animating the symbolic repertoire of the tribe to nourish 'a radical form of hope that constituted courage and made it possible'.[24] The cultural idea of courage must change; more, what it means to be Crow must change, by finding a Crow path through land abstracted by white settlers, to be *actually* Crow where mastery is impossible and submission unthinkable. This *actually* is poetic work, as Lear acknowledges: 'What would be required ... would be a new Crow poet: one who could take up the Crow past and – rather than use it for nostalgia or ersatz mimesis – project it into vibrant new ways for the Crow to live and to be.'[25] The exemplary symbolic agent of the past and future appears to the Crow leader Plenty Coups in a dream, as the Chickadee – which/who is a listener, flexibly responsive to changed conditions, constantly correcting course. As Lear states, 'A crucial aspect of psychological health depends on the internalization of vibrant ideals – the formation of a culturally enriched ego-ideal'. Faced with conceptual devastation, 'Plenty Coups drew on traditional tribal resources – the chickadee – to formulate an ego-ideal of *radical hope*'.[26]

Early in this chapter I referred to poetic enactment which can stage 'life *as it would be if it had had existence*' and now I find myself situating the actual in the dance of agency. What then is the fate of embodiment between what Edward Dorn calls 'the inside real and the outsidereal' – where is the missing middle?[27] Only in pain's clenching of the body?

> I point my mineral eye towards an outward telescope of snow, the static pours from the stars, circles us, the static streams out our bodies
>
> & all the other bodies particulate, superconducting a relentless pulse, my nanotech eyeball constricts in the sudden light, spin, pain is a needle of noise arcing across the synaptic globe, glow, digitalsun digitalstarling.[28]

These paragraphs from Cody-Rose Clevidence's book *Perverse, All Monstrous* both dissolve and re-embody, taking shape as planetary bodies reabsorbed into multiplicity, zooming in from the 'outsidereal'. Their digital universe contracts, expands and re-galaxies like a flock of starlings. Here pain's needle stuck into the organ of seeing, the optic nerve and the receptive cortex, can become an individuating stimulus, against the depletion of streaming where streaming is particulate and digital, a 'destructive attack on a link' to cite W. R. Bion's paper 'Attacks on Linking'. Schizophrenic dreams, according to Bion, consist of material so minutely fragmented that they are devoid of any visual component. When dreams are experienced which the patient can report because visual objects have been experienced by him in the course of the dream, he seems to regard these objects as bearing much the same relationship to the invisible objects of the previous phase as faeces seem to him to bear to urine

– and this streaming material consists of 'what we should call functions and not morphological structures', exactly such dispersed agent-things as global warming, nuclear spread and financialization.[29] Clevidence however sees the creation of the universe as digital orgasm and revels in fragmentation, because she conceives functions as pulses of reforming multiplicities. Individuation and ego-formation do not interest Clevidence, a post-Deleuzian poet for whom 'integration' would be a reterritorializing fiction. Their writing (this being the preferred pronoun) seduces with a cosmic effervescence of inutile expenditure and dissolution of boundaries – but the gratification it offers recalls what troubled me as I gave way to the consoling needles of my false haiku.

Yet the needle of pain cannot be the only agent of individuation; pleasure must be admitted or pain's alleviation (to put it less strongly) whether with or without the use of needles, while resisting the ecstasy which leaves the nameable site behind. Between the abstraction of endless snow and trust in snow's beneficence, pleasurable comfort can be found – 'I slide my arms into a wool coat and put my hand to the door knob' writes Long Soldier, formed and staged through this micro-drama of human development, prepared to open doors. If the snow is alive, if we become our becoming selves by walking through snow and by woollen coats and door knobs and someone who says a word when it's needed, brought alive in the dance of agency, perhaps 'life *as it would be if it had had existence*' is not merely compensatory but is the actual place where life as well as art *takes place*. Even the must-be-protected non-communicative core would then be wrapped in the conditional-subjunctive (to give a name to this grammatical mood). Life is not bound to a thing of motile flesh with its prostheses; it works in a conditional-subjunctive embodiment, in the actual of poeisis. It didn't exist until made actual in the dance of agency; it is a set of coordinates or a probability until it takes place.

Drew Milne's 'Lichens for Marxists' is a group of poems to which Stephen Collis offers a useful background in lichen biology – lichens are 'collaborative interspecies collectives' – and about their use by ecologists as an environmental litmus, before asking the questions that agitate this discussion:

> Milne comes out of an experimental poetic lineage where culled and typically unmarked source materials are worked into a sonic poetic texture, and where a poem's 'argument' *is* its form. Reading his work returns me to the kinds of questions I so often find myself asking: what *is* the social/political 'work' of the work of art? What can something so small as poetry actually *do* in the face of something so vast as capitalist climate change?[30]

'Culled' is perfect here since 'cull' like 'anthology' is a word applying to both literary and floral selection, although more typically with the acknowledgement of sources. A lineage of poets using 'typically unmarked source materials' would include Louis Zukofsky and J. H. Prynne. What is the effect of such a practice? Milne's lichen poems differ from such earlier culling since the dance of agency involved in reading them performs a litmus test on the reader, not so much a diagnosis of her state of knowledge as of adeptness in making links both in the act of reading and through praxis. Their argument may be their form in an Aristotelian sense, and describing Milne as a formalist seems an increasingly agreed way of managing the difficulty of his poems – and yes, the 'collaborative interspecies collective' of lichen coexists with an exceedingly various diction tightly packed stanzaically and syntactically. The trouble with privileging form is that it introduces a foreground/background distinction with the poems' material reduced to the accidental, whereas their texture, their timbre, inhering in the poems' pixilation and the gaps between bits where the poems' airs become audible, is equally telling. To call the poems 'formalist' knocks back the 'sonic poetic texture' onto the printed page, an ever-present temptation given the intricacy of Milne's visual patterning, and leaves the reader to contemplate a set of silhouetted objects. But 'praxis' is another dodge with regard to Collis's questions; what would be an adequate response to reading 'Lichens for Marxists' on a scale between refusing plastic bags and chaining yourself to the gates of a nuclear establishment? Or from another angle, what aesthetic practices would connive with 'capitalist climate change'?

Relish for English 'landscape', those 'lark relics made into airs' as Drew Milne nails the genre, which so repelled me when I was listening to a poet's radio talk, connives with nature as a high-yielding fund through omission of the unsightly and despoiling, confident in landscape's maternal benison and the rhythms of English pastoral verse.[31] The importance of native landscape for poets in their childhood need not be denied or suppressed; but the shuddering of nineteenth-century commentators at the despoliation of the Cornish landscape by mine workings now admired as picturesque, reminds us that landscape as a genre shows an ability to guzzle on any cartographic feature – even the edge zones of industrial cities delight the connoisseur with a newly appreciable eyeful. What has been unusual is representation of landscape as process, beyond the effects of storm in coastal scenes, and beyond the retrospection that discerns the formative agency of enclosure and changes in agriculture depicted in paintings by Constable. Meteorological turmoil in Turner does not displace the surveying eye, though putting it under duress. To be lashed to the mast allows the siren song of sublimity to be heard. By contrast Peter Lanyon's paintings of the 1950s investigate the Cornish landscape geologically, morphologically, historically and industrially – not only the 'lunar' effects of china clay extraction and its white slag-heaps. Lanyon's visual allusion to the 'ruthless suppression of the riots that broke out in 1785 in support of the miners' demands for better treatment' in his painting *St Just* (1953), central to my final chapter, stands at another pole from the taste for industrial ruins and relish for bracken.[32] But even Lanyon's paintings are generically unable to represent a force as dispersed and comprehensive as global warming, or to evidence it in implicature, nor was that their aim; their ambition was intensely local and demanded 'squeezing out empty space', the artist inhabiting the mine's shaft and passages and his body inhabited by its ore's veins.[33]

In their evidentiary detachment Drew Milne's lichen poems propose a valuable litmus test. Attractively lichen-hung trees excepted – and excepting too their scrutiny by black-and-white photographers in love with texture – lichens often pass beneath notice as 'primitive' life-forms and as symbionts, mere surface to more substantial entities. They attach to place but are ubiquitous, they

> live at the mercy of local climate. They absorb and lose water like a sponge, unlike plants, which rely on roots to tap soil water and leaves with waxy coatings to slow water loss. Hot or dry conditions cause a lichen to dry up and become dormant until favorable weather returns.[34]

They are regarded as ideal bioindicators for global warming. Collis confesses he does not know what Milne's new 'symbiont species' of Marxism and lichen might look like outside poems whose argument he claims to be identical with their form – a characterization which happily does not prevent him offering a preliminary gloss to the poem 'Reindeer Lichen', extracting lines that have the potency of slogans and whose potential performativity is at the opposite pole from formalism. While admiring the lichen poems, Adam Piette in a review of Milne's book *In Darkest Capital* offers a darker gloss consistent with my reading of 'Nuclear Song', contending that the poem 'Ideology in the Microscope'

> conceives with some difficult joy the prospect of the rust-bloom on the limestone as both a sign of the extinction event which is the terminus and appropriate punishment for the pride of Anthropocenic destruction, and as a shining sun on the limestone, dawn of a posthuman world given back to the ancient species of this planet.[35]

Piette is good on Milne's self-mockery, his 'high jinx self-dramatizing selving' visible not only in the sardony which must affect anyone anticipating catastrophe from a comfortable nest (such as the writer of this essay), but inscribed in the very grain of the verse:

> so lichens are a sloth's best friend
> to be in sympathy with the symbiotic
> front load stool of oblivion spawned
> out of acronyms set in bone such are
> the lichens of capital the efficient
> flock wallpaper of disaster flicks o[36]

The brilliantly tactile simile of lichen as 'flock wallpaper of disaster' is undercut at once by 'flicks' which abstract lichen into the digital scrim, situated by the poem as the pixilated successor to postage stamps ('the lichens | of industrial revolution'), 'dappled fonts' and 'mosaics in classical montage'.

Pixilated scrim is made into something that enacts, into an *actual* stuff, in Milne's poems because they are at once distributed and boundaried. What holds them in their mesh is Milne's poetic intelligence which is formal and musical and *makes sense*. I might wish for airs less short-winded by the action of distributed grit and plastic, and for thinking, remembering and conceptualizing unhampered by fibrous deterioration. I might wish for the moon; for where are the airs of yesterday? For some they are sewage gas, for some they are the dry drafts of air conditioners. But a formation mobilizes when these poems intersperse with a reader's field of attention. They are active in the universe of things, not addressed to anyone present but active as agents somewhere beyond that field *as it would be if it had had existence,* where we might live vicariously.

4

Friends speak of the dying;
a sharp shower of needles bursts from the pines.

In meditating on 'life as it would be if it had had existence' I have been attentive to needles of pain and of narcosis rather than a more obvious link between the two lines of my pseudo-haiku, shadowed as they are by the imminence of death – suggestive too of natural cycles of renewal and the 'sharp shower' of fertilization. But thoughts of death can be avoided no longer, since in their different ways, Ghosh's, Berardi's and Milne's writings confront death's incommensurability. The apprehension embodied in the major dispersed forces, the hyperobjects of global warming, the nuclear state and financialization, may lack the immediacy of threat experienced in the Black Death or the siege of Stalingrad, and differ fundamentally from the Stalinist and Maoist state-induced famines with their soterial justifications, their quasi-religious kind of radical hope; but it seems more closely akin to the difficulty of imagining one's own death. In Timothy Morton's terminology, hyperobjects are 'futural'; that is, the future annihilation exists in the present but defeats imagining. The sense of an intangibly impending total extinction, or one already upon us but invisibly, beggars the imagination for reasons that Freud articulated in his wartime 'Thoughts for the Times on War and Death':

> It is indeed impossible to imagine our own death; and whenever we attempt to do so we can perceive that we are in fact still present as spectators. Hence the psycho-analytic school could venture on the assertion that at bottom no one believes in his own death, or, to put the same thing in another way, that in the unconscious every one of us is convinced of his own immortality. [37]

Freud is writing of the difficulty of imagining death, an imagining from which people variously protect themselves; and on the deathbed the imminence of death perhaps precludes all imagining besides 'making arrangements' in ways prescribed by a culture's death rituals – the urgings of a priest, or entry onto a psychic pathway of dying as elaborated in *The Tibetan Book of the Dead*. Would a person inflected by plague seek to imagine death? Freud's point is the difficulty of a willed imagining comparable to the exercise of memory on an original trauma; the plague sufferer may however endure bouts of *timor mortis*.

But the idea of a global extinction of humanity makes demands on the imagination that, as Freud proposes, are resisted unconsciously as well as consciously; resistance to imagining the effects of global warming and blindness to their implicature is not confined to investors in carbon fuels. Not the most self-abnegating revolutionary would blithely forfeit his own consciousness, to be denied the justification of surveying an earth of concrete cracked and overwhelmed by jungle and cockroaches, or one of communist joy and perfect sustainability. Drew Milne may strive to imagine a posthuman earth, but he nonetheless dedicates *In Darkest Capital* to his wife and children; and publishing his lichen-encrusted 'concrete poems' implies a hope for their survival. More than that, it implies the possibility of writing a place for life as it would be if it had had existence, to be discovered as such, by who-knows-what conscious excavator in the future. A place has been written, because Milne's poems are built sturdily to resist collapse into streaming. His poems may be 'concrete poems' according to his own pun, and concrete is cooked with cement, commodities more prevalent and permeated by state and capitalist corruption than any other besides petroleum oil, but the poems' facture does not homogenize their ingredients – Milne's poems are built from conglomerate more like pudding-stone than smooth-faced concrete. The bonding is prosodic, and the survival of rhythm's ghosts in these strong entities awaits revival – poetic tardigrades as on the edge of sleep Milne is nagged by a punning tune: 'the rumbled sleeper tracks | the tardigrade tun to tune'.[38]

In 1972, the year of his death, the art critic, poet and psychoanalytical theorist Adrian Stokes published an essay titled 'The Future and Art', anticipating this discussion in his apprehensiveness and his description of present threats – 'an urgent feeling we share; namely unease about, lack of belief in, the future; a terrible ingredient in our living to which we have become accustomed'.[39] To what have we become accustomed? According to Stokes, the imminence of atomic warfare, 'the depleting of natural riches that are unlikely [...] to be permanently replaced by substitute endeavours', consumption which must entail pollution, the destruction of 'other forms of life' and the 'man-made proliferation of dead material', chiefly plastic, all of which represent in short 'a survival problem for mankind as a whole spread over much of the earth'. He was dead right about plastic. There are, however, as both Milne's and Long Soldier's poems show, other ways to respond to such threats than by succumbing to Stokes's unrelieved existential and aesthetic pessimism. First, Stokes regards urban life and modern media including film and television, as catastrophic psychologically, lamenting an environment where 'no-one is truly at home' and which has been denuded of 'custom, legend, religion'. Stokes's worries about media have only intensified in present alarm over smartphone and internet addiction. But whatever the dangers and frustrations of life in New York, London and other metropolises, they have not proved lacking in custom and legend; and although Stokes's lament that art is subject to 'vogues expressing corporate life' remains true enough, fashionable and empty art didn't wait on late capitalism. No moment in the artistic life of the West has surpassed the late 1950s in New York City, a city and a time especially identified with the triumph of 'corporate life'; and more recently Berlin and Beijing have produced compelling art in the consumerist belly. Stokes was wrong, unable to recognize the liveliness in urban niches, and ignorant of the strength of minority cultural and religious communities. Books such as those of Tyehimba Jess and Danez Smith reproach such short-sightedness. More fundamentally, Stokes's Kleinian aesthetic dogma demands art whose values are integration, balance, measure and containment, and essentially functional in promoting the healthy integration of individuals living in small communities. The extreme violence of human development in the Kleinian account, pits art as an instrument of reparation against destructiveness and despair in a gesture analogous to Berardi's idea that poetry can counter financial totalitarianism. Stokes frankly espouses classical humanist virtues, and while more than once he protests he is not attacking 'Expressionism' or 'abstraction', that is exactly what he is doing. His ideal remains the Renaissance Italian city-state, its myth of perfect order visible in its architecture, and centred on the universal individual – implicitly male and white. Stokes's horror of overpopulation, typical of environmentalist thinking in his time, has a misogynistic tinge. Yet for all the intervening erosion of high humanism values, it is sobering to read 'The Future and Art' almost half a century later and to recognize how stuck we are, with cosmic man dethroned and twitching somewhere on the response range between delusory and faltering, restored in his own regard only through spasms of Dostoevskian despair. As China Miéville comments in an interview:

> It is hard to avoid the sense that these are particularly terrible days, that dystopia is bleeding vividly into the quotidian, and hence, presumably, into 'realism', if that was ever a category in which one was interested. At this point, however, comes an obligatory warning about the historical ubiquity of the questionable belief that Things Have Got Worse, and of the sheer arrogance of despair, the aggrandisement of thinking that one lives in the Worst Times.[40]

Resisting such aggrandisement, the best Stokes can imagine is 'a handful of men' surviving a polluted world and re-learning 'diversity of relationship between mind and external object from the angle of contemplation', an un-Darwinian vision of survival lacking only celestial harps and the organs necessary for reproduction. Himself facing death, Stokes projects the persistence of witness, a scarcely embodied contemplative principle brooding over the ruined planet and making art; no longer, he conceives, the prerogative of an artist but a principle distributed among all people and therefore (ironically) tending to abstraction. This reads like biblical creation recast as eternal return, of a Stoical rather than Nietzschean temper.

Sharing Stokes's desire for persistence a year or two earlier, D.W. Winnicott wrote rather less than stoically in a notebook, 'Oh God! May I be alive when I die.' Dodi Goldman comments:

> What is striking about the prayer is how Winnicott yearns for a psychic space in which he can simultaneously hold both life and death. His desire, in other words, is not simply to survive omnipotently but to find a way to bridge the ultimate dissociation *between* life and death. Winnicott is recognizing that aliveness and death have meaning only to the extent that a link can be retained between the two.[41]

In one sense this sounds like Winnicott responding to Freud with a counterfactual – yes I *will* remain present as a spectator. You have to be alive (or have been alive) in order to die, just as pine needles must have been green to turn brown and fall, but how do you 'bridge the ultimate dissociation' with more than the weak hyphen suggested by Goldman? To not 'survive omnipotently', lording it over death, but yet in some way to stay alive, must entail a displacement of liveliness from embodiment in the self-as-flesh. To be vicarious is a shining thing if it can achieve this. Quantum physics fantasies aside, displacement from one's docketed universe must be sponsored by individual consciousness, entering into a dance of agency that finds a place for the actual where forces and things are not ontologically distinct, re-configuring life as it would be if it had had existence. Such displacement refuses to compensate for a psychic–carnal hollow with a false self, but achieves a dispersal in entities whose oscillation, whose self-contradictory rhythms, substantiate in liveliness. This is not a 'bridge' or 'link' but something more like the 'collaborative interspecies collectives' of lichen, including gaps that are something and nothing, the spaces of rhythm, of musical airs. Thinking of death is the exemplary conditional-subjunctive exercise. The needles fall where they will and make their thatch or mesh or nest.

If this sounds too abstract, if following a train of thought across the abstract snow is where my liveliness now takes place, it would be better to turn to poems, to find liveliness in W. S. Graham's 'Malcolm Mooney's Land' for example, its 'words drifting on words. | The real unabstract snow'.[42] These lines are usually read as a terminal and brutal incursion of the real Arctic encountered by Fridtjof Nansen, his vessel trapped in the ice, into the poet's world of 'words drifting on words'. But what if Graham's words make the snow real and unabstract, as Long Soldier's do? Earlier he prays 'Make my impediment mean no ill | But be itself a way'. 'Impediment' is a word deriving from the Latin for shackled feet; the impediment itself becomes a way because the shackled feet of verse make this way on snow (the paper/snow simile is at times too blatant in this poem). The poem goes also to the edge of the world, to the drifts of disembodied voices:

> Out at the far-off edge I hear
> Colliding voices, drifted, yes,
> To find me through the slowly opening leads.

> Tomorrow I'll try the rafted ice.
> Have I not been trying to use the obstacle
> Of language well? It freezes round us all.

Graham's words are making from the abstract snow a raft of ice, a resistance that does not kill with disappearance into the infinite but supports, even if this were an impossible, contradictory thing, life as it un-abstracts into creatures. 'Malcolm Mooney's Land' is the polar opposite from the landscapes relished by poets for their original, maternal, succouring truth. Drawing on such Romantic prototypes as Shelley's 'Mont Blanc', its universe is all desolation and abandonment. Or so it would seem. But the 'dumb' creatures and the hostile environment are, as we might say, brought to life in verse, articulating. 'The glacier calves': reproduction is not restricted to the domain of animals, and 'the new ice falls from canvas walls'. Meanwhile seabirds are a 'honking choir'. A seal 'makes his play' and listens. Lice are 'my good bedfellows', as are 'grammarsows' (woodlice), Graham's favourite hybrid word-animals although an improbable presence in the Arctic. 'My words go through the smoking air | Changing their tune on silence.' The words go out and change their tune; the air will smoke again when another mouth utters them, this reader's, yours. The whole of 'Malcolm Mooney's Land' forms an elaborate hyphen between aliveness and death; and the poems that follow 'Malcolm Mooney's Land' in the 1970 collection to which it gives its title, are filled with suddenly animated linguistic creatures composed of 'Clusters Travelling Out' (a title derived from the kinetic art contraptions of Graham's friend Bryan Wynter, IMOOSs, Images Moving Out Onto Space) – not only grammarsows but 'the beast that lives on silence', 'the quick brown pouncing god', 'a creature in its abstract cage' and numerous birds. Most startlingly, creatures like 'new ice' can be animated by prosody as vicarious part-selves: 'The map of damp | Behind me, up, formed | Itself to catch the look' ('The Lying Dear').

> But first I must empty my shit-bucket
> And hope my case (if it can be found)
> Will come up soon. I thought I heard
> My name whispered on the vine.[43]

Language is shit. Poems come alive as like infants we play with language, and put ourselves out there. Dead stuff, expelled stuff, can be revivified, transformed by verse.

Chapter 9

ON THE TIP OF THE TONGUE

This chapter investigates some formal adaptations of poetic thinking in British and American poetry since the mid-twentieth century. Section 1 analyses lyric poems by Ivor Gurney, John Wieners and Mark Hyatt exhibiting extreme stress in their adaptation of individual proto-syntax (the way a writer connects thoughts to produce thinking) to social proto-syntax embodied in poetic form. Rhythmic conflict gives rise to compelling, unresolvable events. Section 2 connects proto-syntax with the tip-of-the-tongue phenomenon, imagining that form yearns for thoughts whose connection will bring it to life. I apply this idea to recent North American cosmological epics by Christopher Dewdney and Cody-Rose Clevidence. The emergence into syntax of earth at the microbiological level and linguistically in the stuttering epic poem challenges post-Romantic aesthetics represented here by the writing of Adrian Stokes.

1

Rhythm, not just poetic rhythm, can be regarded as a binding principle that supervenes on otherwise disorganized, centrifugal or inert objects and functions, whether linguistic, visual or musical; or else – or simultaneously – as a pre-existing and unconscious disposition towards objects and functions, forming at an early stage of development in an individual or collective as a kind of proto-syntax. I apprehend syntax as rhythmic forms emergent through thinking (thinking in the broadest sense); therefore music and film have their syntax, and since syntax implies temporality, paintings and sculptures could be said to present formal diagrams which an adept viewer unfolds into syntax. What I am keeping in mind is both the external, inherited patterns of rhythmic–syntactical organization – iambic pentameter in relation to balanced phrasing for example – as incorporated and adapted by an individual; and an individual's internal rhythmic formations founded in unconscious emotional linkages forming a pre-figuration particular to him or her. Moods might be untranslated expressions of such pre-figurations. In artistic practice, a compromise or at least a shuttle between social inheritance and the rhythmic pre-figuration emergent through individual development becomes active. To accede prematurely to an affinity between internal and inherited rhythm, having easy recourse to rhythmic apperception, would forestall emergence of figurative and linguistic syntax which can enrich the inherited resource; fear of madness may prompt such premature apperception corresponding to what Deleuze and Guattari have termed 'reterritorialization', the iambic pentameter or ballad metre regulating rhythm as a bondage and reassurance, much as in digital electronics a system is governed by a master clock. On the other hand, internal rhythmic pre-figuration may falter in its task of binding elements apt to become fissiparous, which are 'streaming' and no more susceptible of external than of internal regulation. Internal pre-figuration can fail in various ways; in the most insane, every fragment in the stream is felt to be splitting into infinite links, an infinity which is unbearable, not so much a plenitude as terrifying stellar–inter-stellar space, a dissolution of all bounds. In a saner psychic economy, infinity is tolerated and as it were constellated by proto-syntax, most securely if a compromise develops between internal and external rhythmic clocks and syntactical unfolding.

An example follows in a poem by Ivor Gurney, best known as one of the foremost twentieth-century English composers of art song as well as a significant First World War poet. Gurney was committed to an asylum for the last fifteen years of his life. Although his mental state was often attributed to shell shock, biographical research suggests a bipolar disorder preceded Gurney's voluntary enlistment as a private, destined to serve longer in the trenches than any other British war poet. His letters from the year of his commitment, originally to a hospital in Gloucester, read as more characteristic of a schizo-affective than a strictly diagnosed bipolar disorder – for example, 'I was brought here by friends out of Electrical tricks', 'I rise and am in electrical influence immediately'.[1] Gurney's army trade as a signaller in the Gloucesters may have influenced this technology of external control. Gurney could be described as an outsider poet despite his war-interrupted musical training at the Royal College of Music and the beginnings of recognition both as a composer and as a poet who published two well-reviewed collections. His life did not conform to the narrative of success and breakdown familiar in prodigies; according to his biographer, even as a boy his behaviour was 'frankly disconcerting' and one motivation for volunteering for active service was his belief that 'the physical effects of army life would somehow cure his "neurasthenia"' – and to some extent this seems to have happened, with external danger easing or at least distracting from internal torment.[2] The poem here dates from after 1926 and was written in the City of London Mental Hospital, which geographically was located in Dartford, Kent. The sylvan setting however is more likely to derive from Gloucestershire, Gurney's home county, although abstracted into literary tropes.

Here, If Forlorn

When to Mediterranean the birds' thoughts turn
Watching the lessening days
And the silver glow
Of sunset, 'Goodbye' shall I say

And praise their beauty, and pray winter stern
To hurt nothing those feathers and fairy grace.
But after a week, in a place
Of coppices
I will count the kinds of birds that do not go
But for a Shakespeare and rare courage
Keep here, if forlorn
Despite sleeting scorn, and bitter hate of snow.[3]

It may be helpful to start from the idea that there are no objects in this poem – indeed, there are no objects in any poem meriting long consideration. I do not mean something as banal as that instead of objects there are images or words, but rather that in a poem an object is always a function. Therefore 'Mediterranean', significantly deprived of its definite article, does not refer to the (inland) sea of that name. The birds are not the feathered creatures we can study with binoculars. Days are not conventional temporal units. And so forth. The poem is an analogical system whose most compelling internal linkages are determined by unconscious configurations. Turning to the Mediterranean arrays thoughts that otherwise would be liable to stray all over the place, in some sense bird-brained and split between a wheeling flock's elements, into orderly direction. Bringing a flock of birds or revolving thoughts into such accord makes it possible to say goodbye to them calmly as they leave either for the middle of the earth or the 'silver glow | Of sunset', a sentimental haze, fading into a good, tolerable infinity. Goodbye then to these thoughts, evacuated in good order and with the word 'silver' infiltrating, as Daniel Tiffany has shown, a hint of kitsch – 'fairy grace'.[4] Such poetic stock phrases evacuate all meaning, leaving only a diagrammatic link. Yet while the syntax of this line may be problematic – could 'grace' be a verb? – the triplet rhythm lands on 'grace' with absolute certainty. Thoughts may still be multifarious but they are also diaphanous and harmless; more, they can confer grace.

Wait though: there is retribution ahead. Coppices are characterized by chopping – a coppice is a wood cultivated to be chopped, and the word's origins refer to the act of chopping. There may also be a pun reversing Barbara Guest's copies-coppice pun in 'An Emphasis Falls on Reality' discussed in Chapter 7. A flock and an infinity turn into a multiplicity to be counted – impossible! How to manage these chopped and brutalized thoughts that surely will insist on revenge? 'Rare courage' is needed, and in Gurney's writing is strongly associated with military action – he tirelessly reminds us and himself that he was a 'war poet' – and 'Shakespeare' here is metonymic of poetry (birds being linked with the thoughts of the poet), of Englishness, and more perilously, of a proverbial myriad-mindedness. Coppiced thoughts get chopped into short lines, detained in language's foliage, in 'Shakespeare', and associated with the 'rare courage' of English yeomen (post First World War) against the assaults which flying thoughts will surely engender; true to this military lineage Gurney shakes his spear against them. Superficially the future tense respects a progress in the poem to the final assault performed by sleet and snow;

but the poem does not observe the temporal order of consciousness. Governed by the atemporal unconscious, now it is daytime, it is sunset, it is Mediterranean, it is wintery. The sleet's scorn, the snow's hate, the thoughts that watch, the emphasis on striking ground 'here' (although the title is not Gurney's but applied by his editor), when at once departing and not-going and *forlorn*, that is, 'not to be found' – here is a world knowing no contradiction that recalls the bleak nulling of *King Lear*. Its unbearably powerful tendency is splintering and centrifugal and persecutory, as the final line makes clear. What then holds the poem together?

The emotional rhythm is straightforward. An explosion–implosion pulse is sandwiched between elongated lines having six beats. The first line echoes Shakespeare's 'When to the sessions of sweet silent thought'; but whereas Shakespeare's Sonnet XXX bemoans what has vanished before finding consolation in the continuing presence of a dear friend, Gurney contemplates the bird-thoughts' departure with equanimity: it is bird-thoughts 'that do not go' which shake his fortitude. Triplet runs resonate through 'Mediterranean', 'lessening days', 'feathers and fairy grace', before damping down into 'Shakespeare'. 'Of coppices' is brutally foreshortened and offends the rhyme scheme. The ninth line is set on bringing broken and assailed thoughts into line, with a string of monosyllables launched into iambics off the word 'count'. There is a rhythmic contest in the poem between iambics and triplet flurries. The syntax divides the poem exactly into two quite regularly unfolding sentences, exercising a strong grip on the proto-syntax of thinking and feeling. A long 'a' governs the sonic texture of the poem, driving towards 'hate'. There are one or two curious sonic twists – 'thoughts turn' punningly becomes 'winter stern' (say it), and the final line's rhythm splits out the 'spite' in 'despite'. The first person singular is asserted strongly as an agent, 'shall I say', 'I will count' – the emphatic form 'will' contradicted by the rhythm, for it is impossible to stress the word 'will' in oral performance.

What does this add up to? One subsidiary question is of a reader's feeling response. The first thing to acknowledge is, yes, we have words on a page and they must produce their effect; but those words are composed necessitously. To say that it is the poem's language which produces a feeling response in a reader is true, but the communicable properties of language have been shaped in the matrix of the poet's proto-syntax – they are not so much translating previously formulated messages as performing an emotional shunt. The interposition of the poetic medium makes the impress non-mimetic, more unpredictable and complex than if it were a piece of writing by someone less adept than Gurney in the ordering that poetic composition, shaped by centuries of practice, can impose over alarming disorder. If Gurney seems to have found military discipline and comradeship in the trenches a container for mental disorder, perhaps lineation, rhyme and rhythm can serve this function in poetry too.

A small stepping out of line can trouble poetic order. In prose the opening of the second sentence, 'after a week in a place of coppices', would be a bland report; however the line-break makes 'coppices' a scissor-like assault and governs my response to the entire poem. By contrast the syntactical snarl of line 6 does not trouble me but feels coherent as an emotion, as does the final line for all its attribution of intentionality to sleet and snow. These lines are consolidated formally and strike me as resolved emotions rather than active assaults on the poem's fabric, on the poet and on the reader. After all, a coppice is a pleasing thing, lacking the sinister connotations of a forest or the potential disorientations of a wood.

The stereotyped poetic diction of 'silver glow' and 'those feathers and fairy grace' is a common feature of Outsider Writing, especially by poets who may have suffered from schizophrenia.[5] Opening with the bizarre line 'Your lips in a cloud' the following brief poem is by John Wieners, a poet who determinedly sought outsider status in imitation of Villon and Rimbaud and the jazz musicians he admired, only to become entrapped there. Andrea Brady records that having deranged his senses with heroin and other drugs

> although Wieners eventually broke his drug addiction, he became chronically afflicted by mental illness. After an opium- and benzadrine-fuelled roadtrip from San Francisco via Washington and New York, he found his way back to his family home in Massachusetts. He was then hospitalized from January to July 1960 at Medfield State, and from March to August 1961 in the Metropolitan State Hospital, where he was treated with electric shock therapy.[6]

In his dress and behaviour Wieners was a spectacular sexual outsider, and his poems, in later years often written in a female persona, are saturated with sexual longing. The late and rewritten poems collected in *Behind the State Capitol* (1975) invite reading as pathological, an invitation I have resisted in earlier essays; what follows is a mid-period poem from *Nerves* (1971) which might at first appear straightforwardly referential, albeit with some linguistic distortion drawing attention to its artifice.[7]

TRIMETERS

Your lips in a cloud
the spirit that visited
before I died
still assigned to the dead

the cyanide garments
that spirit vented
with tears in payment
from provincial rent

Without personal burden
only refuge denied
such taking allowed
as federal government

        6.27.69[8]

Pain is accepted, even welcomed here, but unlike in many earlier poems by Wieners does not seem to be suffered; instead it becomes a function in an economy. The distinction between acceptance and suffering can be caught in the opening line and becomes unavoidable by the end of the stanza: this poem starts in hallucination. Consider it therefore in the light of the following psychoanalytical formulations: 'Hallucinations are not representations: they are things-in-themselves born of intolerance and desire. Their defects are due not to their failure to represent but to their failure to be.' 'Frustration and intense pain are equated.' 'Pain is sexualized; it is therefore inflicted or accepted but is not suffered'. And 'all felt emotion is a no-emotion. In this respect it is analogous to "past" or "future" as representing the "place where the present used to be" before all time was annihilated'.[9] Time evidently has been annihilated since 'I' am writing while 'assigned to the dead'. Although it would be possible to press hard on 'assigned', arguing that all writing entails assignment to the dead with every mark anticipating the writer's demise, this poem is governed more by the reassembly of syllables than semantic ingenuity: 'assigned' becomes 'cyanide', so to be assigned is deemed poisonous, and 'garments' oppress as 'federal government'. Words are encrypted weapons designed to kill the spirit. And who is assigned to death in this first stanza, you or me? Neither of us survives into stanzas 2 and 3. 'The spirit that visited' transforms into 'that spirit vented' – so love and perhaps poetic inspiration are stolen through those very words in which they are bestowed. 'Taking' rapidly becomes language's depredation, as 'payment', 'rent' and taxation. 'Personal burden' may be a 'refuge' because it is felt as a real thing, not an evacuated emptiness. Underlying this protest at governmental larceny is a self-arraignment: since I dyed the cyanide garments with my tears I'm responsible for this catastrophe. The imposition of a four-line stanza only exacerbates syllabic churn and the weaponization of words against their wielder; re-reading links 'tears' to 'rents' for instance. As for the poem's title, Wieners fails even to count to three, with many of his 'trimeters' reduced to two feet. So this is a space without time, without number, without a you and an I, reduced to a movement of abstract spirit visiting and venting. Only the terminal date offers something to hang onto. 'Trimeters' begins with a hallucination and ends in time-honoured American paranoia about the federal government's theft of money and individual property. Afflicted with infinite pain, the poet abandons reality.

What could be more forlorn than this? Well, many poems by John Wieners might qualify, such as 'In Public' whose second stanza runs:

> Continue our relationship apart
> under surveillance, torture, persecuted
> confinement's theft; no must or sudden blows
> when embodied spirits mingled
> despite fall's knock
> we rode the great divide
> of falsehood, hunger and last year[10]

The echo of Gurney's poem in the paranoid and courageous schism of these lines and in their prosody is uncanny; in a world of cuts and divides and malign changes of weather, from 'fall's knock' to 'sleeting scorn, and bitter hate of snow', both poets struggle to survive division. Gurney's recourse lies in English countryside and in Shakespeare, both functional links quite unlike the detailed observation of his earlier pastoral poems, born of compulsive walking like John Clare's; and Wieners's recourse lies in memory of an American road trip. Each of them though rides divisions in verse enforced by weird disjunctions – Gurney's 'Keep here' pivoting from birds to the forlorn poet and Wieners's 'mingled | despite fall's knock'. Both poems end in compacted final lines that for all their pain sound like resolutions, albeit rushed as though hazardous and imperilled, liable to be snatched away. It is a remarkable thing to embrace cosmic unkindness so as to forge links across division; for these extremely vulnerable poets, it is heart-rendingly true that verse embraces, and the solace their poems offer is that of a proto-syntax returning to the maternal embrace that can assuage scorn, hatred, falsehood and hunger with 'taking allowed'.

I return now to a forlorn and incoherent poem of splitting by Mark Hyatt, a British poet who committed suicide at the age of thirty-three in 1973, its verse resolving into what might be an impatient act of aggression, a pitting of singular corporeality against the intolerable, streaming infinity of thought, or the animation, performed by language, of the child's body relinquished in adolescence (or all three of these). This poem has long haunted me, and I have written about it previously in a paper on Hyatt, where I advanced an interpretation based on discovering in the first stanza 'the derealised body of severe post-traumatic stress'.[11] I am less inclined to offer such a diagnosis now; the poem seems more like a drama of 'the pain and the pleasure of words', to use Mutlu Konuk Blasing's phrase, as these feelings were experienced in the belated entry into language of a poet whose literacy was hard-won and whose poetry depended on the support, encouragement and editing of his lovers, male and female. Throughout Hyatt's poetry sexual and linguistic activity are entwined, often in masturbation or in sex fusing lovers in a single body. The masturbatory charge levelled against lyric by hostile critics and philistines is embraced by Hyatt as it is accepted implicitly in Keats's poetry and brazenly in Dylan Thomas's as I argue in Chapter 3. The sexuality of 'Puberty of Puck' configures however into a womb of self, untainted by Thomas's misogynistic disgust. Reading Hyatt's poem as describing entry into and being entered by language and as a pleasure-giving manipulation of language, would find the poem stalking a body embraced in maternal reverie, an infant and pre-genital state still accessible in post-coital passivity and repleteness ('infant' whose Latin original means 'unable to speak', that is, not having entered language). This embrace will be shattered then by 'laws of the alphabet', a disciplinary infliction leaving childhood behind as a multiplying or enlarged 'corpse' or 'the sad hole of this new void'. While the linguistically raped pubescent consoles himself as 'alone', language simultaneously is launching his buoyant linguistic self, the boy, the 'I' of the alphabet, who on getting 'beneath my hair' has sponsored this new body 'that wants to fight any wild space'. Where thoughts had been penetrating 'pangs' that 'once my mind wouldn't look at', in the world of language they become endued with 'thrills of urgency'; and even as their potential links multiply round 'the corpse of childhood', they are electrifying in their forked urgency. The linguistically torn body represented as 'somebody else' is now charged and ready to enter adolescence, leaving 'the corpse of childhood behind'. As Blasing writes:

> Learning language is both an emotional training and a physiological disciplining of the organic body, to make it produce recognizable phonemes, the elements of a linguistic code. This is a primal history, so to speak, of the training of the oral zone – a sexually charged zone because of its link to alimentary functions and survival – to produce linguistic sounds. Infants are seduced into discipline, and the individuated/socialized subject is formulated at a crux of pain and pleasure. [12]

Lyric poetry resonates with this primal history, and with the longing to be re-embraced of free choosing. Hyatt's poem 'Puberty of Puck' was transcribed from his unpublished typescript, and apparently not subject to his partner's revision like the poems published in his lifetime:

PUBERTY OF PUCK

It's slow writing
on re-admission of the abyss
so if this body is sleepy-tired
please walk around.

Suddenly there's nothing
in the laws of the alphabet
that breaks open revealing
what buoyancy am I.

Surely the corpse of childhood
can't multiply any greater?
Only the sad hole of this new void
revisiting old headaches,

I realise the image of myself
coils round soft the life,
nolonger am I wise or otherwise
but alone;

exhausted by the birth of aching,
thoughts reach me
with pangs of emptiness,
once my mind wouldn't look at,

split in thrills of urgency
growing beneath my hair,
there's somebody inside me
that wants to fight any wild space. [13]

The synopsis with which I introduced this poem risks making it too legible as a completed train of thought, and does not reckon with its extraordinary idea that the body might be a soft or violent entity *within* the carapacial self or self-image. Representation provides the medium within which the body can grow. I am not contending that Hyatt set out to write a poem making such an outlandish claim, but that the alphabet's release of 'what buoyancy am I' leads to 'somebody inside me' (a boy) where there had been a void or an abyss, by dint of an enwombing the poem formally enacts. 'Coils round soft the life' and 'exhausted by the birth' conform the conception of the 'I' in the alphabet to autogenetic biological life. The template for this poeisis can be seen and heard in the poem's stanzas, each of which, with the part-exception of the third, coils around an inner core which may exist in any state from dead or somnolent to wildly alive. The wrapping or womb of the first stanza is 'slow writing', of the second 'the alphabet', of the fourth 'the image', of the fifth 'thoughts' and of the sixth 'me' – with the linguistic body now translated into the self's core. In all these stanzas the wrapping is performed prosodically and frequently at the expense of regular syntax although syntax remains easy to follow, its deviations contained within stanzas which are repeated autogenetic units even where terminal commas signal continuity. Every stanza wraps and protects its core, with the exception of the third dividing between multiplicity and void, its linguistic wrapping breaking in half. The rhythm of this poem is not therefore governed predominantly by in-line patterns characteristic of verse's autogenetic momentum, but by the eternal return of parturition, creature by stanzaic creature. Once again there are no objects here; the poem's stanzas are entirely functional as bizarre modes of linking achieved by enwombing and replication. The effect and function are somewhat like a lonely child beating his head against his pillow, striving for the impossible reconciliation of the desire for sleep and the desire 'to fight any wild space' in a single repeated act of conjoined self-stunning and excitement – a kind of frigging of thought.

The following section from a poem sequence is by Cody-Rose Clevidence, the author of two notable full-length books, BEAST FEAST (2014) and ~~FLUNG~~ THRONE (2017 – actually 2018). Their poems give an impression of extreme disorder, succeeded by a contrary impression of refinement and control, extending from the large-scale formation of poetic sequences down to a fearsomely precise disposition of phonemes, philologically and sonically. The verses below from *Perverse, All Monstrous*, a chapbook which acts as an abbreviated version of the subsequently published ~~FLUNG~~ THRONE, appear to be based in genetic replication, specifically the transcription of RNA to DNA, and to celebrate the faults that might make for replicata distorted and 'elated | by noise', generating rhythm irreducible to repetition.

From 'By Gaze'

//be corrupt in xchange :: is gem is copy, swapped
thin membrane, mucus is nest then//hustle//to eat
is born anew | | replica//replicata//mingled, elated
by noise. mimic enter. mimic war. anoxic, is permeable, shore.

mock animal what small sensation. self as secretion
be as if / / impelled / / bilateral– diurnal, nocturnal, arhythmic
& yet rhythmic; own, owned or otherwise is an oil-droplet
is a fragment of a moment, flee.

nothing is formless. all is aggregate//all is gated//gutted
glutted w being & hungry w being & sore.

save by a thin wall, a cell, begotten by being got
by being eaten, enmeshed in marsh or swamp of being
held, beheld, beaten into some semblance of submission
each hour erected where wrecked, in wreckage, born. [14]

I hear a powerful echo of Gerard Manley Hopkins in this prosody where phonemes stutter into verbal strings – 'all is gated//gutted | glutted w being' – or more to the point, where 'to be corrupt in xchange' is essential to creativity as opposed to mimetic replication. Biological transcription does not line up with digital transmission because faults or errors in linking serve adaptation (even if adaptation might suit a retrovirus at the expense of its human hosts). Thus the aim of replication, 'some semblance of submission', is frustrated in 'a fragment of a moment' when a cell that encodes the larger entity, escapes its nest, and in the 'swamp of being' the phagocytotic cell devours its *semblable* and divides internally; or when an oil droplet flees the medium where it has been engulfed or rendered unimaginable.

This artfully speech-disordered poem prompts a fundamental question: Could attacks on linking be desirable, or even necessary for communication to become creative? If attacks on linking characterise psychotic thought, perhaps artistic process depends on transcriptase whose error-proneness yields the opening to new thinking. And indeed, psychoanalysts have followed W. R. Bion in proposing a vital function for 'sane psychosis':

> The phenomenon of 'attacks on linking' can be seen, at the level of transformation in knowledge, as attacking the stream of waking dream thought or unconscious, creative, automatic linking. Bion supposes the patient then has to make links at the level of Reason, which results in links that are logical, but sterile and dead as far as emotions are concerned.

However, in order to allow transformations in O, which are concerned with direct intuitive contact, to take place, such attacks on linking of pre-existing thoughts are fundamental. [15]

'O' is a difficult and controversial idea in Bion's late writings, 'the realization that I have variously described as ultimate reality, the thing-in-itself, or truth' and which Bion's editor glosses as 'the unknowable dimension of real life that lies behind what we can apprehend through the senses or articulate in language', evoking Wittgenstein's adage 'Whereof one cannot speak, thereof one must be silent'. [16] Of minatory interest to literary critics as well as to psychoanalysts is Bion's remark that 'the *reality* of the psychic experience – the O in the human personality – is such that the more the analyst is in contact, the more real will be that part of it that he has been able to interpret'. [17] The converse is that what one has been unable to contact owing to 'sterile and dead' preconceptions may be exactly where transformations occur, not least through the devouring of stereotyped interpretations by the amnesiac, anti-linking force of 'O'. What I have named 'proto-syntax' in formations that precede linguistic articulation must be an aspect of 'O', albeit limited to the part it has been possible to interpret. Interpreting a poem relies on a recurrence which anyone returning to his notes at a later date recognizes as partial at best and drained of life; only with this replica can the critic, in Clevidence's words, 'mimic enter. mimic war'. Which is why the continued eventuation of Gurney's, Wieners's, Hyatt's and Clevidence's poems will reproach any critic's efforts at consolidation.

The proto-syntax of Clevidence's poem then is to be found in its phonemic stutter, in failed replication saturated with the predictability and unpredictability of the infant's faecal gift, inside and outside, part and separate. As a later poem in 'By Gaze' puts it:

nether, tether, thither, asunder
ass-under neither I nor I
in excess, be but thrown from it[18]

But the 'ass-under' faecal gift in its proto-syntax is not 'O'. Should I re-read 'By Gaze' by gaze rather than penetratively? The gaze of this poem is encountered as animal at a depth where no species distinction is operative and where a gaze holds to life at the threshold of death, challenging and imploring, entirely alien and intimate. This gaze cannot be the basis of an ethics of the other, since the gaze threatens to annihilate, to drag down into the unsayable at the same time as it enters and hollows out the one behind the returning gaze. This is indeed the point 'Whereof one cannot speak, thereof one must be silent'. To remain forlorn and unattainable might be a condition necessary for survival.

Each of the four poems read here can be understood as determined by a kind of sane psychosis – a core of inner reality whose evidence can be intuited only from its imprint in proto-syntax and rhythm. The poems are governed by a compulsion to repeat as though coinage were being minted from their proto-syntactical matrices;

but varying tactics in attacks on linking and in compromise with prosodic and philological history, frustrate repetition and result in powerful new experience, where experience is understood as an amalgam of thinking and feeling. Perhaps all the lyric poems I value are 'outsider poems' in that they disrupt the society of poems, 'the pre-existing disposition or pre-conception' of poetic communication (which includes the ossified gestures of avant-gardism). [19] This may be achieved through creating linguistic worlds that cannot be digested without reconfiguring the culture, or through sharp revisions that demand to be met with a different gaze.

2

The similarities discovered in the art of sane psychosis neglect a signal difference between the poems by Gurney, Wieners and Hyatt on the one hand, and Clevidence's on the other: a difference testifying to a break with an aesthetic regime dominant in Anglo-American art. The idea of an artwork as autogenic from conception to independence has a long history; Coleridge asserted 'the organic form on the other hand is innate, it shapes as it develops itself from within, and the fullness of its development is one & the same with the perfection of its outward Form', and the dogma of organic form attaining resolution in working simulacra of the human body and its physiology continues to exercise its spell. [20] But Clevidence's work is epic in propensity, and epic presents a problem for such formal aesthetics, as do long poems in general unless metrically, syntactically and semantically cellular. A characterization of epic form based on oral performance and its mnemonic imperatives cannot work for Modernist American epic, canonically *The Cantos*, *'A'*, *Patterson* and *The Maximus Poems*, because all are assertively textual – even *'A'* whose music is as much a visual patterning as embodied in vocalization. Lyric rebellion against 'organic form' in the name of artifice, tradition, economic determinism or cultural transgression is nothing new, but Clevidence's poetry participates in a more specific rebellion against the human body figured as template for a restored unity, as reparation for human assaults on earth and its creatures. It is cosmological, which precludes lyric reparation since cosmology is the setting out of how things are.

Clevidence's rebellion against a reparative role for art can be appreciated by comparing a forerunner, the Canadian poet and natural historian Christopher Dewdney whose early career from 1973 to 1991 spawned ambitious works of ecopoetics *avant la lettre*. Although also extending an 'elemental' lineage back to Robinson Jeffers and discernible in George Oppen's late poems, Dewdney's writing is more celebratory than misanthropic; recalling Olson's *Maximus Poems*, it rhapsodizes the love-making of earth and water that culminates in life's 'spillover' on dry land:

> She is beyond you now. Her piscine features embryonic & dissipated with wisdom. Her nakedness possessed each time a seething harlequin of erectile sequins. Her lips aching with honey. The sky darkening with dreams.

There is a language to predicate the adoration.

And the water, its essence an alarming grace unfolding past the edge of your control. Breeding miraculous witness. Command spillover. Trembling mica electron thunder. Distant blue spruce shimmer vaguely translucent pagodas rising like glass temples in the dusk. The ammonoid's nacreous lustre, iridescent stage lights in a cretaceous theatre. Slow-motion August trees, the Huron clay bluffs blue in the lake haze & at night the stars rain glittering onto the beach. Pyritized mother of pearl a refraction so ancient the dreams are blackened. This most devonian of raptures. A vowel away from the discrete crystals wherein her rude beauty gives way to angels. [21]

This rapturous embodiment, a vowel away from rupture, arrives as a longed-for relief from the irony patrolling Dewdney's first published poems, as in the following stanza:

In the critical half light
a remote personal operation
is performed with mirrors.
'ground zero' of the poem[22]

Dewdney's hall-of-mirrors poetic irony leads to a predicament more extreme than the poems of W. S. Graham considered in the next chapter. While Graham's poems fret over the alienation from human sociality entailed in lyric address, Dewdney's irony lacks the prosodic weight, the word-pavement Graham depends on to offset the abstracting of pronouns in lyric. Graham further assails the lyric impasse through a dialogic intimacy conjuring life *as it would be if it had had existence*, whereas to heal the rifts of consciousness, language and exploitative detachment from the natural world commits Dewdney to a full-bore coupling with Demeter. Although his epic project is formally various and doesn't rely on prosodic recurrence, it returns to the enveloping lover repeatedly: how things are seems to demand a continually re-performed *poeisis* to sustain a 'shimmer' of potential, Dewdney's dream of angels. The wonder is a constant work. But for Dewdney angels share the same ontological status as bacteria, crystals, fish and stars, and their advent is longed-for as a churning creation, far from a depressive reconciliation.

The theoretical high point of a reparative aesthetics, emblematized by Pound in the shimmering, watery suspensions that relieve instruction in *The Cantos*, arrives in the critical writings of Adrian Stokes, most compellingly in his *Michelangelo* (1955). Here Stokes imagines the fully achieved artwork as the outcome of a dialectic between oceanic oneness and self-sufficient otherness, drawing on Kleinian developmental theory and privileging the human figure in integrated self-contemplation, in supreme self-sufficiency:

Now, if we are to allot pre-eminence in aesthetic form to an underlying image of the body, we must distinguish two aspects of that image, or, rather, two images which are joined in a work of art. There is the aspect which leads us to experience from art a feeling of oneness with the world, perhaps not dissimilar from the experience of mystics, of infants at the breast and of everyone at the deeper points of sleep. We experience it to some extent also from passion, manic states, intoxication, and perhaps during a rare moment in which we have truly accepted death; above all, from states of physical exaltation and catharsis whose rhythm has once again transcribed the world for our possession and for its possessiveness of us. [23]

Building on foundational German Romantic aesthetics, Stokes echoes Winckelmann's aesthetic ideal: 'The beautiful statue is one whose muscles are not stretched by any action, but melt into one another like waves whose perpetual movement evokes the smooth and calm surface of a mirror.' [24] The fantastic quality of this image is highlighted by Winckelmann having inferred such perfection from a disarmed and decapitated torso: no risk of motivated action, and how obliging to provide a mirror for the contemplative mind, shimmering with ideal but inert forms! The limitless potential Stokes discovers in the moving but unfocused musculature of Michelangelo's sculpture could be described (less exaltedly) as muscle-bound; and the aesthetic tradition of which Stokes's art writings are a fine example, unapologetically figure-bound. Stokes finds in Michelangelo's poetry the same muscular proto-syntax he finds in the artist's sculpture and painting – to write of the sonnets' 'concise welter' is apt, but Stokes's focus on inaction and the unconstrained potential encapsulated in this phrase means that in a chapter on Michelangelo's poems, he will not specify the beloved's gender. [25] His reserve is congruous with his insistence on the 'bisexuality' of Michelangelo's sculptures, focused on the moving surface of muscles that 'melt into one another like waves' and 'are not stretched by any action'. Such so-called bisexuality is zero sexuality: implicitly it is the aim of art to achieve a reparation that will baulk desire. Health and wholeness, means No Sex, although No Sex by no means implies no possession. What Stokes describes is pure possession, an almost parodic humanism that claims everything, the human here, the object there, and through the aesthetic encounter gets it all, here and now, a shimmering plenitude. We're closing in on the therapeutics of mindfulness where world and consciousness approach equivalence, while in the light of my readings of Gurney, Wieners and Hyatt I want to assert the value of directed, organized stress before returning to Clevidence.

'Stress' in prosody manifests a now-unusual positive usage of the word. It acknowledges that the power of verse depends on felt inflection, a forcible bending in performance (silent or vocalized) of what stands on the page in straight lines. Inwardly they must be bent like a wicker basket, outward like communicative cables. Invariant rhythm mars verse; even the most regular verse must be disturbed by irregularity if not to self-confound into the doldrums. But I would go further and link stress to *resistance*. There must be moments of interruption and retaliation, cross-rhythms, blocks to the intolerable repetition entailed in reparative art, the need to be forgiven again and again. Leo Bersani writes of theories of the restitutive or redemptive power of cultural forms and activities [which] give us extraordinarily diminished views of both our sexuality and our cultural imagination. [...] Everything can be made up, can be made over again, and the absolute singularity of human experience – the source, undoubtedly, of both its tragedy and its beauty – is thus dissipated in the trivializing nobility of a redemption through art. [26]

Following Bersani I reject the divorce Stokes celebrates between the artist and her artwork, and the reader and the poem – the divorce W. S. Graham deplored repeatedly. Art does not make up for failed experience; what can be shattering in art is the momentary breakdown of the crust of sensory attributes of both reader and poem, activating a new compound object-event, instinct with an evanescent hark of life *as it would be if it had had existence*, from behind mere recognition. The experience is repeatable, but its repetition does not sustain a shimmering whole; it produces a new amalgam every time, inauthentic, unsustainable. Nothing is redeemed because the core of its object-event is subjunctive and conditional, born of the art encounter, and in relation to the suffering and damaged poet or reader remains oblique. The object-event arises elsewhere from reader and poem, shattering both.

While such experience shatters and composes, its core is unapproachable. The hypothesis of an unattainable, non-communicative core, a *withdrawing* of objects' reality owing to their incomparable and 'absolute singularity', is of central importance to D. W. Winnicott: 'This core never communicates with the world of perceived objects [...] the individual person knows that it must never be communicated with or be influenced by external reality. [...] *each individual is an isolate, permanently non-communicating, permanently known, in fact unfound*' – that is to say, singular, perhaps even forlorn. [27] Following Heidegger the move then made by the OOO philosopher Graham Harman is to assert that any object (I prefer object-event), not just the human self, has a core that cannot be reached. Sensory accidents fall away at the lyric touch. Rhythmic stress, confluence and cross-currents act as catalyst for the object-event, engendering the amalgam at its birthing core. What Actor-Network Theory would describe as a transient event, OOO thinks of as a new object born of the flash encounter of True Self-Object with True Art-Object. I locate the repeatably evanescent object-event somewhere between these designations, eschewing any claim to the true in favour of creative multiplicity in the aesthetic encounter and comparable disruptions. How then does this differ from Dewdney's shimmer of potential?

Writing of Michelangelo's sonnets, Stokes refers to their 'genitalization of the act of seeing', rendering looking 'a mode of impregnation' of the viewer by objects that appear beautiful. [28] Beautiful things enter through the eyes only to be suspended in a surface undulation, anything but phallic. Impregnation is effected through merger, not penetration. For all the insistence on a oneness/otherness dialectic, rhythm becomes monotonous. To say Stokes's aesthetics are figure-bound therefore needs further qualification; identifying figures (separating them out) implies marking boundaries against a ground, whereas Stokes is more taken with fluctuations and shimmering as figures gather into a discernible oneness out of the oceanic 'ground' from which they cannot tolerate separation. In Dewdney's writing such shimmer and glitter mark a pregnancy: new life will emerge, and the calm surface will soon disgorge. There is an *awaiting* rather than a production, a tense anticipation of a shattering.

Dewdney's anticipation is predicated on responsiveness to an unfolding cosmology; what emerges has not been foretold. The forms of life will be new. For poets assailed by paranoid, disintegrative forces, such anticipation is inconceivable; the sustaining of a boundaried identity would be an immense boon, and acts of reparation, of supplication to an authority which for Wieners is maternal, remain an essential motive for much compelling lyric. In the poems by Gurney, Wieners and Hyatt this neediness is nonetheless transcended. The directed force of *despite*, the strong rhythmic stresses, work to accommodate paranoid, disintegrative tendencies to the compact forms in which and about which they achieve their 'concise welter', their array – 'despite sleeting scorn' (Gurney) and 'despite fall's knock' (Wieners's 'In Public'). The poems clench against dissolution, and their relatively conventional poetic forms necessitate violent, even procrustean twists into prosodic matrices. Gurney's poem is the more clearly outlined in formal binding by rhyme and iambics, and Wieners's 'Trimeters' the more tightly, if not obsessionally bound sonically (by the sequence garments-payment-rent-government, following cloud-died-dead); but semantically and rhythmically both poems feel forced against disintegrative counter-pressure towards separation as artistic entities. Yearning to leave, fearing to be snatched or on the brink of collapse, the poets seek reparation through poetry, desperately; and a formal unity more or less explicitly returning to the (male) human figure becomes a crucial attribute to contain fragmentation and to 'Keep here, if forlorn'. These poems continue to invest faith in the first person singular, in the capacity for fullness of a human *voice* as reparative, however distorted, tortured or suppressed – for this is true even and especially in 'Trimeters' whose voice is 'taken' 'by federal government'. Voice in these poems does not abstract to the lyric 'first person transactional' as it might be termed, but expresses either a separate, isolated body or a body distorted in a bureaucratic machine. Voice is forced back to origins in cries, exclamations and howls of protest.

Such agonized containment differs radically from the Apollonian celebrated by Stokes in that Stokes finds 'the outcome of conflict' shaping 'a touchable homogenous condition' where oneness and otherness fluctuate across the artwork's surface. Resolution feels compelled in the poems by Gurney, Wieners and Hyatt, and the conflict they struggle to contain persists and resonates semantically and prosodically to the extent that their boundaries are ever imperilled. The poems betray an aesthetic as well as personal crisis, in relation to physical unity. Gurney must fight against dissolution into flocks and Wieners against eradication by malign federal powers; Hyatt contends with 'any wild space'. Such a continual crisis is scarcely peculiar to poets harried by mental disorders, although these poetic expressions are distinctive and powerful. It is now general. The aesthetic regime of the perfected human body was crumbling at the time cybernetics evolved, when

Wieners and Hyatt were writing, and looks truly anachronistic when digital culture routinely violates the contours of embodied cognition. The untoward body contorts, goes into paroxysms or disjoints, off-shores its eyes and ears. Disembodiment became the ineluctable logic of cybernetics as it developed into the research field and technologies of Artificial Intelligence. The trajectory from cybernetics to post-humanism heralded the demise of the fantasy of the autonomous human subject, inscribed according to gendered and 'racial' privilege; thus enabling a new conception of 'embodied actuality' no longer formed in that matrix but in a form 'conducive to the long-range survival of humans and of other life-forms, biological and artificial, with whom we share the planet and ourselves'. [29] How striking now is the sound of entitlement in Stokes's writing when invoking 'the world for our possession', and in its appeal to 'nature'. Such stock humanism demanded radical revision; the breakdown it otherwise engenders is felt painfully in the self-flocks of Gurney and the theft of Wieners' own imagined autonomy. To invoke 'an underlying image of the body' has become as anachronistic in language art as in visual.

Shelley's *A Defence of Poetry* provides a compass for embodied actuality 'within the human being, and *perhaps within all sentient beings*' (my emphasis), which I modify with the claim that poetry develops or encounters monadic thought-feeling-things through connective thinking channelled by the proto-syntax they further shape. Reuven Tsur's sophisticated elaboration of cognitive poetics attributes a force to poetic practice and its conventions not far out of keeping with Shelley and my processual revision. Tsur summarizes: 'Poetic language is organised violence against language and poetic conventions' which he claims 'renders the working of the relevant linguistic and cognitive mechanisms and their perceived effects accessible to conscious introspection' – although I would argue this distancing arrives as secondary gain beyond a restored and shocking coherence of thought and feeling, stressing, distorting and re-setting channels of thinking, communication and introspection. [30] Tsur sees the marks of violence settle historically into new conventions apt to become mere decorative style; dread of thinking through such fossilized forms and pathways presses on the serious poet.

Textbook cognitive poetics echoes the Romantic aesthetic tradition's distinction between oneness and otherness in the distinction between figure and ground, reproduced in the cybernetic binary of signal and noise. Competence to pick up cues for foregrounding the message (signal) certainly is important for reading, but in cognitive poetics becomes over-privileged. There can be no irrelevant noise in a poem. A relatively low level of obtrusive noise, redundancy and resistance reduces a poem's aesthetic potential (not that a high level corresponds to quality): to read a poem demands a willed and learnt suspension of the skill, experience and memory enabling a reader in other contexts to distinguish a message.

Tsur's invocation of TOT (tip-of-the-tongue) states, where 'suppressed semantic and phonetic features constitute some intangible and invisible condensed mass that induces a thick atmosphere' describes exactly the emergence of 'thought-emotion-things' that proto-syntax assembles; such thinking depends on a resistance to automatic and conventional separation of figure and ground and the acceptance of a relationship between oneness and otherness which remains unstable, for no word or phrase in lyric poetry can definitively settle the TOT crisis. In poetry the TOT crisis can demand violent adjustments in the proximate language field to align thoughts to proto-syntax. [31] Proto-syntax with its 'thick atmosphere' precedes thinking, but awaits thoughts for activation – thoughts that in this atmosphere stress, distort and re-set the tormented physiology of poems like those of Gurney, Wieners and Hyatt, poems supplicating an impossible redemptive return to a figure free of damage.

Cody-Rose Clevidence's *Perverse, All Monstrous* revises the aesthetic regime of the autonomous human subject, and it reanimates Olson's field poetics. Olson's 'human universe' (the title of his major essay in poetics) should not be misread as a humanistic universe, but is one where according to the Uncertainty Principle entities exist only in relation to the state of other entities, to a field. Reitha Pattison offers a lucid account, asserting that for Olson:

> Myth was the cosmology that was spoken, not a rite of referral but an instantiation in the act of speaking, its enactment. Space, like myth, had to be as actual, solid, and factual as everything else in Olson's 'Kosmos', written and spoken. [32]

I'd like to place emphasis on the word 'actual' here. Space *acts*. Time *acts*. And the poem affects time and space. What primarily distinguishes Olson's cosmology from, say, Milton's, is that it eschews a singular foundational text or story for overlaid temporalities extending from the quotidian to the mythological, and activating thought in their cross-rhythms. Given the documents folded into *The Maximus Poems* and many references to Greek myth and philosophy, this may seem an odd claim, but *The Maximus Poems* are unique in epic for their churning quality, a feeling of incessant emergence that becomes more pronounced with the work's addenda and revisions, ending firmly but *diminuendo* with 'myself' understood in its littleness and descent from the figure of Maximus, in its dependence on others for its shaping. Olson's cosmology is performed in a way that is tentative, adjusting and ever-emergent into new and mutually re-configurative forms.

Clevidence's poem '[AGATE/ALGAE]' in *Perverse, All Monstrous* rewrites creation as the enlivening of a cooling earth, starting with the emergence of amino acid and syntactical chains out of a background genetic and linguistic radiation, a TOT world where collectively arising genomes accommodate to cellular proto-syntax. In strophes reminiscent of pre-Socratic philosophy filtered through *The Maximus Poems*, Clevidence tells of earth struggling to evolve sensory organs competent to apprehend planetary transformations as thoughts that will in turn struggle to conceive the consciousness that will eventuate them (not yet and not only human) – for as Shelley asserts, 'Every original language near to its source is in itself the chaos of a cyclic poem' (*A Defence of Poetry*). Clevidence stretches back in a trans-corporeal re-inscription to a time prior to cellular life, scaling between nanobiological and cosmic events. Epic ambitions are announced by their book's title and '[AGATE/ALGAE]'s epigraph, taken from *Paradise Lost*. By no means the first perversion of *Paradise Lost*, Clevidence's invites comparison with Ronald Johnson's *Radi os* first published in 1977. At first sight Johnson's poem may look more radical in its paratactical disposition of fragments surviving his erasure of Milton's text, but it hews closer to Milton's patriarchal cosmology than Clevidence's, even if the word 'God' is lost to *Radi os* (a title continuing to claim oracular authority). Johnson's poem begins:

O

              tree
      into the World,
                    Man

           the chosen

Rose out of Chaos: [33]

The first two pages of Clevidence's poem could scarcely be more different; they present a typographically abstract score, a background radiation or 'thick atmosphere' within which chemical elements form contemporaneously with language, 'glyc' and 'sulpH' but also 'gly', then 'agate' and 'iron' before 'Oxy' and 'breathe'. Cosmic speculation returns to a history and space prior to humanity's emergence – no proper names, whether of persons or places, appear. Dewdney may catch his glitter in the sediment of named and loved places, while Olson stations himself on Watchhouse Point in Gloucester MA, shaped by continental drift and geological time. Clevidence's lyric presence self-dissolves in a kind of retrospeculation where their first person singular is mutative as a cloud of knowing condensed according to the formations of proto-syntax, or as organs of perception imagined into being by the perceptible-to-be. The thinking process is commanded by the precedence of thoughts:

                            the rock sky

hung, pony, like the moon, hard up in heaven, then by fire built the sky
lit round the rock-crowned earth that grew an eye to see it

I ache, I arc, I archaic, I arch, I eon, Ion, archembryonic, vie, vision
as minerals ache toward light, as crystals crowd toward heat

      (p. 15)

Might 'pony' bear the unusual sense of a summary, crib or abridgement, so 'the rock sky' first concentrates into the moon and the moon as a reflective entity, then becomes an observation post nascent from 'the rock sky', developing as, in short, 'an eye'? Unlikely since 'pony' grows into a stallion a few lines later, or reverts to a proto-stallion of froth and scum; these are sea horses, then (or previously) sulphuric spray, then (or previously) Olsonian chrysanthemums exploding. Either way, the eye/I plunges back in time from the eye-ache of the present through the archaic human record, to aeons before human development and to primitive, embryonic life, and back yet further to non-organic but responsive matter, 'crystals crowd toward heat'. The eye reverses the zoom of the opening score. What '[AGATE/ALGAE]' decidedly is not is patriarchal or a drama of the achievement by humans of grace – even if its retrospection can exalt 'how things are' as though born of Necessity encoded in rock.

To quote from Clevidence's work of continuous emergence and reversion risks representing a clipping as a bounded entity, but needs must to offer some way of approaching. Tracking the consolidation of silt into 'BIZARRE FORMS TO CROWD OVER IMMENSE AND ANIMATE EARTH', a short passage reads:

FERMENTING THE DEAD & SHINY BODIES INTO
AIR MADE SHELLS MADE ENEMIES MADE PALACE OF
THEMSELVES MADE TOWER TO LIVE IN MADE OF THEIR
BODIES RADIAL DIALS MADE OF THEIR BODIES PRISMS &
TUBES MADE OF THEIR BODIES WHIPS & PROPELLERS

(p. 20)

—referring to flagella since these whips and propellers go on to wriggle and swim. This richly detailed writing describes and responds to what the poem later describes as 'data of the echo, tidal rhythm condenses to an order, heaving signifier of the place marked by urge' (p. 28). Rhythm condenses at the urging of the moon whose presiding over the rhythms of ovulation is confirmed by a 'heaving signifier', a version of the postmodern 'floating signifier' endowed with the force of birth labour. 'The earth's crust rises tidal to the dumb moon': birth labour is eruptive from the rising earth as a 'thumb-in-the-eye || of the dumb moon', disembodied consciousness reverting to a 'sightless glucocorticoid receptor in the interstice' (the glucocorticoid receptor 'regulates genes controlling a cell's development, metabolism, and immune response') (p. 29). Self-constructing through feedback loops building data in layers or waves impelling towards consciousness in the entire planet's corporeality, the poem loops back to 'the rock sky', the horizon of earth's substance, its stuff, looping back and forth continuously. '[AGATE/ALGAE]' eventuates in a fold-out page typeset as a double helix, executing a turn and reverse boost forward to a Now put under surveillance by the 'dude moon grin', and with the moon's masculine degeneration of 'my garland all spangled' into 'the endless grey | gauntlet of my eyes | what my dirty hands | have touched'.[34] Transfigured from tidal femaleness into this disembodied but dude-gendered viewer the moon has become stupid, as in eyes that merely copy and confirm 'what my dirty hands | have touched'.

W. R. Bion's dictum that 'thinkers might be likened to objects sensitive to certain wave lengths of thought, as the eye or radio-telescope is sensitive to a particular range of electromagnetic waves' corresponds uncannily to the I/eye of Clevidence's poem. [35] Such awaiting thoughts are discerned in a TOT state and take shape linguistically: 'there is a wept in the distance' Clevidence writes and *Perverse, All Monstrous* ends by recognizing 'come tomorrow, all this 'open' will be | overgrown'. '[AGATE/ALGAE]' exceeds the prescriptions of open form and better answers Olson's call for a field poetics; it is a new, ancient epic bearing no mythically sanctioned apology for nation state or cultural patrimony. In the poem's creation myth the figure 'I' is 'a reciprocating thinker' who has been impinged on by thoughts, and acting as agent of proto-syntax comprises their stressed connective tissue. Isolated fragments do not exist; the demiurge lives on the tip of the tongue, ready to insert the word or the neurotransmitter into place in life's proto-syntax or the poem's. There is no true openness to be colonized; nothing could be more 'overgrown' than the world where each of us invents our own self – it was overgrown from the start and rubbish strewn. But the man on the dump must get to work, and in Clevidence's poem Wallace Stevens's 'stanza my stone' (quoted in my first chapter) will birth crystals and sludge knowing the promise of life before birth.

But what does this require of a reader? The proto-syntax of Clevidence's poem is governed by yielding and resistance to the rhythmic urge of the moon, to and against the tides. To extend the passage cited earlier:

nether, tether, thither, asunder
ass-under neither I nor I
in excess, be but thrown from it
gelding, glimmer
in the eye in the eye
of a storm.

The storm's eye and the I's eye merge and push-pull. Clevidence's 'I' is not the resisted and surveying eye of the moon, but is battered, devoured and exultant, a receiver who 'becomes an emitter or intermittent'. Despite changes in how things are since Dewdney published his Natural Histories, Clevidence's writing shares his poems' rapture, while their polymorphous perversity overtakes Dewdney's heterosexual world-conception; indeed, Clevidence's rapture is less compromised than Dewdney's in part because its grammar is so fractured and its first person a function of condensation which could never be mistaken for a consistently embodied and nameable human subject. Dewdney writes impersonal and elegantly phrased prose mutating into the first person singular or plural chiefly for sexual acts. The cosmic timescale of Clevidence's ~~FLUNG~~ *THRONE* makes negligible the present blink of an eye while Dewdney reflects on an exactly dated present. *Spring Trances in the Control Emerald Night* (1978) is announced as written in spring 1974, and scrutinizes Southwestern Ontario at that moment:

PETROLIA BATHED IN A neo-carboniferous glow. Oil and gas flow from the taps of every household. Tar sand abound, some with live trapped smilodons snarling & surprisingly lean. In Petrolia the limestone is so soft farmers ploughing theiyr [sic] fields feel only a slight drag as their blades slice through boulders. Fossils are dragged through the rock like crumbs through butter. [36]

The present-orientation means Dewdney's rapture has to work *in despite* – depredations on the earth are all too apparent in an economy dependent on the filthy extraction of oil from tar sands. Monsters emerge from the shimmer as well as angels. Yet Dewdney's prose remains largely unruffled where Clevidence's verse, breaks, digitises, streams and so is absolutely contemporary; but it seeks too to remake the world from its birth – and the impetus to undertake this re-eventuation has to be more than merely formalist. Their poetry yearns for an inside that corresponds to hieroglyphs and alphabets:

> Do all minerals strain toward living? Porous silicates, clay, pyrite, both code & catalyst, the silver spray catches in the light, would it have caught in the darkness also, made an inside out of it, an instant out of it, the ragged shore is wide & bright with its patterns etched in rock. [37]

Here we have it again: from inscribed rock and the scrim of silver spray an inside evolves. For both cosmological poets the earth precedes us but originates in poetic syntax: such a claim revises Shelley's claim that poets are 'the unacknowledged legislators of the world' by clarifying the distinction between earth and world implicit in his 'Defence'. The earth wants to world itself.

The receiver/emitter, the intermittent poetic 'I' effects the languaging of earth into world for each of us as also for our communities; our entry into language creates the world. At the same time each of us continues to be enveloped in the earth and lonely in the universe, protecting as best we can a forlornness necessary for psychic endurance. The limitations of consciousness press back on us in continuous action–reaction with the extension of our earthed-ness, a mutative re-embodiment. Again and again Clevidence turns things around; exulting in schiz-flows, going with the dissolute flows of language and of cellular nuclei, the flows which Gurney, Hyatt and Wieners must fight so as to stay intact and forlorn. Clevidence shapes the emergence of the forlorn kernel, the inside, at every scalar point from the microbiological to the cosmic; is this restoring or originating life as it would be if it had had existence, or both? The kinship of this cosmogony to Heidegger's 'worlding' and to Blake's 'orbs' is clear. Worlding means that "by the opening of a world, all things gain their lingering and hastening, their distance and proximity, their breadth and their limits." [38] What clears within the circle of the poem, transforms into the clearing that surrounds the cosmogenic poem:

> From every one of the four regions of human majesty
> There is an outside spread without & an outside spread within,
> Beyond the outline of identity both ways, which meet in one –
> An orbed void of doubt, despair, hunger, & thirst & sorrow. [39]

But in the clearing outside that orb, might be found not only human majesty, but love of all the now-creatures. I have to believe it, or anticipate an environment of cockroaches and scuttling orbs 'of doubt, despair, hunger, & thirst & sorrow'.

I would propose in place of a psychoanalytically derived oneness and otherness, or a gestalt or cognitive figure-and-ground, that dissolution and reformation occurring around nodes of language would be a way to describe how thinking happens in certain extended poetic works, including Clevidence's and Prynne's, and that their rhythmic, lunar pulsation guides how such poems might be read. Beginning by reading according to normal protocols, I engage the default activity of compiling linguistic acts into implicit paraphrase – I don't need actually to paraphrase but to experience a sense of 'grasping' similar to finding the word felt and sought on the tip of my tongue. A thick atmosphere urges towards momentary resolution into a figure. The figure of thought dissolves and I return to a tolerable floating above the text, perhaps while preoccupied – anticipating an e-mail – and so experience my dilation across the text's surface; I move between grasping and floating, with periodic *interruptions* that can fracture the train of reading–thinking and demand a conscious 'picking up' of what has been read when resuming. Interruption can have the baleful effect of making me attentive to myself as a reading subject, an intrusive kind of distraction – I might hear my own blood pulse; an intrusion which also doubles down on the text as a material thing. (There is no such thing as a thing, but thingliness is one pole of an event.) Let go then and start again. Let us arise and go now. Opposed to self-objectification and art-objectification as epitomised by Stokes's retreat into contemplating of 'self-sufficiency' and his own 'turned phrases and fine passages', dissolution–reformation and expansion–contraction are biomorphic processes, that also oppose the fragmentation and bit-perfect shiny reassembly characterizing the digital. Such language-immersion also opposes digital streaming by virtue of its interfering and amplifying pulsation between form as recognized in its social and historical density, and form discovered according to individual rhythmic pre-figuration – what I have here called proto-syntax. It is a rule that a single set rhythm becomes stupefying or authoritarian, inducing 'oneness', while polyrhythms create multiple worlds on earth. We may each of us press on forlorn and necessarily so, but disruption in aesthetic encounter childs us repeatedly into strange unions. Frail, tentative and short-lived, such fleeting insults to time, space and separate consciousness continue to propose a defence of poetry.

Such an extensive conception of *poeisis* can be illustrated by a metaphor. Imagine a jellyfish swimming by expanding and contracting. This jellyfish is at once a figment of ocean, an individual life and belongs to the life of a shoal or welter. This jellyfish is colourless and shimmers with variegated colour. This jellyfish is beginning to think with its tentacles. The ocean's waves pull the shoal back and forth, impeding and accelerating its movement. Lifeless medusae abound. There is evidence that shoals of shrimp can affect the ocean's currents.

Chapter 10

TRYING TIMES

Figure 8 Peter Lanyon, *St Just*.

This final chapter recapitulates the themes of *Lyric in Its Times* through analysis of a painting by the St Ives artist Peter Lanyon that responds to a mining disaster, and of an elegy for Lanyon by the poet W. S. Graham. I find contrarious rhythms in both works and a struggle against the petrifaction threatened by memorializing, before at last through a reading of Graham's 'The Constructed Space' I return to the temporal, local and methodological claims animating the book from the start.

*

For Frank O'Hara both 'The Day Lady Died' and 'Ode on Causality' ended in the air and in the inspiration granted by great art, whether in breath held by the audience at Billie Holiday's Five Spot performance or the cloud that gives birth to an artwork named Bird in Flight.[1] Poets are more inclined to air and airs (and to air their views) than they are to keep their feet on the ground, but Graham fights to restore the airy, the abstracted, and abstracting to earth. Graham has an antipathy to air, and it's personal. His superb elegy 'The Thermal Stair' is dedicated 'For the painter Peter Lanyon killed in a gliding accident 1964' and while it asks Lanyon to

> Find me a thermal to speak and soar to you from
> Over Lanyon Quoit and the circling stones standing
> High on the moor over Gurnard's Head[2]

It is the named quoit, a stone dolmen, that links Lanyon with Cornwall (as the only major St Ives artist of Cornish extraction and birth) and more narrowly with the Penwith peninsula where both he and Graham lived. Lanyon Quoit, the oddly mobile 'circling stones' and the poem's later granite 'carn to carn' culminate in a monumental declaration of purpose:

> The poet or painter steers his life to maim
>
> Himself somehow for the job. His job is Love
> Imagined into words or paint to make
> An object that will stand and will not move.

Air itself becomes a rigid support under a buzzard's wings, and the poem honours Lanyon's resistance to the Cornish picturesque, citing the industry of tin miners and beam engine and the 'vesselled men' who were 'maintained' by the sea. In the face of a more obvious narrative of leaving the wounded earth for open space, Graham's poem sees Lanyon's flying as a way of getting closer to earth, of surveying its topography and geology, connected umbilically to place – so the poem ridicules a woman who 'turns to mention space' at an exhibition opening, and reverts to the homosocial place of the pub, opening time being signalled by 'the phallic boys', the Godrevy and Wolf lighthouses reliably signalling charted places. Yet this is also an elegy for a flier who 'steers his life to maim | Himself somehow for the job' and did eventually maim himself horribly, and a painter who had little interest in making 'an object that will stand and will not move', whose paintings from the start were restless and would not adopt the proprietorial stance of a fixed perspective. The poem remembers Lanyon saying 'Shall we go down' and go down he did, into the earth in his paintings, and rise he did on the thermals before eventually going down.

Both Graham and O'Hara insist on the social origin and hoped-for destination of lyric even when isolation and loss are felt most deeply, and hold out against the lure of abstraction by absorbing it through idioms New York poetry connects characteristically to Surrealism and Graham to Constructivism.[3] O'Hara's air in his two elegies is palpable not metaphysical, and 'The Thermal Stair' invites Lanyon, who may well have been grasping air as his glider crashed and his life ended, to 'Climb here where the hand | Will not grasp on air'. The waymarks of 'The Thermal Stair' are the shared places of artist and poet as in 'Dear Bryan Wynter'. Both of Graham's poems go walking to re-evoke the presence of the departed, along tracks familiar to him and his companions and quite possibly to them only. Yet the reader does not demur and feels the same solid ground underfoot. In a recent book on Lanyon, the artist Tacita Dean comments in a way equally applicable to O'Hara that the

> intimacy of the poem beguiles you into feeling you know the place that Lanyon knew. Both poet and painter understood that to evoke a sense of place is to do so indirectly, and that place is about the local, and about biography, actual or assumed, and that place is felt.[4]

The inventions of 'The Thermal Stair' are its title, constructed from the thermals on which Lanyon's glider rose and fell, and the attribution of 'Lanyon's stair' after 'Lanyon Quoit' to suggest a kind of Jacob's ladder dreamt up to heaven out of 'one of the stones of the place' (Gen. 28:11). Graham reconciles with air by making steps from it, a fancy corresponding to Lanyon's preparations for his aerial paintings with jury-rigged objects which he called 'airscapes', 'precipitations rather than constructions'.[5] But Graham's construction of a 'thermal stair' is followed immediately by the appeal: 'Uneasy, lovable man, give me your painting | Hand to steady me taking the word-road home.' W. S. Graham is a great poet of male friendship, taciturn and down to earth. His response to loss, rooted in the particulars of shared life and a friend's gestures, is to lay down his suffered taciturnity in words, a pavement others may walk beside him.

The structural armature of Lanyon's paintings is braced and buckled and decidedly resists finish. Lanyon came into his own as a painter through transfiguring landscape into worked surface, the product of both geological and meteorological forces and of human labour. Such labour is evident not only in the work of farming the refractory fields and meagre soil of Land's End, but crucially in the shaping of land by mining. Lanyon's family was long employed in Cornish tin mining, and thus in creating the typical Cornish postindustrial landscape of derelict chimneys, smelting houses and mineheads set against the granite outcrops and wind and wave violence of the Penwith peninsula. Mines extended far under the sea and their buildings clung to battered rock ledges. It was Lanyon's practice to subject his body to the utmost stress in order to work the surface of his painting as a broken whole-body analogue of this land's surface formation; he tunnelled underground, drove recklessly, rock-climbed, and eventually took to gliding overhead. He remarked that 'starting in an extreme awareness of oneself in a place ends in an extreme awareness of oneself in a painting'; so-called landscape painting therefore cannot be a mimetic practice for Lanyon but becomes a full phenomenological equivalent to terrene investigation and exploitation.[6]

Lanyon's masterpiece of painting-as-excavation is *St Just* of 1952–3, a painting I mentioned briefly in Chapter 7, named after the centre of Cornish tin mining, and roughly contemporary with de Kooning's early masterpiece *Excavation* of 1950. Both artists obsessively excavated the painted surface. De Kooning's painting is shallower in its layering; and while *St Just* may look very distant from Naum Gabo's immaculately finished constructions, so influential on Lanyon and Bryan Wynter, its worked surface relies on an armature first fabricated as a maquette, an underpinning rather than an airscape, made mostly of glass 'held precariously with bostik and painted only with black'.[7] Lanyon's designs for the painting were complex and contradictory; he began with studies for a crucifixion, a subject to which British painters turned in the early 1950s regardless of religious affiliation – Francis Bacon's crucifixions accord with William Empson's description of Christianity as a torture cult. Lanyon's crucifixion does not depict Christ's suffering, but commemorates workers killed in the Levant mining disaster of 1919, at a Cornish mine producing tin, copper and arsenic in harsh conditions. The 'man-engine' carrying miners up and down the main shaft collapsed, leaving, as Lanyon put it in a letter, 'those bits of miners, so much meat hanging from the man-engine collected up into shovel-fulls and processed to St Just for the laying in state'.[8] The painting's syncretic mythology also refers to 'welding together the bits of Osiris', and as Lanyon's letter suggests the *via dolorosa* is as much present as the crucifixion. Procession-processing relates *St Just* to Lanyon's established practice of hard trekking as groundwork for a landscape painting based on physical response rather than the eye's comprehensive survey. At the same time a contrary urge to pure abstraction survived through the painting's early states to the extent that in a December 1952 letter to the painter Ivon Hitchens he announced 'I have at last painted a painting with no colour like glass', before then subjecting it to sustained assault, as though the painting could survive only through incorporating its negative in colour opacity, thickness and the evidence of labour.[9]

Where hung in 2018 in the newly extended Tate St Ives, *St Just* is difficult to look at in one go. Its length forces me back further and further in the effort to take it in, and at any distance and angle one or another portion disappears in reflected glare. But the painting could never be grasped in its entirety as Clement Greenberg came to demand of 'advanced painting', ironically restating the possessive ambition of landscape painting; the Tate hanging enforces reception of *St Just* as a narrative, and that's part of what it is, although its continuous movement of swallowing and regurgitating forfends resolution. The painting may seem deprived of air, but its central shaft can be recognized as a windpipe as much as a digestive system, with a ribcage visible in the near-horizontal slashes across the pulmonary shapes or shields on either side of the black shaft in the painting's upper half. Although breath may conjure air, spirit, lightness and (literally) aspiration, here I find myself forced to see it as a physical process of intake and exhalation, in a depiction of going down into the earth and coming up 'over grass' (as miners call the surface). At the base of the shaft and the painting lies a confused tangle of roots or a pile of smashed flesh or an alimentary bonfire, with a looser tangle at the summit, perhaps of breath exhaled but also alluding to minehead winding gear.

Roughly contemporary paintings by Lanyon help to identify the hatched boundaries of the fields of Penwith through which a procession would pass from Levant to St Just (about nine miles). The shaft from this perspective rises through fields and settlements, to be laid out over grass even as its vertical is also the vertical of the painting, the dominant colour being a dull green evoking not only grass but the copper oxide staining of the Levant cliffsides. The dual perspective and the colour might suggest the corpse of the mine itself being dragged to rest. The painting's layering is troubled and troubling; at one moment I see the shaft with its top V-shape emerge like one of Giacometti's etiolated figures, powerful in its pathos; at another I see it recede cradled by the fields' shallow hollow. Physical experience of the land, below, above, along and offshore, does not allow separation of figure and ground, but nor does it reduce to a dead flatness. The painting breathes, it rises and falls, it eats and expels, and there is a generative conflict between the front-back and up-down rhythmic forces, further complicated by its horizontals and tangles.

The three poems addressed to painters in W. S. Graham's *Malcolm Mooney's Land*, published in 1970 and written over the preceding fifteen years, draw on intense debate in St Ives during this period about abstraction and landscape, and each poem is carefully attuned to the distinct practices of the painters. 'The Thermal Stair' excavates and overflies, and in keeping with Lanyon's respect for the work of fishermen and miners, thinks about the solitude of a poet's work and its dependence on the shaping work of generations of users of the language, its social proto-syntax. The poem comprises an exacting meditation on time, space, surface, landscape and abstraction in Lanyon's painting and in its own practice. Although Graham's poetry sustains a connection with ordinary speech, song and anonymous balladry, it resists the idea of song as spontaneous, autochthonous or readily available; Graham's peculiarly compressed and warped syntax is laborious in 'taking the word-road home' and asserts the origins of ballad and sea-shanty in rhythms of work. 'We all make it again' the poem records Lanyon as saying of the sea and that is true of the rhythm of verse also, which demands human society, a walking and working together across land and sea – a steadiness hard-won.

The stakes for Graham in Lanyon's art as it bears on his poetry and as set out in 'The Thermal Stair' can best be identified by comparison with two other late poems, 'The Constructed Space' and 'The Secret Name'. Both of these poems are obsessed, even anguished by the undecidability of prepositions despite their claim to map spatial relations, and by the problematic orientation of pronouns. The opening stanza of 'The Constructed Space' begins:

> Meanwhile surely there must be something to say,
> Maybe not suitable but at least happy
> In a sense here between us two whoever
> We are. Anyway here we are and never
> Before have we two faced each other who face
> Each other now across this abstract scene
> Stretching between us.[10]

The greater the effort at precision, the more apt to slip are the words laid down. 'Meanwhile' and 'between' are attempts at location spatially and temporally, frustrated from the start by an inability to specify who 'us two' might be. The thicket of conditionals, 'surely', 'must be', 'maybe', 'at least', 'whoever' and 'anyway', makes ground extremely difficult to establish. Characteristic of Graham is the extraordinary weight invested in everyday, usually weightless communicative phrases: 'in a sense', 'us two'. 'Us' and 'we' oscillate between internal and external reference, and 'faced each other who face' reduces the participants in 'this abstract scene' to coordinates, but coordinates that can be mapped only in relation to each other since 'this abstract scene' cannot be referred to a mappable place. But at the same time that such uncertainty jitters the phrasing, the two enjambed sentences make a performance of 'stretching between us'; this abstracted act of saying becomes an oddly intimate connective tissue allowing us to be 'at least happy'. 'The Constructed Space' belongs among the many Graham poems disturbed by the paradox of the poet's exclusion from human community through an artistic pursuit able to offer hospitality to a distant audience only through abstraction, but which overcome abstraction through intimate dialogue and tone.

Graham yearns for a poetry which feels as intimate as the verbal exchange between loving friends in a loved place, while abstract enough to embrace readers far removed in space and time. This poetic work might be compared with Lanyon's work on *St Just* between his preparatory 'Construction for St Just' and the eventual painting, a procession-processing that brings the abstract into sociality, place and history, retrospectively identifying the horizontals of the construction as machinery for descending into the earth. 'The Constructed Space' ends 'Yet here I am | More truly now this abstract act become'. 'Here I am' has become a recognized voice through verse. What is the abstract act? What is the action of abstraction, and the relation to it of the first person pronoun? The question bears on the poem's earlier contention that 'we know what we are saying | Only when it is said and fixed and dead'. How can a work of art be at once an object and an act, a construction and a space that admits new pronominal identifications, that is, new readers and lookers-in – how can a poem be both speech and text, and how can it be true to the poet and his love for another while true to the experience of unknowable, immitigably abstract others? In this poem 'you' might be a direct addressee, maybe after a pub discussion about pictorial abstraction with an artist, or the 'you' now reading these lines, or the 'you' that the poet's own words form in their transfer from imaginary speech to page to a voice-effect that cannot be the poet's or the reader's either, but an abstract voice both distant and near, both disembodied and entirely familiar as Graham's.

A closer focus on the stakes in 'The Thermal Stair' is afforded by the later three-part poem 'The Secret Name'. Naming is critical for Graham in pushing back against abstraction and the threat it bears of disembodiment into a mere coordinate, a pronoun. The first stanza of the poem announces almost belligerently:

> Whatever you've come here to get
> You've come to the wrong place. It
> (I mean your name.) hurries away
> Before you in the trees to escape.[11]

The highly irregular full stop inside the parentheses after 'name' enacts the stamp of naming; the name of a place or a person establishes place or person as an identifiable fixture. But here the name 'hurries away' from its referent and escapes into a wood of language divorced from signifying, a linguistic mass from which poems may possibly be made but into which the talking of people is sucked as into a black hole. All living creatures can be trapped in its syntactical vortex: 'Neath the boughs of the last black | Bird fluttered frightened in the shade | I think you might be listening'. Familiar speech is wrested away from its speakers, and in the wood the words 'move | As a darkness of my family'. There is only one name in this thirty-eight-line poem, and that is Madron Wood, visible from Graham's Madron home as his friends and diligent readers know. For them and for those unfamiliar with Graham, the name also resonates with the regular ballad form of the poem's first two sections. Names in ballad commemorate the named and make it legendary. Although the poem declares of Madron Wood 'It is only an ordinary wood' at the same time it is the fearful wood of folk tales and the language thicket that traps the poet, the devourer of familial, intimate, friendly speech. The final stanza of the poem brings a chilling interpellation by 'The long sigh of Outside' left at the end of the first section; now exhaled as 'The terrible, lightest wind in the world' it streams in a loosened rhythm, its signifiers seeking objects to possess. We are named by others. Or perhaps this lightest wind might be leading a reader deep into Madron Wood. The poem ends in a riddle:

> You maybe
> Did not know you had another
> Sound and sign signifying you.

You entered this poem looking for something and became the poem's 'you'. That now is the only name you have. In reflecting on this poem, the poignancy of Graham's practice of naming emerges; those whom his poems name most tenderly have died, and their names have escaped from their living referents. But as Elizabeth Helsinger writes of the nineteenth-century poetic attachment to song and ballad, Graham's frequent return to these genres

> opens prospects of impersonality or plurality, voices that may be heard as ghostly tunes or figures behind the poet's particular poem, the singer's present performance, summoning other voices present, past and future as it moves its listeners together, to a half-remembered tune.[12]

Such ghostliness is yet more disturbing in Graham's poems owing to their greater degree of abstraction, a constructed space and a language lifted from the earth and the living.

Peter Lanyon's last paintings track along the air-paths that would fail to support him. It is striking how closely in their abstract structure these paintings resemble his first constructions and recall the paintings of Ben Nicholson in that earlier period. Nicholson's bleached and standardized field systems with their exact divisions, little resembling the Cornish snatches of scanty cultivation, are now viewed from above, but through buffetings of wind, the stresses on the glider's fabric, sudden breaks in cloud, and rapid rises and descents. Dividing lines become scarifications, while swaths of atmospheric, meteorological colour pull even the colour-field abstraction vaunted by Greenberg into sharply urgent evidence of the earth. Lanyon's studies for these paintings are instructively described by Chris Stephens as designs rather than drawings. The paintings are at once constructivist and action painting, and also landscape painting although no longer named cartographically; instead they are *Solo Flight*, *Offshore*, *Thermal* and *Cloud Base*. For Lanyon there was no opposition between 'subject painting' and 'landscape painting'; at the time he was making his aerial canvases and 'precipitations' he wrote 'I believe in the subject as awareness in myself of place and time and in abstraction as the process of making'.[13]

'The Thermal Stair' is W. S. Graham's most sustained, determined exercise in naming. Its naming not only defers to Lanyon's ambivalence about abstraction and assertion of his work's primary loyalty to the English landscape painting tradition, but is generated too out of the coincidence of Lanyon's name with the megalithic Lanyon Quoit. Lanyon Quoit collapsed in the nineteenth century and its orientation was changed in re-erection, but there are few humanly contrived landscape features of West Cornwall of more massive and time-defiant presence; its capstone is 5.5 metres long, and weighs more than 12 tonnes. Thus while Peter Lanyon's name hurried away from him on his death, abandoning its living referent, his name remains installed both formidably and fortuitously on the moor he walked with Sydney Graham. Graham's poem names abandoned tin mines, Botallack, Ding Dong and Levant, as well as the coastal promontory of Gurnard's Head where the poet lived in a coastguard's hut before moving to Madron. Lanyon's home, Little Parc Owles, is named, as are Morvah and St Just, the population centres of the mining industry. The lighthouses Godrevy and the Wolf may stand for Lanyon's sexual magnetism, but also allude to his partiality for Lawrentian and Jungian sexual symbolism. The one painting by Lanyon named in the poem is *SARACINSECO*, Italian rather than Cornish, and the foreignness of this name from the poem's other named places may lead an unnamed woman to 'mention space', a degree of abstraction Lanyon was unlikely to approve. The poem also names the St Ives 'primitive' fisherman-painter Alfred Wallis, further insisting on place and all with a certain gruff sexism.

Graham makes two significant verbal coinages in 'The Thermal Stair'. Peter Riley, in his sensitive discussion of this poem, declares that the puzzling '"tin singers" are the old miners of the defunct Cornish tin mines who made paths from the moors down to the settlements, singing as they walked home (with the possible involvement of The Wizard of Oz)' Beyond the yellow brick road, there is the entailment of Tin Pan Alley – that is to say, popular song in general, and song here associated with physical labour and the homosociality of the pub. Riley continues:

> The writing has not really changed from the simple and direct mode of address of the rest of the poem; it has merely shifted into a local intimacy, continuing to address Lanyon in ways he would have understood perfectly.[14]

This identifies a characteristic of all Graham's poems addressed to friends; 'Dear Bryan Wynter' is full of in-jokes and private allusions which remarkably do not obstruct the accessibility of the poem – and this feature makes 'Dear Bryan Wynter' a masterpiece of Graham's art in reconciling intimate voice and abstracted universality. 'Lanyon's stair', the other invention in 'The Thermal Stair', names both the rising thermal that carries a glider high over land, an airy equivalent to the immensely ponderous Lanyon Quoit, and also puns as does the poem's title, on the fierce quality of Lanyon's looking as an artist, that is, Lanyon's stare. Not only does (or did) Lanyon stare, but he steers his body fearlessly in his art's service to the point of damage and even death: 'The poet or painter steers his life to maim | Himself somehow for the job.'

Song and ballad offer abstraction in rhythmic, corporeal and social form and also as blocks of 'stanza stone'. It was a dream of early Russian constructivists that their art would be recognized as truly popular in its origins and impulse, eliciting a unifying response in support of the new Revolutionary order. The tin singers track between places of work and dwelling, but the abstraction of names into a linguistic thicket or whisper of predatory signifiers can be resisted through the thickening of the dissevered names. Even as they hurry from their deceased and derelict referents, they may be restored in song, as at the end of this poem the names of Lanyon and of Ding Dong mine join with the tin singers' departing voices. 'Lanyon' has become a refrain, a touchstone:

> Lanyon, why is it you're earlier away?
> Remember me wherever you listen from.
> Lanyon, dingdong dingdong from carn to carn,
> It seems tonight all Closing bells are tolling
> Across the Duchy shire wherever I turn.

The repetition of 'wherever' induces none of the disorientation of unmoored deictics felt in 'The Secret Name'. Death may be tolled everywhere by 'Closing bells' as they strike the end of licensing hours, and the sense of loss pervades this poem palpably. Yet Lanyon is everywhere and may still, as the line preceding these asks of him, 'steady me taking the word-road home'. Home to Madron, where words lurk. But Lanyon Quoit, Lanyon stair, and the name 'Lanyon' are turning into song, a sounding 'dingdong dingdong'.

Graham's recorded reading of 'The Thermal Stair' is instructive, making it sound more akin to 'The Constructed Space' than at first it looks.[15] The relationship between the weight of simple words as blocks placed in syntactical and linear rows, their function as names asserted by the hard-edged Cornish names and the edge given to all words by Graham's Scottish accent, their activity as felt in an intimate address to the departed Peter Lanyon, and their urge towards song verging on nonsense or sonic abstraction (dingdong dingdong) – lead to an audible indecision between the dictates of metrical line (there are two patterns, one of five and one of three beats), the continuity of dialogue speech even if only one half is audible, and the particularity of stressed single-syllable words. Named place and abstract space are involved through Graham's song, as constructivist abstraction and tracked land are involved through Lanyon's painting which can be described by its measurements, 'Seventy-two by sixty', identified by place, *SARACINESCO*, and felt intimately through 'your painting | Hand'. The position from which Graham addresses Lanyon may be from 'a thermal', a warm breath rising high above, but the thermal is located – 'over Lanyon Quoit and the circling stones standing | High on the moor over Gurnard's Head'. The stones in Graham do not constitute a stone circle; they are 'circling stones standing' as though in mourning tribute about Lanyon Quoit, the stone representative of the painter. Like 'stanza my stone' the stones live. And the poem turns from present to past to the future perfect, life *as it would be if it had had existence*, talking to a dead man as though he were alive. As Graham writes in 'The Constructed Space': 'And yet I say | This silence here for in it I might hear you'. But who is heard in this 'abstract act', 'abstraction in the process of making' as Lanyon puts it?

Temporally 'The Constructed Space' starts in the suspended time of 'meanwhile'. Owing to Graham's preoccupation in earlier poems with the relationship between writer and reader, it is tempting to read the poem as continuing this negotiation, but that would be too straightforward. What is awaited is not the reader's response, but the emergent voice of the poem – awaited by both poet and reader. The amalgam grammared in the first person plural brings 'I' as poet or reader into transient unity with the poetic voice, into an unprecedented 'whoever | We are'. It is necessary to read the statement that these stanzas are 'mainly an obstacle to what I mean' as a positive achievement, allowing me or the poet to be met 'by some intention risen up out of nothing'. The silence of the text prepares for the poem's voice. As for *my* voice it will be engulfed in the event, in the 'abstract act', as act is engulfed in abstraction and as abstraction gives rise to act. Such coming-together is enacted in the assertive rhyming of the third and last stanza, brought to a limit-case in the simple repetition of 'mortal'. Perhaps the uncanniest effect of this poem is the last stanza's oscillations in rhyme and phrasal variation gradually coming to rest in death's invariant repetition, after the fluent syntax of the earlier stanzas stretching to cover the distance between those 'who face | Each other'.

What is 'our home'? Evidently it is death in its inevitability, but it is also 'stanza my stone' which unifies the reader with the poem in the aesthetic experience, the repeatedly evanescent act of the poem which must wear a changeable, mortal disguise in order to make this poetic enlivening possible, again and again breaking through 'the caught habits of language', Reuven Tsur's 'cognitive fossils'. The poem survives 'meanwhile', in its conditional-subjunctive hibernation, reanimated in our reading and reanimating us as we so need in these 'trying times'.

NOTES

Chapter 1

1. In 'Notes on a Poetry of Release', appendix to W. S. Graham, *The Nightfisherman. Selected Letters of W.S. Graham*. Manchester: Carcanet 1999, p. 379.
2. J. Hillis Miller, 'Anachronistic Reading', *Derrida Today*, Vol. 3, No. 1 (2010), p. 75.
3. Adrian Stokes, *Stones of Rimini in the Critical Writings of Adrian Stokes, Volume 1 1930–1937*. London: Thames and Hudson 1978, p. 194.
4. Adrian Stokes, 'The Future and Art', in Stokes, *A Game That Must Be Lost. Selected Papers*. Cheadle Hulme: Carcanet 1973, pp. 146–160.
5. Christopher Dewdney, *Concordat Proviso Ascendant. A Natural History of Southwestern Ontario. Book III*. Great Barrington, MA: The Figures 1991, p. 16.
6. Martin Thom, *Fair*. London: infernal methods 2018, pp. 3–4.
7. Quoted in Derek Attridge, *The Work of Literature*. Oxford: Oxford University Press 2015, p. 57.
8. Attridge, *Work of Literature*, p. 56.
9. Kevin Powers, 'What Kept Me from Killing Myself', *New York Times*, June 16, 2018.
10. https://www.poetryfoundation.org/poems/42657/the-day-lady-died
11. Ted Berrigan, *The Sonnets*. New York: Penguin Poets 2000. The 5:15 time-stamp occurs in Sonnets II, XVIII, XXX, XLII, LXXX, LXXXII and the final Sonnet, LXXXVIII. Another recurrent time-stamp is 3:17, in Sonnets LXXVII, LXXXI and LXXXIII.
12. Barbara Guest, 'A Noise of Return', in *The Collected Poems of Barbara Guest*, ed. Hadley Haden Guest [henceforward, Guest *CP*]. Middletown, CT: Wesleyan University Press 2008, p. 500.
13. https://www.poetryfoundation.org/poems/43434/the-man-on-the-dump
14. Miller, 'Anachronistic Reading', p. 81.

Chapter 2

1. The lyric to the song written by Bob Crewe and Kenny Nolan can readily be discovered online, for instance at www.lyricstime.com/patti-labelle-lady-marmalade-lyrics.html.
2. Eve Kosofsky Sedgwick, 'A Poem Is Being Written', *Representations*, No. 17, Special Issue: The Cultural Display of the Body (Winter 1987), pp. 110–143.
3. Sigmund Freud, 'An Outline of Psycho-Analysis', *Standard Edition*, Vol. 23 (1940a [1938]), p. 148.
4. Robert Herrick, *Hesperides: Or, The Works Both Humane and Divine of Robert Herrick*, Vol. 1. London: William Pickering 1846, p. 220.
5. Isabelle Stengers, *Thinking with Whitehead: A Free and Wild Creation of Concepts*, trans. Michael Chase. Cambridge, MA: Harvard University Press 2011, p. 216.

6   Henri Meschonnic, 'The Rhythm Party Manifesto', trans. David Nowell Smith, *Thinking Verse* I (2011), p. 165. [Internet journal: www.thinkingverse.com]
7   Mutlu Konuk Blasing, *Lyric Poetry. The Pain and the Pleasure of Words*. Princeton, NJ: Princeton University Press 2007, p. 53.
8   *Shakespeare's Sonnets*, ed. Katherine Duncan-Jones. London: The Arden Shakespeare 2010, pp. 144–145.
9   Duncan-Jones notes regarding 'filled': 'Q's 'fild' has been modernized as *filled*, but the possibility of a play on "filed," = polished, rhetorically refined, cannot be excluded.' *Shakespeare's Sonnets*, p. 144, n. 2.
10 Denise Riley, *Time Lived, Without Its Flow*. London: Capsule Editions 2012, p. 56.
11 Charles Baudelaire, *Les Fleurs du Mal*, edition critique ed. Jacques Crépet et Georges Blin, refondue par Georges Blin et Claude Pichois. Paris: Librairie José Corti 1968, pp. 143–144.
12 Charles Baudelaire, *Flowers of Evil: From the French of Charles Baudelaire*, trans. George Dillon and Edna St. Vincent Millay. New York: Harper & Bros 1936, pp. 150–153 (parallel French: English text). The translation of this poem is attributed to Millay alone.
13 Algernon Charles Swinburne, review of Charles Baudelaire, *Les Fleurs du Mal* published *Spectator* 35, September 6, 1862, http://www.uni-due.de/lyriktheorie/texte/1862_swinburne.html.
14 Brian Massumi, *Semblance and Event. Activist Philosophy and the Occurrent Arts*. Cambridge, MA: MIT Press 2011, p. 21. Alain Badiou, 'Language, Thought, Poetry', in Badiou, *Theoretical Writings*, ed. and trans. Ray Brassier and Alberto Toscano. London: Continuum 2004, p. 233.
15 Allen Grossman, 'On Communicative Difficulty', in *True-Love, Essays on Poetry and Valuing*. Chicago, IL: Chicago University Press 2009, p. 160.
16 W. R. Bion, 'Commentary', in *Second Thoughts. Selected Papers on Psycho-Analysis*. New York: Jacob Aronson 1984, p. 163.
17 Blasing, *Lyric Poetry*, p. 47. Here I conflate her argument with a Kleinian developmental story.
18 John Berryman, 'Homage to Mistress Bradstreet', in Berryman, *Collected Poems 1937–1971*, ed. and int. Charles Thornbury. New York: Farrar, Straus and Giroux 1989 [1953], pp. 131–148. In the first book publication of this poem, illustrated by Ben Shahn, the numbered stanzas are divided by bold lines crossing the full width of the print area, legitimating a narrow focus of attention on a particular stanza, as here on stanza 55. John Berryman, *Homage to Mistress Bradstreet*. New York: Farrar, Straus & Cudahy 1956.
19 Berryman glosses 'wet brain' as 'edema' in a footnote.
20 Petrarch's canzone 'Nel dolce tempo de la prima etade' may have provided Shakespeare with his sonnet's pen, ink and stone.
21 Allen Grossman, 'Hard Problems in Poetry', in *True-Love*, p. 33.
22 Jonathan Culler, 'Why Lyric?' *PMLA*, Vol. 123, No. 1 (January 2008), pp. 201–206 (6).
23 I borrow this summary phrase from a review by Paul D. Myers of Nicolas Abraham, 'Rhythms: On the Work, Translation, and Psychoanalysis', *MLN*, Vol. 111, No. 5 (December 1996), p. 1040.
24 Collected in ed. Donald Allen, *The Collected Poems of Frank O'Hara*. New York: Knopf 1972, pp. 252–257. [Henceforward, O'Hara *CP*.]
25 Adrian Stokes, *Smooth and Rough* in *The Critical Writing of Adrian Stokes Volume II, 1937–1958*. London: Thames and Hudson 1978, p. 245.

26 Bill Brown, 'Martial Art', *PMLA*, Vol. 124, No. 5 (October 2009), pp. 1787–1793.
27 See, for instance, Finlay's brief exposition of 'The Boat's Blueprint' cited in Alec Finlay's excellent introductory essay to Ian Hamilton Finlay, *Selections*. Berkeley: California University Press 2012, p. 3.
28 Drew Milne, 'Adorno's Hut: Ian Hamilton Finlay's Neoclassical Rearmament Programme', *Jacket*, Vol. 15 (December 2001), http://jacketmagazine.com/15/finlay-milne.html.
29 D. W. Winnicott, *Playing and Reality*. Harmondsworth: Penguin Books 1974, p. 111.
30 O'Hara *CP*, pp. 302–303.
31 As Paulina cries in *The Winter's Tale*, Act V, Scene III.

Chapter 3

1 Geoffrey Hill, 'September Song', in *Broken Hierarchies: Poems 1952–2012*. Oxford: Oxford University Press 2013, p. 44.
2 Ben Jonson, 'On My First Son', in *Ben Jonson (The Oxford Authors)*, ed. Ian Donaldson. Oxford: Oxford University Press 1985, pp. 236–237.
3 Diana Fuss, *Dying Modern: A Meditation on Elegy*. Dunham, NC: Duke University Press 2013, p. 8.
4 David Kennedy, *Elegy*. London: Routledge 2007, p. 7.
5 Fuss, *Dying Modern*, p. 3; Sam Ladkin, 'Ornate and Explosive Grief. A Comparative Commentary on Frank O'Hara's "In Memory of My Feelings" and "To Hell with It," Incorporating a Substantial Gloss on The Serpent in the Poetry of Paul Valéry, and a Theoretical Excursus on Ornate Poetics', *Glossator*, Vol. 8 (2013), p. 201.
6 Ed. Anthony and Ben Holden, *Poems That Make Grown Men Cry: 100 Men on the Words That Move Them*. New York: Simon & Schuster 2014.
7 W. H. Auden, 'In Memory of W.B. Yeats', in W. H. Auden, *Collected Poems*, ed. Edward Mendelson. New York: The Modern Library 2007, pp. 245–247.
8 Peter M. Sacks, *The English Elegy. Studies in the Genre from Spenser to Yeats*. Baltimore, MD: Johns Hopkins University Press 1985, p. 15.
9 William Wordsworth, 'A Slumber Did My Spirit Seal', in William Wordsworth, *The Poems. Volume One*, ed. John O. Hayden. Harmondsworth: Penguin Books 1977, p. 364.
10 O'Hara *CP*, pp. 302–303.
11 Graham insisted on capitalizing titles of poems, so: THE CONSTRUCTED SPACE. See, for example, his letter of 4 May 1979 to Peter Moldon of Faber and Faber regarding the first *Collected Poems*: 'It is necessary that the titles of the poems should be printed in caps, every word. Please believe that this is not an affectation. It goes with the kind of "word-conscious" poetry I try to write' (Graham, *The Nightfisherman*, p. 356). Since this decision was related to stipulations about a poem's appearance on the page in his published collections, I have decided against applying it to citations within the text of this book.
12 Fiona Green, 'Achieve Further through Elegy', in *W. S. Graham: Speaking Towards You*, ed. R. Pite and H. Jones. Liverpool: Liverpool University Press 2004, esp. pp. 152–154.
13 W. S. Graham, 'Dear Bryan Wynter', in W. S. Graham, *New Collected Poems* ed. Matthew Francis. [Henceforward, Graham, *NCP*.] London: Faber and Faber 2004, pp. 258–260.

14 Angela Leighton, 'Only Practicing How to Speak to Speak. W.S. Graham's Art of Letter Writing', *PN Review* 200, Vol. 37, No. 9 (June–July 2011), pp. 54–58.
15 Hannah Brooks-Motl, 'W. S. Graham: "Dear Bryan Wynter": How a Poem Brings Language to Loss and Speaks to the Dead', A Poetry Foundation Poem Guide on-line at, http://www.poetryfoundation.org/learning/poem/242916#guide
16 Green, 'Achieve Further through Elegy', p. 153.
17 The Housman poem is as follows:

LII. Far in a western brookland

FAR in a western brookland
   That bred me long ago
The poplars stand and tremble
   By pools I used to know.

There, in the windless night-time,
   The wanderer, marvelling why,
Halts on the bridge to hearken
   How soft the poplars sigh.

He hears: no more remembered
   In fields where I was known,
Here I lie down in London
   And turn to rest alone.

There, by the starlit fences,
   The wanderer halts and hears
My soul that lingers sighing
   About the glimmering weirs.

18 Accessible at The Poetry Archive, https://www.poetryarchive.org/poem/dear-bryan-wynter
19 W. S. Graham, 'Two Poems on Zennor Hill', in *NCP*, p. 209.
20 Peter Riley, review of W. S. Graham, *New Collected Poems*, *Jacket* 26, October 2007, http://jacketmagazine.com/26/rile-grah.html
21 Graham, *NCP*, p. 37 and pp. 178–182, respectively.
22 James Schuyler, 'Buried at Springs', in *Collected Poems*. New York: Farrar, Straus and Giroux 1993, pp. 42–44.
23 Adam Phillips, 'Contribution to "A Symposium on Forsaken Favorites"', *The Threepenny Review*, 117 (Spring 2009), http://www.threepennyreview.com/samples/phillips_sp09.html (Accessed 1 September 2014).
24 Daniel Tiffany, *My Silver Planet: A Secret History of Poetry and Kitsch*. Baltimore, MD: Johns Hopkins University Press 2014, see esp. chapter 1.
25 'Poem in October', first publ. in *Horizon* and *Poetry* (Chicago), February 1945; repr. in ed. John Goodby, *The Collected Poems of Dylan Thomas*. London: Weidenfeld & Nicolson 2014, pp. 160–162. [Henceforward, Thomas *CP*.] Goodby traces the poem's composition to the summer of 1944, but follows previous editors in admitting the possibility of an earlier date (Thomas *CP*, p. 385).
26 I'm referring here to 'The seed-at-zero', Thomas *CP*, pp. 87–88.
27 Paulo César Sandler, *The Language of Bion: A Dictionary of Concepts*. London: Karnac 2005, p. 97.
28 This notebook poem, 'Now the Thirst Parches Lip and Tongue' does not appear in Thomas *CP*. See ed. Daniel Jones, *The Poems of Dylan Thomas*. New York: New

Directions, revised edition 2003, p. 37. Or in another early poem of heterosexual intercourse, 'Their faces shone under some radiance', which ends a little more subtly: 'the suicides parade again, now ripe for dying' (Thomas *CP*, pp. 19–20 (p. 20)).

29 Isobel Armstrong, 'The Caesura', lecture given at the conference, 'The Languages of Literature: Attridge at 70', University of York, May 2015.
30 *Dylan Thomas: The Caedmon Collection* [CD set] intro. Billy Collins (2002).
31 Jacques Derrida, *Monolingualism of the Other; or, The Prosthesis of Origin*, trans. Patrick Mensah. Stanford, CA: Stanford University Press 1998, p. 48. Qtd by David Nowell Smith, *On Voice in Poetry: The Work of Animation*. Basingstoke: Palgrave Macmillan 2015, p. 65.
32 Édouard Glissant, 'Open Circle, Lived Relation', in *Poetics of Relation*, trans. Betsy Wing. Ann Arbor: University of Michigan Press 1997, p. 200.
33 John Goodby, *The Poetry of Dylan Thomas. Under the Spelling Wall*. Liverpool: Liverpool University Press 2013, p. 389.
34 Specifically, 'Poem in October' 'has seven ten-line stanzas with a syllabic count of 9, 12, 9, 3, 5, 12, 12, 5, 3, 9', as Alan Bold notes in *Dylan Thomas: Craft or Sullen Art*. London: Vision Press and New York: St. Martin's Press 1990, p. 160.
35 Armstrong, 'The Caesura'.
36 John Hollander, 'Marianne Moore's Verse', in *The Work of Poetry*. New York: Columbia University Press 1997, pp. 250–270 (pp. 261 and 257).
37 'Poem in October', Thomas *CP*, pp. 160–162 (p. 160).
38 'Syllabic Verse', in *The Princeton Encyclopaedia of Poetry and Poetics*, fourth edition. Princeton, NJ: Princeton University Press 2012, pp. 1388–1390 (p. 1389).
39 'The Origin of the Work of Art', in Martin Heidegger, *Off the Beaten Track*, ed. and trans. Julian Young and Kenneth Haynes. Cambridge: Cambridge University Press 2002, esp. p. 23.
40 'I Know This Vicious Minute's Hour', *Poems of Dylan Thomas*, p. 48; Thomas *CP*, pp. 4–5.
41 Geoffrey Grigson, 'How Much Me Now Your Acrobatics Amaze', in *The Harp of Aeolus*. London: Routledge 1947, p. 157: '(Here perhaps I should interpolate that the second, just-construable piece which I quoted from Mr. Thomas, is one made up by myself of disconnected lines from three stanzas of one poem [...] it reads, I am convinced, as authentically as most of Mr. Thomas's stanzas.)' Needless to say, it doesn't.
42 'Poem in October', Thomas *CP*, p. 160.
43 'Poem in October', Thomas *CP*, pp. 161–162.
44 Sigmund Freud, *Inhibitions, Symptoms and Anxiety*, in *The Standard Edition of the Complete Psychological Works of Sigmund Freud*, Vol. 20, trans. James Strachey, in collaboration with Anna Freud, assisted by Alix Strachey and Alan Tyson. London: Vintage 2001 [1925–1926], pp. 87–156 (p. 138).
45 Cited in John Haffenden, *William Empson. Volume II: Against the Christians*. Oxford: Oxford University Press 2006, p. 485.
46 'Before I knocked', Thomas *CP*, pp. 38–39.
47 'Before I knocked', Thomas *CP*, p. 38.
48 W. R. Bion, 'Caesura', in *The Complete Works of W. R. Bion*, 16 volumes, ed. Chris Mawson and Francesca Bion. London: Karnac 2014, Vol. 5, pp. 1–51 (p. 40).
49 'Before I knocked', Thomas *CP*, p. 39.
50 Thomas to Vernon Watkins, 26 August 1944, *CL*, p. 580.
51 Friedrich Hölderlin, 'Remarks on *Oedipus*', (1803), trans. Stefan Bird-Pollan in *Classic and Romantic German Aesthetics*, ed. J. M. Bernstein. Cambridge: Cambridge University Press 2003, pp. 194–202 (p. 195).

52 'A Refusal to Mourn the Death, By Fire, of a Child in London', Thomas *CP*, pp. 172–173.
53 Bion, 'Caesura', p. 49.
54 David Nowell Smith, *Sounding/Silence: Martin Heidegger at the Limits of Poetics*. New York: Fordham University Press 2013, p. 52.
55 'Poem in October', Thomas *CP*, p. 161.
56 Bion, 'Caesura', p. 38.
57 'Fern Hill', Thomas *CP*, pp. 177–179.
58 'Fern Hill', Thomas *CP*, pp. 177–178.
59 'The seed-at-zero', Thomas *CP*, p. 87.

Chapter 4

1 Roger Caillois, *The Writing of Stones*, trans. Barbara Bray. Charlottesville: University Press of Virginia 1985, p. 11.
2 Caillois, *The Writing of Stones*. p. 75.
3 Jennifer Scappettone, *Killing the Moonlight: Modernism in Venice*. New York: Columbia University Press 2014, p. 232.
4 Ezra Pound, *The Cantos of Ezra Pound*. London: Faber and Faber 1987, p. 76.
5 Pound, *Cantos*, p. 607.
6 Ezra Pound, 'Swinburne Versus Biographers', *Poetry*, Vol. 11, No. 6 (March 1918), p. 328.
7 Caillois, *Writing of Stones*, p. 74.
8 Tim Dayton, *Muriel Rukeyser's The Book of the Dead*. Columbia: University of Missouri Press 2003, esp. chapter 1, 'Muriel Rukeyser and the Gauley Tunnel Tragedy', pp. 5–29.
9 'Rukeyser's association with documentary film began at an early age, and *The Life of Poetry* contains several references to Rukeyser's experiences cutting, editing and writing for motion pictures, as well as her admiration for the "unity of imagination" in American and British documentary film efforts. Having studied film editing in 1935 […]'. Catherine Gander, *Muriel Rukeyser and Documentary: The Poetics of Connection*. Edinburgh: Edinburgh University Press 2013, p. 8.
10 Muriel Rukeyser, 'The Dam', in *The Collected Poems of Muriel Rukeyser*, ed. Janet E. Kaufman and Anne F. Herzog. Pittsburgh: University of Pittsburgh Press 2005 (henceforward, Rukeyser *CP*), pp. 99–102 (p. 100).
11 It should however be noted that in his review of Rukeyser's *U.S. 1*, the first third of which consists of *The Book of the Dead*, William Carlos Williams noted approvingly Rukeyser's use of original documents, comparing it with Pound's in *The Cantos*. *New Republic* 94, 1938, pp 141–142, cited by Dayton, *Rukeyser's The Book of the Dead*, p. 121.
12 Charles Altieri, *Painterly Abstraction in Modernist American Poetry: The Contemporaneity of Modernism*. Cambridge: Cambridge University Press 1989, p. 389.
13 George Oppen, 'Daybook I', in *Selected Prose, Daybooks, and Papers* [henceforward Oppen *SP*], ed. Stephen Cope. Berkeley: California University Press 2007, p. 53.
14 Oren Izenberg, 'Oppen's Silence, Crusoe's Silence, and the Silence of Other Minds', *Modernism/Modernity*, Vol. 13 (January 2006), pp. 787–811.

15 Robert Duncan, letter to Denise Levertov, 7 May 1963, *The Letters of Robert Duncan and Denise Levertov*, ed. Robert J. Bertholf and Albert Gelpi. Stanford: Stanford University Press 2004, p. 401.
16 Étienne Gilson, quoted in Daniel B. Gallagher, 'Integritas and the Aesthetic Appreciation of Incomplete Artworks', PsyArt, 2006, http://psyartjournal.com/article/show/b_gallagher-integritas_and_the_aesthetic_appreciatio
17 Oppen, letter to Charles Tomlinson, 5 May 1963, *The Selected Letters of George Oppen*, ed. Rachel Blau DuPlessis. Durham, NC: Duke University Press 1990, p. 82. [Henceforward Oppen *SL*].
18 Oppen, letter to Serge Fauchereau, [14 October 1966], Oppen *SL*, p. 146.
19 Oppen, letter to Tomlinson, Oppen *SL*, p. 82.
20 Oppen, letter to Fauchereau, [25 July 1966] and letter to John Crawford, [Summer 1966], Oppen *SL*, pp. 141, 144.
21 Oppen, 'The Poem', in *New Collected Poems*, ed. Michael Davidson. New York: New Directions 2002 [henceforward, Oppen *NCP*], p. 270.
22 Oppen, letter to Fauchereau, [14 October 1966], Oppen *SL*, p. 146.
23 Andrea Brady, 'Object Lessons', review of *New Collected Poems* by Oppen, *Poetry Review*, Vol. 94 (Spring 2004), p. 66.
24 Peter Nicholls, *George Oppen and the Fate of Modernism*. Oxford: Oxford University Press 2007, p. 92.
25 Oppen, ['The Knowledge Not of Sorrow, You Were'], ['Closed Car—Closed in Glass'], and ['This Land':], *NCP*, pp. 5, 13, 16.
26 Oppen, letter to Julian Zimet, [late April or May 1966], Oppen *SL*, p. 33.
27 See Oppen, ['Fragonard'], *NCP*, p. 27 and ['She Lies, Hip High'], ['Near Your Eyes—'], ['O City Ladies'], Oppen *NCP*, pp. 20, 26, 29.
28 Oppen, 'Technologies', Oppen *NCP*, p. 93. Rather startlingly, Mary Oppen records that on returning from the Great War her brother 'Wendell vowed, "After working in a bank, never again will I work at anything that requires that I look through a window at the world"' (Mary Oppen, *Meaning a Life*. Santa Barbara, CA: Black Sparrow 1978, p. 43).
29 Oppen, letter to Diane Meyer, [1963 or 1964], Oppen *SL*, p. 97 and 'Statement on Poetics', Oppen *SP*, p. 49. This latter document is dated 1975.
30 Oppen, letter to Diane Meyer, [Fall 1973], Oppen *SL*, pp. 266–267.
31 Oppen, 'Daybook V', Oppen *SP*, p. 226.
32 Nicholls, *George Oppen*, pp. 118–119.
33 See John Wilkinson, 'Frostwork and the Mud Vision', in *The Lyric Touch: Essays on the Poetry of Excess*. Cambridge: Salt Publishing 2007, pp. 176–188.
34 See Monique Claire Vescia, 'The Lyrical Apertures of George Oppen's Discrete Series', in *Depression Glass: Documentary Photography and the Medium of the Camera Eye in Charles Reznikoff, George Oppen, and William Carlos Williams*. New York: Routledge 2006, pp. 63–95.
35 Oppen, 'Daybook III', Oppen *SP*, p. 167.
36 Guest *CP*, pp. 81–82. See John Ashbery, 'The Instruction Manual', in *Some Trees*. New Haven, CT: Yale University Press 1956, pp. 26–30.
37 'Daybook II:V', Oppen *SP*, p. 137. Oppen's immediate target is the magazine *The New Yorker*, but through personification the invective extends to the city's denizens.
38 Oppen, *Meaning a Life*, p. 200.
39 Heidegger, 'Origin of the Work of Art', p. 16.
40 Oppen, letter to Donald Davie, [after 20 February 1973], Oppen *SL*, p. 258.

41 'Daybook V', Oppen *SP*, pp. 222, 218, 224.
42 'The Mind's Own Place', Oppen *SP*, p. 32.
43 Norma Cole, 'The Poetics of Vertigo', *Denver Quarterly*, Vol. 34 (Winter 2000), p. 71.
44 Jacques Rancière, *The Politics of Aesthetics: The Distribution of the Sensible*, trans. Gabriel Rockhill. London: Continuum 2004, p. 34.
45 'Twenty-Six Fragments', Oppen *SP*, fragment 20, p. 239.
46 Cope, headnote to 'Twenty-Six Fragments', in Oppen, *SP*, p. 231.
47 See *From Fin-de-Siécle to Negritude* and *From Postwar to Millennium*, Vols. 1 and 2 of *Poems for the Millennium: The University of California Book of Modern and Postmodern Poetry*, ed. Jerome Rothenberg and Pierre Joris. Berkeley: California University Press 1995, 1998, and ronsilliman.blogspot.com
48 Oppen, letter to Tomlinson, 31 August 1964, Oppen *SL*, p. 386 n. 8.
49 See Barrett Watten, *The Constructivist Moment: From Material Text to Cultural Poetics*. Middletown, CT: Wesleyan University Press 2003, pp. xvi–xvii.
50 Cary Nelson, 'Developing the Cultural Epic: Muriel Rukeyser's Documentary Testament (Part 5)', transcribed at https://www.coursera.org/learn/modern-american-poetry/lecture/Uu56U/developing-the-cultural-epic-muriel-rukeysers-documentary-testament-part-5
51 Rukeyser *CP*, pp. 73–74.
52 W. H. Auden, *The English Auden. Poems, Essays, and Dramatic Writings, 1927–1939*, ed. Edward Mendelson. New York: Random House 1977. The quotations are from poem X 'We made all possible preparations', p. 26, and XII 'From scars where kestrels hover', p. 28.
53 Dayton, *Rukeyser's The Book of the Dead*, p. 17.
54 Dayton, *Rukeyser's The Book of the Dead*, pp. 8, 15.
55 Muriel Rukeyser, *The Book of the Dead*, intr. Catherine Venable Moore. Morgantown: West Virginia University Press 2018.
56 Michael Davidson, *Ghostlier Demarcations: Modern Poetry and the Material World*. Berkeley: University of California Press 1997, p. 148.
57 Muriel Rukeyser, *The Life of Poetry*. New York: Current Books 1949, pp. 24–25.
58 Rukeyser *CP*, pp. 77–78.
59 Both quotations are from 'The Face of the Dam: Vivian Jones', Rukeyser *CP*, pp. 76–77.
60 Rukeyser *CP*, p. 76.
61 'Mearl Blankenship', Rukeyser *CP*, p. 83.
62 Caillois, *The Writing of Stones*, p. 75.
63 'The Book of the Dead', Rukeyser *CP*, pp. 106–111, both quotations p. 110.
64 Muriel Rukeyser, 'The Usable Truth', *Poetry*, Vol. LVIII, No. 4 (July 1941), p. 207.
65 The interview is printed as Appendix III to Dayton, *Rukeyser's Book of the Dead*, pp. 143–148.
66 Gander, *Muriel Rukeyser and Documentary*, esp. 'The Melville Revival', pp. 126–130.
67 Rukeyser, *The Life of Poetry*, pp. 117–178.
68 Rukeyser, *The Life of Poetry*, p. 158.
69 Rukeyser, *The Life of Poetry*, p. 152.
70 Rukeyser *CP*, p. 107.
71 Rukeyser, *The Life of Poetry*, p. 223.
72 Muriel Rukeyser, 'Gauley Bridge'. *Films. A Quarterly Discussion and Analysis*, Vol. 1, No. 3 (Summer 1940). New York: Kamin Publishers, pp. 51–64.
73 Rukeyser, 'Gauley Bridge', p. 52.

74 Dayton, *Rukeyser's The Book of the Dead*, p. 19. See also Catherine Venable Moore, intro. to Rukeyser, *The Book of the Dead*, pp. 1–51.
75 Rukeyser, 'Gauley Bridge', p. 55.
76 Rukeyser, 'Gauley Bridge', p. 53.
77 Rukeyser *CP*, pp. 110–111.

Chapter 5

1 Michael Beggs, 'The Flattest Kind of Picture: Texture and Matière in Photography at Black Mountain College', in *Begin to See: The Photographers of Black Mountain College*, ed. Julie J. Thomson. Asheville, NC: Black Mountain Museum + Arts Center 2017, p. 79.
2 'Adventures of Children: A Portfolio of Photographs. Narrative by Muriel Rukeyser', *Coronet*, Vol. 6, No. 5 (1 September 1939), pp. 23–38. The double-page spread is on pp. 26–27.
3 'Worlds Alongside: A Portfolio of Photographs. Narrative by Muriel Rukeyser', *Coronet*, Vol. 6, No. 6 (1 October 1939), pp. 83–98. The contrasted photographs are on p. 88.
4 Rukeyser, 'Worlds Alongside', pp. 90–91. The caption is printed on p. 90.
5 Rukeyser, 'Worlds Alongside', p. 97.
6 Walter Benjamin, 'The Author as Producer', trans. Anna Bostock in *Art in Theory 1900–2000: An Anthology of Changing Ideas*, ed. Charles Harrison and Paul Wood, New edition. Oxford: Blackwell 2003, p. 496.
7 Maurice Merleau-Ponty, 'Cézanne's Doubt', in *The Merleau-Ponty Aesthetics Reader*, ed. Galen A. Johnson. Evanston, IL: Northwestern University Press 1993, p. 65.
8 Joes Segal, *Art and Politics. Between Purity and Propaganda*. Amsterdam: Amsterdam University Press 2016, p. 8.
9 Barbara Savedoff, 'Documentary Authority and the Art of Photography', in *Photography and Philosophy*, ed. Scott Walden. Oxford: Blackwell 2008, p. 121.
10 Roland Barthes, *Camera Lucida*, trans. Richard Howard. London: Vintage Books 2000, p. 4.
11 Quoted in James Rhem, *Aaron Siskind*. London: Phaidon Press 2003, p. 11.
12 Simon Baker, 'Photography's Sense of Abstraction', in *Shape of Light: 100 Years of Photography and Abstract Art*, ed. Simon Baker and Emmanuelle de l'Ecotais. London: Tate Publishing 2018, p. 92.
13 See Rhem, *Aaron Siskind*, p. 6 and Michael Reid, *Convergence/Divergence. Exploring Black Mountain College + Chicago's New Bauhaus/Institute of Design*. Exhibition catalogue. Asheville, NC: Black Mountain Museum + Arts Center 2015, p. 51.
14 Rhem, *Aaron Siskind*, p. 3.
15 Thomas B. Hess, 'Introduction', in *Places. Aaron Siskind Photographs*. New York: Light Gallery and Farrar, Straus and Giroux 1976, pp. 6–7.
16 *Aaron Siskind 100*. New York: Powerhouse Books, a Blind Spot Book 2003, np.
17 Gilles Mora, *Aaron Siskind. Another Photographic Reality*. Austin: University of Texas Press 2014, p. 22. Quoted from a draft of an interview in the Aaron Siskind archives.
18 Schuyler, *Collected Poems*, pp. 42–44.

19 The phrase 'substratum of instantaneity' is the photographer Jeff Wall's, quoted in Kaja Silverman, *Miracle of Analogy, or, The History of Photography, Part 1*. Stanford: Stanford University Press 2015, p. 68.
20 John Ashbery, *Reported Sightings: Art Chronicles, 1957–1987*, ed. David Bergman. Manchester: Carcanet 1989, p. 317.
21 Fairfield Porter, 'Class Content in American Abstract Painting', in Fairfield Porter, *Art in Its Own Terms. Selected Criticism 1935–1975*, ed. Rackstraw Downes. New York: Taplinger Publishing Company 1979, p. 253.
22 Ed. Ted Leigh, *Material Witness. The Selected Letters of Fairfield Porter*. Ann Arbor: The University of Michigan Press 2005, p. 145.
23 Rhem, *Aaron Siskind*, p. 62–63.
24 Reproduced in Mora, *Aaron Siskind*, p. 75.
25 Sheryl Conkelton, essay in *Aaron Siskind: The Fragmentation of Language*, catalogue accompanying the exhibition at the Robert Mann Gallery, New York 1997, p. 5.
26 Reproduced in Mora, *Another Photographic Reality*, p. 74.
27 Conkelton, *The Fragmentation of Language*, p. 4.
28 https://www.metmuseum.org/art/collection/search/266507
29 Reproduced in Mora, *Aaron Siskind*, p. 91.
30 Lesley Stonebridge, *The Destructive Element: British Psychoanalysis and Modernism*. Basingstoke: Macmillan Press 1998, p. 84.
31 Ella Freeman Sharpe, 'Similar and Divergent Unconscious Determinants Underlying the Sublimations of Pure Art and Pure Science (1935)', in *Collected Papers on Psycho-Analysis*, ed. Marjorie Brierley. New York: Brunner/Mazel 1978, pp. 140–141.
32 Carl Chiarenza, *Aaron Siskind. Pleasures and Terrors*. Boston, MA: Little, Brown and Center for Creative Photography 1982, p. 147.
33 https://www.moma.org/collection/works/56277
34 http://www.artic.edu/aic/collections/artwork/102581
35 Phillip Barcio, *Ideelart* Blog, http://www.ideelart.com/module/csblog/post/365-1-aaron-siskind.html
36 Chiarenza, *Aaron Siskind*, p. 171.
37 Chiarenza, *Aaron Siskind*, pp. 189–190.
38 Roger Caillois, *The Mask of Minerva*, trans. George Ordish. New York: Clarkson N. Potter Inc. 1964, p. 126.
39 Silverman, *Miracle of Analogy*, p. 105.
40 Merleau-Ponty, 'Cézanne's Doubt', p. 65.
41 Charles Olson, *Mayan Letters*, ed. Robert Creeley. London: Jonathan Cape 1968, p. 64.
42 David Trotter, *Literature in the First Media Age: Britain between the Wars*. Cambridge, MA: Harvard University Press 2013, p. 149.
43 Hugh MacDiarmid, 'On a Raised Beach', in *Complete Poems*, ed. Michael Grieve and W. R. Aitken. London: Penguin 1994, Vol. 1, pp. 422–433.
44 Trotter, *Literature in the First Media Age*, p. 153.
45 MacDiarmid, 'First Hymn to Lenin', *Complete Poems*, Vol. 1, p. 199.
46 MacDiarmid, 'On a Raised Beach', p. 422. Trotter notes that the promised turn from optic to haptic is not realized in the return to 'synthetic English' at the end of the poem. Trotter, *Literature in the First Media Age*, p.157.
47 J. H. Prynne, *Poems*, third edition. Hexham: Bloodaxe Books 2015, pp. 637–662.
48 MacDiarmid's political thinking and activity is surveyed in Bob Purdie, *Hugh MacDiarmid. Black, Green, Red & Tartan*. Cardiff: Welsh Academic Press 2012.
49 Trotter, *Literature in the First Media Age*, p. 157.

Chapter 6

1. Lisa Robertson, *Nilling: Prose Essays on Noise, Pornography, The Codex, Melancholy, Lucretius, Folds, Cities and Related Aporias*. Toronto: Bookthug 2012. "Time in the Codex" pp. 11–12, and citing Erich Auerbach, 'Figura' (1938), in n.1.
2. As noted by Alessandra Zamperini, *Paulo Veronese*. London and New York: Thames & Hudson 2014, p. 292.
3. *Treasures of the Fitzwilliam Museum*. London: Scala Publishing 2005, p. 32.
4. Richard Cocke, *Paolo Veronese: Piety and Display in an Age of Religious Reform*. Aldershot: Ashgate 2001, p. 31.
5. The absence in the English-language literature on Veronese of any mention of this extraordinary passage of paint mystifies me. I have expected to find a reference to clumsy restoration, vandalism, an incompetent assistant etc., but so far as I can find it is simply ignored.
6. Cocke, *Paolo Veronese*, p. 1.
7. All quotations and citations are from Ovid, *Metamorphoses*, trans. A. D. Melville. Oxford: Oxford University Press 1986, pp. 46–49.
8. So Heidegger: 'Hermes is the divine messenger. He brings the message of destiny; *hermeneuein* is that exposition which brings tidings because it can listen to a message'. 'A Dialogue on Language', in Martin Heidegger, *On the Way to Language*, trans. Peter D. Hertz. New York: Harper & Row 1971, p. 29.
9. Wenn der Schnee ans Fenster fällt,
   Lang die Abendglocke läutet,
   Vielen ist der Tisch bereitet
   Und das Haus ist wohlbestellt.

   Mancher auf der Wanderschaft
   Kommt ans Tor auf dunklen Pfaden.
   Golden blüht der Baum der Gnaden
   Aus der Erde kühlem Saft.

   Wanderer tritt still herein;
   Schmerz versteinert die Schwelle.
   Da erglänzt in reiner Helle
   Auf dem Tische Brot und Wein.

   The translation is by Albert Hofstadter, from Martin Heidegger, *Poetry, Language and Thought*, trans. and ed. Albert Hofstadter. New York: Perennial Classics 2001, pp. 194–195.
10. See, for instance, Jacques Derrida, *Of Spirit*, trans. Geoffrey Bennington and Rachel Bowlby, Chicago, IL: Chicago University Press 1989.
11. 'Language in the Poem', in Heidegger, *On the Way to Language*, p. 181.
12. Wallace Stevens, 'The Noble Rider and the Sound of Words', in *The Necessary Angel: Essays on Reality and the Imagination*. New York: Vintage 1951, p. 25.
13. Throughout this discussion of Hölderlin and Heidegger, for consistency I use Michael Hamburger's translation of Hölderlin's 'Brod und Wein' rather than that supplied in *On the Way to Language*. See Friedrich Hölderlin, *Poems and Fragments*, trans. Michael Hamburger. Cambridge: Cambridge University Press 1980, pp. 242–253 (parallel German and English texts). See also Heidegger, *On the Way to Language*, p. 139.

14 Heidegger, *On the Way to Language*, p. 149.
15 David Farrell Krell, 'Marginalia to Geschlecht III: Derrida on Heidegger on Trakl', *CR: The New Centennial Review*, Vol. 7, No. 2 (Fall 2007), pp. 175–199. My quotations are both from p. 182.
16 J. H. Prynne, *Field Notes: 'The Solitary Reaper' and Others*. Cambridge, privately printed 2007.
17 William Blake, *Visions of the Daughters of Albion*, First published by William Blake in 1793. *Blake: The Complete Poems*. ed. W.H. Stevenson, third edition. Harlow: Pearson Longman 2007, pp. 179–193. I have followed the lineation and consulted the notes to this edition, but resisted its modernized orthography and punctuation. http://www.blakearchive.org has been consulted for reproductions of the original plates.
18 'The thought of the poem begins only after the complete disobjectification of presence'. Badiou, 'Language, Thought, Poetry', p. 238.
19 Heidegger, 'Language in the Poem', in *On the Way to Language*, p. 160.
20 '"An Einen Frühverstorbenen"/"To One Who Died Young"', in Georg Trakl, *Poems & Prose*, trans. Alexander Stillmark, bilingual edition. London: Libris 2001, pp. 74–77. The lines in German are 'Seele sang den Tod, die grüne Verwesung des Fleisches | Und es war das Rauschen des Walds'.
21 '"Frühling der Seele II"/ "Springtime of the Soul II"', in Trakl, *Poems & Prose*, pp. 98–101.
22 Trakl, *Poems & Prose*, p. 176.
23 Ed. Michael Rossington, Cian Duffy, Kelvin Everest, and Michael Rossington, *The Poems of Shelley*, Vol. 3, 1819–1820. Harlow: Pearson Education 2011, pp. 221–222. All quotations are from this edition.
24 *The Poems of Shelley*, Vol. 3, p. 223.
25 Ed. Michael Rossington, Jack Donovan, and Kelvin Everest, *The Poems of Shelley*, Vol. 4, 1820–1821. London: Routledge 2014, pp. 35–43.
26 Julia Kristeva, *Revolution in Poetic Language*, trans. Margaret Waller. New York: Columbia University Press 1984, pp. 25–26.
27 Ed. Ian Brinton, *An Andrew Crozier Reader*. Manchester: Carcanet 2012, p. 246.
28 By Ian Brinton, in a review of ed. Rod Mengham and John Kinsella, *Vanishing Points, New Modernist Poems* where Crozier's poem first appeared. *The Use of English*, Vol. 56, No. 3 (Summer 2005), pp. 266–270.
29 Philip Larkin, 'Aubade', in *Collected Poems*, ed. Anthony Thwaite. New York: Farrar, Straus and Giroux 2004, pp. 190–191.
30 Kristeva, *Revolution in Poetic Language*, p. 26.
31 J. H. Prynne, 'Die a Millionaire', in *Kitchen Poems*. London: Cape Goliard Press 1968, np. The cover of this book also features a grid.
32 William Blake, 'Introduction' [first two stanzas of four], in *Songs of Innocence and Experience*. Oxford: Oxford University Press 1970, p. 29.

Chapter 7

1 Percy Bysshe Shelley, 'The Cloud', *The Poems of Shelley*, Vol. 3 (2011), pp. 355–364.
2 David Trotter, 'Voices-Off', in *The L=A=N=G=U=A=G=E Book*, ed. Bruce Andrews and Charles Bernstein. Carbondale and Edwardsville: Southern Illinois University Press 1984, p. 252. Originally published in *Twisted Wrist*, 4, Paris 1979, np.

3   Hart Crane, 'The Broken Tower', in *Complete Poems and Selected Letters*, ed. Langdon Hammer. New York: The Library of America 2006, pp. 106–107.
4   Prynne, *Poems*, p. 499.
5   J. H. Prynne, *The Oval Window*, ed. N. H. Reeve and Richard Kerridge. Hexham: Bloodaxe 2018.
6   See David Nowell-Smith, 'The Art of Fugue: Heidegger on Rhythm', *Gatherings: The Heidegger Circle Annual*, Vol. 2 (2012), p. 56, quoting Heidegger, *Introduction to Metaphysics*, trans. Gregory Fried and Richard Polt. New Haven, CT: Yale University Press 2000, p. 164.
7   Badiou, 'Language, Thought, Poetry', p. 235.
8   Justin Katko, 'Sex – *Triodes* – Gilgamesh', in *On the Late Poetry of J.H Prynne: Hix Eros No.4*, ed. Joe Luna and Jow Lindsay Walton. Brighton: High Zero and Sad Press, 2014, pp. 43–60.
9   J. H. Prynne, *Triodes*. Cambridge: Barque Press 1999. Robin Purves, 'J.H. Prynne's *Triodes*'. *The Paper*, Vol. 7 (November 2003), pp. 47–63. Passage quoted on p. 49.
10 Barbara Guest, 'An Emphasis Falls on Reality' in Guest *CP*, pp. 221–222. However the line 'The necessary idealizing of you reality' is incorrectly printed as *your* reality, as confirmed by both the poem's earlier inclusion in the collection Barbara Guest, *Fair Realism*. Los Angeles, CA: Sun & Moon Press 1989, and in Barbara Guest's reading of the poem online at Penn Sound.
11 Allen Grossman, *True-Love*. Chicago: Chicago University Press 2009, p. 149.
12 Barbara Guest, *Poems. The Location of Things; Archaics; The Open Skies*. New York: Doubleday 1962. The poem is reprinted in Guest *CP*, pp. 9–10.
13 Barbara Guest, *Quill, Solitary* APPARITION. Sausalito, CA: The Post-Apollo Press 1996.
14 Barbara Guest, *Dürer in the Window: Reflexions on* Art. New York: Roof Books 2003, item, p. 13.
15 Hartigan's comment is to be found at http://library.syr.edu/digital/exhibits/i/imagine/section8.htm. The four lithographs are reproduced alongside the poem in Terrence Diggory, *Grace Hartigan and The Poets: Paintings and Prints*, the catalogue of an exhibition at Skidmore College. Saratoga Springs, NY 1993, pp. 42–47. The first two lithographs seem to represent window spaces in ruins overlooking a Mediterranean scene.
16 Theodore W. Adorno, *Aesthetic Theory*, trans. Robert Hullot-Kentor. Minneapolis: University of Minnesota Press 1997, p. 89.
17 See Rachel Blau DuPlessis, 'The Gendered Marvelous: Barbara Guest, Surrealism and Feminist Reception', in *The Scene of My Selves: New Work on New York School poets*, ed. Terence Diggory and Stephen Paul Miller. Orono, ME: The National Poetry Foundation 2001, pp. 189–203.
18 'Barbara Guest and Kathleen Fraser, in conversation with Elisabeth Frost and Cynthia Hogue', *Jacket*, 25, http://jacketmagazine.com/25/guest-iv.html
19 See Jennifer Ashton, 'The Numbers Trouble with 'Numbers Trouble', *Chicago Review*, Vol. 53, No. 2/3 (Autumn 2007), pp. 112–120.
20 Geoffrey Ward, *Statutes of Liberty*, second edition. Basingstoke: Palgrave Macmillan 2001, p. 197.
21 Veronica Forrest-Thomson, *Poetic Artifice: A Theory of Twentieth-Century Poetry*. Manchester: Manchester University Press 1978, p. 156.
22 Barbara Guest, *The Blue Stairs*. New York: Corinth Books 1968, pp. 32–33; Guest *CP*, pp. 81–82.

23   Guest *CP* pp. 85–91.
24   *The Blue Stairs*, p. 17. A detailed analysis of the sonic texture of 'Saving Tallow' is presented in my paper '"Couplings of Such Sonority": Reading a Poem by Barbara Guest', *Textual Practice*, Vol. 23, No. 3 (2009), pp. 481–502.
25   *The Türler Losses*, p. 8.
26   Guest's reading of *The Türler Losses* is available through the Penn Sound site: http://mediamogul.seas.upenn.edu/pennsound/authors/Guest/Location-of-Things/Guest-Barbara_15_TurlerLosses_NY_1984.mp3. The first print publication was: Barbara Guest, *The Türler Losses* M.B.M. Monograph Series no.5. Montréal: Book Mart Ltd. 1979. The revised version appears in Guest, *Fair Realism*, pp. 91–114 as 'Türler Losses', and in Guest *CP* pp. 169–188 as 'The Türler Losses'.
27   *The Türler Losses*, p. 14. *The Türler Losses* is unpaginated; page references here are numbered from the opening page of the poetic text.
28   Barbara Guest, *Herself Defined: The Poet H.D. and Her World*. New York: Doubleday 1964.
29   Guest confirms 'that poem did come out of those trips' in 'Barbara Guest and Kathleen Fraser, in conversation with Elisabeth Frost and Cynthia Hogue', *Jacket* 25, February 2004, http://jacketmagazine.com/25/guest-iv.html
30   *Herself Defined*, p. ix–x.
31   *Herself Defined*, p. 228.
32   Erika Duncan, 'ENCOUNTERS: Hearing a Poet, but Understanding Little', *New York Times*, (25 September 1994).
33   *The Türler Losses*, p. 17.
34   Barbara Guest, *The Confetti Trees*. Los Angeles, CA: Sun & Moon Press 1999.
35   'Letter from Barbara Guest to Susan Gervitz, excerpt', *HOW(ever)*, Vol. 4, No. 4 (April 1988), http://www.asu.edu/pipercwcenter/how2journal/archive/print_archive/0488post.html
36   Barbara Guest, *Biography*. Providence, RI: Burning Deck 1980, part Four, np.
37   H. D., *Collected Poems 1912–1944*. New York: New Directions 1983, pp. 509–511.
38   *Biography* part Six. The 'e's appear in part Three.
39   Blasing, *Lyric Poetry*, pp. 37–38.
40   *The Türler Losses*, p. 3.
41   *The Türler Losses*, pp. 26, 28.
42   *The Türler Losses*, p. 25.
43   Barbara Guest, *The Red Gaze*. Middletown, CT: Wesleyan University Press 2005. See, for instance, 'Echoes', 'Composition'.
44   'Barbara Guest and Kathleen Fraser, in conversation with Elisabeth Frost and Cynthia Hogue', *Jacket* 25.
45   'The Barbara Guest Memory Bank' is at http://www.asu.edu/pipercwcenter/how2journal/bg_memorybank/bg_memory.html
46   'Letter from Barbara Guest to Susan Gervitz, excerpt', www.asu.edu/pipercwcenter/how2journal/archive/print_archive/0488post.html; Duncan, 'ENCOUNTERS',
47   For Marjorie Welish's poems see, for instance, *The Annotated 'Here' and Selected Poems*. Minneapolis, MN: Coffee House Press 2000.
48   Barbara Guest, *Rocks on a Platter*. Hanover, NH: Wesleyan University Press 1999. Guest *CP* pp. 425–448. References in the text are to the first publication.
49   *Rocks on a Platter*, p. 35; Adorno, *Aesthetic Theory*, p. 6.
50   Barbara Guest, *If So, Tell Me*. London: Reality Street Editions 1999, p. 25; Guest *CP*, p. 380.

51 Robert Kaufman, 'A Future for Modernism: Barbara Guest's Recent Poetry', *American Poetry Review*, Vol. 29 No. 4 (2000), p. 14. Kaufman also notes the allusion to Adorno in the book's subtitle.
52 Guest *CP*, pp. 71–72.
53 Susan Stewart, *Poetry and the Fate of the Senses*. Chicago: University of Chicago Press 2002, p. 111.
54 At 'The Barbara Guest Memory Bank', http://www.asu.edu/pipercwcenter/how2journal/bg_memorybank/bg_memory.html
55 Barbara Guest, *Biography*, np. The line occurs in part Six, Guest *CP*, p. 186.
56 Both in the 'Barbara Guest Feature' at *Jacket* 10 (January 2000), http://jacketmagazine.com/10/index.shtml
57 *Rocks on a Platter*, pp. 8, 45.
58 Sara Lundquist, '"Two Voices, One Joking": The Metapoetic Comedy of Barbara Guest's Poetry', *Jacket* 25, February 2004, http://jacketmagazine.com/25/guest-lund.html
59 Barbara Guest, *Forces of Imagination, Writing on Writing*. Berkeley, CA: Kelsey St Press 2003.
60 Barbara Guest, *Seeking Air*. Los Angeles, CA: Sun & Moon Press 1997, p. 84.
61 *Seeking Air*, p. 168.
62 *If So, Tell Me*, p. 27. Guest *CP*, pp. 381–382.
63 Forrest-Thomson, *Poetic Artifice*, pp. 65–80.
64 Ian Patterson, *The Glass Bell*. London: Barque 2009, np. The line is from the first sonnet in the sequence 'Glossolalia'.

Chapter 8

1 Jack Spicer, 'After Lorca', in Spicer, *My Vocabulary Did This to Me. The Collected Poetry of Jack Spicer*, ed. Peter Gizzi and Kevin Killian. Middletown, CT: Wesleyan University Press 2008, p. 123.
2 'A Step away from Them', O'Hara *CP*, p. 257.
3 Timothy Morton, *Hyperobjects. Philosophy and Ecology after the End of the World*. Minneapolis: University of Minnesota Press 2013, p. 20.
4 Drew Milne, 'Nuclear Song', *Angelaki: Journal of the Theoretical Humanities*, Vol. 22, No. 3 (2017), pp. 77–85.
5 Adam Phillips, *Winnicott*. Harmondsworth: Penguin Books 2007, p. 136.
6 D. W. Winnicott, 'Ego Distortion in Terms of True and False Self' (1960), in Winnicott, *The Maturational Processes and the Facilitating Environment*. London: Karnac 1990, p. 147.
7 D. W. Winnicott, 'Communicating and Not Communicating Leading to a Study of Certain Opposites', in Winnicott, *The Maturational Processes*, p. 185.
8 Layli Long Soldier, '*Example:*', in *Whereas*. Minneapolis, MN: Greywolf Press 2017, p. 27.
9 Winnicott, 'Communicating and Not Communicating', p. 187.
10 Morton, *Hyperobjects*, p. 14.
11 Drew Milne, 'Poetry after Hisoshima?' *Angelaki: Journal of the Theoretical Humanities*, Vol. 22, No. 3 (2017), pp. 87–102.
12 Morton, *Hyperobjects*, p. 43.

13. Amitav Ghosh, *The Great Derangement. Climate Change and the Unthinkable.* Chicago, IL: University of Chicago Press 2016, p. 7.
14. Ghosh, *The Great Derangement*, p. 84.
15. Tyehimba Jess, *Olio*. Seattle, WA and New York: Wave Books 2016; Shane McCrea, *In the Language of My Captor*. Middletown, CT: Wesleyan University Press 2017.
16. Forrest Gander and John Kinsella, *Redstart. An Ecological Poetics*. Iowa City: University of Iowa Press 2012, p. viii.
17. See Ghosh, *The Great Derangement*, p. 87.
18. Franco 'Bifo' Berardi, *Uprising: Poetry and Finance*. Los Angeles, CA: Semiotext(e) 2012, pp. 157–158. Several intermediate paragraphs omitted.
19. Joshua Kotin, *Utopias of One*. Princeton, NJ: Princeton University Press 2017, p. 78.
20. Andrew Pickering, 'Poesis in Action: Doing Without Knowledge'. Paper given at the conference, *Weak Knowledge: Forms, Functions, and Dynamics*, Goethe University, Frankfurt, 2–4 July 2017. My thanks to Judith Farquahar for the transcript.
21. Sam Solnick, *Poetry and the Anthropocene. Ecology, Biology and Technology in Contemporary British and Irish Poetry*. London: Routledge 2017, p. 172.
22. J. H. Prynne, 'Poetic Thought', *Textual Practice*, 24, No. 4 (2010), pp. 595–606, p. 596.
23. Long Soldier, *Whereas*, p. 64.
24. Jonathan Lear, *Radical Hope. Ethics in the Face of Cultural Devastation*. Cambridge, MA: Harvard University Press 2006, pp. 145–146.
25. Lear, *Radical Hope*, p. 51.
26. Lear, *Radical Hope*, pp. 140–141.
27. Edward Dorn, *Slinger*. Berkeley, CA: Wingbow Press 1975, p. 111.
28. Cody-Rose Clevidence, *Perverse, All Monstrous*. Berkeley, CA: Nion Editions 2017, p. 28.
29. W.R. Bion, 'Attacks on Linking', in *Second Thoughts*. London: H. Karnac 1984, pp. 93–109 (p. 98).
30. Stephen Collis, 'Drew Milne's Marxist Lichens", *Jacket 2*, 21 August 2017, https://jacket2.org/commentary/drew-milnes-marxist-lichens
31. Drew Milne, "News from Lichen Times', in Milne, *In Darkest Capital. Collected Poems*. Manchester: Carcanet Press 2017, p. 373.
32. Sam Smiles, 'Representation and Reality in West Country Landscapes', in *Places of the Mind: British Watercolour Landscapes 1850–1950*, ed. Kim Sloan. London: Thames & Hudson and The British Museum 2017, p. 136.
33. Andrew Causey, *Peter Lanyon, Modernism and the Land*. London: Reaktion Books 2006, p. 149.
34. 'Summary' of research by Dr Sarah Jovan, 'Lichen Are Indicators of Climate Change in Southern Alaska's Forests', USDA Forest Service, 2014, https://www.fs.fed.us/research/highlights/highlights_display.php?in_high_id=662
35. Adam Piette, reviews of Rachel Blau DuPlessis, *Days and Works*, Drew Milne, *In Darkest Capital: Collected Poems* and Iain Britton, *The Intaglio Poems* http://www.manifold.group.shef.ac.uk/issue19/AdamPietteBM19.html
36. Milne, 'Symboliste Propaganda', *In Darkest Capital*, p. 423.
37. Sigmund Freud, 'Thoughts for The Times on War and Death', in *The Standard Edition of the Complete Psychological Works of Sigmund Freud*, Vol. XIV (1914–1916): *On the History of the Psycho-Analytic Movement, Papers on Metapsychology and Other Works*, p. 288.
38. Milne, 'Thence This Must', *In Darkest Capital*, p. 405.
39. Stokes, 'The Future and Art', pp. 146–160.

40 'A Strategy for Ruination. An Interview with China Miéville', *Boston Review* online, 8 January 2018, http://bostonreview.net/literature-culture-china-mieville-strategy-ruination
41 Dodi Goldman, 'Vital Sparks and the Forms of Things Unknown', in *Donald Winnicott Today*, ed. Jan Abram. New York: Routledge 2013, p. 331.
42 Graham, 'Malcolm Mooney's Land', in Graham *NCP*, pp. 153–157.
43 Graham, 'Clusters Travelling Out', pt.7, Graham *NCP*, pp. 194–195.

Chapter 9

1 Ivor Gurney, *Collected Letters*, ed. R. K. R. Thornton. Ashington: The Mid Northumberland Arts Group and Manchester: Carcanet 1991, p. 547 & p. 549.
2 Michael Hurd, *The Ordeal of Ivor Gurney*. Oxford: Oxford University Press 1978, pp. 24 and 53.
3 Ivor Gurney, *Collected Poems*, ed. P. J. Kavanagh. Manchester: Carcanet 2004, p. 315.
4 Tiffany, *My Silver Planet*, p. 13.
5 I have discussed this previously in 'Too-Close Reading: Poetry and Schizophrenia', in John Wilkinson, *The Lyric Touch*. Cambridge: Salt 2007, pp. 157–167.
6 Andrea Brady, 'The Other Poet: John Wieners, Frank O'Hara, Charles Olson', in *Don't Ever Get Famous: Essays on New York Writing after the New York School*, ed. Daniel Kane. Champaign, IL: Dalkey Archive Press 2006, pp. 317–347.
7 See my 'Chamber Attitudes', in *The Lyric Touch*, pp. 215–250.
8 John Wieners, *Selected Poems, 1958–1984*, ed. Raymond Foye. Santa Barbara, CA: Black Sparrow Press 1986, p. 109.
9 W. R. Bion, *Attention and Interpretation, in the Complete Works of W. R. Bion*, ed. Chris Mawson, Vol. VI. London: Karnac Books 2014, pp. 235–238.
10 'In Public', in Wieners, *Selected Poems, 1958–1984*, p. 148.
11 John Wilkinson, 'Mark Hyatt's Poésie Brut', in *Hidden Agenda. Unreported Poetics*, ed. Louis Armand. Prague: Literaria Pragensia 2010, pp. 48–62.
12 Blasing, *Lyric Poetry*, p. 13.
13 Mark Hyatt, *A Different Mercy*. Cambridge: infernal methods 1976, p. 29.
14 Clevidence, *Perverse, All Monstrous*, p. 44.
15 Rudy Vermote, 'The Sane and the Insane Psychotic', in *'Attacks on Linking' Revisited. A New Look at Bion's Classic Work*, ed. Catalina Bronstein and Edna O'Shaughnessy. London: Karnac Books 2017, p. 85.
16 Bion, *Attention and Interpretation*, p. 270, and Chris Mawson's introduction, pp. 215–216.
17 Bion, *Attention and Interpretation*, p. 280.
18 Clevidence, *Perverse, All Monstrous*, p. 45.
19 Bion, *Attention and Interpretation*, p. 315.
20 S. T. Coleridge, 'Shakespeare's Judgment Equal to His Genius', in *The Critical Tradition. Classic Texts and Contemporary Trends*, ed. David H. Richter. Boston, MA: Bedford/St Martin's, third edition 1994, pp. 323–325.
21 Dewdney, *Concordat Proviso Ascendant*, pp. 15–16.
22 Christopher Dewdney, *A Palaeozoic Geology of London, Ontario*. Toronto: The Coach House Press 1973, np.
23 Adrian Stokes, *Michelangelo. A Study in the Nature of Art in the Critical Writings of Adrian Stokes Volume III 1955–1967*. London: Thames and Hudson 1978, p. 37.

24 Jacques Rancière, *Aisthesis. Scenes from the Aesthetic Regime of Art*, trans. Zakir Paul. London: Verso 2013, p. 7.
25 Stokes, *Michelangelo*, p. 57.
26 Leo Bersani, '"The Culture of Redemption": Marcel Proust and Melanie Klein", *Critical Inquiry*, Vol. 12, No. 2 (Winter 1986), p. 414.
27 Winnicott, 'Communicating and Not Communicating', p. 187.
28 Stokes, *Michelangelo*, pp. 64-65.
29 N. Katherine Hayles, *How We Became Posthuman. Virtual Bodies in Cybernetics, Literature, and Informatics*. Chicago, IL: University of Chicago Press 1999, pp. 286-291.
30 Reuven Tsur, *Poetic Conventions as Cognitive Fossils*. Oxford: Oxford University Press 2017, p. 258.
31 Tsur, *Poetic Conventions*, p. 245.
32 Reitha Pattison, 'Empty Air: Charles Olson's Cosmology', in *Contemporary Olson*, ed. David Herd. Manchester: Manchester University Press 2015, p. 62.
33 Ronald Johnson, *Radi os*. Chicago, IL: Flood Editions 2005, p. 3.
34 This section appears less spectacularly in Clevidence, ~~FLUNG~~ THRONE. Boise, ID: Ahsahta Press 2018, pp. 91-92.
35 W.R. Bion, *Further Cogitations. 1968-1969* in *The Complete Works of W. R. Bion*, ed. Chris Mawson, Vol. XV. London: Karnac Books 2014, p. 80.
36 Christopher Dewdney, *Spring Trances in the Control Emerald Night*. Berkeley, CA: The Figures 1978, p. 37.
37 Clevidence, ~~FLUNG~~ THRONE, p. 8.
38 Heidegger, 'The Origin of the Work of Art', p. 23.
39 William Blake, *Jerusalem*, plate 18. My thanks to Tom Mitchell for drawing my attention to these lines.

Chapter 10

1 This provides an opportunity to correct a careless error in my paper on O'Hara's Odes, where I mistake 'Bird in Flight' for Brancusi's 'Bird in Space', misnaming Brancusi's sculpture. There may be an allusion but not an identity. John Wilkinson, '"Where Air Is Flesh": The *Odes* of Frank O'Hara', in *Frank O'Hara Now. New Essays on the New York Poet*, ed. Robert Hampson and Will Montgomery. Liverpool: Liverpool University Press 2010, p. 112.
2 Graham *NCP*, pp. 163-166.
3 I say more about abstraction and Graham in 'Drift and Pop: On Writing about W.S. Graham', *Poetry*, Vol. 206, No. 4 (July/August 2015), pp. 427-433.
4 Tacita Dean, 'Then the Wind's Hand Brushed the Picture Away', in *Peter Lanyon*, ed. Chris Stephens. London: Tate St Ives 2010, p. 120.
5 ed. Toby Treves and Barnaby Wright, *Soaring Flight. Peter Lanyon's Gliding Paintings*. London: The Courtauld Gallery and Paul Holberton Publishing 2015, p. 125.
6 Lanyon quoted in Causey, *Modernism and the Land*, p. 189.
7 Chris Stephens, *Peter Lanyon: At the Edge of Landscape*. London: 21 Publishing 2000, p. 110.
8 Stephens, *At the Edge of Landscape*, p. 108.
9 Stephens, *At the Edge of Landscape*, p. 110.

10 Graham *NCP*, pp. 161–162.
11 Graham *NCP*, pp. 237–238.
12 Elizabeth K. Helsinger, *Poetry and the Thought of Song in Nineteenth-Century Britain*. Charlottesville: University of Virginia Press 2015, p. 32.
13 Treves and Wright, *Soaring Flight*, p. 125.
14 Riley, review of Graham *NCP*.
15 Reading accessible on The Poetry Archive, https://www.poetryarchive.org/poem/thermal-stair

BIBLIOGRAPHY

Adorno, Theodore W. *Aesthetic Theory*, translated by Robert Hullot-Kentor. Minneapolis: University of Minnesota Press, 1997.
Altieri, Charles. *Painterly Abstraction in Modernist American Poetry: The Contemporaneity of Modernism*. Cambridge: Cambridge University Press, 1989.
Ashbery, John. *Reported Sightings. Art Chronicles, 1957–1987*, edited by David Bergman. Manchester: Carcanet, 1989.
Ashbery, John. *Some Trees*. New Haven: Yale University Press, 1956.
Ashton, Jennifer. 'The Numbers Trouble with "Numbers Trouble"'. *Chicago Review* 53, no. 2/3 (Autumn 2007): 112–20.
Attridge, Derek. *The Work of Literature*. Oxford: Oxford University Press, 2015.
Auden, W. H. *Collected Poems*, edited by Edward Mendelson. New York: The Modern Library, 2007.
Auden, W. H. *The English Auden: Poems, Essays, and Dramatic Writings, 1927–1939*, edited by Edward Mendelson. New York: Random House, 1977.
Badiou, Alain. *Theoretical Writings*, edited and translated by Ray Brassier and Alberto Toscano. London: Continuum, 2004.
Baker, Simon. 'Photography's Sense of Abstraction'. In *Shape of Light: 100 Years of Photography and Abstract Art*, edited by Simon Baker and Emmanuelle de l'Ecotais, 87–95. London: Tate Publishing, 2018.
Barcio, Phillip. 'How Aaron Siskind Found Abstraction on the Streets'. *Ideelart* Blog. March 2018. Available online: http://www.ideelart.com/module/csblog/post/365-1-aaron-siskind.html (accessed 24 April 2018).
Barthes, Roland. *Camera Lucida*, translated by Richard Howard. London: Vintage Books, 2000.
Baudelaire, Charles. *Flowers of Evil: From The French of Charles Baudelaire*, translated by George Dillon and Edna St. Vincent Millay. New York: Harper & Bros., 1936.
Baudelaire, Charles. *Les Fleurs du Mal*, critique edition, edited by Jacques Crépet and Georges Blin, reworked by Georges Blin and Claude Pichois. Paris: Librairie José Corti, 1968.
Beggs, Michael. 'The Flattest Kind of Picture: Texture and Matière in Photography at Black Mountain College'. In *Begin to See: The Photographers of Black Mountain College*, edited by Julie J. Thomson, 79–81. Asheville: Black Mountain Museum + Arts Center, 2017.
Benjamin, Walter. 'The Author as Producer', translated by Anna Bostock. In *Art in Theory 1900–2000: An Anthology of Changing Ideas*, edited by Charles Harrison and Paul Wood, 493–98, New edition, Oxford: Blackwell, 2003.
Berardi, Franco "Bifo". *Uprising: Poetry and Finance*. Los Angeles: Semiotext(e), 2012.
Berrigan, Ted. *The Sonnets*. New York: Penguin Poets, 2000.
Berryman, John. *Collected Poems 1937–1971*, edited and introduced by Charles Thornbury. New York: Farrar, Straus and Giroux, 1989.
Berryman, John. *Homage to Mistress Bradstreet*. New York: Farrar, Straus & Cudahy, 1956.
Bersani, Leo. '"The Culture of Redemption": Marcel Proust and Melanie Klein'. *Critical Inquiry* 12, no. 2 (Winter 1986): 399–421.

Bion, W. R. *The Complete Works of W. R. Bion*, 16 volumes, edited by Chris Mawson and Francesca Bion. London: Karnac, 2014.

Bion, W. R. *Second Thoughts: Selected Papers on Psycho-Analysis*. New York: Jacob Aronson, 1984.

Blake, William. *Blake: The Complete Poems*, edited by W. H. Stevenson, third edition. Harlow: Pearson Longman, 2007.

Blake, William. *Songs of Innocence and Experience*. Oxford: Oxford University Press, 1970.

Blake, William. *Visions of the Daughters of Albion*, First published by William Blake, 1793.

Blasing, Mutlu Konuk. *Lyric Poetry: The Pain and the Pleasure of Words*. Princeton: Princeton University Press, 2007.

Bold, Alan. *Dylan Thomas: Craft or Sullen Art*. London: Vision Press; New York: St. Martin's Press, 1990.

Brady, Andrea. 'Object Lessons, George Oppen, New Collected Poems'. *Poetry Review* 94, no. 1 (Spring 2004), 64–70.

Brady, Andrea. 'The Other Poet: John Wieners, Frank O'Hara, Charles Olson'. In *Don't Ever Get Famous: Essays on New York Writing after the New York School*, edited by Daniel Kane, 317–47. Champaign: Dalkey Archive Press, 2006.

Brinton, Ian. 'Review of *Vanishing Points, New Modernist Poems*, edited by Rod Mengham and John Kinsella'. *The Use of English* 56, no. 3 (Summer 2005): 266–70.

Brooks-Motl, Hannah. 'W.S. Graham: "Dear Bryan Wynter": How a Poem Brings Language to Loss and Speaks to the Dead'. *Poetry Foundation*. Available online: http://www.poetryfoundation.org/learning/poem/242916#guide (accessed 19 August 2013).

Brown, Bill. 'Martial Art'. *PMLA* 124, no. 5 (October 2009), 1787–93.

Caillois, Roger. *The Mask of Minerva*, translated by George Ordish. New York: Clarkson N. Potter Inc., 1964.

Caillois, Roger. *The Writing of Stones*, translated by Barbara Bray. Charlottesville: University Press of Virginia, 1985.

Causey, Andrew. *Peter Lanyon, Modernism and the Land*. London: Reaktion Books, 2006.

Chiarenza, Carl. *Aaron Siskind: Pleasures and Terrors*. Boston: Little, Brown and Center for Creative Photography, 1982.

Clevidence, Cody-Rose. ~~FLUNG~~ THRONE. Boise: Ahsahta Press, 2018.

Clevidence, Cody-Rose. *Perverse, All Monstrous*. Berkeley: Nion Editions, 2017.

Cocke, Richard. *Paolo Veronese: Piety and Display in an Age of Religious Reform*. Aldershot: Ashgate, 2001.

Cole, Norma. 'The Poetics of Vertigo'. *Denver Quarterly* 34 (Winter 2000): 71–99.

Coleridge, S. T. 'Shakespeare's Judgment Equal to his Genius'. In *The Critical Tradition: Classic Texts and Contemporary Trends*, third edition, 323–24. Boston: Bedford/St Martin's, 1994.

Collis, Stephen. 'Drew Milne's Marxist Lichens'. *Jacket* 2. 21 August 2017. Available online: https://jacket2.org/commentary/drew-milnes-marxist-lichens (accessed 13 January 2018).

Conkelton, Sheryl. Essay in *Aaron Siskind: The Fragmentation of Language*, catalogue accompanying exhibition. New York: Robert Mann Gallery, 1997.

Crane, Hart. *Complete Poems and Selected Letters*, edited by Langdon Hammer. New York: The Library of America, 2006.

Crozier, Andrew. *An Andrew Crozier Reader*, edited by Ian Brinton. Manchester: Carcanet, 2012.

Culler, Jonathan. 'Why Lyric?' *PMLA* 123, no. 1 (January 2008): 201–06.

Davidson, Michael. *Ghostlier Demarcations. Modern Poetry and the Material World.* Berkeley: University of California Press, 1997.

Dayton, Tim. *Muriel Rukeyser's The Book of the Dead.* Columbia: University of Missouri Press, 2003.

Dean, Tacita. 'Then the Wind's Hand Brushed the Picture Away'. In *Peter Lanyon*, edited by Chris Stephens, 118–20. London: Tate St. Ives, 2010.

Derrida, Jacques. *Monolingualism of the Other; or, The Prosthesis of Origin*, translated by Patrick Mensah. Palo Alto: Stanford University Press, 1998.

Derrida, Jacques. *Of Spirit*, translated by Geoffrey Bennington and Rachel Bowlby. Chicago: University of Chicago Press, 1989.

Dewdney, Christopher. *Concordat Proviso Ascendant: A Natural History of Southwestern Ontario. Book III.* Great Barrington: The Figures, 1991.

Dewdney, Christopher. *A Palaeozoic Geology of London, Ontario.* Toronto: The Coach House Press, 1973.

Dewdney, Christopher. *Spring Trances in the Control Emerald Night.* Berkeley: The Figures, 1978.

Diggory, Terrence. *Grace Hartigan and The Poets: Paintings and Prints.* Saratoga Springs: Skidmore College, 1993.

Dorn, Edward. *Slinger.* Berkeley: Wingbow Press, 1975.

Duncan, Erika. 'ENCOUNTERS: Hearing a Poet, but Understanding Little'. *New York Times* Section 13 25 (September 1994): 21.

Duncan, Robert and Denise Levertov. *The Letters of Robert Duncan and Denise Levertov*, edited by Robert J. Bertholf and Albert Gelpi. Palo Alto: Stanford University Press, 2004.

DuPlessis, Rachel Blau. 'The Gendered Marvelous: Barbara Guest, Surrealism and Feminist Reception'. In *The Scene of My Selves: New Work on New York School Poets*, edited by Terence Diggory and Stephen Paul Miller, 189–203. Orono: The National Poetry Foundation, 2001.

Étienne Gilson, quoted in Daniel B. Gallagher, 'Integritas and the Aesthetic Appreciation of Incomplete Artworks', PsyArt. 2006. Available online: www.clas.ufl.edu/ipsa/journal/2006/gallagher01.shtml

Finlay, Ian Hamilton. *Selections.* Berkeley: California University Press, 2012.

Fitzwilliam Museum. *Treasures of the Fitzwilliam Museum.* London: Scala Publishing, 2005.

Forrest-Thomson, Veronica. *Poetic Artifice: A Theory of Twentieth-Century Poetry.* Manchester: Manchester University Press, 1978.

Freud, Sigmund. *The Standard Edition of the Complete Psychological Works of Sigmund Freud, Vol.14: On the History of the Psycho-Analytic Movement, Papers on Metapsychology and Other Works*, translated by James Strachey, in collaboration with Anna Freud, assisted by Alix Strachey and Alan Tyson, 1914–16. London: Hogarth Press and the Institute of Psycho-analysis, 1957.

Freud, Sigmund. *The Standard Edition of the Complete Psychological Works of Sigmund Freud. Vol. 20, An Autobiography Study, Inhibitions, Symptoms and Anxiety, The Question of Lay Analysis and Other Works*, translated by James Strachey, in collaboration with Anna Freud, assisted by Alix Strachey and Alan Tyson, 1925–26. London: Vintage, 2001.

Freud, Sigmund. *The Standard Edition of the Complete Psychological Works of Sigmund Freud. Vol. 23. Moses and Monotheism, An Outline of Psycho-Analysis and Other Works*, translated by James Strachey, in collaboration with Anna Freud, assisted by

Alix Strachey and Alan Tyson. 1937–39. London: Hogarth Press and the Institute of Psycho-analysis, 1964.

Fuss, Diana. *Dying Modern: A Meditation on Elegy*. Dunham: Duke University Press, 2013.

Gallagher, Daniel B. '*Integritas* and the Aesthetic Appreciation of Incomplete Artworks'. *PSYART: A Hyperlink Journal for the Psychological Study of the Arts*. 19 March 2006. Available at: http://psyartjournal.com/article/show/b_gallagher-integritas_and_the_aesthetic_appreciatio (accessed 12 February 2008).

Gander, Catherine. *Muriel Rukeyser and Documentary: The Poetics of Connection*. Edinburgh: Edinburgh University Press, 2013.

Gander, Forrest and John Kinsella. *Redstart: An Ecological Poetics*. Iowa City: University of Iowa Press, 2012.

Ghosh, Amitav. *The Great Derangement: Climate Change and the Unthinkable*. Chicago: University of Chicago Press, 2016.

Glissant, Édouard. *Poetics of Relation*, translated by Betsy Wing. Ann Arbor: University of Michigan Press, 1997.

Goldman, Dodi. 'Vital Sparks and the Forms of Things Unknown'. In *Donald Winnicott Today*, edited by Jan Abram, 331–57. New York: Routledge, 2013.

Goodby, John. *The Poetry of Dylan Thomas: Under the Spelling Wall*. Liverpool: Liverpool University Press, 2013.

Graham, W. S. Graham reading 'Dear Bryan Winter'. *The Poetry Archive*. Available online: https://www.poetryarchive.org/poem/dear-bryan-wynter (accessed 12 July 2014).

Graham, W. S. Graham reading 'The Thermal Stair'. *The Poetry Archive*. Available online: https://www.poetryarchive.org/poem/thermal-stair (accessed 16 December 2017).

Graham, W. S. *New Collected Poems*, edited by Matthew Francis. London: Faber and Faber, 2004.

Graham, W. S. *The Nightfisherman: Selected Letters of W.S. Graham*, edited by Michael and Margaret Snow. Manchester: Carcanet, 1999.

Green, Fiona. 'Achieve Further through Elegy'. In *W. S. Graham: Speaking Towards You*, edited by Ralph Pite and Hester Jones, 132–59. Liverpool: Liverpool University Press, 2004.

Greene, Roland, Stephen Cushman, Clare Cavanaugh, Jahan Ramazani, and Paul F. Rouzer, editors. *The Princeton Encyclopaedia of Poetry and Poetics*, fourth edition. Princeton: Princeton University Press, 2012.

Grigson, Geoffrey. *The Harp of Aeolus: And Other Essays on Art, Literature and Nature*. London: Routledge, 1947.

Grossman, Allen. *True-Love, Essays on Poetry and Valuing*. Chicago: Chicago University Press, 2009.

Guest, Barbara. *Biography*. Providence: Burning Deck, 1980.

Guest, Barbara. *The Blue Stairs*. New York: Corinth Books, 1968.

Guest, Barbara. *The Collected Poems of Barbara Guest*, edited by Hadley Haden Guest. Middletown: Wesleyan University Press, 2008.

Guest, Barbara. *The Confetti Trees*. Los Angeles: Sun & Moon Press, 1999.

Guest, Barbara. *Dürer in the Window: Reflexions on Art*. New York: Roof Books, 2003.

Guest, Barbara. *Fair Realism*. Los Angeles: Sun & Moon Press, 1989.

Guest, Barbara. *Forces of Imagination, Writing on Writing*. Berkeley: Kelsey St. Press, 2003.

Guest, Barbara. *Herself Defined: The Poet H.D. and Her World*. New York: Doubleday, 1964.

Guest, Barbara. *If So, Tell Me*. London: Reality Street Editions, 1999.

Guest, Barbara. 'Letter from Barbara Guest to Susan Gervitz, Excerpt'. *HOW(ever)* 4, no. 4 (April 1988). Available online: http://www.asu.edu/pipercwcenter/how2journal/archive/print_archive/0488post.html (accessed 3 June 2007).
Guest, Barbara. *Poems: The Location of Things; Archaics; The Open Skies*. New York: Doubleday, 1962.
Guest, Barbara. *Quill, Solitary* APPARITION. Sausalito: The Post-Apollo Press, 1996.
Guest, Barbara. *The Red Gaze*. Middletown: Wesleyan University Press, 2005.
Guest, Barbara. *Rocks on a Platter*. Hanover: Wesleyan University Press, 1999.
Guest, Barbara. *Seeking Air*. Los Angeles: Sun & Moon Press, 1997.
Guest, Barbara. *The Türler Losses*, M.B.M. Monograph Series no.5. Montréal: Book Mart Ltd., 1979.
Guest, Barbara and Kathleen Fraser. 'In Conversation with Elisabeth Frost and Cynthia Hogue'. *Jacket* 25. Available online: http://jacketmagazine.com/25/guest-iv.html (accessed 1 June 2007).
Gurney, Ivor. *Collected Letters*, edited by R. K. R. Thornton. Ashington: The Mid Northumberland Arts Group, and Manchester: Carcanet, 1991.
Gurney, Ivor. *Collected Poems*, edited by P. J. Kavanagh. Manchester: Carcanet, 2004.
H. D. *Collected Poems 1912–1944*. New York: New Directions, 1983.
Haffenden, John. *William Empson, Volume II: Against the Christians*. Oxford: Oxford University Press, 2006.
Hayles, N. Katherine. *How We Became Posthuman: Virtual Bodies in Cybernetics, Literature, and Informatics*. Chicago: University of Chicago Press, 1999.
Heidegger, Martin. *Introduction to Metaphysics*, translated by Gregory Fried and Richard Polt. New Haven: Yale University Press, 2000.
Heidegger, Martin. *Off the Beaten Track*, edited and translated by Julian Young and Kenneth Haynes. Cambridge: Cambridge University Press, 2002.
Heidegger, Martin. *On the Way to Language*, translated by Peter D. Hertz. New York: Harper & Row, 1971.
Heidegger, Martin. *Poetry, Language and Thought*, translated and edited by Albert Hofstadter. New York: Perennial Classics, 2001.
Helsinger, Elizabeth K. *Poetry and the Thought of Song in Nineteenth-Century Britain*. Charlottesville: University of Virginia Press, 2015.
Herrick, Robert. *Hesperides: Or, The Works both Humane and Divine of Robert Herrick*, Vol. 1. London: William Pickering, 1846.
Hess, Thomas B. 'Introduction'. In *Places: Aaron Siskind Photographs*, edited by Aaron Siskind. New York: Light Gallery and Farrar, Straus and Giroux, 1976.
Hill, Geoffrey. *Broken Hierarchies: Poems 1952–2012*. Oxford: Oxford University Press, 2013.
Holden, Anthony and Ben Holden, editors. *Poems that Make Grown Men Cry: 100 Men on the Words that Move Them*. New York: Simon & Schuster, 2014.
Hölderlin, Friedrich. '"Remarks on *Oedipus*" (1803)', translated by Stefan Bird-Pollan. In *Classic and Romantic German Aesthetics*, edited by J. M. Bernstein, 194–202. Cambridge: Cambridge University Press, 2003.
Hollander, John. *The Work of Poetry*. New York: Columbia University Press, 1997.
Hurd, Michael. *The Ordeal of Ivor Gurney*. Oxford: Oxford University Press, 1978.
Hyatt, Mark. *A Different Mercy*. Cambridge: infernal methods, 1976.
Izenberg, Oren. 'Oppen's Silence, Crusoe's Silence, and the Silence of Other Minds'. *Modernism/Modernity* 13 (January 2006), 787–811.
Jess, Tyehimba. *Olio*. Seattle and New York: Wave Books, 2016.

Johnson, Ronald. *Radi os*. Chicago: Flood Editions, 2005.
Jovan, Dr. Sarah. 'Lichen Are Indicators of Climate Change in Southern Alaska's Forests'. USDA Forest Service. 2014. Available online: https://www.fs.fed.us/research/highlights/highlights_display.php?in_high_id=662 (accessed 19 December 2017).
Katko, Justin. 'Sex – *Triodes* – Gilgamesh'. In *On the Late Poetry of J.H Prynne: Hix Eros No. 4*, edited by Joe Luna and Jow Lindsay Walton, 43–60. Brighton: High Zero and Sad Press, 2014.
Kaufman, Robert. 'A Future for Modernism: Barbara Guest's Recent Poetry'. *American Poetry Review* 29, no. 4 (2000): 11–16.
Kennedy, David. *Elegy*. London: Routledge, 2007.
Kinnes, I. The Cattleship Potemkin: Reflections on the First Neolithic in Britain'. In *The Archaeology of Context*, edited by J. Barrett and I. Kinnes, 308–11. Sheffield: University of Sheffield, 1988.
Kotin, Joshua. *Utopias of One*. Princeton: Princeton University Press, 2017.
Krell, David Farrell. 'Marginalia to Geschlecht III: Derrida on Heidegger on Trakl'. *CR: The New Centennial Review* 7, no. 2 (Fall 2007): 175–99.
Kristeva, Julia. *Revolution in Poetic Language*, translated by Margaret Waller. New York: Columbia University Press, 1984.
Ladkin, Sam. 'Ornate and Explosive Grief: A Comparative Commentary on Frank O'Hara's "In Memory of My Feelings" and "To Hell with It," Incorporating a Substantial Gloss on The Serpent in the Poetry of Paul Valéry, and a Theoretical Excursus on Ornate Poetics'. *Glossator* 8 (2013): 189–316.
Larkin, Philip. *Collected Poems*, edited by Anthony Thwaite. New York: Farrar, Straus and Giroux, 2004.
Lear, Jonathan. *Radical Hope: Ethics in the Face of Cultural Devastation*. Cambridge: Harvard University Press, 2006.
Leighton, Angela. 'Only Practicing How to Speak to Speak. W.S. Graham's Art of Letter Writing'. *PN Review* 37, no. 6 (July–August 2011): 54–58.
Long Soldier, Layli. *Whereas*. Minneapolis: Greywolf Press, 2017.
Lundquist, Sara. '"Two voices, one joking": The Metapoetic Comedy of Barbara Guest's Poetry'. *Jacket* 25. February 2004. Available online: http://jacketmagazine.com/25/guest-lund.html (accessed 3 June 2007).
MacDiarmid, Hugh. *Complete Poems Volume I*, edited by Michael Grieve and W. R. Aitken. London: Penguin, 1994.
Massumi, Brian. *Semblance and Event: Activist Philosophy and the Occurrent Arts*. Cambridge: MIT Press, 2011.
McCrea, Shane. *In the Language of My Captor*. Middletown: Wesleyan University Press, 2017.
Merleau-Ponty, Maurice. 'Cézanne's Doubt'. In *The Merleau-Ponty Aesthetics Reader*, edited by Galen A. Johnson, translated by Michael B. Smith, 59–75. Evanston: Northwestern University Press, 1993.
Meschonnic, Henri. 'The Rhythm Party Manifesto', translated by David Nowell Smith. *Thinking Verse* I (2011): 161–73. Available online: http://www.thinkingverse.org/issue01/Henri%20Meschonnic,%20The%20Rhythm%20Party%20Manifesto.pdf (accessed 21 December 2013).
Miéville, China. 'A Strategy for Ruination. An Interview with China Miéville'. *Boston Review*. 8 January 2018. Available online: http://bostonreview.net/literature-culture-china-mieville-strategy-ruination (accessed 29 January 2018).
Miller, J. Hillis. 'Anachronistic Reading'. *Derrida Today* 3, no. 1 (2010): 75–91.

Milne, Drew. 'Adorno's Hut: Ian Hamilton Finlay's Neoclassical Rearmament Programme'. *Jacket* 15. December 2001. Available online: http://jacketmagazine.com/15/finlay-milne.html (accessed 3 January 2014).
Milne, Drew. *In Darkest Capital: Collected Poems*. Manchester: Carcanet Press, 2017.
Milne, Drew. 'Nuclear Song'. *Angelaki: Journal of the Theoretical Humanities* 22, no. 3 (2017): 77–85.
Milne, Drew. 'Poetry After Hisoshima?' *Angelaki: Journal of the Theoretical Humanities* 22, no. 3 (2017): 87–102.
Mora, Gilles. *Aaron Siskind: Another Photographic Reality*. Austin: University of Texas Press, 2014.
Morton, Timothy. *Hyperobjects: Philosophy and Ecology after the End of the World*. Minneapolis: University of Minnesota Press, 2013.
Myers, Paul D. 'Review of Nicolas Abraham'. *Rhythms: On the Work, Translation, and Psychoanalysis*. *MLN* 111, no. 5 (December 1996): 1037–41.
Nelson, Cary. 'Developing the Cultural Epic: Muriel Rukeyser's Documentary Testament (Part 5)'. From the Modern American Poetry course by University of Illinois at Urbana-Champaign. Transcribed and available online: https://www.coursera.org/learn/modern-american-poetry/lecture/Uu56U/developing-the-cultural-epic-muriel-rukeysers-documentary-testament-part-5 (accessed 9 October 2017).
Nicholls, Peter. *George Oppen and the Fate of Modernism*. Oxford: Oxford University Press, 2007.
Nowell Smith, David. 'The Art of Fugue: Heidegger on Rhythm'. *Gatherings: The Heidegger Circle Annual* 2 (2012): 41–64.
O'Hara, Frank. *The Collected Poems of Frank O'Hara*, edited by Donald Allen. New York: Knopf, 1972.
O'Hara, Frank. 'The Day the Lady Died'. *Poetry Foundation*. Available online: https://www.poetryfoundation.org/poems/42657/the-day-lady-died (accessed 9 January 2018).
Olson, Charles. *Mayan Letters*, edited by Robert Creeley. London: Jonathan Cape, 1968.
Oppen, George. *New Collected Poems*, edited by Michael Davidson. New York: New Directions, 2002.
Oppen, George. *The Selected Letters of George Oppen*, edited by Rachel Blau DuPlessis. Durham: Duke University Press, 1990.
Oppen, George. *Selected Prose, Daybooks, and Paper*, edited by Stephen Cope. Berkeley: California University Press, 2007.
Oppen, Mary. *Meaning a Life*. Santa Barbara: Black Sparrow, 1978.
Ovid. *Metamorphoses*, translated by A. D. Melville. Oxford: Oxford University Press, 1986.
Patterson, Ian. *The Glass Bell*. London: Barque, 2009.
Pattison, Reitha. 'Empty Air: Charles Olson's Cosmology'. In *Contemporary Olson*, edited by David Herd. Manchester: Manchester University Press, 2015.
Phillips, Adam. 'On Forsaken Favorites'. *The Threepenny Review* 117 (Spring 2009). Available online: http://www.threepennyreview.com/samples/phillips_sp09.html (accessed 1 September 2014).
Phillips, Adam. *Winnicott*. Harmondsworth: Penguin Books, 2007.
Pickering, Andrew. 'Poesis in Action: Doing Without Knowledge'. Paper Given at the Conference, *Weak Knowledge: Forms, Functions, and Dynamics*. Goethe University, Frankfurt, 2–4 July 2017.
Piette, Adam. Review of Rachel Blau DuPlessis, *Days and Works*; Drew Milne, *In Darkest Capital: Collected Poems*; and Iain Britton, *The Intaglio Poems*. *Blackbox Manifold* 19

(Winter 2017). Available online: http://www.manifold.group.shef.ac.uk/issue19/AdamPietteBM19.html (accessed 9 March 2018).

Porter, Fairfield. *Art in Its Own Terms: Selected Criticism 1935–1975*, edited by Rackstraw Downes. New York: Taplinger Publishing Company, 1979.

Porter, Fairfield. *Material Witness: The Selected Letters of Fairfield Porter*, edited by Ted Leigh. Ann Arbor: University of Michigan Press, 2005.

Pound, Ezra. *The Cantos of Ezra Pound*. London: Faber and Faber, 1987.

Pound, Ezra. 'Swinburne Versus Biographers'. *Poetry* 11, no. 6 (March 1918): 322–29.

Powers, Kevin. 'What Kept Me from Killing Myself'. *New York Times*. 16 June 2018: SR5.

Prynne, J. H. *Field Notes: 'The Solitary Reaper' and Others*. Cambridge: privately printed, 2007.

Prynne, J. H. *Kitchen Poems*. London: Cape Goliard Press, 1968.

Prynne, J. H. *The Oval Window: A New Annotated Edition*, introduction by Richard Kerridge, edited by N. H. Reeve and Richard Kerridge. Hexham: Bloodaxe Books, 2018.

Prynne, J. H. *Poems*, third edition. Hexham: Bloodaxe Books, 2015.

Prynne, J. H. 'Poetic Thought'. *Textual Practice* 24, no. 4 (2010): 595–606.

Prynne, J. H. *Triodes*, Cambridge: Barque Press, 1999.

Purdie, Bob. *Hugh MacDiarmid: Black, Green, Red & Tartan*. Cardiff: Welsh Academic Press, 2012.

Purves, Robin. 'J.H. Prynne's *Triodes*'. *The Paper* 7 (November 2003): 47–63.

Rancière, Jacques. *Aisthesis: Scenes from the Aesthetic Regime of Art*, translated by Zakir Paul. London: Verso, 2013.

Rancière, Jacques. *The Politics of Aesthetics: The Distribution of the Sensible*, translated by Gabriel Rockhill. London: Continuum, 2004.

Reid, Michael. *Convergence/Divergence: Exploring Black Mountain College + Chicago's New Bauhaus/Institute of Design*. Exhibition catalogue. Asheville: Black Mountain Museum + Arts Center, 2015.

Rhem, James. *Aaron Siskind*. London: Phaidon Press, 2003.

Riley, Denise. *Time Lived, Without its Flow*. London: Capsule Editions, 2012.

Riley, Peter. 'Review of W.S. Graham'. *New Collected Poems*. *Jacket* 26 (October 2007). Available online: http://jacketmagazine.com/26/rile-grah.html. (accessed 5 October 2017).

Robertson, Lisa. *Nilling: Prose Essays on Noise, Pornography, The Codex, Melancholy, Lucretius, Folds, Cities and Related Aporias*. Toronto: Bookthug, 2012.

Roese, H., 'Some Aspects of Topographical Locations of Neolithic and Bronze Age Monuments in Wales', *Bulletin of the Board of Celtic Studies* 29, no. 1 (1982): 763–65.

Rothenberg, Jerome and Pierre Joris, editors. *From Fin-de-Siècle to Negritude* and *From Postwar to Millennium*, vols. 1 and 2 of *Poems for the Millennium: The University of California Book of Modern and Postmodern Poetry*. Berkeley: California University Press, 1995, 1998.

Rukeyser, Muriel. 'Adventures of Children. A Portfolio of Photographs. Narrative by Muriel Rukeyser'. *Coronet* 6, no. 5 (1 September 1939): 23–38.

Rukeyser, Muriel. *The Collected Poems of Muriel Rukeyser*, edited by Janet E. Kaufman and Anne F. Herzog. Pittsburgh: University of Pittsburgh Press, 2005.

Rukeyser, Muriel. 'Gauley Bridge'. *Films: A Quarterly Discussion and Analysis* 1, no. 3 (Summer 1940). New York: Kamin Publishers: 51–64.

Rukeyser, Muriel. *The Life of Poetry*. New York: Current Books, 1949.

Rukeyser, Muriel. 'The Usable Truth'. *Poetry* LVIII, no. 4 (July 1941): 206–09.

Rukeyser, Muriel. 'Worlds Alongside. A Portfolio of Photographs. Narrative by Muriel Rukeyser'. *Coronet* 6, no. 6 (1 October 1939): 83–98.
Sacks, Peter M. *The English Elegy: Studies in the Genre from Spenser to Yeats*. Baltimore: Johns Hopkins University Press, 1985.
Sandler, Paulo César. *The Language of Bion: A Dictionary of Concepts*. London: Karnac, 2005.
Savedoff, Barbara. 'Documentary Authority and the Art of Photography'. In *Photography and Philosophy*, edited by Scott Walden, 111–37. Oxford: Blackwell, 2008.
Scappettone, Jennifer. *Killing the Moonlight: Modernism in Venice*. New York: Columbia University Press, 2014.
Schieffelin, E., editor. *The Sorrow of the Lonely and the Burning of the Dancers*. New York: St Martin's Press, 1976.
Schuyler, James. *Collected Poems*. New York: Farrar, Straus and Giroux, 1993.
Sedgwick, Eve Kosofsky. 'A Poem Is Being Written'. *Representations*, no. 17, Special Issue: The Cultural Display of the Body (Winter 1987): 110–43.
Segal, Joes. *Art and Politics: Between Purity and Propaganda*. Amsterdam: Amsterdam University Press, 2016.
Shakespeare, William. *Shakespeare's Sonnets*, edited by Katherine Duncan-Jones. London: The Arden Shakespeare, 2010.
Sharpe, Ella Freeman. 'Similar and Divergent Unconscious Determinants Underlying the Sublimations of Pure Art and Pure Science (1935)'. In *Collected Papers on Psycho-Analysis*, edited by Marjorie Brierley, 137–54. New York: Brunner/Mazel, 1978.
Shelley, Percy Bysshe. *The Poems of Shelley, Volume 3 1819–1820*, edited by Michael Rossington, Cian Duffy, Kelvin Everest and Michael Rossington. Harlow: Pearson Education, 2011.
Shelley, Percy Bysshe. *The Poems of Shelley, Volume 4, 1820–1821*, edited by Michael Rossington, Jack Donovan and Kelvin Everest. London: Routledge, 2014.
Silverman, Kaja. *Miracle of Analogy, or, The History of Photography, Part 1*. Palo Alto: Stanford University Press, 2015.
Siskind, Aaron. *Aaron Siskind 100*. New York: A Blind Spot Book, published by powerHouse Books, 2003.
Smiles, Sam. 'Representation and Reality in West Country Landscapes'. In *Places of the Mind: British Watercolour Landscapes 1850–1950*, edited by Kim Sloan, 118–39. London: Thames & Hudson and The British Museum, 2017.
Smith, David Nowell. *On Voice in Poetry: The Work of Animation*. Basingstoke: Palgrave Macmillan, 2015.
Smith, David Nowell. *Sounding/Silence: Martin Heidegger at the Limits of Poetics*. New York: Fordham University Press, 2013.
Solnick, Sam. *Poetry and the Anthropocene. Ecology, Biology and Technology in Contemporary British and Irish Poetry*. London: Routledge, 2017.
Spicer, Jack. *My Vocabulary Did This To Me: The Collected Poetry of Jack Spicer*, edited by Peter Gizzi and Kevin Killian. Middletown: Wesleyan University Press, 2008.
Stengers, Isabelle. *Thinking with Whitehead: A Free and Wild Creation of Concepts*, translated by Michael Chase. Cambridge: Harvard University Press, 2011.
Stephens, Chris. *Peter Lanyon: At the Edge of Landscape*. London: 21 Publishing, 2000.
Stevens, Wallace. 'The Man on the Dump'. *Poetry Foundation*. Available online: https://www.poetryfoundation.org/poems/43434/the-man-on-the-dump (accessed 4 May 2018).
Stevens, Wallace. *The Necessary Angel: Essays on Reality and the Imagination*. New York: Vintage, 1951.

Stewart, Susan. *Poetry and the Fate of the Senses*. Chicago: University of Chicago Press, 2002.
Stokes, Adrian. *A Game That Must Be Lost: Collected Papers*. Cheadle: Carcanet, 1973.
Stokes, Adrian. *The Critical Writings of Adrian Stokes, Volume 1, 1930–1937*. London: Thames and Hudson, 1978.
Stokes, Adrian. *The Critical Writing of Adrian Stokes Volume II, 1937–1958*. London: Thames and Hudson, 1978.
Stokes, Adrian. *The Critical Writings of Adrian Stokes Volume III, 1955–1967*. London: Thames and Hudson, 1978.
Stonebridge, Lesley. *The Destructive Element: British Psychoanalysis and Modernism*. Basingstoke: Macmillan Press, 1998.
Swinburne, Algernon Charles. "Review of Charles Baudelaire." *Les Fleurs du Mal. Spectator* 35 (6 September 1862): 998–1000.
Thom, Martin. *Fair*. London: infernal methods, 2018.
Thomas, Dylan. *The Collected Poems of Dylan Thomas*, edited by John Goodby. London: Weidenfeld & Nicolson, 2014.
Thomas, Dylan. *Dylan Thomas: The Caedmon Collection* [CD set], introduction by Billy Collins. New York: Caedmon, 2002.
Thomas, Dylan. *The Poems of Dylan Thomas*, edited by Daniel Jones, revised edition. New York: New Directions, 2003.
Tiffany, Daniel. *My Silver Planet: A Secret History of Poetry and Kitsch*. Baltimore: Johns Hopkins University Press, 2014.
Trakl, Georg. *Poems & Prose*, bilingual edition, translated by Alexander Stillmark. London: Libris, 2001.
Treves, Toby and Barnaby Wright, editors. *Soaring Flight: Peter Lanyon's Gliding Paintings*. London: The Courtauld Gallery and Paul Holberton Publishing, 2015.
Trotter, David. *Literature in the First Media Age: Britain between the Wars*. Cambridge: Harvard University Press, 2013.
Trotter, David. 'Voices-Off'. In *The L=A=N=G=U=A=G=E Book*, edited by Bruce Andrews and Charles Bernstein, 251–53. Carbondale and Edwardsville: Southern Illinois University Press, 1984.
Tsur, Reuven. *Poetic Conventions as Cognitive Fossils*. Oxford: Oxford University Press, 2017.
Vermote, Rudy. 'The Sane and the Insane Psychotic'. In *'Attacks on Linking' Revisited: A New Look at Bion's Classic Work*, edited by Catalina Bronstein and Edna O'Shaughnessy, 75–86. London: Karnac Books, 2017.
Vescia, Monique Claire. *Depression Glass: Documentary Photography and the Medium of the Camera Eye in Charles Reznikoff, George Oppen, and William Carlos Williams*. New York: Routledge, 2006.
Ward, Geoffrey. *Statutes of Liberty*, second edition. Basingstoke: Palgrave Macmillan, 2001.
Watten, Barrett. *The Constructivist Moment: From Material Text to Cultural Poetics*. Middletown: Wesleyan University Press, 2003.
Welish, Marjorie. *The Annotated 'Here' and Selected Poems*. Minneapolis: Coffee House Press, 2000.
Wieners, John. *Selected Poems, 1958–1984*, edited by Raymond Foye. Santa Barbara: Black Sparrow Press, 1986.
Wilkinson, John. '"Couplings of Such Sonority": Reading a Poem by Barbara Guest'. *Textual Practice* 23, no. 3 (2009): 481–502.
Wilkinson, John. 'Drift and Pop: On Writing about W.S. Graham'. *Poetry* 206, no. 4 (July/August 2015): 427–33.

Wilkinson, John. *The Lyric Touch: Essays on the Poetry of Excess*. Cambridge: Salt Publishing, 2007.

Wilkinson, John. 'Mark Hyatt's Poésie Brut'. In *Hidden Agenda: Unreported Poetics*, edited by Louis Armand, 48–62. Prague: Literaria Pragensia, 2010.

Wilkinson, John. '"Where Air is Flesh": The *Odes* of Frank O'Hara'. In *Frank O'Hara Now: New Essays on the New York Poet*, edited by Robert Hampson and Will Montgomery. Liverpool: Liverpool University Press, 2010.

Winnicott, D. W. *The Maturational Processes and the Facilitating Environment*. London: Karnac, 1990.

Winnicott, D. W. *Playing and Reality*. Harmondsworth: Penguin Books, 1974.

Wordsworth, William. *The Poems: Volume One*, edited by John O. Hayden. Harmondsworth: Penguin Books, 1977.

Zamperini, Alessandra. *Paulo Veronese*. London and New York: Thames & Hudson, 2014.

INDEX

Aaron Siskind 100 (Siskind, Aaron) 100
Aaron Siskind: Pleasures and Terrors (Chiarenza, Carl) 109
abstract act 230, 234
Abstract Expressionism 3–4, 65, 96–8, 198
abstraction 105–8, 198, 231–4
    in painting 96–7
    photography 105, 107–8, 110
Actor-Network Theory 1, 215
Adams, Ansel 73, 103
Adorno, Theodore W. 172, 187
Adventures of Children: A Portfolio of Photographs (Rukeyser, Muriel) 94–5
aesthetics 2, 5, 97, 216
    Adrian Stokes's 215
    constructivist 4
    experience 3, 6–7, 10, 117–18, 136, 185, 235
    of George Oppen 68
    aesthetic regime 212, 216–18
    return to aesthetics 1
    romantic 25, 214, 217
Aesthetic Theory (Adorno, Theodore W.) 169
Agamben, Giorgio 21
'[AGATE/ALGAE]' (Clevidence, Cody-Rose) 218–21
Albers, Josef 93, 95–6, 102, 111
Altieri, Charles 65
American Modernist poetry 65, 68, 90, 172
anachronistic reading 2, 13
Apollinaire, Guillaume 38
Armstrong, Isobel 48–9
art critic/criticism 45, 93
    Adrian Stokes 3, 29, 197
    Clement Greenberg 3
artists, St Ives 3–4, 226
Ashbery, John 7, 52, 68, 103–4, 152, 174
    The Instruction Manual 75
    They Dream Only of America 153
Ashton, Jennifer 156

'as it would be if it had had existence' 9, 14, 179, 183–5, 192–3, 196–7, 199, 213, 215, 222, 234
Attacks on Linking (Bion, W. R.) 192, 210–12
Attridge, Derek 6, 38
Aubade (Larkin, Philip) 137–8
Auden, W. H. 35, 80–1, 190
avant-garde art 67, 79, 90, 152, 186

Badiou, Alain 24, 148
bad naturalisation 14, 167, 175
Barcio, Phillip 109
Barker, George 47
Barthes, Roland 98, 100
Bataille, Georges 61
Baudelaire, Charles 7, 15
    The Sphinx 23–4
    Spleen II 22–3, 129
The Bay (painting by Porter, Fairfield) 103
Beast Feast (Clevidence, Cody-Rose) 209
Before I knocked (Thomas, Dylan) 54–6
Beggs, Michael 244 n.1
Behind the State Capitol (Wieners, John) 205
Bellmer, Hans 61
Benjamin, Walter 96, 115
    and Aaron Siskind 108–9
    on photography 96, 108
Benson, E. F. 174
Berardi, Franco 'Bifo' 189–91
    and Amitav Ghosh 190
    on death 196
    Uprising: Poetry and Finance 189
Berrigan, Ted 8
Berryman, John 15, 26–8, 237 n.18
Bersani, Leo 214–15
binding/unbinding rhythm 16–19, 31, 52, 201–2, 216
Biography (Guest, Barbara) 161–3, 173

Bion, W. R. 58-9
  Attacks on Linking 192, 210-12
  Caesura 55, 57
  'O' in writings of 211
  psycho-analysis of 1, 25
  on sane psychosis 210-11
Bishop, Elizabeth 162-3
Blake, William 7, 15, 117, 139-40, 149
  and orbs 222
  Visions of the Daughters of Albion 127-30, 148
Blank Misgivings (Crozier, Andrew) 137-8
Blasing, Mutlu Konuk 19, 25, 163, 207-8
The Blue Stairs (Guest, Barbara) 157
  Saving Tallow 158, 171
Bonnefoy, Yves 69
The Book of the Dead (Rukeyser, Muriel) 11, 61, 63-4, 81, 86, 91, 94
  The Dam 65, 84, 86
  and glass 80, 82-3, 89
  and photography 63, 84, 87-90
  and racism 82, 88-9
  and sexual exploration 89
  on tunnel disaster 64, 81-2, 88
Brady, Andrea 69, 205
The Bridge (Crane, Hart) 86
The Broken Tower (Crane, Hart) 143-4, 151
Brooks, Gwendolyn 90
Brooks-Motl, Hannah 39
Brown, Bill 30
Buried at Springs (Schuyler, James) 44-5, 102-3
By Gaze (Clevidence, Cody-Rose) 209-11
Byzantine Proposals of Poetry (Guest, Barbara) 171

Caesura 141-2
  as *aporia* 47
  of birth 47-8, 50-1, 54-6, 138
  in Dylan Thomas's poetry 47-8
  Isobel Armstrong on 48
  line-ending 47-8, 114
  visual 49
Caesura (Bion, W. R.) 55, 57, 59
Cage, John 8
Caillois, Roger 84
  on insect behaviour 110
  The Writing of Stones 61, 63-4
Call Me Ishmael (Olson, Charles) 86
The Cantos of Ezra Pound (Pound, Ezra) 61-2, 72, 76, 87, 175, 212-13
Cartier-Bresson, Henri 97
Cézanne, Paul, paintings of 96, 111
Chiarenza, Carl 109
chora 136, 139
clatter-montage, H. D.'s 161
Clevidence, Cody-Rose 7, 192-3, 201, 215, 220-3
  Beast Feast 209
  Flung Throne 209, 221
  By Gaze 209-11
  Perverse, All Monstrous 192, 209, 218, 221
  proto-syntax in poem of 211, 221
The Cloud (Shelley, Percy Bysshe) 141-5, 151
Clough, Arthur Hugh 138
Cocke, Richard 119
cognitive poetics 3, 217
Cole, Norma 77-8
Coleridge, S. T. 184, 212
The Collected Poems (Guest, Barbara) 158, 162-3, 168
Collis, Stephen 193-5
Compton-Burnett, Ivy 174
The Confetti Trees (Guest, Barbara) 161
Conkelton, Sheryl 245 n.25
The Constructed Space (Graham, W. S.) 226, 229-30, 234, 238 n.11
Construction for St Just (Lanyon, Peter) 230
The Constructivist Moment: From Material Text to Cultural Poetics (Watten, Barrett) 79
contradiction/fault-lines, poetry 48, 52, 114, 141-2, 144
  George Oppen's 75-6
  in *Triodes* (Prynne, J. H.) 147
Cope, Stephen 78
'"Couplings of Such Sonority": Reading a Poem by Barbara Guest' (Wilkinson, John) 249 n.24
Crane, Hart 86, 145
  The Broken Tower 143-4, 151
Creeley, Robert 49
cross-rhythm 8, 13, 114, 214, 218

Crozier, Andrew 117, 137–9
  Blank Misgivings 137–8
Culler, Jonathan 5, 29, 100
Cunningham, Merce 8

'*das Ge-läut der Stille*' 126
Davidson, Michael 82
Davis, Miles 7, 11
Daybook V (Oppen, George) 77
The Day Lady Died (O'Hara, Frank) 7–9, 16, 33, 35, 226
  semantic/rhythmic levels 9–10
  and stone 11
Dean, James 35
Dean, Tacita 227
Dear Bryan Wynter (Graham, W. S.) 34, 36–7, 227, 233
  Hannah Brooks-Motl on 39
  and 'meanders' 42
  musical note 37
  reference to A. E. Housman's poem 42
Deaths and Entrances (Thomas, Dylan) 60
A Defence of Poetry (Shelley, Percy Bysshe) 18, 31, 217–18, 222
de Kooning, Willem 7, 28, 98–100
  Excavation 100, 228
  and Fairfield Porter 104
  Woman I (painting) 100–2
Deleuze, Gilles 1, 191, 202
Depression Glass (Vescia, Monique Claire) 73
Derrida, Jacques 48, 124, 246 n.10
Dewdney, Christopher 201, 212–13, 216, 219, 221
dialectical lyric 142
Dickinson, Emily 2
Die a Millionaire (Prynne, J. H.) 139
Diggory, Terrence 248 n.15
Discrete Series (Oppen, George) 69–70, 73–4
Donne, John 138
Dorn, Edward 192
Dufy, Raoul 154
Duncan-Jones, Katherine 236 n.9
Duncan, Robert 67, 78
DuPlessis, Rachel Blau 248 n.17
Dürer in the Window: Reflexions on Art (Guest, Barbara) 154

Ein Winterabend (Trakl, Georg) 246 n.9
  Friedrich Hölderlin on 126
  Martin Heidegger's claims on 124
  and threshold 124–5, 128
  wanderer 124–5, 130–1
Elegy in a Country Churchyard (Gray, Thomas) 33
Eliot, T.S. 113, 156
An Emphasis Falls on Reality (Guest, Barbara) 141, 149–51, 203
Empson, William 54, 228
Excavation (painting by de Kooning, Willem) 100, 228

Fern Hill (Thomas, Dylan) 58–9
Field Notes: 'The Solitary Reaper' and Others (Prynne, J. H.) 127
Finlay, Alec 238 n.27
Finlay, Ian Hamilton 7, 15, 238 n.27
  art of 30–1
  Marble the Revolution 32
  The Present Order 30–1
The Fish (Moore, Marianne) 49
Flowers by the Sea (painting by Porter, Fairfield) 103
Flung Throne (Clevidence, Cody-Rose) 209, 221
Forces of Imagination (Guest, Barbara) 174
The Forms of Love (Oppen, George) 72
Forrest-Thomson, Veronica 14, 25, 153, 156, 167
Frankenthaler, Helen 104, 152
Fraser, Kathleen 155
Freud, Sigmund 16, 47, 196–7
  birth caesura 57
  D. W. Winnicott responds to 199
  Inhibitions, Symptoms and Anxiety 54
  Thoughts for the Times on War and Death 196
Fuss, Diana 34
The Future and Art (Stokes, Adrian) 4, 3, 197–8

Gabo, Naum 3–4, 228
Gander, Catherine 86, 241 n.9
Gevirtz, Susan 166
Ghosh, Amitav 187–9, 196
  and Franco 'Bifo' Berardi 190
  The Great Derangement 187–8

Gilgamesh, clay tablets of 182
Ginsberg, Allen 80
glass 63, 65, 72–3, 82
    and *The Book of the Dead* 80, 82–3, 89
    and *Discrete Series* 69–70, 74
    George Oppen's poetry on 63, 69–70, 73–5, 77
    and stone 63, 69, 77, 83
Glinn, Burt 97
Glissant, Édouard 48, 52
Gloucester Rocks 1 (Siskind, Aaron) 105–6
Goldman, Dodi 199
Goodby, John 50, 239 n.25
    levelling effect 48–9
    The Poetry of Dylan Thomas: Under the Spelling Wall 48
    sonic web 51
Gottlieb, Adolph 3, 99
Graham, Martha 95–6
Graham, W. S. 2, 7, 33, 36–7, 213, 215, 232, 238 n.11
    abstract act 230, 234
    The Constructed Space 226, 229–30, 234, 238 n.11
    Dear Bryan Wynter (see Dear Bryan Wynter (Graham, W. S.))
    Malcolm Mooney's Land 199–200, 229
    and Peter Lanyon 226–7
    The Secret Name 229–31, 234
    The Thermal Stair 226–7, 229, 231–4
Gray, Thomas 31, 33
The Great Derangement (Ghosh, Amitav) 187–8
Greenberg, Clement 3, 228, 232
Green, Fiona 37, 40
Grigson, Geoffrey 52, 240 n.41
Grossman, Allen 24–5, 28, 151
Guattari, Félix 191, 202
Guest, Barbara 1, 4, 7, 68, 151–2, 154–6, 166–7, 170
    and Ann Lauterbach 172
    Biography 162–3, 173
    block-like resistance 156–7
    The Blue Stairs 157
    Byzantine Proposals of Poetry 171
    The Collected Poems 158, 162–3, 168
    The Confetti Trees 161
    consonance in poems of 152, 154–6, 176–7
    Dürer in the Window: Reflexions on Art 154
    on ellipsis 166–7, 176
    An Emphasis Falls on Reality 141, 149–51, 203, 248 n.10
    Forces of Imagination 174
    The Hero Leaves His Ship 152–4, 156
    Herself Defined: The Poet H.D. and Her World 159–61, 174
    If So, Tell Me 169, 175
    and Kathleen Fraser 155
    The Location of Things 152–3
    Marjorie Welish on 166–8, 170
    Moscow Mansions 159
    A Noise of Return 11–13
    Poems: The Location of Things; Archaics; The Open Skies 152
    poetic voice of 153
    Quill, Solitary APPARITION 153
    The Red Gaze 165
    and Robert Kaufman 170–1
    Rocks on a Platter 11, 141, 149–51, 157–8, 166–9, 171–4
    Sara Lunquist on 173
    Seeking Air 159, 174
    Selected Poems 158
    The Strum 169
    Susan Gevirtz and 166
    syntax in poems of 155, 176–7
    The Türler Losses (see The Türler Losses (Guest, Barbara))
    A Way of Being 75
Gurney, Ivor 201–4, 207, 211–12, 216–18, 222
    Here, If Forlorn 202–4
Guston, Philip 3

Hamburger, Michael 246 n.13
Harman, Graham 215
Hartigan, Grace 152, 154, 248 n.15
Hayles, N. Katherine 253 n.29
H. D. 152, 159–61, 163
Heidegger, Martin 52, 117, 181, 215, 246 n.8
    and George Oppen 68, 76
    and Georg Trakl 124, 131–2
    on human–environmental interactions 190
    Introduction to Metaphysics 147–8

Language in the Poem 57, 131
  on petrifying pain 131
  on rhythm and song 127, 131–2
  on Vincent Van Gogh's painting 76
  Words 126
Helsinger, Elizabeth 232
Hepworth, Barbara 3–4
Here, If Forlorn (Gurney, Ivor) 202–4
Hermes, Herse and Aglauros (painting by Veronese, Paulo) 15, 117–21, 125, 136
  female satyr 119–20, 123
  paragone 119–20
  phallicism 120
  and spectator 120–1, 123
The Hero Leaves His Ship (Guest, Barbara) 152–4, 156
Heron, Patrick 3
Herrick, Robert 15
  To Daisies, Not to Shut So Soone 17–18
Herself Defined: The Poet H.D. and Her World (Guest, Barbara) 159–61, 174
Hess, Thomas 99–100
Hill, Geoffrey 34
Hitchens, Ivon 228
Holden, Anthony 34
Hölderlin, Friedrich 56–7, 117, 124, 126
Holiday, Billie 8–10, 17, 33, 35
Hollander, John 49
Homage to Franz Kline photographs (Siskind, Aaron) 109–10
Homage to Mistress Bradstreet (Berryman, John) 26–8, 237 n.18
Hopkins, Gerard Manley 210
  The Windhover 54
  The Wreck of the Deutschland 34, 36
Horatian logic 28
Housman, A. E. 42, 44, 239 n.17
Howe, Susan 86–7
Hulme, T. E. 62
Human Universe (Olson, Charles) 218
'the hum pouring into another' 170
Hurd, Michael 252 n.2
Hyatt, Mark 201, 211–12, 214, 216–18, 222
  Puberty of Puck 207–9

iambic pentameter 12, 16, 85, 201–2, 216
If So, Tell Me (Guest, Barbara) 169, 175
In Darkest Capital (Milne, Drew) 197
  Adam Piette's review of 195

Inhibitions, Symptoms and Anxiety (Freud, Sigmund) 54
In Memory of My Feelings (O'Hara, Frank) 29
In Memory of Sigmund Freud (Auden, W. H.) 35
In Memory of W.B. Yeats (Auden, W. H.) 35
In Public (Wieners, John) 206
'The Instruction Manual' (Ashbery, John) 75
In the American Grain (Williams, William Carlos) 86
In the Language of My Captor (McCrae, Shane) 188
Introduction to Metaphysics (Heidegger, Martin) 147–8
Izenberg, Oren 67

James, Henry 69
Jarvis, Simon 51
Jeffers, Robinson 212
Jess, Tyehimba 188, 198
Johns, Jasper 105, 155
Johnson, Ronald 219
Jones, LeRoi 7
Jonson, Ben 34
Jovan, Sarah 251 n.34

Katko, Justin 149
Kaufman, Robert 170–1, 250 n.51
Kazoo Dreamboats (Prynne, J. H.) 113
Kennedy, David 34
Kline, Franz 98–9
  and Aaron Siskind 109
Koch, Kenneth 152
Kotin, Joshua 190
Krell, David Farrell 126–7
Kristeva, Julia 136

Labelle, Patti 15–16
Ladkin, Sam 34
Lady Marmalade (Labelle, Patti) 15, 19
Language in the Poem (Heidegger, Martin) 57, 131
language poetry 25
Lanyon, Peter 3–4, 33, 45, 194, 226, 229–30
  abstract act 230, 234
  Construction for St Just 230
  on crucifixion 228

paintings by 227, 232–4
St Just 194, 225, 228–30
Tacita Dean on 227
W. S. Graham and 226
Lanyon Quoit 226–7, 232–4
Larkin, Philip 2, 46
   Aubade 137–9
Latour, Bruno 1, 30
Lauterbach, Ann 172
Lear, Jonathan 192
Leighton, Angela 37–8
Les Fleurs du Mal (Baudelaire, Charles) 22–4
Levertov, Denise 67, 76
Lichens for Marxists (Milne, Drew) 193–5
The Life of Poetry (Rukeyser, Muriel) 87–8, 241 n.9
line breaks 19, 38–40, 49, 55, 141–2, 154, 204
linguistic constructivism 25
linguistic cryptograms 2
The Location of Things (Guest, Barbara) 152–3
Long Soldier, Layli
   Whereas 179, 184, 188–9, 191–3, 199
Lowell, Robert 2
Lunquist, Sara 173
Lycidas (Milton, John) 33
lyric/lyric event 2, 16–18, 148
   art of forgetting/remembrance 25
   Barbara Guest's 13
   formal unity 19–20
   formulation for 10
   step-by-step movement 19–20

MacDiarmid, Hugh 93, 114–15
   On a Raised Beach 65, 111–13
Malcolm Mooney's Land (Graham, W. S.) 199–200, 229
The Man on the Dump (Stevens, Wallace) 13–14
Mao Zedong 113–14
'Marble the Revolution' (Finlay, Ian Hamilton) 32
'Marginalia to Geschlecht III: Derrida on Heidegger on Trakl' (Krell, David Farrell) 126
Maritain, Jacques 67–8, 70
'Mark Hyatt's Poésie Brut' (Wilkinson, John) 252 n.11

Mars and Venus United by Love (painting by Veronese, Paulo) 117, 121–3, 138
Martha's Vineyard Rocks (Siskind, Aaron) 104, 106–7
The Mask of Anarchy (Shelley, Percy Bysshe) 4–5
Massumi, Brian 24
The Maximus Poems (Olson, Charles) 86, 212, 218
Mayakovsky, Vladimir 11, 79
McCrae, Shane 188
Meaning a Life (Oppen, George) 66
Medusa (serpent)
   Adrian Stokes's rejection of 29
   in Frank O'Hara's poem 29
   in Percy Bysshe Shelley's poem 132–4
   in Petrarch's poem 28
   Shield of Achilles 30
Merleau-Ponty, Maurice on Cézanne's painting 96, 111
Meschonnic, Henri 18–19
Metamorphoses (Ovid) 117, 120–1
Michelangelo
   Adrian Stokes on 215
   and bisexuality 214
Michelangelo (Stokes, Adrian) 213
Miéville, China 198
Millay, Edna St. Vincent 23–5
Miller, J. Hillis 14
   on anachronistic reading 2, 13
Milne, Drew 31, 179, 181, 188, 196
   In Darkest Capital 195, 197
   Lichens for Marxists 193–5
   Nuclear Song 182–3, 185–6, 195
   Poetry after Hiroshima? 186–8
   and Theodore W. Adorno 187
Milton, John
   Lycidas 33
   Paradise Lost 219
The Mind's Own Place (Oppen, George) 77
Mitchell, Joan 7, 11
mondegreen/misheard line 15–16, 19, 21
Monk, Thelonious 8
Mont Blanc (Shelley, Percy Bysshe) 85, 200
Moore, Catherine Venable 82
Moore, Marianne 49
Morton, Timothy 196
Moscow Mansions (Guest, Barbara) 159
Motherwell, Robert 3, 106

Muriel Rukeyser and Documentary (Gander, Catherine) 86
My Silver Planet: A Secret History of Poetry and Kitsch (Tiffany, Daniel) 46
Myth of the Blaze (Oppen, George) 72, 77–8

Naumburg, Nancy 63–4, 82
Nelson, Cary 80, 83
Nerves (Wieners, John) 205
Newman, Barnett 97–9
New York, West Street 14 (painting by Siskind, Aaron) 100–1, 110
Nicholls, Peter 72
  on George Oppen 67, 69
  on Yves Bonnefoy 69
Nicholson, Ben 3, 232
A Noise of Return (Guest, Barbara) 11–13
The Norton Anthology of Poetry 5
Nowell Smith, David 57, 240 n.31
Nuclear Song (Milne, Drew) 182–3, 185–6, 195

object-events 1–2, 6, 215
objectification 11, 15, 25, 61, 68, 87, 131, 223
objectivism, poetic 1, 14, 25, 63, 68, 90
Ode on Causality (O'Hara, Frank) 32–3, 35–6, 148, 226
  linked to *Buried at Springs* 44
Ode to a Skylark (Shelley, Percy Bysshe) 18, 76–7
Ode to the French Negro Poets (O'Hara, Frank) 11
Ode to the West Wind (Shelley, Percy Bysshe) 54
Of Being Numerous (Oppen, George) 63, 67, 71, 74
O'Hara, Frank 1, 7, 10–11, 15, 36, 75, 79–80, 110, 152, 157, 180, 226
  and *Buried at Springs* (Schuyler, James) 44–5
  and coterie 10
  The Day Lady Died (see *The Day Lady Died* (O'Hara, Frank))
  elegy for 33, 35, 102–3
  and Henri Cartier-Bresson 97
  In Memory of My Feelings 29
  Ode on Causality (see *Ode on Causality* (O'Hara, Frank))

Ode to the French Negro Poets 11
  on social origin 227
  Standing still and walking in New York 36
Olio (Jess, Tyehimba) 188
Olson, Charles 49, 65, 105, 111, 219
  Call Me Ishmael 86
  on cosmology (*Human Universe*) 218–19
  The Maximus Poems 86, 212, 218
On a Raised Beach (MacDiarmid, Hugh) 65, 111–13
On Contradiction (Mao Zedong) 113
On My First Son (Jonson, Ben) 34
On the Medusa of Leonardo da Vinci, in the Florentine Gallery (Shelley, Percy Bysshe) 132–6
Oppen, George 61, 77, 80, 91, 114–15, 212
  and Andrea Brady 69
  Of Being Numerous 63, 67, 71, 74
  Daybook V 77
  Discrete Series 69–70, 73–4
  The Forms of Love 72
  and glass 63, 70, 73–5, 77
  'little word' 69, 78
  and Martin Heidegger 68, 76
  Meaning a Life 66
  The Mind's Own Place 77
  Myth of the Blaze 72, 77–8
  Oren Izenberg on 67
  O Western Wind 76
  Peter Nicholls on 67, 69
  poetry of 66–9, 75, 77–9
  Robert Duncan on 67, 78
  Seascape: The Needle's Eye 71–2, 77
  This in Which 70–1
Oppen, Mary 66, 72–3, 75, 242 n.28
Ovid 119, 123, 129, 170, 175–6
  consonant 169
  Metamorphoses 117, 120–1
O Western Wind (Oppen, George) 76
Ozymandias (Shelley, Percy Bysshe) 21
  and *Spleen II* (Baudelaire, Charles) 22–3

'the pain and the pleasure of words' 207
Paradise Lost (Milton, John) 219
Patterson (Williams, William Carlos) 86, 212

Patterson, Ian 177
Pattison
   Reitha on Olson's cosmology 218–19
Perverse, All Monstrous (Clevidence, Cody-Rose) 192, 209, 218, 221
   '[AGATE/ALGAE]' in 219–21
Petrarch 7, 10, 16, 28, 237 n.20
Philip, M. NourbeSe 86–7
Phillips, Adam
   on D. W. Winnicott 183
   and Dylan Thomas 46, 59
phonotextual clusters 51
photography 93–4, 102
   Aaron Siskind and (*see* Siskind, Aaron)
   and abstraction 105, 107–8, 110
   black-and-white 96, 100, 105, 195
   and *The Book of the Dead* (Rukeyser, Muriel) 63, 84, 87–90
   of Burt Glinn 97
   car travel and 80
   documentary 108
   Josef Albers on 96
   of Martha Graham 95–6
   Nancy Naumburg's 82
   of rocks 103–8
   taking *vs.* making 102
   Thomas Hess on 99
   Walter Benjamin on 96, 108
Picasso 154
Pickering, Andrew 190–1
Piette, Adam 195
Plato, *Timaeus* 136
Poem in October (Thomas, Dylan) 47–9, 51–3, 56, 58
   de-hyphenation 50–1
   present participle 53
   sonic reality of 52
   suppression of punctuation 49–50
Poems That Make Grown Men Cry (Holden, Anthony) 34
Poems: The Location of Things; Archaics; The Open Skies (Guest, Barbara) 152
Poetic Conventions as Cognitive Fossils (Tsur, Reuven) 235
The Poetics of Vertigo (Cole, Norma) 77–8
Poetry after Hiroshima? (Milne, Drew) 186–8
The Poetry of Dylan Thomas: Under the Spelling Wall (Goodby, John) 48

'*point de capiton*' 166, 171
Pollock, Jackson 7, 32, 33, 36, 107
Porter, Fairfield 102, 104, 107
   The Bay (painting) 103
Pound, Ezra 77, 167
   The Cantos of Ezra Pound 61, 63, 76, 87, 175, 212–13
   on glass 63
   on limestone 62
   'reified identity' 72
Powers, Kevin 7
The Present Order (Finlay, Ian Hamilton) 30–1
The Princeton Encyclopedia of Poetry and Poetics 51
The Protocols of the Elders of Zion 66
proto-syntax 201–2, 204, 207, 211, 214, 217–19, 221, 223, 229
Proust, Marcel 88
Prynne, J. H. 52, 114, 167, 191, 194, 223
   Die a Millionaire 139
   Field Notes: 'The Solitary Reaper' and Others 127
   Kazoo Dreamboats 113
   Triodes 12, 145–7, 149, 151
   Unanswering Rational Shore 147
Puberty of Puck (Hyatt, Mark) 207–9
Purdie, Bob 245 n.48

The Quattro Cento (Stokes, Adrian) 61
Quill, Solitary APPARITION (Guest, Barbara) 153

Radical Hope (Lear, Jonathan) 192
Radi os (Johnson, Ronald) 219–20
Ramazani, Jahan 34
Rancière, Jacques 78
'reactor piles' 26–8
The Red Gaze (Guest, Barbara) 165
Renaissance art/poetry 3, 118
'repeatable evanescence' 10–11, 15–16, 130, 148
Rhem, James 99
rhyme/rhymes 9, 21, 28, 142
   Dylan Thomas's 56
   Sonnet 17 19–20, 25–6
   triple 135
rhythm(s) 87, 110, 113–14, 201, 214, 220

appreciable 105–6, 109, 111
binding/unbinding 16–19, 31, 52, 201–2, 216
  with embodiment 29
  Jacques Derrida on 48
  Martin Heidegger's 127, 131–2
  Percy Bysshe Shelley's 18–19
  and phonotext 52
  primal 106, 108–11, 148–9
  rhythmic stress 40, 216
  rhythmic voice 51
  in stone 29–30, 65
  subject-form(er) 18–19
  wave power 7
Rich, Adrienne 90
Richards, I. A. 6
Riley, Denise 21
Riley, Peter 43, 45, 233
The Road (Rukeyser, Muriel) 80–2, 85
Robertson, Lisa 117
'rock platter' 175–6
rocks 4, 12, 32, 44, 62, 102–3, 106, 158, 174
  Aaron Siskind's pictures of 103–5, 111
  in Fairfield Porter's paintings 104, 107
  and Muriel Rukeyser 91
  stone and 3, 75, 104
Rocks on a Platter (Guest) 11, 141, 149–51, 157–8, 166–9, 171–4
romantic poetics 25, 129
Rosenberg, Harold 97
Rotha, Paul 87
Rothko, Mark 3
Rousseau, Le Douanier (epitaph by Apollinaire, Guillaume) 38
Rukeyser, Muriel 4, 7, 108, 115
  Adventures of Children: A Portfolio of Photographs 94–5
  The Book of the Dead (see *The Book of the Dead* (Rukeyser, Muriel))
  documentary project of 83–4
  The Life of Poetry 87–8, 241 n.9
  Marxism 90–1
  and Nancy Naumburg 63–4, 82
  and photography 4, 64, 84, 94
  The Road 80–2, 85
  U.S. 1 80, 88
  The Usable Truth 86–7
  Worlds Alongside: A Portfolio of Photographs 94

St Ives artists 3–4, 226
St Just (painting by Lanyon, Peter) 194, 225, 228–30
Savedoff, Barbara 98–100
Saving Tallow (Guest, Barbara) 158, 171
Scappettone, Jennifer 62
Schuyler, James 4, 33, 108, 110, 152, 174
  Buried at Springs 44–5, 102–3
Seascape: The Needle's Eye (Oppen, George) 71–2, 77
Seaweed 8 (Siskind, Aaron) 105
The Secret Name (Graham, W. S.) 229–31, 234
Sedgwick, Eve Kosofsky 16
Seeking Air (Guest, Barbara) 159, 174
September Song (Hill, Geoffrey) 34
Shakespeare, William 7, 203–4, 207
  sonnets (see Sonnet (Shakespeare, William))
  The Winter's Tale 238 n.31
Sharpe, Ella Freeman 107–8
Shelley, Percy Bysshe 2, 7, 117
  The Cloud 141–5, 151
  A Defence of Poetry 18, 31, 217–18, 222
  incomplete poems by 132
  The Mask of Anarchy 4–5
  Mont Blanc 85, 200
  Ode to a Skylark 18, 76–7
  Ode to the West Wind 54
  Ozymandias 21
  post-Lucretian organicist philosophy 25
Shomei, Tomatsu 108
singularity of art (poem) 5–6
Siskind, Aaron 4, 7, 63, 65, 96–9, 102, 108, 244 n.17
  Aaron Siskind 100 100
  Aaron Siskind: Abstractions exhibition 109
  Abstract Expressionism and 96–8
  Barbara Savedoff on 98
  Homage to Franz Kline photographs 109–10
  James Rhem on 99
  New York, West Street 14 (painting) 100–1, 110
  photograph and viewer 99
  photograph's characteristics 109

principle of conversation 109
rocks and stones photography 10–11, 103–7
Seaweed 8 105
Thomas Hess on 99–100
and Walter Benjamin 108–9
Smith, Danez 188, 198
Smith, David 3
Solnick, Sam 191
Sonnets (Shakespeare, William) 15, 18
Sonnet 17 19–21, 24–6
Sonnet 30 204
Sonnet 43 21
Sonnet 81 21
The Sonnets (Berrigan, Ted) 8
Sounding/Silence: Martin Heidegger at the Limits of Poetics (Nowell Smith, David) 57
The Sphinx (Baudelaire, Charles) 23–4
Spicer, Jack 180
Spleen II (Baudelaire, Charles) 22–4, 129
and *Ozymandias* (Shelley, Percy Bysshe) 23
Springtime of the Soul (Trakl, Georg) 132–3
Spring Trances in the Control Emerald Night (Dewdney, Christopher) 221
Standing still and walking in New York (O'Hara, Frank) 36
'stanza my stone' 13–14, 221, 234–5
Stengers, Isabelle 18
Stephens, Chris 232
Stevens, Wallace 65, 68, 125, 153, 221
The Man on the Dump 13–14
Stewart, Susan 172
Stillmark, Alexander 132
Stokes, Adrian 3, 31, 199, 201, 223
aesthetics of 215
The Future and Art (*see The Future and Art* (Stokes, Adrian))
in history of St Ives art 3–4
Kleinian aesthetic dogma of 198
on limestone 61
on media 197
Medusa (serpent) and 29
Michelangelo 213
and Michelangelo 214–15
and stone 3
stone 3, 114–15, 134

and abstraction 13
in Barbara Guest's poetry 157
carved/carving of 62, 64–5, 94–5
The Day Lady Died and 11
and glass 63, 69, 77, 83
headstones 3
limestone 61–2, 64
in *Mars and Venus United by Love* 121
A Noise of Return (Guest, Barbara) 11–13
'rhythm in stone' 29–30, 65
and rocks 3, 75, 104
and truth 113
Stonebridge, Lesley 107–8
The Stones of Rimini (Stokes, Adrian) 61–2
The Strum (Guest, Barbara) 169
subject-form(er), rhythm 18–19
subjectivity, poem 16–17, 19–20, 24, 28, 30
The Sun Rising (Donne, John) 138
syntax 49–50, 71, 134, 201, 203, 209, 222. *See also* proto-syntax
in Barbara Guest's poem 155, 176
conventional 50, 112
Here, If Forlorn (Gurney, Ivor) 204
multivalent 154
Puberty of Puck (Hyatt, Mark) 209

'thee GLOSS GLOSS' 166, 177
The Thermal Stair (Graham, W. S.) 226–7, 229–34
They Dream Only of America (Ashbery, John) 153
'they will have been' 147
This in Which (Oppen, George) 70–1
This is Just to Say (Williams, William Carlos) 37
Thomas, Dylan 2, 7, 57, 207
Adam Philips and 46, 59
caesura 47–8
Deaths and Entrances 60
Fern Hill 58–9
gross catastrophe 48, 54
Before I knocked 54, 56
intercourse in poem of 55
Poem in October 47–9
rhymes of 56
universing poetry 57, 60

and Vernon Watkins 56
verse of 47–8, 51–2, 59
voice–text 46–7, 49
Thom, Martin 5
Thompson, E. P. 187
Thoughts for the Times on War and Death (Freud, Sigmund) 196
The Tibetan Book of the Dead 197
Tiffany, Daniel 203
  My Silver Planet: A Secret History of Poetry and Kitsch 46
Timaeus (Plato) 136
time-stamp in sonnets 8, 236 n.11
To Daisies, Not to Shut So Soone (Herrick, Robert) 17–18
'Too-Close Reading: Poetry and Schizophrenia' (Wilkinson, John) 252 n.5
TOT (tip-of-the-tongue) 217–18
The Tower of Famine (Shelley, Percy Bysshe) 132, 135
Trakl, Georg 15, 117, 125, 246 n.9
  and Alexander Stillmark 132
  Ein Winterabend (see *Ein Winterabend* (Trakl, Georg))
  and Martin Heidegger 124, 131–2
  Springtime of the Soul 132
Trilogy (H. D.) 163
Triodes (Prynne, J. H.) 12, 145–7, 149, 151
Trotter, David 112, 115, 142, 245 n.46
Tsur, Reuven 217
  Poetic Conventions as Cognitive Fossils 235
  TOT (tip-of-the-tongue) crisis 217–18
The Türler Losses (Guest, Barbara) 151, 157–166, 171, 249 n.26
  metatextual suppression in 158–9, 162–4
  off-text/metatext 157
  revisions of 160–2, 164–6
  ruses of Barbara Guest 157, 164
  travelogue 158
  and Cy Twombly paintings 158
Twombly, Cy 158, 170, 175

Unanswering Rational Shore (Prynne, J. H.) 147

universing poetry 52, 57, 60
Uprising: Poetry and Finance (Berardi, Franco 'Bifo') 189
U.S. 1 (Rukeyser, Muriel) 80, 88
The Usable Truth (Rukeyser, Muriel) 86–7

Van Gogh, Vincent 76
Vermote, Rudy 252 n.15
Veronese, Paulo 7, 15, 125
  female satyr of 126
  Hermes, Herse and Aglauros (see *Hermes, Herse and Aglauros* (painting by Veronese, Paulo))
  Mars and Venus United by Love (see *Mars and Venus United by Love* (painting by Veronese, Paulo))
Vescia, Monique Claire 73
Visions of the Daughters of Albion (Blake, William) 127–30, 148
Vitruvius 29
voice–text dichotomy 46–7

Wallis, Alfred 233
Wall, Jeff 245 n.19
Ward, Geoffrey 156
Watkins, Vernon 56
Watten, Barrett 79
wave power, rhythms 7
  of Thomas's verse 47, 59
A Way of Being (Guest, Barbara) 75
Weil, Simone 71–2
Welish, Marjorie 166–8, 170, 172, 177
Wharton, Edith 70
Whereas (Long Soldier, Layli). See Long Soldier, Layli
Whitehead, Alfred North 1
Wieners, John 201, 205–6, 211, 214, 216–18, 222
  Behind the State Capitol 205
  Nerves 205
  In Public 206
  trimeters 205–6, 216
Williams, William Carlos 79, 173, 241 n.11
  In the American Grain 86
  Patterson 86, 212
  This is Just to Say 37
  variable foot 49

Wilkinson, John
   '"Couplings of Such Sonority": Reading a Poem by Barbara Guest' 249 n.24
   'Mark Hyatt's Poésie Brut' 252 n.11
   'Too-Close Reading: Poetry and Schizophrenia' 252 n.5
Winckelmann, Johann Joachim 214
The Windhover (Hopkins, Gerard Manley) 54
Winnicott, D. W. 3, 199, 215
   Adam Phillips on 183
   Dodi Goldman on 199
   hallucinations 31
   responds to Sigmund Freud 199
   True Self/False Self 181, 183–4, 215
The Winter's Tale (Shakespeare, William) 238 n.31
Woman I (painting by de Kooning, Willem) 100–2
Words (Heidegger, Martin) 126
Wordsworth, William 36, 127, 138, 160, 169
Worlds Alongside: A Portfolio of Photographs (Rukeyser, Muriel) 94
The Wreck of the Deutschland (Hopkins, Gerard Manley) 34, 36
The Writing of Stones (Caillois, Roger) 61, 63
Wynter, Bryan 4, 33, 36, 38–42, 200

Yeats, W. B. 35, 171

Zukofsky, Louis 66, 194